A yankee in de Valera's Ireland

* The memoir of David Gray *

A YANKEE IN DE VALERA'S IRELAND

EDITED BY PAUL BEW

A yankee in de Valera's Ireland: the memoir of David Gray

First published 2012

by Royal Irish Academy
19 Dawson Street
Dublin 2

www.ria.ie

The editor and publisher are grateful to the John J. Burns Library, Boston College, for permission to reproduce the material in this book.

ISBN 978-1-908996-05-3

Front cover: Eamon de Valera with David Gray at the US Legation (1 January 1940), photograph by William Vandivert, © Getty Images, original has been altered.
Reverse of front cover: *Irish Press*, 20 May 1940, 6.
Reverse of back cover: *Irish Independent*, 15 April 1940, 5.
The prelim pages begin on the half title.

The editor and publisher are grateful to the John J. Burns Library at Boston College for permission to reproduce David Gray's memoir 'Behind the Emerald Curtain', and to Cambridge University Press for permission to reproduce the biography of David Gray from the *Dictionary of Irish biography*.

British Library Cataloguing in Publication Data. A CIP catalogue record for this book is available from the British Library.

Design: Fidelma Slattery
Copy-editing: Maggie Armstrong
Typesetting: Carole Lynch
Index: Helen Litton

Printed in Poland by Drukarnia Skleniarz.

10 9 8 7 6 5 4 3 2 1

Contents

INTRODUCTION

There can be no doubt in the mind of any reasonable man that if Ireland were given complete independence, with its own army and control of its own ports and powers to enter into treaties with foreign nations, whether they were friendly or hostile to us, that would place Britain in a position of such peril that I should hesitate to think what would befall in the event of either the great struggle with Napoleon or the great struggle with Germany.

David Lloyd George[1]

In 1993 Tim Pat Coogan said of David Gray's historical memoirs, here published for the first time: 'Its splenetic tone was such that the reaction from de Valera followers would have eclipsed the reaction to Salman Rushdie's *Satanic Verses*.[2] But Coogan added that it was nevertheless 'a valuable historic document'. Since 1993 David Gray's reputation has declined somewhat. In 2009 a distinguished Irish historian of intelligence matters, Professor Keith Jeffery, described him as an 'ineffably ill-informed Hibernophobe'.[3] In 2009 also R.M. Douglas, who has—more than any other scholar—sought to insist on the relative strength of pro-Axis sentiment in Ireland, nonetheless portrayed Gray as an obsessive, receiving intelligence information—albeit surprisingly accurate information—by means of spiritualist séance.[4] In 2010, Professor Tully wrote: 'Gray was hardly the ideal candidate for the

[1] Centurion, 'The Irish treason and its authors', *National Review* 79 (1922), 697–8.
[2] Tim Pat Coogan, *De Valera: long fellow, long shadow* (London, 1993), 527.
[3] Review of Eunan O'Halpin, 'Spying on Ireland: British intelligence and Irish neutrality during the Second World War', *Irish Historical Studies* XXXVI (143) (May 2009), 471.
[4] R.M. Douglas, *Architects of the resurrection: Ailtirí na hAiséirighe and the fascist New Order in Ireland* (Manchester, 2009), 217. In an article in *History Ireland* (September/October 2009), 41, Douglas describes Gray simply as 'erratic'.

position. His early career was a series of failures ... . He brought with him no experiences with Ireland, other than a few hunting trips in the 1930s'.[5] In 2010 also Maurice Walsh described Gray as 'petulant ... unhelpful ... unbalanced', authoring alarmist and wildly inaccurate diplomatic reports on Irish security.[6]

Who then was David Gray? It is important to note that he was nearly 70 years old—ten years beyond the usual retirement age in the UK diplomatic service—when he took up his position as US minister plenipotentiary and envoy extraordinary to Ireland in 1940 (twenty years later, Gray was still active enough to be elected vice-president of the Harvard Club in Sarasota).[7] Gray was a well-connected member of the East Coast elite: the son of a Buffalo newspaper proprietor. He graduated from Harvard in 1892—where he acquired his interest in spiritualism—and was admitted to the Bar. Gray pursued a legal career unsuccessfully[8] but achieved more as a journalist—working as an editorial writer in New York.

Gray then had an impressive spell of military service in World War One. He was decorated with the Croix de Guerre and was made a Chevalier of the Légion d'honneur and a Chevalier de la Couronne. He was a commandant captain of aviation in the French airforce in France. Gray, however, saw himself, above all, as a literary man rather than a soldier. For example, in 1919 he co-authored the play *Smith* with William Somerset Maugham; in 1924 he co-authored a play with the 'playboy playwright' Avery Hopwood, *The best people*, which was filmed in 1925 and again in 1930 as *Fast and loose* (which starred Carole Lombard and had Preston Sturges as a scriptwriter). *The best people* ran for almost a year in the London theatre.[9] Two volumes of Gray's short stories, *Ensign Russell* and *Gallops*, were in print in the years immediately after his death, published by the Books for Libraries Press in Freeport, New York. Gray incidentally maintained his literary interests even at the height of international crisis in the summer of 1940. On 18 June he offered to read a play of Micheál MacLiammóir of the Gate Theatre in Dublin.[10] On 25 July he was engaged in a correspondence with Twentieth Century Fox about the script *Where stars walk*. In the 1930s

---

[5] John Day Tully, *Ireland and Irish Americans: the search for identity 1932–1945* (Dublin and Portland, 2010) 80.

[6] Maurice Walsh, *G2: In defence of Ireland—Irish military intelligence 1918–45* (Dublin, 2010), 250.

[7] Elizabeth Shannon, *Up in the Park: diary of the wife of the American ambassador in Ireland* (Dublin, 1983).

[8] T. Ryle Dwyer, *Behind the green curtain: Ireland's phony neutrality during World War II* (Dublin, 2009), 53.

[9] *Daily Telegraph*, 3 April 1940.

[10] Beth Kane to David Gray, 25 July 1940, David Gray papers, University of Wyoming.

he went into agribusiness in Florida and liked to tell Irish audiences that he was a farmer. The Dublin appointment was, in effect, his sixth career.

Yet, all these attributes or activities do not explain Gray's appointment as a United States minister plenipotentiary. That appointment, as he liked to say himself, was in part nepotistic. As the historian Stephen Hess has pointed out, President Roosevelt appointed several other relatives to significant positions.[11] Gray's wife was the aunt of Franklin D. Roosevelt's wife, Eleanor; this gave him the edge when the president considered who was the best man to replace another old friend, John Cudahy, as the American representative in Dublin. This family connection has another significance. It meant that Gray had an intimacy with the White House denied to other diplomatic representatives to small neutral countries in the Second World War. It gives his time in Dublin a very special interest. Roosevelt, for example, on 18 May 1940 wrote to Queen Wilhelmina of Holland that she should organise an escape to the USA through Ireland, 'where the Minister David Gray … is my cousin'.[12]

In the aftermath of the outbreak of the Second World War in 1939, a significant part of the US establishment remained isolationist. Indeed, men such as Joseph Kennedy, Roosevelt's minister to Britain, the republican Senate leader Robert Taft and the celebrated aviator Charles Lindbergh had all said they believed England could not survive and publicly predicted a complete Nazi victory in Europe. Roosevelt did not share this thinking, but in the summer and fall of 1940 he was still manoeuvring between the desire for a more interventionist foreign policy and the difficult context of a reluctant American public and his re-election. Roosevelt told a cheering crowd, which included many Irish-Americans, in isolationist Boston: 'I have said this before, but I shall say it again and again; your boys are not going to be sent into any foreign wars'.[13] Unsurprisingly, some Irish diplomats seem to have accepted the authenticity of this declaration. David Gray, on the other hand, was sufficiently close to the president not to believe it. Roosevelt's rhetoric was not simply hypocritical, but rather was 'a necessary feature of the odd dialectic between president and people, in which FDR gave assurances he did not mean and they pretended to believe him'.[14]

David Gray knew Ireland rather well. His literary interests had created connections to the Irish intellectual and artistic worlds. In June

[11] Stephen Hess, *America's political dynasties: from Adams to Kennedy* (New York, 1966), 201.
[12] E. Roosevelt (ed.), *F.D.R.: his personal letters 1918–45* (New York, 1950), 1027.
[13] Michael Barone, *Our country: the shaping of America from Roosevelt to Reagan* (New York, 1990), 134–5.
[14] William O'Neill, *A democracy at war: America's fight at home and abroad in World War II* (New York, 1993), 31.

1933 he visited Drishane House in Castletownshend, west Cork, as guest of the celebrated Anglo-Irish writer and fellow spiritualist Edith Somerville. Gray enjoyed the rural Irish lifestyle so much—hunting and fishing, in particular—that he and his wife spent the winter in the country.[15] He started to write a serious and sympathetic book on Ireland.

The appointment of David Gray, a 'passionate Anglophile', has been seen by Professor Eunan O'Halpin as a clear sign that 'the [Roosevelt] administration had no sympathy for Ireland's position'.[16] In fact, Gray was considered to be a friend of Ireland. It is true that G. Hall Roosevelt could write to Gray on 2 July: 'This is July 2nd. I give you ten days to haul down the Irish flag in Dublin', but a bad joke is just a bad joke.[17] Gray was initially well disposed towards Eamon de Valera. In fact, as we also know from Professor O'Halpin's excellent research—'a State Department official noted that Gray "knows a great deal about Ireland, and is friends with 'all the right people'—the degree of rightness nowadays depending upon the length of time they spent in jail" during the war of independence'.[18] This is clearly a reference to Gray's friendship with the family of Robert Brennan (1881–1964), de Valera's old comrade and diplomatic representative in the United States.[19] Incidentally, Brennan's memoir reveals that Roosevelt considered himself to be part of that group of Irish-American politicians and journalists who played a role in 1920–1 in negotiating the Anglo-Irish settlement.[20] When Gray left for Ireland, the Brennans sent him a telegram: 'May the road rise with you and the winds in your back'.[21] Professor Girvin has argued that 'Gray was extremely sympathetic to Ireland's position in the summer of 1940, making various suggestions about how American support might

[15] Gifford Lewis, *Edith Somerville: a biography* (Dublin, 2005), 382; *Southern Star*, 19 August 1933, records the presence of Gray at a fête in Drishane: his first known mention in an Irish newspaper. When Edith Somerville's brother Boyle was murdered by the IRA, Gray published a tribute to him in the *Irish Press*—it is interesting that he should have chosen to place it in de Valera's paper rather than the *Irish Times* (favoured by the Anglo-Irish) or the pro-Treaty conservative *Irish Independent*.

[16] Eunan O'Halpin, *Spying on Ireland: British intelligence and Irish neutrality during the Second World War* (Oxford, 2008), 140.

[17] Letter from G. Hall Roosevelt to David Gray, Gray papers, University of Wyoming, American Heritage Centre (Box 23).

[18] O'Halpin, *Spying on Ireland*, 133.

[19] For Brennan, see Richard A. Ruppe's introduction to Robert Brennan, *Ireland standing firm: my wartime mission in Washington* (Dublin, 2002).

[20] *New York Times*, 12 December 1920; Carl Ackerman's Diary, Library of Congress.

[21] The telegram was sent on 9 March 1940, see Gray manuscript, University of Wyoming. The Brennans were a literary family. Their daughter Maeve Brennan (1917–93) became a celebrated short story writer and journalist. She was close to Charles Addams, creator of the macabre cartoon series 'The Addams Family'. It has been suggested that Morticia Addams—beautiful, aloof, highly intelligent—is modelled on Maeve Brennan.

be provided'.[22] Not only did Gray admire de Valera on first contact but he even compared Mrs de Valera to Maude Adams, the famous New York actress. This was significant, because Gray's besotted rhapsodies in prose about Maude Adams were well known.[23]

In the light of such controversy, it has to be noted that Gray's draft book on Ireland, designed to help the reader 'comprehend' his 'new Ireland', can hardly be described as Hibernophobe or unsympathetic in tone: he describes 'a courteous and efficient police, the agreeable absence of a military caste and a people intensely kind and sympathetic. There is little evidence of the extremes of wealth or of poverty in the countryside. The people seem decently clad and fed; the children a good flesh and colour'.[24] De Valera himself would hardly have challenged his description, and he might especially have admired Gray's praise of this 'small significant land whose influences penetrate not only the British empire but the United States and the rest of the Americas'. Gray's final assessment was hardly a challenge to Irish nationalist orthodoxy: 'The race which this green earth has nurtured and impressed has been vital and resistant through a succession of conquests and, at last, has achieved independence and a place of its own'.[25]

On the other hand, Gray was clearly more sympathetic to the policies of the Cosgrave government in the 1922–32 period, as opposed to the de Valera government actually in power. Gray wrote: 'To comprehend this new Ireland one must hold in mind the fact that, during the past 20 years, she has participated not only in world war but experienced national revolution, Partition, independence and war, a decade of orderly reconstruction, and is now in the throes of a major depression brought on by a new dispute with England'.

The tone of this remark clearly favours the Cosgrave government. But not too much should be made of it. Gray regarded policies of agrarian radicalism like self-sufficiency so beloved, rhetorically at least, by Fianna Fáil in its early years in power, as 'idiotic'. But he was a shrewd observer. As early as 1935, the agrarian radical supporters of the government were inclined to admit defeat on the self-sufficiency issue.[26] In short, in 1940 Fianna Fáil attitudes were beginning to change, and Gray knew this well.

[22] Brian Girvin, *The Emergency: neutral Ireland 1939–45* (London, 2006), 183.
[23] Kim Marra, *Strange duets: impresarios and actresses in the American theater 1865–1914* (University of Iowa Press, 2006), 130.
[24] Gray papers, University of Wyoming, 'Ireland', 4.
[25] Gray manuscript, University of Wyoming, 'Ireland', 3.
[26] *Mayo News*, 18 February 1935.

At the very moment David Gray returned, in Ireland, in 1940, the Irish agrarian revolution was beginning its internal decomposition. The Fianna Fáil government, elected in 1932, had presented itself as the logical completion of the tradition of Irish agrarian radicalism, first expressed in a rather complex way in the Fenian movement, the Land League and then Sinn Féin. Gray understood the historical basis of this appeal. 'Irish land', he liked to say, moulded the 'race mind'. The displaced Cosgrave government was characterised as timid in this respect: in thrall to the rural bourgeoisie, the English market for Irish agricultural produce. By way of sharp contrast, Fianna Fáil offered a further phase of land redistribution in order to appeal to the rural poor, whose votes they successfully gained.

By 1940, however, the results of this process were decidedly mixed. Always a sceptic, the *Dundalk Democrat and People's Journal* felt free to observe: 'The division of land meets, to an extent, that condition of the rural mind known as land hunger. But it does not seem to have produced, in general, satisfactory results, though some of the new land owners, industrious and skilled in rural pursuits, are doing well'. The striking development in 1940, however, was the willingness of key people in Fianna Fáil to echo the sentiment. Erskine Childers, the son of the executed republican martyr, told the Dáil that 'examination of the methods by which small farms are run is long overdue'.[27] Also significant was the declaration by Micheal Clery, a Fianna Fáil deputy from Mayo, that to give land to 'landless men' was a 'good political ramp', but it was bad economically. They were, he said, only creating new rural slums. (Clery's departure from agrarian radicalism was limited; his hostility to 'landless men' reflected his belief that land division should be carried out for the benefit of migrants from the West.) Gray was a friend of Childers and well aware of the new mood within Fianna Fáil. He even notes how de Valera was uncomfortable when presented with an American politician's sentimental traditional picture of rural Ireland. Gray's characteristic economic and social views, therefore, hardly explain his later radical fall-out with Fianna Fáil.

The reasons lie elsewhere. Gray was no cultural relativist. He believed that the lessons of history since Magna Carta were clear: he believed in a capitalism which was liberal and progressive. Gray was aware of the dark side of Western imperialism and colonialism; nonetheless, it did not

---

27 *Dundalk Democrat and People's Journal*, 18 May 1940. For Clery's speech see Dáil Éireann debates, vol. 80 (15 May 1940), col. 525–38, especially 528–9. For comments in the same debate on the 'political ramp' of land division by another deputy, Colonel Jeremiah Ryan, Fine Gael TD for Tipperary, see 16 May 1940, col. 578–84.

undermine his belief that, in the Second World War, the British were defending a democratic heritage shared by America. A firm anti-Nazi in the Roosevelt mould, Gray, on arrival in Dublin, threw himself into the task of winning Irish support for the struggle against Hitler. Gray's friends—Chauncey Hamlin of Buffalo is a typical example—were drawn from the public-spirited progressive WASP elite which despised American isolationism.[28] Gray assumed, and it was from his point of view a compliment, that de Valera shared his values. At first he believed that the Craigavon Ulster Unionist leadership's unwillingness to make sacrifices was the principal obstacle to his strategy. He assumed that de Valera was, at heart, a principled anti-Nazi. Sir John Maffey, the British representative in Dublin, has left us the picture of Gray in mid-June 1940:

> The American minister, Mr David Gray, does a great deal of wishful thinking in regard to the partition issue. He is convinced that, if a solution of the partition problem could be found *now*, Ireland would be in the war on our side. He would make it the *quid pro quo* and he is convinced that Mr De Valera would be forced by the best opinion in this country to fall into line. He may be right. He informs that in his opinion nothing but swift and dramatic action now can secure these results ... . He said that he sympathised with the people of the North in their difficult situation and he could fully understand Lord Craigavon's attitude. Nevertheless, he thought that attitude today was ruinous to the Commonwealth and that the British government ought to have 'him out'.[29]

Later Gray came to believe not only that de Valera would never have given up Irish neutrality whatever the North did—which is correct—but also, which is more controversial, that de Valera had made a private deal with Berlin to stay out of the war and be rewarded with Irish unity later.

To understand the negotiations of May/June 1940, in which the British attempted to barter an end to Partition for an end to Irish neutrality, it is essential to understand the two principal actors, Eamon de Valera (1882–1975) and Winston Churchill (1874–1965). Both had actually gone to some pains to outline their views on these issues before the outbreak of war, and it is to an exposition of these views which we now turn.

[28] Hamlin to Gray, 19 June 1940, Gray manuscript, University of Wyoming.
[29] Maffey to Sir Ernest Machtig, 15 June 1940. Dominions Office Records, National Archives, Kew, CAB 123/196/XC 19173.

Churchill had an unusually shrewd and cynical take on the controversies of Irish history. His own experience of Ireland included a period as a child in the Viceregal Lodge and he was aware that his father's career in the 1880s had been much taken up with Irish issues.[30] At the time of the Anglo-Irish Treaty of 1921, in which he was intimately involved, he observed with some aplomb: 'Mr Asquith had denied that they had any right to claim that in

> their Irish settlement they were following in the footsteps of Mr Gladstone. In what happened before, as well as in the settlement as it appeared, if they studied the facts, they would see that they were following, to a very large extent, and in many respects with painful accuracy, in the footsteps of Mr Gladstone. For the best part of five years, Mr Gladstone pursued a regime of coercion in Ireland, and it was only at the end of that period that he turned round and offered a Home Rule solution to the men he had previously described as marching through rapine to the disintegration of the Empire.[31]

There is a crude brutality in this portrait of Gladstone's policies in 1880–5, but it can not be denied that it contains a very important element of truth.

In March 1926 Churchill, then Chancellor of the Exchequer, made a visit to Belfast in which he addressed not only economic policy but his own record on Irish affairs. Amid much humorous reference to the turmoil which had attended his visit on behalf of the Home Rule cause in February 1912,[32] he explained his own position: 'At the moment when Ulster accepted the 1920 Act and withdrew her opposition to a measure of autonomy for the rest of Ireland, he became one of the defenders of the rights of Ulster'. He insisted that Irish unity could only come about by the exercise of the 'free and unfettered' choice of the Northern unionists. Churchill made it clear that he was totally opposed to any London effort to exert 'unfair economic pressure'. His long-term preference was for Irish unity within the empire; but he accepted that many in Ireland felt that this was unrealistic. At any rate, these were merely abstract rather than theoretical considerations. As far as his audience was concerned, the Irish question had entered a 'stable phase',

---

[30] Celia Lee and John Lee, ' "An Irish Exile" 1876–80', in *The Churchills* (London, 2009), 11–19.

[31] *County Cork Eagle*, 28 January 1922.

[32] Paul Bew, *Ideology and the Irish question* (Oxford, 1994), chapter 3; see also Paul Bew, 'What did Churchill really think about Ireland?', *Irish Times*, 8 February 2012.

and there would be no constitutional change for many years ahead. Thus far, Churchill had merely repeated—quite accurately—the principles, if not quite the precise political history, which had informed his highly influential conduct in 1921–2, when the future of the Partition settlement had been at stake.[33] Speaking in the Ulster Hall, where his father, Randolph Churchill, had so famously in 1886 rallied to the cause of loyalist militancy (and where he himself had been prevented from advocating Home Rule in 1912), Winston Churchill then added a final flourish. He concluded by acknowledging 'old friends, good comrades, my father's work'.[34]

In April 1938 the British government made the decision to cede to de Valera the three ports of Berehaven, Queenstown and Lough Swilly, which London had retained under the terms of the 1921 Treaty. It was, in some ways, a surprising and controversial decision, driven, above all, by the decision of the Chamberlain government to advertise compromise and peaceful dialogue as the way forward for Europe. A key figure in the pro-Irish drift of British policy was Malcolm MacDonald (successively secretary of state in the Dominions Office and the Colonial Office). From the British viewpoint this policy, intended as an act of good authority, or, at least, of example to Hitler, failed on its own terms. Gray suggests that the British had reason to believe there was some kind of gentleman's understanding that, in the event of some great international peril, they could use the ports. Another celebrated American diplomat, Joe Kennedy, did not agree: 'I was in England when all the original discussions were taking place for the turning over of the ports, and I must say that, strictly from a personal point of view, I was never very impressed that the English arguments would prevail. However, that's neither here nor there. They don't, and there we are'.[35] More significantly, the deal failed also to transform the attitude of Irish public opinion towards Britain. It was an action bitterly opposed by Churchill—'a more feckless act can hardly be

[33] Paul Bew, Peter Gibbon and Henry Patterson, *The state in Northern Ireland: political forces and social classes* (London, 1994), 21–55.
[34] See *Irish Times*, 3 March 1926; for the complex context of his father's speech; see R.F. Foster, 'To the Northern Counties Station: Lord Randolph Churchill and the prelude to the Orange Card', in F.S.L. Lyons and R.A.J. Hawkins (eds), *Ireland under the union: varieties of tension* (Oxford, 1980), 237–88; Paul Bew, *Ireland: the politics of enmity, 1789–2006* (Oxford, 2007), 434–45.
[35] Joe Kennedy to David Gray, 6 January 1943, Gray manuscript, University of Wyoming. The tone of this letter is friendly and Gray's account of Joe Kennedy in 'Behind the Emerald Curtain' is equally amiable. Gore Vidal's *Palimpsest* (London, 1995), 341–2, however, records Gray as being rather dismissive of Kennedy. Vidal describes a dinner with David Gray and Eleanor Roosevelt in which Gray described Kennedy as a 'damn coward' and 'an unpleasant fellow who thought he knew everything and wanted us to make a deal with Hitler'. Eleanor Roosevelt backed this up by saying that Franklin D. Roosevelt had said of Joe Kennedy 'I never want to see that man again as long as I live'.

imagined'—he declared. On his return to the admiralty in September 1939, Churchill tried unsuccessfully to persuade the Cabinet to take back Berehaven.[36] For this reason, as much as any other, Churchill's arrival in No. 10, Downing Street, worried Dublin. It was always suspected that he would launch some military adventure against Ireland. Churchill was keen to point out that Fianna Fáil represented the most Anglophobic element in Irish society. In this context, his theoretical support for Irish unity meant nothing; he always saw it as coming about by means of a new understanding between conservatives, North and South.[37] In turn, and logically enough, the Irish government regarded Churchill with dislike—but also fear. Lieutenant General Dan McKenna, de Valera's 'inspired' choice as chief of state of the Irish army, when somewhat in his cups, was to tell the US military attaché in Dublin, Colonel Hathaway, that Churchill 'was the greatest enemy to Ireland since Cromwell'. The feeling that Churchill was a natural friend of the Ulster Unionists but worse, ill-intentioned and unpredictable in his attitude towards Dublin, constituted a kind of conventional wisdom in Dublin. How then would Eamon de Valera deal with the problem thus created?[38]

In August 1940 de Valera told the *Christian Science Monitor*, published in Boston, that he had laid out the basis of his war-time policy some seven months before the outbreak of war in a speech on the Partition issue. 'He had stated in the Senate that unity could not be purchased at a price which would indicate taking from the Irish nation the right to decide for itself whether or not it would participate in a war'.[39] It was a true (if incomplete) statement and yet, in a way, a surprising one. De Valera had not wanted to speak in the Senate at all; he regarded the debate—initiated by one of his own appointees, Senator Frank MacDermot—as ill-timed. Nonetheless, the debate turned out to be a significant one.

In its reaction to the broad sweep of Irish history, the debate was of considerable general interest. MacDermot recalled: 'My mind goes back to a spring day in 1916, when I was in the orchard of a monastery a couple of miles away from Ypres, and when I first heard to me the shameful, the heart-breaking news of the rebellion of 1916, I believed then, as I still believe, that it was a frightful blunder'.[40] He recalled

[36] Andrew Baker, 'Anglo-Irish relations 1939–41: a study in multi-lateral diplomacy and military restraint', *Twentieth-Century British History* 16 (4) (2005), 363.
[37] Douglas Savory, *A contemporary history of Ireland* (Belfast, 1958), 36.
[38] O'Halpin, *Spying on Ireland*; University of Wyoming, Gray manuscript, Report 472 (12 May 1944).
[39] For the coverage, see *Dundalk Democrat and People's Journal*, 17 August 1940.
[40] *Seanad Éireann*, vol. 22–07 (February 1939).

sympathetically Lord Balfour's declaration of 1919 that it would be better if Northern Ireland was properly integrated with the rest of the United Kingdom rather than given its own parliament and state apparatus. MacDermot was strongly supported by Professor Joseph Johnston, a self-confessed 'rotten Protestant' from the North—that is to say, a Protestant who had become a nationalist.[41] Even so, he was frustrated by nationalism's refusal to think seriously about unionism. Johnston argued that one third of northern Protestants were liberal and two thirds were illiberal and reactionary: all were united by a common sense of Britishness.[42] He responded to nationalist rhetoric in the Senate—of which there was a significant quantity—about claiming the North with a dry 'Heil Hitler'.[43]

De Valera's own intervention contained some interesting elements.[44] At one level, entirely traditional, he reiterated Mussolini's recent reference to natural geographic boundaries of a nation as having a special significance, in defiance of the view of his old Sinn Féin colleague, Fr Michael O'Flanagan, that while geography had tried to make one nation of Ireland, history had made it a duality. He insisted that he would not accept a united Ireland in exchange for the abandonment of the aim of 'restoring its national language [Irish] to be the spoken language of the Irish people'. To the anger of many, MacDermot dismissed the promotion of 'pidgin Irish' as entirely counterproductive.[45] De Valera did not rule out the use of force to transfer nationalist areas of the North into his own state. But he did insist that coercion could not be used to end Partition as such. The taoiseach insisted that unionists held their views as sincerely as nationalists: he made it clear that he did not consider that either Irish unionists or nationalists were motivated by selfish economic interest.

> I think that we, both north and south, would be prepared to sacrifice our material interests for the convictions we have of a sentimental character. I think that it is true of both, and it is one of the difficulties of the problem, as I wish that would get this far:

[41] Joseph Johnston, *Civil war in Ulster* (Dublin, 1913, reprint 1999) attacks the pre-1914 Ulster Unionist campaign as reactionary. Johnston was the father of Roy Johnston, the Marxist republican intellectualist who played a significant role in the politics of the civil rights crisis in the late 1960s. In 1918 he published *The handbook for rebels*, a compilation of seditious pre-1914 statements by unionists, implying that they had set the precedent for the subsequent activities of Sinn Féin; this was banned by the British authorities (J.J. Horgan, *Parnell to Pearse: some recollections and reflections* (Dublin, 1949, reprint 2009), 335.
[42] *Seanad Éireann*, vol. 22–07 (February 1939), col. 923.
[43] *Seanad Éireann*, vol. 22–07 (February 1939), col. 1012.
[44] *Seanad Éireann*, vol 22–07 (February 1939), cols 970, 995.
[45] http://debates.oireachtas.ie/seanad/1939/02/07/00004.asp (accessed 7 February 2011).

that each side would give the other credit for that; foolish in attributing to the other side a certain amount of weakness which we pride ourselves upon not having ourselves. I do not think that weakness exists at all. I have never acted, at any rate, on that basis. I always held that the people who differ from me hold their views as tenaciously as I hold mine and that if force is ruled out, I must try to meet them half-way.

De Valera even went so far as to say that he thought the British government probably wanted an end to Partition. He added: 'I did not go over to ask them to coerce any section of the northern people. In fact, I made it quite clear that if the British government was going to use coercion against a section of our people, they would, probably, find us standing by other Irishmen against them'.[46] But where, precisely, was the 'half-way' de Valera talked about; where was the envisaged line of compromise? De Valera's remarks are most revealing: he defined the Irish state after the 1937 Constitution as an 'internal republic', the remaining exiguous forms of association with Westminster (such as Commonwealth membership) were the best he could offer the unionists. Most importantly, of all, was the right of Ireland to remain neutral in a conflict involving Great Britain.

There is another price I would not pay. Suppose we were to get unity in this country, provided we were to give up the principles that are here in the first Article of the Constitution—the 'sovereign right of the nation to choose its own form of government, to determine its relations with other nations, and to develop its life, political, economic and cultural, in accordance with its own genius and traditions'—I would not sacrifice that right, because without that right you have no freedom at all. Although freedom for a part of this island is not the freedom we want—the freedom we would like to have, this freedom for a portion of it, freedom to develop and to keep the kernel of the Irish nation is something, and something that I would not sacrifice, if by sacrificing it we were to get a united Ireland, and that united Ireland was not free to determine its own form of Government, to determine its relations with other countries, and, amongst other things, to determine, for example, whether it would or would not be involved in war.

[46] *Seanad Éireann*, vol 22–07 (February 1939), col. 982.

David Gray was aware of this speech, as his manuscript reveals, but he appears to have hoped that it did not represent a final and finished statement of Irish policy. In this hope he was to be disappointed. De Valera had articulated the core principles of his policy before the crisis and he simply stuck to it. There is, however, a broader story to be told. It is a useful exercise to look at rural currents of opinion—as both reflected and manipulated in the Irish media in 1940. It helps to give a more proper sense of the context within which political decisions were taken. In particular, it throws light on the pressure placed on Eamon de Valera.

De Valera also felt the pressure coming from his republican left. This was not just a matter of the IRA. At the beginning of 1940 the English journalist, Harold A. Albert, in his 'World Searchlight' column in *Everybody's*, praised de Valera for pursuing a policy of 'dignity' in 'dominionhood': such allegedly patronising praise was, to say the least, unwelcome. It genuinely raised a question for some critics. Barry Mayo asked in the *Connaught Telegraph*: 'Surely De Valera has a higher and worthier purpose in governing? Surely he has not sunk so low?'[47] When the British, in February 1940, executed two IRA men involved in the IRA's murderous British bombing campaign of 1939–40, the *Roscommon Herald*—by no means the most Anglophobic element in the Irish provincial press—declared: 'At the moment we can only say that the British government blundered badly in executing these men, just as they blundered badly in executing the leaders of Easter Week'.[48]

Eamon de Valera felt compelled to spell out his position on the northern issue—the issue, which, above all, was exploited against his leadership. At the Cavan county convention of Fianna Fáil in mid-February, de Valera made his position clear on the use of force to resolve Partition. The Irish people had voted for a Constitution which fixed the power to wage war in its name on one body only: the democratically elected government of the country. In his view, that government should not employ force. 'They had got to solve Partition by force or by good will, and getting the people who were not ready to fall in with them—to see eye to eye with them. They were determined to use this second means, because they did not believe the first would be successful. Even if it was successful, they would leave them with a problem, *a canker in*

[47] *Connaught Telegraph*, 20 January 1940.
[48] *Roscommon Herald*, 10 February 1940. For a lucid analysis of Irish public opinion on this issue, see Eunan O'Halpin, *Defending Ireland: the Irish Free State and its enemies since 1922* (Oxford, 1999), 247. See also M. Manseagh, 'Dev's effort to counter IRA campaign', *Irish Times*, 1 April 2011.

the heart of the nation, which ultimately would bring this nation to disaster, as nations on the continent had been brought'.[49]

But if de Valera determined to prosecute a constitutional republicanism, he was well aware that this seemed feeble to many. Germany now threatened British power—but should republicans not ally with Germany to bring about the reunification of the country and the humiliation of Britain? The IRA leadership had no hesitation about such a project. There was little confusion, even in provincial Ireland, as to the nature of Nazi doctrine. In an article, 'This Man—Hitler', specially commissioned for the *Connaught Telegraph,* it was explained: 'From his past historical studies, Hitler had learned that a nation's strength lies in its preserving racial purity'. The author added: 'Regarding the Jews as the greatest menace to racial purity, Hitler proceeded to use every means in his power to exterminate them'.[50] Few republicans, however, seem to have been deterred by Nazi racial theory. De Valera himself estimated in 1940 that a majority of the Irish wanted Germany to prevail.[51] It is noticeable, however, that, while the Irish nationalist press appears to have concentrated on the intentions of the Nazis towards the Jews, in the North more space was given to the voice of Irish Jews themselves. The celebrated Rabbi Jacob Schachter's statement in April 1940 on the 'Feast of the Passover' was publicised in the Belfast press: 'The Jews in celebrating the feast of Passover declare to the world the ancient principle of the right of all to be free, which has been accepted by democracy and liberalism for many centuries'.[52]

There were, however, strongly Anglophile writers active in the Irish nationalist media. Michael MacDonagh, the *Independent's* veteran London Irish correspondent whose career went back to the Parnell era, kept up a flow of comment designed to stress the closeness of the Anglo-Irish connection. Ben Tillet, the 80-year old socialist campaigner, offered his services to his country in any capacity: MacDonagh reminded Irish readers that Tillet's mother was from Connemara and that he had been a great ally of Michael Davitt in the 1890s.[53] The British minister in

---

[49] *The Dundalk and People's Journal,* 24 February 1940.

[50] *Connaught Telegraph,* 13 January 1940.

[51] R.M. Douglas, *Architects of the resurrection,* 54.

[52] *Belfast Newsletter,* 13 April 1940; Schachter was a close friend of the influential Presbyterian Professor J. Ernest Davey. See Zevi Herah Chajer, *The students' guide through the Talmud: a pre-eminent scholar's overview of Talmudic literature and history* (New York, 2005). Schachter was a leading Talmudic scholar. In this epoch the small Belfast Jewish community nurtured, among others, Chaim Hertzog, Abba Eban, the Hollywood director Benjamin Glazer, the businessman Leonard Steinberg (later Lord Steinberg) and Ya'akov Morris, 'poet of the Negev' and father of the historian Benny Morris.

[53] *Irish Independent,* 19 April 1940.

Belgrade, Sir George Campbell, was a direct descendent of the martyred Irish patriot hero of 1798, Lord Edward Fitzgerald.[54] When Churchill became premier, Michael MacDonagh was there to remind Irish readers of his many contacts with Ireland, going back to his childhood experience both in Dublin Castle and the Phoenix Park, when his father was aide to the duke of Marlborough.[55] The ageing Lloyd George, nobbled in the House of Commons Lobby by MacDonagh, was quoted as saying kindly things about Irish leaders. Sympathetic accounts of London facing the onslaught of German bombing appeared both in the national and provincial press—before the Irish Censor decided that they inevitably favoured the British. The total Irish death toll in the British forces for the fall of France and Norway was probably about 500; Irish newspapers initially carried details but again the Censor soon intervened to stop such a public record.[56]

Other writers in the *Independent* were not so Anglophile. Consider the account of the German representative's visit to an art exhibition in Dublin. Hempel had attended the opening day showing of William Conor's paintings in Dublin. He was reported as admiring the work which in his view portrayed the Irish as they really were—sincere and not snobbish.[57] The *Independent* journalist did not say it but an implied contrast with another neighbouring nationality soon was rather obvious. Neutral Ireland had little choice but to placate both Britain and Germany.

At the beginning of May, Sir John Maffey accompanied two of de Valera's ministers, Seán Lemass and James Ryan, to London on a 'trade mission'.[58] Maffey arranged, with de Valera's consent, for the two Irish ministers to call at Buckingham Palace.[59] On 10 May, Neville Chamberlain—much liked by de Valera—resigned and Winston Churchill became prime minister. 'I hope it is not too late,' Churchill muttered.[60] On 13 May he told parliament: 'I have nothing to offer but blood, sweat and tears'—it was a message which left many in the House

---

[54] *Irish Independent*, 18 April 1940.

[55] *Irish Independent*, 11 May 1940. The duke of Marlborough, Winston Churchill's grandfather, was Disraeli's viceroy in Dublin in the late 1870s.

[56] Kevin Myers, 'Why it is wrong to airbrush the Fighting Irish from our history', *Belfast Telegraph*, 11 June 2010. See also Brian Girvin 'The forgotten volunteers of World War II', *History Ireland* 6 (1) (1998) and the remarkable essay by Carol Acton ' "Stepping into history": reading the Second World War through Irish women's diaries', *Irish Studies Review* 18 (2010) 39–56.

[57] *Irish Independent*, 11 May 1940.

[58] *Irish Independent*, 4 May 1940. The *Independent* reported that the two ministers were returning to London the following week.

[59] National Archives, Kew, DO 130/84/275/29.

[60] John Lukacs, *Five days in London: May 1940* (Yale University Press, 1999), 13.

of Commons rather cold. News of devastating German strikes against the British position commanded the headlines almost daily in May and June. On 15 May the Dutch capitulated: reeling under the power of the German offensive, the Allied armies retreated towards Dunkirk and began their evacuation on 26 May. Hitler stopped his Panzers eighteen miles short of Dunkirk, predicting that the 'British won't come back in this war'.[61] His mistake helped to allow 338,226 Allied soldiers to escape capture and also, perhaps, Churchill's government to survive. Not that the situation remained anything other than grim: on 28 May, the king of Belgium surrendered. On 21 June 1940, Joe Walshe, the secretary general of the Department of Foreign Affairs, informed de Valera: 'British defeat has been placed beyond all doubt'.[62] The French high command, as if to drive home the point, surrendered the next day. Irish policy was bound to be influenced by the perception that the Germans were, at the very least, unbeatable.

De Valera's words at Galway on 11 May are, on the face of it, a definite condemnation of German actions.

> I was at Geneva on many occasions ... the representatives of Belgium and of the Netherlands were people that I met frequently, because we co-operated not a little with the northern group of nations. Today these two small nations are fighting for their lives, and I think I would be unworthy of this small nation, on an occasion like this, if I did not utter our protest against the cruel wrong which has been done them.

There was a particular additional point to these remarks; de Valera, as he told Malcolm MacDonald, regarded Galway as a hotbed of pro-German feeling.[63] But there was soon to be evidence of back-tracking. The German representative Hempel was told by a nervous Joe Walshe on 14 May 1940 that de Valera's statement was 'intended not as a gratuitous judgement on the rights and wrongs of the German action'—which Gray had rather assumed it was. Rather, the de Valera speech in Galway had been making 'an assertion, in principle, on which our national security depends'.[64]

[61] For a recent discussion, see Andrew Roberts, *The storm of war: a new history of the Second World War* (London, 2009), 64.
[62] Catriona Crowe, Ronan Fanning, Michael Kennedy, Dermot Keogh and Eunan O'Halpin (eds), *Documents on Irish foreign policy, volume VI 1939–1941* (Dublin, 2008), 249. Aengus Nolan, Walshe's biographer, notes that Walshe had a reputation for being pro-German, *Joseph Walshe: Irish foreign policy* (Cork, 2008), 173.
[63] Note of talk between Mr de Valera and Mr MacDonald on 21 June 1940. National Archives, Kew, CAB 123/1–19.
[64] Crowe *et al.* (eds), *Documents on Irish foreign policy, volume VI*, 212.

The Irish envoy in Berlin, William Warnock, wrote to Walshe on 18 May 1940 that de Valera's remarks—though not publicised—had not been 'well received' in Berlin. 'I may say by way of explanation that every German is convinced that the Fuehrer was right in anticipating an Allied attack through these countries, whose governments had ill concealed their enmity to Germany ever since the outset of war'.[65]

The German archives record Warnock as having used some rather striking 'personal' language to reassure the Germans—implying that Ireland was merely waiting for the right moment to strike against Britain, having struck too early in 1916. In mid-June the Department of External Affairs—worried by some talk from Hitler about German compromise with the British empire—asked for reassurance that this did not mean 'the abandonment of Ireland' and the withdrawal of German support for 'the final realisation of Irish demands'.[66] Gray's reaction is recorded in the pages below. For Gray this was a matter of elite betrayal, but popular attitudes have also to be considered.

The response in the provincial press to de Valera's Galway speech was instructive. Given that it was made at an election meeting for a by-election candidate—John J. Keane, a returned emigrant who had fought in the American forces in World War One—it was perhaps inevitable that most interest was aroused in the west of the country. The *Southern Star* in Cork made no comment, for example, nor did the Waterford *Munster Express*, in the immediate aftermath. The *Connaught Tribune* was prepared to echo de Valera's tone by expressing sympathy for Belgium—that most 'unfortunate little country' which 'bore not the slightest responsibility' for the national tragedy it was experiencing.[67] The *Connaught Telegraph*, a week later, however, was explicitly critical of de Valera:

> But the Premier himself, we are bound to say, did not set a very edifying example to the people when he addressed a meeting recently at Galway. He might have assumed that our people needed no hint as to what had happened in Holland or Belgium. They were well aware of the fate of both countries, but, as we have declared for neutrality, we did not expect that our Prime Minister would commit a breach of his own professed faith and set about talking up one side or another.[68]

[65] Crowe *et al.* (eds), *Documents on Irish foreign policy, volume VI*, 215; *Documents on German foreign policy 1918–45, series D (1937–1945)* IX, 401.
[66] Telegram from Dublin from E. Hempel, the German legate, dated 17 June 1940, *Documents on German foreign policy 1918–1948, series D (1937–1945)* IX, no. 473, 603.
[67] *Connaught Tribune*, 18 May 1940.
[68] *Connaught Telegraph*, 25 May 1940.

The *Mayo News* (traditionally pro-Fianna Fáil)[69] summarised the consensus at the end of the month:

> While we sympathise with all those small nations which have been, in most cases, unwillingly and undeservedly made victims of the great powers, there is no reason why we should be forced to participate in any struggle, and any person or body of persons in the state who, by their actions, may be the cause of embroiling us in conflict must be regarded as the worst enemies of their country'.[70]

The British, worried by these developments, moved rapidly to open up a dialogue with de Valera. Churchill, now premier, gave his permission: he disavowed 'coercion', but this traditionally meant economic pressure against the unionists as advocated by some in London in 1921–2. He was clearly open to the idea that an entirely new political context might be created, which favoured his long-term concept of Irish unity. On 17 June, Malcolm MacDonald, the minister for health in the British government, a close personal friend of the Irish leader,[71] engaged de Valera in Dublin. MacDonald stressed how quickly the Germans were capable of taking over a country: 'It was essential that the full weight of resistance that could be brought to bear should be ready, awaiting the Germans in the territorial waters and on the shores of the island'. De Valera replied:

> his people did not appreciate this. They knew too little of what happened in the other small neutral countries. Their information service was not good. Moreover, too many Irishmen actually thought that the Germans would make them more free. Prejudice against Britain was still strong, it would still take a long time to remove such an old sentiment. Indeed, his countrymen would actually fight with greater zeal if we were the first to violate Eire's neutrality than they would if the Germans were the first aggressors. He was only able to keep national unity at its present unprecedented level by making it clear that the government would resist whichever belligerent invaded the country.[72]

[69] For the general ethos and history of the *Mayo News*, see Harry Hughes and Áine Ryan, *Charles Hughes: Lankill to Westport 1876–1949* (Westport, 2007).
[70] *Mayo News*, 1 June 1940.
[71] Deirdre McMahon, 'Malcolm MacDonald', in Deirdre McMahon, *Republicans and imperialists: Anglo-Irish relations in the 1930s* (New Haven, 1984). See also Martin Gilbert, *Winston S. Churchill, volume 6: finest hour 1939–1941* (London, 1983), 577. On this topic see also Robert McNamara (ed.), *The Churchillls and Ireland* (Dublin, 2012), 191.
[72] National Archives, Kew, CAB 123/196/7–8.

On 21 and 22 June 1940, de Valera had further conversations in Dublin with Malcolm MacDonald. At this meeting, de Valera argued that if the British agreed to the extension of his 1937 Constitution to cover the whole country, Dublin 'might' enter the war. MacDonald questioned 'the might' and de Valera, almost deliberately it seemed, destroyed his own argument by adding 'there would be a very big question mark after "might"'. As to British prospects in the war, de Valera claimed to have a view which differed from that of his own professional advisors. 'If the French fleet would not fall into German hands, he holds the view that, provided we can withstand invasion in our island for the next two months, we shall defeat Hitler'.[73] Nevertheless, MacDonald was increasingly convinced that, in fact, Dublin was sure that London was a beaten docket.

It is clear that for de Valera neutrality was an absolute value and that no offer to end Partition—however genuine—could trump it. In this sense, as David Gray points out—the traditionalist clique in Stormont, led by Lord Craigavon, grasped the context more correctly than he had himself. It is all the more remarkable because the Craigavon clique, which had been strongly pro-appeasement, had misread all the key political developments up to this point. Yet, for all that, it is important to note that a significant public debate broke out within the leadership of Ulster unionism on the issue. In particular, respected figures raised their voices in favour of making major concessions on the Partition issue in exchange for an end to Irish neutrality. David Gray placed Speaker Sir Harry Mulholland of the Stormont parliament in this category. It also included the Rev. James Little, MP for Down. Little insisted on 24 June that Ireland shared a common Christianity, which, despite all previous internal divisions, was bound to see it present a unified face against Hitler. 'I can not for one moment think that a people who have held firmly by the Cross will ever allow the Holy Cross to be replaced by the Swastika'.[74]

On the same day, one Stormont emissary, Patrick Herdman, the son of the unionist senator Sir Emerson Herdman (the Herdman family ran a linen mill near Strabane on the Tyrone–Donegal border), met de Valera 'quite unofficially' in Dublin for an hour on 25 June. Patrick Herdman was described by his Eton contemporary, the novelist Anthony Powell, as 'a completely philistine personality of the coarsest possible texture'.[75] Herdman was an interesting choice as interlocutor. Powell concluded:

[73] CAB 123/196/14; CAB 123/196/17.
[74] *Belfast Newsletter*, 25 June 1940.
[75] Anthony Powell, *Journals* (London, 1996), 6. For a family history, see Rex Herdman, *They all made me* (Omagh, 1970).

'Pat Herdman was a good example of the complexity of the Irish: on the one hand, a fanatical Ulsterman, on the other, much closer to the South than to Great Britain; I think politically full of duplicity'.[76] But it is doubtful if personality counted for much at this moment. Craigavon informed Chamberlain: 'My friend suggested that if he would declare himself as willing to come in with Britain, I would be glad to meet him anywhere at any time over mutual civil defence, provided no "constitutional questions" were touched upon. Mr de Valera's answer was "Quite impossible"'.[77] Herdman also appears to have worked out that de Valera was simply unwilling to bargain away neutrality at any price.

But there were two interesting developments in Belfast on the same day. Also on 25 June 1940, Colonel Alexander Gordon (1882–1967) resigned his junior ministerial post at Stormont. He denounced governmental inertia in the face of the German threat. More importantly, at his moment of resignation he talked of giving 'all Ireland'[78] a lead. This was widely understood to be a hint that the Craigavon government should pursue a deal with de Valera to end Irish neutrality, whatever the consequences for Partition. Colonel Gordon had been severely wounded in 1914, been mentioned in dispatches five times and received numerous military honours, including the Croix de Guerre. It was difficult to dismiss his patriotism and the Craigavon government reaction was notably nervous.

The Marquis of Dufferin and Ava (1909–45), easily the most brilliant member of the Ulster aristocracy, also took a public stand. A fine scholar at Eton and Oxford, he had an impressive political career in the 1930s, characterised by his strong interest in India, a family tradition. Dufferin and Ava was under-secretary of state for the Colonies in 1937. An intense patriot, he refused a post in Churchill's war-time coalition government, becoming a captain in the Royal Horse Guards in July 1940—he was to lose his life in a covert mission in Mandalay just a few weeks short of his 36th birthday.

In the *Northern Whig*, Dufferin and Ava proclaimed:

It seems to me that the government of Northern Ireland are too obsessed by the memory of past grievances to realise that within a few hours everything that they fought for may be threatened by a foreign invader with little respect for the Orange drum and very doubtfully acquainted with the Westminster Confession.

[76] Powell, *Journals*, 7.
[77] John Bowman, *De Valera and the Ulster question* (Oxford, 1982), 237.
[78] *Belfast Newsletter*, 26 June 1940.

That being so, there is no point in delay and I can not understand why Ulster did not long ago ask De Valera to agree that a united government of Ireland be set up and, upon the consequent renunciation of Eire's neutrality, every German should be cleared out of Ireland within two hours and the defence of Ireland should be undertaken by Great Britain.[79]

It is well known that there were private indications given that the unionist Cabinet would split on age lines if de Valera offered a unity for neutrality deal. Professor Henry Patterson and Dr Brian Barton have pointed out that Basil Brooke, later to be prime minister of Northern Ireland, accepted the logic of a deal on Partition to facilitate the defeat of Hitler.[80] It is perhaps more remarkable how far the debate was conducted in public in Belfast and how little interest there was in Dublin—even though the Irish minister in Canada reported that it was engaging Canadian opinion. Referring to the great *rendez-vous manqué* of the early summer of 1940, a meeting between de Valera and Lord Craigavon, de Valera told the *Christian Science Monitor* in August: 'I met him once in 1921 to discuss differences between us. We agreed on nothing'.[81] But the real issue lay elsewhere—it lay in Dublin's lack of interest in a rather dramatic unionist split in Belfast, which had the potential to bring about Irish unity.

Dublin now had a greater priority: keeping the Germans sweet. The *Irish Independent* on 5 July carried a rather worrying report: At the Wilhelmstrasse it was stated that the position in Ireland is similar to that existing in Belgium before the German invasion. Hitler's general staff drew up detailed plans to invade Ireland under the authority of Field Marshal Fedor von Bock, who had a fearsome reputation as an aggressive campaign officer. Dublin's Gauleiter was to have sweeping executive powers.[82]

Many must have privately cursed de Valera's Galway speech when perusing this report. On 9 July de Valera, in response, told the *New York Times* that he was committed to a policy of 'strict neutrality', even in the context of Irish unity. Craigavon could hardly resist exploiting the opportunity. 'He is demanding the subjection of Ulster to Eire, not in

[79] *Northern Whig*, 25 June 1940.

[80] Henry Patterson, *Ireland since 1939: the persistence of conflict* (London, 2007), 38.

[81] *Dundalk Democrat and Peoples' Journal*, 17 August 1940. For a discussion of his meeting see the introduction to Paul Bew and Patrick Maume (eds), *Wilfrid Ewart: a journey in Ireland in 1921* (Dublin, 2008). *Northern Whig* of 6 July 1940 contains German press threats directed at Ireland.

[82] See Tom Clonan, 'What if Hitler had invaded?', *Irish Times*, 28 June 2010.

order to make Ireland powerful enough to resist an invasion by the strongest military power in Europe but merely to maintain neutrality'.[83] Unionist public opinion agreed with Craigavon. 'De Valera's statement about maintaining and defending Eire's neutrality is regarded by the majority as banging the door on any proposals for a united military command of Ireland'.[84]

There remained a degree of public sympathy for the plight of Britain in the nationalist press. The *Roscommon Herald* commented with some affection:

> On the whole, it must be said that the prospect for Britain is none too bright. Desolation looms ahead, but there are as yet no signs of despair. The British, like ourselves, have many faults, but they have the great qualities of stubborn determination and one hundred per cent national unity in times of danger. These qualities may stand them in good stead in the coming difficult days'.[85]

Sometimes, even a note of wry self-criticism crept into the national discourse. In early August, the *Roscommon Herald* commented: 'And now a tidal wave of despondency sweeps through the island'. The *Herald* felt that this was a little undignified and reflected badly on the Irish character. 'Irishmen who visit London will tell you they hear far less of the dismal talk there. Dublin, whose peril is relatively negligible, wore the long face of a man walking to the scaffold! Isn't this timidity a little unworthy of our national character?' In the end, the *Herald* concluded, either the worst would not happen or, if it did, 'we must face up ... like men'.[86] But for most the Germans seemed likely to win and many hoped it would lead to Irish unity. Some even allowed themselves some wistful reflection on a possible future. The parliamentary sketch writer of the *Irish Independent* allowed himself to dream of the 'summer of 1945, when we hope World War II would be a distant memory'. He concluded: 'Probably I shall be writing then on the speeches of Belfast deputies in the All-Ireland Dublin parliament'.[87] One of Gray's friends, the Kerryman and successful journalist, Viscount Castlerosse (later earl of Kenmare), recalled later in the year: 'Last August there was scarcely a

---

[83] *Irish Independent*, 12 July 1940.
[84] Paul Addison and Jeremy A. Craig, *Listening to Britain: home intelligence reports on Britain's finest hour—May to September 1940* (London, 2010), 193.
[85] *Roscommon Herald*, 22 July 1940.
[86] *Roscommon Herald*, 10 August 1940.
[87] *Irish Independent*, 20 August 1940.

man in Ireland who did not believe that Britain was beaten. I remember assuring my neighbours in Kerry that this was not so. You see, I know the British, but I was not believed'.[88]

The waters closed over that moment when a unionist MP had talked of Ireland's common Christian and anti-fascist identity. In October 1940, the respected figure of Lord Strabolgi slapped down Dr Little for his suggestion that German submarines were being secretly supplied from Éire territory. Irish neutrality, albeit regrettable, was being observed strictly:

> I have had very happy experiences of the west of Ireland. I know it fairly well and know the people there, and the idea that you can convey large quantities of heavy oil fuel or anything else to Bantry Bay or any of the other harbours here to supply German submarines, without it being known, is grotesque. It is bound to be known.[89]

In an earlier life as the MP J.M. Kenworthy, Lord Strabolgi had been a strong critic of the Black and Tans. This was traditional material for Dublin—the 'better type' of English politician slapping down the vulgar Ulsterman. Everyone, it now seemed, could return to their traditional comfort zone. Dr Little's insistence on the shared Christian anti-Nazi value system of both Irish Protestants and Catholics was quite forgotten: he was dismissed in the nationalist press as the 'stormy petrel', 'partisan' and 'very ridiculous'.[90]

Ireland, in the end, was not available for the Allied cause. For David Gray the sense of betrayal was bitter and personal. No reader of this 'Behind the Emerald Curtain' will be surprised to discover that, as the war continued, his distaste for Irish neutrality became ever more marked. In June 1943 Gray recommended to the US government that it exert, jointly with England, a united pressure by withholding raw materials from Irish manufacturers. Ireland was largely dependent on such raw materials. Anthony Eden, however, advised the British government to take no action. For most of 1943 and 1944 Gray worked to 'develop a diplomatic note to be presented to Ireland that would publicise the state's perceived lack of sympathy for the Allied cause'.[91] Initially, this note was to be a request for access to Irish ports; in the end, the note formally

---

[88] *Sunday Express*, 30 November 1940.
[89] Lords Hansard, 22 October 1940, vol. 117, cols 565–8.
[90] *Roscommon Herald*, 26 October 1940.
[91] Korcaighe P. Hale, 'The limits of diplomatic pressure: Operation Safehaven and the search for German assets in Ireland', *Irish Historical Studies*, vol. XXXVI (143) (May 2009), 394.

requested the expulsion of the Axis missions in Dublin. Gray anticipated a refusal but was quite happy to see de Valera's reputation tarnished.

After the war Gray began work on a new history of Ireland. When compared with his 1930s book project, it is considerably less sympathetic in tone. 'By 1900,' he noted, 'the Irish peasantry, noted for being the most oppressed in Europe, had become the most privileged in the world'.[92] He denounced, unsurprisingly, the political leadership of its romantic republicanism as solipsistic and ultimately self-destructive, even though he retained an admiration for de Valera's personal courage as displayed in 1916:

> The Irish masses were hungry for just such a gospel of hope and pride and apocalyptic nationalism as were the Germans after their defeat in the first world war. And while it is not generally recognised, the analogy between Hitler and De Valera in their rise to power is very striking. Each preached the same doctrine of atavistic pagan nationalism: Hitler proclaimed the *Herrenvolk* and their oppressors the Jews. In the De Valera version the Gaels became the *Herrenvolk*, the English the hated oppressors. Each employed 'goon squads' to enforce pretence. As late as the early thirties the IRA made it as unhealthy to oppose De Valera as the Brown Shirts made it painful to oppose Hitler.

Gray rather injudiciously convinced himself that the rhetorical exaggerations of a democratic radical-nationalist party like Fianna Fáil were equivalent in some sense to the Big Lie of the Goebbels machine, and that majority support for the censorship mentality of the era was solely a top-down imposition by de Valera ('de Valeraism had abolished liberalism in Ireland') rather than reflecting deeper-rooted tendencies within Irish culture.

Gray's literary tastes also shifted. He had always admired Anglo-Irish literary achievements. He always enjoyed friendships with Edith Somerville and Elizabeth Bowen. But he had been open to pleasurable exploration of other, more republican, representatives of Irish literary life: his early friendly connections with the Brennans and admiration of the republican Francis Stuart are very evident. He now came to believe, as the book concludes, that Dublin nationalist literary life was essentially hollow and living off past glories. Gray came to believe also that the ultra-imperialist Lord Dunsany was the first lyric poet of the age: a somewhat extravagant judgement, although Dunsany's short stories are

[92] Gray manuscripts (Box 24), Folders 14 and 17.

widely admired. Dunsany responded by dedicating to Gray *The Fourth Book of Jorkens* (1949): this has several stories which—albeit in a fanciful style—portray war-time Ireland as full of Nazi spies.[93] In real life, it should be noted that Gray was not quite so fanciful.[94]

Gray offered the text of 'Behind the Emerald Curtain' (he also considered other titles in his notes, including 'Behind the Green Curtain') to the Northern Ireland Cabinet in the mid 1950s. They considered publication but never got around to making a positive decision. His proposed text came into the possession of the senior Northern Irish civil service official, W.F. Stout. It is the 'Stout' version which appears to include some material—for example, de Valera's discussion of the Schrödinger case—which is not in the Gray material used by other scholars. In the end, Gray was invited to write the introduction to W.A. Carson's *Ulster and the Irish republic*, which was published in Belfast in 1956. Gray took this opportunity to make his principal charge:

> The accumulating evidence supports the view that, even before the fall of France in 1940, De Valera believed that Hitler would win the war and in payment for keeping the Allies out of the Eire ports, he would obtain Northern Ireland on his own terms. This would have enabled him to invoke his formula of exchange of populations, expel 800,000 Ulstermen and invite in an equal number of exiles.[95]

The Department of External Affairs reacted immediately and in its weekly bulletin said:

> It is impossible to reconcile Mr Gray's view with the material facts. The position formerly held by Mr Gray, however, will confer a certain appearance of authority on what he has to say on matters arising during his term of office here. His brief account of that period is so distorted and so grave in its implications that it needs to be publicly refuted.[96]

---

[93] Patrick Maume, 'Dreams of empire, empire of dreams: Lord Dunsany plays the game', *New Hibernia Review*, 13 (4) (winter 2009), 14–33. Admiration for Dunsany's verse was not, however, unusual in inter-war American literary circles; the hero of F. Scott Fitzgerald's *This side of Paradise* is described as reciting it during a 'decadent' phase at Princeton (Laura Miller, 'Minor Magus: the fantastical writings of Lord Dunsany', *New Yorker*, 6 December 2004).
[94] Paul McMahon, *British spies and Irish rebels: British intelligence and Ireland 1916–45* (Woodbridge, 2008), 420.
[95] W.A. Carson, *Ulster and the Irish republic* (Belfast, 1956), v.
[96] *Irish Times*, 12 April 1968.

Carson passed the criticisms on to Gray, who was quite unrepentant in his reply. He did not regard the criticisms as having any 'material' validity.[97] Even so, even John J. Horgan, a close friend of David Gray—as this book makes clear—felt compelled to join in the criticism, describing Gray's criticisms of Irish neutrality as 'unjust and untrue'.[98]

It is possible to doubt significant aspects of Gray's analysis. Gray nowhere makes full allowance for a weak country desperately dodging and weaving in order to preserve its neutrality. De Valera not only had to play off the Germans against the British, but the Germans, as Gray knows, had two strategies against him: one, the threat of outright German victory—the other lay in their alliance with the IRA, which might topple his government. Some of the more embarrassing Irish messages to the Nazi regime—those which exude a tone of complicity—may be explained, in part, in this light. Gray himself appears to have been ignorant of the degree of genuine co-operation, especially in the intelligence field between neutral Ireland and belligerent Britain. The essence of the matter is summed up in the exchange between Seán Lemass and Malcolm MacDonald in Dublin in late June 1940: 'Mr Lemass then said that he gathered from listening carefully to my argument that we were not so much concerned that Éire should enter the war, as that the territory of Ireland should be secured against invasion by the enemy. I replied that this analysis was right'.[99] This helps to explain why Gray is more than a little surprised at the degree of British toleration of Irish ambiguities; a toleration encouraged by the surveys of his Irish public opinion conveyed by his own literary friends like Elizabeth Bowen.[100]

He speaks too, though, as if de Valera reached his policy of population transfer as a means of solving the Partition issue in response to an opportunity which might be created by a German victory in 1940–1. In fact, de Valera had believed in such a policy as early as 1920 and offered a public articulation of it at the Fianna Fáil party conference of 1939.[101] On the second day of the Fianna Fáil Ard Fheis in December 1939, de Valera argued that a transfer of populations between Irish emigrants in Britain and those in Northern Ireland who refused to

---

[97] PRONI D1327/20/4/36, Gray to Carson.
[98] John J. Horgan, 'Ireland: new problems, old policies?', *The Round Table* 48 (189) (December 1957), 71–75: 74.
[99] National Archives, Kew, CAB 123/196/XCI 91973.
[100] Elizabeth Bowen, '*Notes on Éire': espionage reports to Winston Churchill 1940–2* (Aubane, 1999), 12.
[101] Patrick Maume, 'Ulstermen of letters: the unionism of Frankfort Moore, Shan Bullock and St John Ervine', in Richard English and Graham Walker (eds), *Unionism in modern Ireland* (London, 1996), 84.

consider themselves Irish[102] might provide a solution to the Partition question.[103] Undoubtedly, Gray was aware of such a position and based his condemnation of de Valera upon it. The idea, of course, dismays and embarrasses the twenty-first century, when nationalist discourse in Ireland is glutted with talk of a hypothetical reconciliation of the 'two traditions'. We should not forget, however, that, half a century ago, much civilised opinion took a different view of population transfer—under the Treaty of Lausanne in 1923 some two million people moved between Greek and Turkish territory, and it was believed that an appalling loss of life had been averted.[104] More importantly, there is nothing in the archives which specifically connects de Valera's neutrality policy with such an aim. In February 1940, de Valera seemed to publicly disavow any such policy in his Cavan speech. On the other hand, Irish critics of Gray rarely acknowledge his most substantive points: for example, his critique of Dublin offers to manipulate mainstream American politics in the German interest through the utilisation of the Irish lobby. Gray's anger at discovering this offer being made to Berlin is absolutely inevitable, given his own strong anti-isolation stance. This is a fascinating work—throwing much new light on Irish but also British, American and German politics at the one moment in the last century when the fate of Western civilisation stood in the balance.

The controversy concerning the moral and political logic of Irish neutrality has not ended.[105] On one side there is a vigorous defence from the moral and cultural point of view of Irish neutrality policy. It has been convincingly argued that it was politically impossible—certainly highly divisive—for de Valera to enter the war on the Allied side. A survey of the provincial press hardly suggests any popular yearning. It has also been argued that Britain's decision not to invade represents another form of realism, allowing it to retain a degree of the moral high ground, crucial, for example, in the United States of America. There has also been a strong tendency, particularly in the work of Eunan O'Halpin and Michael Kennedy, to stress the ways in which Irish policy from late 1940 onwards effectively assisted the Allies.[106] Dr Kennedy, for example, demonstrates that the British naval attaché, Captain Grieg,

[102] For important context, see T. Ryle Dwyer, *De Valera: the man and the myths* (Dublin, 1992), 223.

[103] Bowman, *De Valera and the Ulster question*, 209.

[104] Isaiah Berlin to Johanna Lambert, 20 May 1958, Henry Hardy and Jennifer Holmes (eds), *Isaiah Berlin: enlightening letters 1946–60* (Oxford, 2009), 691.

[105] T.J. White and A.J. Reilly, 'Irish neutrality in World War Two: a review essay', *Irish Studies in International Affairs* (2008), 142–250.

[106] Michael Kennedy, *Guarding neutral Ireland: the coastwatching service and military intelligence* (Dublin, 2008).

was satisfied with Irish co-operation against German U-boat activity from late 1940.

Even some contemporary opponents of de Valera and of the policy agreed with this analysis. The ultra-republican journalist and former TD Brian O'Higgins (1882–1963), who believed for the rest of his life that de Valera and his successors were mere British vassals, sarcastically informed readers of the 1957 issue of his *Wolfe Tone Annual* that during the war:

> The Twenty-Six Counties Dáil had declared the neutrality of 'this part of Ireland' in the war being waged on the Continent of Europe, proofs of that neutrality being shown in heated speeches by the Taoiseach of the day, by the sending of cargoes of food to Britain, of tens of thousands of young people to work in British factories and in the fields of Britain and by freedom of movement out of the Twenty-Six Counties of all who wanted to join the British army.[107]

On the other hand, Geoffrey Sloan[108] cites the evidence of Admiral Eberhard Gott, who told his British interlocutors that German U-boats were able to surface, rest and repair in Irish territorial waters throughout the war and to the end of the war were receiving very considerable information about anti-U-boat minefields from the German intelligence service. It can not be denied, moreover, that Irish neutrality undermined the Irish state's official anti-Partition policy.

There is no escaping the logic of Malcolm MacDonald's remarks to Eamon de Valera, Frank Aiken and Seán Lemass on 27 June 1940:

> I said that I would like to speak for a moment, not as representative of the United Kingdom government, but as a private individual whose sympathies were on the side of the establishment of a united Ireland, and who, at the same time, knew British politics and the British parliament pretty well. The present was the best

---

107 Brian O'Higgins, *Wolfe Tone Annual* 15 (1957). I owe this reference to Dr Patrick Maume. O'Higgins's definition of national freedom is sufficiently indicated by his statement in the same volume (64–7), that Ireland would only be truly free when it was a criminal offence to verbally deny 'the right of Ireland to an independent, a separate national existence ... [to advocate] the dragging down of all the children of Ireland to his own level by leaving them ignorant of God's gift to Ireland, the Irish language ... to belittle Ireland's games by refusing to play and promote them, by uttering the slave's cry that 'one game is as good as another' ... to play and foster the vulgar, sensual, imported noise called music ... jungle jazz' and when anyone who transgressed in this manner 'would be punished so effectually that others like him would think oftener than twice before following his pernicious example'.

108 Geoffrey Sloan, 'Ireland and the geopolitics of Anglo-Irish relations', *Irish Studies Review* (15) (2007), 239–75. See also Robert Fisk, 'German U-boats refuelled in Ireland? Surely not', *Independent*, 17 September 2011.

opportunity that had yet offered itself of a union of the whole of Ireland against the Nazi attack, then that union would not be broken afterwards. But if the leaders of Eire now stayed out of the war and, perhaps contributed to German strength by doing so, whilst the people of Northern Ireland and of the United Kingdom, were joined in the supreme struggle against the Nazis, then none of us in Britain would be very concerned to create a united Ireland afterwards. My private, most sincere advice to them was to seize this opportunity which might never recur.[109]

Earlier in the month, Malcolm MacDonald had put it even more brutally in a private conversation with de Valera on 17 June:[110]

If they showed they were not prepared to fight for the freedom of Ireland, the United Kingdom and the other democratic countries of Europe—if they, who had spoken so much about liberty, now shrank from its defence in its supreme hour of danger, whilst Ulster fought fully for that defence—then the differences between the 26 and the six counties would certainly be aggravated and enlarged, and we politicians, who had gone through the fight, would never agree to handing Ulster over to Eire against the former's will.

As David Gray points out, even Malcolm MacDonald, in February 1945, acknowledged the cost of Irish neutrality to the Allied cause. Denial of the Irish ports to the Royal Navy was reckoned by the admiralty to have cost 368 ships and 5,070 lives during the Second World War.[111] It is hardly a surprise, therefore, that the most recent British study of the conflict is sharply sarcastic about the role of the Irish state.[112]

Professor Geoffrey Roberts has argued that the 'pragmatic pro-neutrality narrative' dominates academic and popular approaches to the issue in the Irish republic. In this interpretation, neutrality was a necessary policy which benefited Ireland and the Allies alike.[113] In a later article, Professor Roberts has acknowledged a greater 'official' Irish willingness to stress the heroism of the 150,000 Irish volunteers who served in the British forces during the Second World War: volunteers

---

[109] National Archives, Kew, CAB 123/196/6.
[110] National Archives, Kew, CAB 123/196/10.
[111] Patterson, *Ireland since 1939*, 56. For a different perspective, see Patrick McCarthy, 'The Treaty ports and the battle of the Atlantic', *Irish Sword* XXVIII (111) (2011), 57–100.
[112] Andrew Roberts, *The storm of war*, 114–16.
[113] Geoffrey Roberts, 'Three narratives of neutrality: historians and Ireland's war', in Brian Girvin and Geoffrey Roberts (eds), *Ireland in the Second World War: politics, society and remembrance* (Dublin, 2000), 67.

who were not made to feel very welcome when they returned to post-war Ireland.[114] But in the decade that has passed since he articulated the concept, the 'pragmatic pro-neutrality narrative' has, if anything, grown stronger. Even Jewish authors write with sentimental affection of de Valera, although it is now clear that Irish neutrality would not have saved Irish Jews.[115] David Gray's reputation has been a casualty, his spiritualism making him an easy target—a kind of WASP Brahmin eccentric.[116] It should be noted that Gray's text and argument here makes no reliance on the paranormal, and—while it cannot settle the argument—can redress the balance and enliven the discussion. It was not messages from the next world, but the content of the files captured by Allied troops in Berlin, which provoked Gray's anger. For example, he was infuriated by the German representative Hempel's message to Berlin on 17 June 1940, in which Joseph Walshe appeared anxious that Hitler's apparent desire to compromise with the British empire would not harm the fulfilment of Irish nationalist aspirations: 'Walshe remarked that he hoped that the statement by the *Fuehrer* ... [denying] an intention to destroy the British empire did not mean the abandonment of Ireland. In this connection it interested him, especially what I had told him about the importance of the outcome of the war for the final realisation of Irish demands'.[117]

Gray's work is instructive in another respect. It evokes a moment in which the special relationship with Britain is very real to certain American elites; though even then it was not uncontested. His admiration for Churchill is unstinting; it makes suggestive reading in the aftermath of President Obama's decision to return the Bush White House bust of Winston Churchill to the British government. Gray was an unapologetic supporter of Anglo-American democratic capitalism— in this period the only real Irish challenge was the radical chic Nazi anti-commercialism of an Irish republican like Francis Stuart.[118] Gray dismissed this with contempt—a moral clarity which in more recent times some have found unsettling and oversimplified.[119]

Paul Bew

[114] Geoffrey Roberts, 'Neutrality, identity and the challenge of the Irish volunteers', in D. Keogh and M.O. Driscoll (eds), *Neutrality and survival: Ireland in World War Two* (Cork, 2004), 284.
[115] Stanley Price, *Somewhere to hang my hat* (Dublin, 2002), 119; Roberts, *The storm of war*, 239.
[116] The 1983 RTÉ drama series about German spies in war-time Ireland, *Caught in a Free State*, plays Gray (O.Z. Whitehead) largely for laughs, and extracts some mileage out of his attendance at a séance.
[117] *Documents on German foreign policy 1918–45, series D (1937–1945)* X, 601.
[118] Brendan Barrington (ed.), *The wartime broadcasts of Francis Stuart, 1942–1944* (Dublin, 2000), 99.
[119] But see Michael Burleigh, *Moral combat: a history of World War II* (London, 2010).

BEHIND THE EMERALD CURTAIN

PREFACE

At the end of World War Two, Eamon de Valera, the Irish statesman, attributed the 'frictions' which arose between his government and Washington during the war years as due to 'divergence of national interest'. He expressed this opinion in a friendly talk at a dinner which he gave to the writer as retiring American minister to Éire in June 1947.

What doubtless he had in mind was that at the outbreak of hostilities both nations proclaimed neutrality; that after Pearl Harbor the United States became a belligerent while Éire continued as a proclaimed neutral. From this stemmed the divergence of interest which produced the frictions. But nothing begins in Ireland. It became evident that Mr de Valera's 'divergence of national interest' stemmed from causes lost centuries before Munich and the outbreak of World War Two. Although at the outbreak of the war both nations proclaimed neutrality neither was neutral within the classic definition of Dr Grotius.[1] As early as 1936 American Military Intelligence had convinced President Roosevelt that Hitler intended to make war. If victorious he would control Europe, the British empire, the Atlantic Ocean and South America. The United States would be left without democratic allies to meet a Germany controlling the industrial resources of the European continent.

It was a choice between fighting alone for survival or with allies for victory. The president thereupon embarked upon his ill-fated effort to 'preserve the peace of Europe' by a conference of European powers in which the United States would participate. Failing in this he formulated

[1] Hugo Grotius (1583–1645). With Francisco de Vitoria and Alberico Gentili he laid the foundations for international law, based on natural law.

his policy of American preparedness, as the 'Arsenal of Democracy', the keystone of which became 'all aid to Britain short of war'. This un-neutral keystone produced what the historians Langer and Gleason have termed the 'Undeclared War' which led to Pearl Harbor.[2]

On September 3rd, 1939 the president proclaimed American neutrality because at that time no other course was politically practicable. The German Bundists, the Irish Anglophobes and the American Firsters had captured American isolationist opinion and controlled the Congress. But the executive branch of the United States government upon which lay the responsibility of formulating foreign policy could never have been neutral in conviction or aim. For since 1936 it had recognised Hitler's Germany as a menace to American vital interest and Western democracy.

The professed neutrality of Éire was even more unreal, for two years before World War Two began there existed an undivulged understanding between the British and Éire governments currently referred to as 'The Gentleman's Agreement', the import of which, as the British government understood it, was to make Éire a secret ally of England. The importance of this not merely to the Anglo-Irish relation but to Irish-American relations after Pearl Harbor is such as to compel examination of the background facts.

In 1927 Mr de Valera with a majority of his new Fianna Fáil party took the oath of allegiance to the Irish Free State and entered the Dáil, forming a 'Constitutional Opposition'. This was five years after he had launched his ill-fated Civil War against the parliamentary majority which in 1922 had concluded the 'Treaty' with Britain and set up of the Irish Free State in the southern part of Ireland. The reasoning behind his action then had been that they should have held out for republican instead of dominion status and for the whole of Ireland instead of just the southern part. Now in accepting the Treaty and the Free State established under it, he accepted the Free State's obligations and responsibilities. One of these was the promise made by the government in 1925 to live in peace and amity with the other part of the island, Northern Ireland. The latter had opted to remain a part of the United Kingdom when the South broke away to form the Irish Free State.

Another was collection and remittance to the British treasury of 'Annuities'. About the turn of the century the British public had subscribed upwards of a hundred million sterling to finance the new Irish Land Acts. These Acts authorised the purchase of Irish lands and

[2] William L. Langer and S.E. Gleason, *The undeclared war, 1940–1941* (New York, 1953).

their resale to tenant farmers on the instalment plan, and on favourable terms. They were primarily a lien on the land but guaranteed by the British treasury. The payments of capital, amortisation and interest, were known as 'the Annuities'.

In the general election of 1932 Mr de Valera's Fianna Fáil party repudiated this obligation. This won them the election but he had not considered the consequences. The British government imposed a 40 per cent retributive duty on Irish cattle. Mr de Valera promised the farmers alternative markets. But there were none. He declared an 'economic war' on England, and rallied supporters by beating the old anti-British drums. The Irish people could tighten their belts as exhorted, but this did not feed livestock. By 1934 the Éire government was slaughtering calves by the thousand which the Irish farmer could not feed, and the English government was collecting the annuities and something over. In 1937 the Irish cattle industry, the chief source of Irish national income, was all but ruined, and the Éire government was politically bankrupt. They threw in the sponge and went to London as it was said, 'cap in hand'.

Apparently they found Neville Chamberlain illuminated by his dream of European peace by appeasement.[3] The prime minister apparently was not interested in punishing the Irish government for their violation of Treaty obligations, but in using their predicament to test the appeasement formula and end the ancient and profitless Anglo-Irish quarrel. For the Éire government Mr Chamberlain's attitude offered not only immediate escape from Irish economic disaster for which they were responsible, but an opportunity which in the nature of things Mr de Valera could not reasonably have hoped for, to retrieve his political fortunes. It was an opportunity to retain the benefits of remaining in the British system yet on such conditions as would tend to justify his repudiation of the Treaty in 1922.

In return for ending the ancient quarrel on terms which were as advantageous to the Irish people as to Fianna Fáil's political fortunes, the English government was prepared to give him practically everything he asked for except Northern Ireland. And not only were they prepared to grant these concessions, but in part secretly and in the somewhat devious ways which the Éire government apparently suggested. In April 1938, the British government not merely repealed the retributive cattle duties which were ruining Ireland, but condoned the repudiation of the annuities and waived them entirely for the future.

[3] For the outstanding modern scholarly treatment of these negotiations, see Deirdre McMahon, *Republicans and imperialists: Anglo-Irish relations in the 1930s* (New Haven, 1984), 237–84.

Item I of the Trade Agreement reads: 'The Government of Éire agree to pay to the Government of the United Kingdom, on or before the 20th November, 1938, the sum of £10,000,000'. This was the token payment recognising the validity of the annuities obligation.

The amount which Mr Chamberlain forgave the Irish people was between four and five hundred million dollars at the rate of exchange then prevailing. It was the equivalent of nearly 170 dollars to every man, woman and child in Éire. A gift proportionally large to the American people today[4] would be over 29 billion dollars, yet no mention was made of it in the formal agreement. Nor yet was mention made of other provisions of the Treaty which, had they not been waived secretly, would have prevented Mr de Valera from promulgating his new Constitution in 1937. This replaced the Anglo-Irish Treaty Constitution of the Free State and established Éire as an 'Independent state voluntarily associated with the British Commonwealth'. This new Éire was essentially the 'republic' for which Mr de Valera had split the Irish people in 1922.

It cannot be asserted that the Éire government enjoyed the *right* to modify the Treaty under the Statute of Westminster,[5] enacted in 1931, for the Irish Free State had refused to accept the Statute. In 1931 the Cosgrave government had been apprehensive lest the British parliament should unilaterally modify the Treaty in a sense adverse to Free State interest. They therefore filed the Treaty with the League of Nations at Geneva with the declaration that they elected to base their rights upon its terms rather than on the new Statute. The Treaty therefore was in force at the time of the Chamberlain-de Valera negotiation. Its provisions for common defence and the use by England of the Irish ports were also in full force and necessarily would be until modified by mutual agreement.

The great concession which concerned British security and eventually American vital interest was the surrender of the Irish ports. These were the areas reserved by the Anglo-Irish Treaty of 1922 for the common defence of the two islands. It was now proposed that these ports should be surrendered 'without conditions'. Prime Minister Chamberlain made the official statement on the matter in the House of Commons on May 5th, 1938 (italics mine):

There was no part of our discussions with the ministers from Éire which gave us more prolonged and anxious thought than the

[4] At time of writing, 1959.
[5] The Statute of Westminster adopted by the British parliament in 1931 declared the inherent right of the Commonwealth Dominions to autonomy.

subject of defence. A request was made to us that we should hand back to the Government of Éire the full and unrestricted possession of certain ports.[6] After consideration of all the circumstances and after due consultation with the Chiefs of Staff we came to the conclusion that a *friendly Ireland* was worth far more to us both in peace and in war than these paper rights which could only be exercised at the risk of maintaining, and perhaps increasing their sense of grievance, and so we agreed that, subject to Parliamentary confirmation, the ports shall be handed over unconditionally to the Government of Éire.

The implication is clear that the consideration for the return of the ports was a friendly Ireland. There was English opposition to this policy. Mr Winston Churchill, then in opposition, during the debate on the Éire bill said:

Now we are to give them (the ports) up unconditionally, to an Irish Government composed of men—I do not wish to use hard words—whose rise to power has been proportionate to the animosity with which they have acted against this country, no doubt in pursuance of their own patriotic impulses, and whose present position is based on the violation of solemn treaty engagements.[7]

Professor Sir Douglas Savory in 1938 was a member of the faculty of Queen's University, Belfast, Northern Ireland. In 1940 he entered parliament and continued there till 1948. During this period he represented the interests of Northern Ireland. His historical writings with first-hand knowledge of this controversial period have made him not only its 'authoritative' historian but 'source material'. Sir Douglas, in his brochure reprinted from the *Contemporary Review* (1958) under the title 'The Irish Treaty Ports in 1938' tells us that opposition came not only from Winston Churchill but from within the Cabinet also. He quotes the late Lord Maugham, who succeeded Lord Hailsham as Lord Chancellor, as telling him that the matter had been settled in the Cabinet before he took his place there; that he, Hailsham, had protested strongly but had been overruled. Sir Douglas further notes:

[6] Several paragraphs intervene between this and the next sentence—see Hansard for 5 May 1938. http://hansard.millbanksystems.com/commons/1938/may/05/eire-confirmation-of-agree-ments-bill (accessed 19 August 2011). In the Hansard record of this speech the following sentence begins 'After most careful consideration…'.
[7] See Hansard for 5 May 1938.

At the time of the negotiations Mr Andrews, Minister of Labour in the Northern Ireland Government, journeyed to and from London many times to plead with the British Government to stay their hand. 'I saw Mr MacDonald myself', said Mr Andrews, 'and told him it was an act of folly. He answered "no, it is an act of faith"'.[8]

Though there was difference of opinion and strong dissent in parliament, agreement was reached in the Cabinet and there were no resignations on the issue. Even the admiralty accepted the proposal. Sir Douglas quotes Admiral Lord Chatfield, First Sea Lord, who approved the surrender as follows:

A new and safer Agreement with Ireland (than that of 1921) was very necessary and the political wheels were beginning to turn slowly in that direction. If a friendly Agreement would increase the assurance that we could rely on the use of the Irish ports, should we become involved in war, and by creation of a better feeling, make it safe to base our defensive and offensive strategy on such an assurance, the Admiralty anxiety would be greatly reduced. The political aim as expressed by the Dominions Secretary, Mr Malcolm MacDonald, was the creation of the prospect of a more abundant friendship with the Irish people.

Obviously, the undisclosed agreement, whatever its terms, in Admiral Chatfield's opinion was a 'safer' agreement for England than the Treaty provided.

Mr Chamberlain's personal convictions as to Mr de Valera's assurances are revealed in an extract from his diary dated March 18th, 1938, which his biographer, Mr Feiling, releases:

I shall be accused of having weakly given way when Éire was in the hollow of my hand. Only I and my colleagues (who are

[8] Sir Douglas Lloyd Savory (1878–1969), the most respected of the Ulster Unionist parliamentary representatives. An English academic, of proud Huguenot extraction, he was regarded by nationalists as a strident Protestant bigot. Savory was educated at Marlborough College, the University of Paris and at St John's College Oxford and was a man of some ability. In 1943 he was asked by the Polish government in exile to investigate the mass murder of Polish officers in Katyn Forest. His report correctly concluded that Russian forces were responsible but was not published until several years after the war. Gray's account here is accurate enough as far as it goes. But it omits the fact that Craigavon supported the appeasement policy in broad terms and merely asked to be 'bribed' with contracts for Belfast firms as the price of his acquiescence in the Chamberlain/de Valera deal. D.W. Harkness, *History and the Irish* (Belfast, 1976), 313.

unanimous) can judge of this. But I am satisfied that we have only given up the small things (paper rights and revenues that would not last) for the big things—the ending of a long quarrel, the beginning of better relations between North and South Ireland and the Co-operation of the South with us in trade and defence.[9]

Mr de Valera obviously had convinced Mr Chamberlain that he had ended the long quarrel; that this was the 'final settlement'; that they were united 'for Trade and Defence'. Trade and defence were the key words. Together with the prime minister, Sir John Simon, Sir Samuel Hoare, Malcolm MacDonald, minister for dominions, and T.W.H. Inskip, then minister for the co-ordination of defence, afterwards Lord Chancellor and subsequently, as Viscount Caldecote, chief justice of England, signed the agreement for England. These were not political amateurs, starry-eyed idealists or the conscience-haunted aristocrat inheritors of unearned privilege but representatives of the tough, successful British businessman type which had made the British empire. They believed that in surrendering the Treaty ports they were doing a good thing for England; they believed, like Admiral Chatfield, that the assurances which Mr de Valera had given them were a better guarantee of Irish support in case of war—and war was threatening—than the Irish Treaty provisions. They trusted de Valera.

As Mr Chamberlain set out upon his tragic pilgrimage to Munich in 1938 Mr de Valera wrote:

You will have succeeded or failed when you receive this. I merely write to tell you that one person at least is completely satisfied that you are doing the right thing, no matter what the result. I believe you will be successful. Should you not be so, you will be blamed for having gone at all. To stop half way, to stop short of any action which held out even the slightest chance of success, in view of what is involved, would be wrong. Should you fail you need have no qualms. What a business man would do, you, who have at this moment, the fate of millions who cannot help themselves, depending on you, are certainly entitled to do so and should do so. May God bless your efforts.[10]

[9] See Keith Feiling, *Neville Chamberlain* (London, 1946).
[10] For de Valera's support of Chamberlain, see T.P. Coogan, *De Valera: long fellow, long shadow* (London, 1993) 529–30.

The sincerity of this letter suggests that Mr Chamberlain's confidence in the Éire leader was not unwarranted.

And why should he not have been sincere? The great opportunity had come to him to fulfil what had been the manifest destiny of the Irish people since 1168, to lead them to strength and fulfilment through co-operation. What shrewder move could an Irish statesman have made than to assure the Irish economy by co-operation with England's, and to insure Ireland's security by agreement for common defence with England, an agreement presumably soon to be underwritten by a hundred and fifty million Americans whose vital interest lay palpably in the defeat of National Socialism? Any other policy would have been irrational. Thus in 1938 and '39 in the English view Éire was a secret ally under the terms of the 'Gentleman's Agreement'. As London understood it the Éire government had pledged themselves to promote the common interest in trade and defence. Their price had been remission of the annuities, the Coal-Cattle pact, the ports without strings and other valuable considerations, and Britain had paid it. Éire therefore was not at that time neutral.

But on September 3rd, 1939, the day England declared war on Germany, de Valera 'explained' matters to a specially summoned Dáil and was authorised to proclaim Irish neutrality.

What did this mean? Outside of Mr de Valera's circle of intimates no one knew. At the time in London it seemed to mean that the Éire government was having a bad time politically in Ireland. The IRA were accusing them of having sold out to England. They did not believe that the government could have got the ports unless he had given assurances to Prime Minister Chamberlain that in case of war Britain would be able to use them. They (the IRA) therefore in January 1939 had declared a private war on England, and when World War Two began in September they proclaimed themselves the ally of Germany. Their underground propaganda put the issue to the Irish people thus: 'Are we for the traditional English enemy or the German friend?'.

Since the Éire government had not taken the Irish people into their confidence and explained the advantages of 'common defence and trade', they had no good answer. They were caught trying to get the best of both possible worlds. Presumably they explained their plight to Neville Chamberlain and asked to be allowed to temporise. With France intact, the British navy did not then need the Irish ports. Apparently Mr Chamberlain acquiesced. He certainly had faith in Mr de Valera and 'Irish Friendship', as late as the first week in April 1940, for [on] the 3rd of that month he sent me a message in London, breaking an appointment for that day. He said that on second thoughts he was of the opinion that to receive the United States minister on the way to his post might be regarded by Mr de Valera as a breach of confidence even though there were no grounds for it. His faith in Mr de Valera appeared to be warranted, for on April 11th, Mr de Valera's newspaper[11] in Dublin condemned the German invasion of Denmark and Norway and on May 12th, Mr de Valera himself, after consultation with Sir John Maffey, United Kingdom Representative in Éire, in a speech delivered in Galway condemned German aggression in the Low Countries.

Based presumably on reports from its representatives in London and Dublin, Washington's view of Éire at this time was substantially that of London—that it was 'No Enemy'.

We know today that no view could have been more erroneous. For eight days before the Second World War began, without withdrawing the pledges of 'Irish friendship' and acceptance of the principles of common interest in trade and defence, or returning the thirty pieces of silver, the Éire government secretly offered Hitler assurance of Irish sympathy in the impending conflict and the promise of an Irish neutrality which would bar Britain from the ports.

Further, as if they controlled the American government, they offered Hitler the exercise of Irish influence in the United States described as 'perhaps decisive', to prevent an Anglo-American alliance and what Hitler most feared, American intervention.

Since Éire was dependent on England for markets and supplies which Germany could not provide, the Éire government proposed that the German government permit them to take the necessary measures to maintain England's trust in them, thus assuring continuance of supply and immunity from attack.

The price which the Éire government proposed for these not inconsiderable services was Northern Ireland. Only a few months before, in the Irish Senate, Mr de Valera had denounced any coercion of Ulstermen as unthinkable. Now Hitler was to hand over to Éire all eight hundred thousand Ulstermen and their territory for a price. This despite the fact that in 1925 the Dublin government had renounced all territorial claim to the North.

How do we know this? The information is set forth in a series of telegrams sent by the German minister in Dublin to Ribbentrop in Berlin, the first dated August 26th, 1939. They were in the German

---

[11] *Irish Press.*

Foreign Office files captured by the American army when it entered Berlin. The British government has published them in Vol. VII Series D. of *Documents on German foreign policy 1918–1945* by H.M. Stationery Office.[12] The Irish government has not challenged their authenticity. The texts will be examined in Chapter I of this book.

Why when they discovered their mistake did the Allies never take the Éire ports? They always had the power, and there were periods when the need was grave. From the Hitlerian viewpoint not to take them was lunacy.

Realistic as Winston Churchill was, realism to him meant respect for the Moral Order. International law recognises that 'Necessity knows no Law'. This posed the question: what and when is 'Necessity'? In Mr Churchill's view the point that would justify seizure never was quite reached. After the war he had this to say:

> I well know the grievous injury which Southern Irish neutrality and the loss of the Southern Irish ports inflicted upon us in the recent war, but always adhered to the policy that nothing save British existence and survival should lead us to regain the ports by force of arms.

After Pearl Harbor this became the American view. The United States equally with Great Britain suffered losses in American lives, ships and treasure which demonstrably could have been reduced had we had use of the bases in Southern Ireland. Not having them, those of Northern Ireland became indispensable, and this indispensability became the measure of America's debt to Northern Ireland. No one less than ex-President Eisenhower has appraised this indispensability and hence the debt. In October 1945, in Belfast, as General of the Armies he said:

> It was here in Northern Ireland that the American Army first began to concentrate for our share in the attack upon the citadel of continental Europe. From here we started the long, hard march to Allied victory. Without Northern Ireland I do not see how the American forces could have been concentrated to begin the invasion of Europe. If Ulster had not been a definite, co-operative part of the British Empire and had not been available for use, I do not see how the build-up could have been carried out in England.[13]

12 HMSO, *The last days of peace, 9 August–3 September 1939* (London, 1956).
13 This phrase was, interestingly, not repeated by President Clinton in his three visits to Belfast during the peace process.

But over and beyond the indispensability of the Northern Ireland bases there was the inspiring spiritual factor in the gesture granting them. The Ulster people welcomed us at the moment when the strength of our Pacific fleet was on the bottom, when the outlook was dark, when we needed friends and friendship; at the moment when de Valera who, on January 13th, 1921, leaving America with 9 million American dollars, had said, 'Ireland will not forget' yet had himself forgotten. At such a moment the warm friendliness of the Ulster people in welcoming American soldiers, their patience during the occupation of their villages and their peculiar staunchness, can never be forgotten. Such Ulster names as James Craig,[14] Basil Brooke,[15] the Abercorns[16] and J.M. Andrews,[17] will pass into our history with the Ulstermen who two centuries before stood by George Washington in his darkest days. They, like the bonds of comradeship forged during the dangerous years, have become part of our American Heritage.

---

[14] Sir James Craig (Viscount Craigavon) (1871–1940), son of a Presbyterian whiskey millionaire and educated at Merchiston School, Edinburgh. Prime minister of Northern Ireland from 1921 to 1940.
[15] Sir Basil Brooke (Viscount Brookeborough) (1888–1973). Educated at Winchester and Sandhurst, lost two sons in the Second World War. From 1943 to 1963 he was prime minister of Northern Ireland.
[16] James Hamilton, 3rd Duke of Abercorn (1869–1953), Ulster Unionist MP for Londonderry City 1900–13, Governor of Northern Ireland 1922–45.
[17] J.M. Andrews (1871–1956). Came from a family with substantial interests in flax-spinning and railways. Held various Cabinet posts from 1921–40, and became prime minister from 1940 to 1943.

CHAPTER I

The United States Department of State in February 1940 had no knowledge of the understanding between the Éire government and the German minister in Dublin, arrived at just prior to the British declaration of war on Germany on September 3rd, 1939. However the historical facts relating to the inception and development of the Sinn Féin Separatist Movement were public knowledge. That they had not been 'evaluated', interpreted and made a basis for an American-Irish policy was probably due to the then long-standing American sentimental predilection for the Irish Cause as against Britain and the power and influence of the Irish Societies in American politics. No American secretary of state, regardless of party, cared to stick his neck out. Regardless of party, therefore, the 'Anglo-Irish relation' and the 'Partition Question' were regarded as '*not* American concerns'.

Similar reasons probably also prevented Department discussion of the results of Mr Chamberlain's 'Policy of Faith', as regards Éire and the presumption that reliance on 'Irish Friendship' had replaced provisions for common defence, embodied in the Anglo-Irish Treaty. Certainly no views on these matters were communicated in 1940 to the minister designate to Éire. The president appointed me to this post on February 4th. The Senate confirmed the nomination on February 26th, I was sworn in and began the usual fortnight of 'indoctrination'.

The preceding introductory matter, as the reader will have noted, is an interpretation of accepted history and of the social forces which had made the Irish people what they were as World War Two began. What follows is the raw material of history in the making. It must be winnowed, weighed and 'evaluated' before acceptance by the historian.

England and the United States have begun publishing official documents relative to the period, and authoritative books written by American and English participants in the drama have appeared. Thus far Éire has not opened her archives.[1] But the captured files of the German Foreign Office are now becoming available to the public and these throw light on Irish war policy. It is revealed as essentially different from what it was proclaimed to be by the de Valera government. The pattern of events disclosed exposes not merely the fantastic blunders in foreign policy inspired by the emotional philosophy of Irish Racial Separatism, but the breakdown of accepted standards of international morals which it entailed. It further exemplifies the universal menace to the Free World of such philosophy whether manifesting in Catholic Ireland or non-Christian Indonesia or Darkest Africa.

Most of my letters to the president and reports to the secretary of state were written before the capture of the German files. In the light of what they divulge, certain views and interpretations expressed in these documents have necessarily to be revised but the quoted texts stand as written.

During the first phase of World War Two, the American people were confused. Here was a war that obviously threatened their vital interests but they were reluctant to recognise the obvious. The First World War was less than a generation away. There was no biological urge for bloodletting. Their repudiation of the League of Nations had left them divided. The Versailles Treaty had left them disillusioned. The Technocrats, pointing to the Great Depression, were suggesting that Democracy was an outworn system. The enemy within the gates, the Bundists, the Ireland Firsters, the America Firsters, all sham patriots, were shouting raucously, 'This is not our war. No more American boys to save England a second time!' It was one of those periods of crisis and indecision in the national life when sinister minorities capture nations. It was in such a period that Lenin and Trotsky had captured Russia, Hitler the Germans, and, in Ireland, Sinn Féin the Irish.

The politicians in Congress were marking time, waiting for repercussions from 'back home'. The administration was professedly waiting on Congress. Actually and secretly it was exploring ways and means effectively to protect America and Western Democracy. The president never doubted Democracy. He said we had not exploited its resources. All that we had to fear about Democracy was our fear about it. At the time I was one of those who believed in what they called 'strong

[1] The *Documents on Irish foreign policy* series edited by Crowe *et al.* has now published material relating to this era: *DIFP VI 1939–41* (Dublin, 2008); *DIFP VII 1941–45* (Dublin, 2010).

leadership', that is blurting out the truth and trusting the people to accept it. Later I realised that this had not been a time for debate. Honest debate was impossible, for un-American influences, among them an Anglophobe Irish Minority were exploiting American ignorance. It was necessary to gain time that the people might see clearly. I realised that the president and Secretary Hull had been right in waiting for the Congress to discover for itself that this was another case of 'hanging together' with those with similar vital interests or 'hanging singly' and to prepare the first step toward co-operation, which was to become prepared.

A somewhat analogous situation had faced Lincoln as the war between the states drew on. Lincoln knew that the true issue was slavery but he also knew that the border states would not support him on slavery but might fight to maintain the Union. So he made the Union the paramount issue. President Roosevelt knew that Americans who would not fight to save Western civilisation would fight for America, so he made defence of America the issue. He would have to wait for the honest isolationists to learn that it was easier to defend America with allies, who would help control the North Atlantic, than alone. He could not announce this self-evident fact because the German Bundists, the America Firsters and the Irish Sinn Féiners would charge him with sacrificing America to save England. They would rather have America beaten than England saved. He, therefore, would have to wait till the people saw the truth for themselves. While he was waiting he would work for as great a measure of preparedness as the Congress would sanction. But here in Washington a newly appointed minister was being 'indoctrinated' for a strategic post in the 'war area' and nobody mentioned the war.

Secretary Hull,[2] to whom I became warmly attached, talked to me for an hour and never mentioned the possibility of war. He said that he understood Dublin was a very pleasant post. He hoped that we would have a good time. Then he told me about education in the Tennessee Mountain Country when he was a boy.

No one in the West European Division, which conducted Irish affairs, seemed interested in the realities of Irish politics which involved Irish neutrality. No one mentioned the state of Anglo-Irish relations, the significance of the Coal-Cattle Pact and the surrender of the ports. No one mentioned the 'Gentleman's Agreement' in London. No one told me anything about the conflict going on in the Irish Societies in the United States between the de Valera supporters and the Irish Republican

[2] Cordell Hull (1871–1955). Longest serving secretary of state (1933–44); Nobel Peace Prize winner in 1945.

Army which now opposed him. Nobody told me that the IRA financed with American funds had declared war on England as of January 1939, and was the avowed ally of Germany and enemy of de Valera.[3]

There was the same war blackout at the White House as in the State Department. We had gone back to Florida to arrange for what I then expected to be at most a year's absence. At the close of a business talk with Homer Whitman,[4] vice-president of the Palmer Bank in Sarasota, he asked, 'What do you think about the war?' I countered, 'What do you think about it?' He said, 'I can't see but what this is *our* war and if a fellow is willing to do our fighting for us, aren't we fools not to give him a gun and cartridges?'

Here was the 'Arsenal of Democracy' and 'Lend Lease'. Mr Whitman was a banker who presumably should have been an isolationist. I thought: 'This is something to tell the President'. But after I had spent the day in Washington I was afraid to tell him. I told it to Steve Warly.[5] 'Don't that beat the Dutch!' he said. 'We keep getting stories like that from all over the country'. But the fact was that the people of the United States were entering a new phase in their political evolution. Four centuries earlier men had learned that the world was round. Now they were beginning to learn, with Wendell Wilkie,[6] that it was One. There was no escape from the responsibilities which living in it imposed. But this realisation came slowly and at first to but the few. The politicians were slow to adjust themselves to the new facts. The war taboo at the White House in February and March 1940 stemmed not from the fact that no one was thinking about it, but from fear that what they were *doing* would leak out. As early as 1936 our Military Intelligence had convinced the president that Hitler was planning to fight and create a world empire. A year later the president made his ill-fated proposal for a peace conference to Prime Minister Chamberlain. He had no illusions about 'Fortress America', but he also realised that the forces of isolationism were strong. Besides the mothers who did not 'raise their boys to be soldiers' and the spiritual heirs of William Jennings Bryan who would stand on the American beaches and oppose invaders with bare arms, there were great masses of sensible people who felt that it was not a good idea to be used by European nations as a cat's paw to pull out their chestnuts. There were also the American quislings with fascist propagandas of hate and

[3] Eunan O'Halpin, *Defending Ireland: the Irish state and its enemies since 1922* (Oxford, 1999), 147–8.
[4] Homer Whitman went on to establish the Selby foundation in 1955.
[5] Stephen Early (1889–1951). White House press secretary.
[6] Wendell Wilkie (1892–1944), former democrat turned senior republican. Republican presidential candidate 1940, eventually moved back into Roosevelt's camp.

disunion. The president was facing the problem how best to save the nation, which also meant how best to educate it to the facts of international life. Thus the Pro-Germans were charging him with warmongering and the 'Idealists' with cowardice in refusing to save civilisation. His great ally was a Free Press.

As Hitler revealed himself, American newspapers reported the revelations and their significance. Slowly American public opinion gelled in the mould of Truth.

In contrast to this groping of the American people toward decision on the basis of augmenting knowledge was the situation in de Valera's Éire. There was no groping in Dublin, no augmenting knowledge, and no indecision. Mr de Valera decided for the Irish people, and that without a mandate, without informing William Cosgrave, leader of the opposition, without notifying the Irish parliament. Such was the de Valera conception of Democracy.

It was probably not the decision that Mr de Valera had wished to make and had planned. The evidence suggests that he would have preferred to be loyal and grateful to Mr Chamberlain but the Coal-Cattle Pact had backfired politically in Ireland. The announcement of it, instead of being hailed by the left-wing IRA as a patriotic achievement, was received with suspicion and challenge. The IRA did not believe that he had got back the ports 'without strings'. They believed what was doubtless the truth, that Mr de Valera had given undertakings, though not in writing, that if the ports were needed they would be available. Soon the IRA were circulating the charge that he had sold Ireland out and had agreed to 'common defence'. It was then that Mr de Valera panicked. His political career had been built on the basis of being always 'on the Left'. He could not endure letting his rivals get to the 'Left' of him. In Ireland 'Left' means 'anti-British'.[7]

It is probable that he returned from London in 1938 prepared to make good his pledge of 'Irish Friendship', of adherence to the principle of common interest with Britain for trade and defence. It was a sound and unquestionably profitable long-range policy. He made the announcement that he would never permit a foreign power to use Éire as a base to attack Britain. He made his speech in the Irish Senate disclaiming force as a method of ending Partition, and advising mutual co-operation and good will. Then about the middle of January 1939 the IRA's announcement of its declaration of war on England frightened him.

[7] Paul Bew, Henry Patterson and Ellen Hazelkorn, *The dynamics of Irish politics* (London, 1989), 41–72.

According to the alleged confession of his alleged stool pigeon in the IRA, for a number of months he had been secretly betraying IRA plans to British Intelligence. But now he felt compelled to come out in the open. He could not avow his 'Gentleman's Agreement' for common defence. He could not allow his party to appear in Irish eyes as pro-British and the IRA as custodian of the 'German Friendship' which had become 'traditional' in patriot circles since the First World War, or of the anti-British issue. He began shifting his position. On February 9th, 1939, he made his notable speech on Partition in the Irish Senate. No one could say that he could not understand what it meant.

There were two opposed opinions on the subject and it gave support to each of them. It seems to have been made in part to fulfil what Prime Minister Chamberlain understood to mean Mr de Valera's pledge to him not to use force or incite the use of force against Northern Ireland. It also assured the advocates of force in Éire that they had the *right* to use force since they had the *right* to the whole national territory, to wit the whole island. In part he said (italics mine):

> If we had behind us *the strength of some of the Continental Powers,* I can say publicly what I have said privately—I would feel perfectly justified in using force to prevent the coercion of the people of South Down, South Armagh, Tyrone, Fermanagh, and Derry City. Would I go further than that? Remember I do not think that I would have solved the question of the partition of this country simply by relieving them of coercion. Even though I would feel justified in doing it and *probably would do it,* still I cannot blind myself to the fact that the problem of the partition of this country would remain, because a portion of it would still be cut off. I think that the whole of this island is the national territory.

This paragraph would have been for the German minister to send to Berlin suggesting that Éire was after all, and in spite of getting back the ports, not in the British Camp. Eight days later on February 17th and about a month after the IRA had declared war on England as well as against him, Mr de Valera in the Dáil proclaimed the government's hopes that in case war should break, the new 'independent' state of Éire would remain neutral. He had taken the first open step in disassociating Éire with 'common defence'. This he was to develop into the specious thesis that Irish independence was the 'equivalent of Neutrality'.

Presumably it would have been about this time that he began to explore the German attitude toward the IRA's declaration of war on England, and toward his own government. He knew that IRA agents in Dublin would have forwarded to Berlin the organisation's charges that he had sold out to Britain with prima facie evidence to support them. He must therefore have been relieved to find out through Mr Walshe's approach to Hempel that Hempel personally had no illusions about the importance of the IRA as an ally, in the event of war; that he realised that an official Irish neutrality which barred England from the Éire ports would be of vastly greater assistance than the belligerence of the group which he referred to as the 'Extreme Nationalists'. Hempel, therefore, who must have been instructed by his ministry that Berlin had written off Éire after the Coal-Cattle Pact, began a new programme of conciliation which included a cautious but consistent deprecation of the IRA.

Mr Joseph P. Walshe, de Valera's secretary of the Department of External Affairs, had established an exceptionally happy personal relation with the German minister and his family. He himself believed in German victory and the inauguration of the 'New Order'. At that time so did most Irish politicians regardless of party. Presumably he influenced Mr de Valera in the framing of his new 'realistic' Irish foreign policy. It had two chief objectives, first the acquisition from a victorious Hitler of Northern Ireland at the end of the war; second the immediate replacement in the mind of the Irish electorate of the IRA by the Fianna Fáil government as the 'anti-British' party and custodian of German friendship, which since the First World War had become a 'traditional' friendship. Thus on August 26th, 1939, Herr Hempel and Mr Walshe lunched together. They must have lunched extremely early for Dublin, for Hempel's dispatch reporting the conversation is dated August 26th, 1939, 12.15 p.m. Berlin received it on the same day at 4 p.m. Here is the text (italics mine):

No. 303

91/100055

The Minister in Eire to the Foreign Ministry

Telegram

No. 47 of August 26   Dublin, August 26, 1939—12:15 p.m.
                                        Received August 26—4:15 p.m.

Secretary General Walsh [*sic*][8] of the Irish foreign ministry lunched with me today and *brought* the conversation around to the Irish attitude in case of war. He stated definitely that Ireland

[8] Walshe is spelled correctly in the *Documents on German foreign policy* version of this telegram.

would remain neutral except in the case of a definite attack, for example, dropping bombs on Irish towns. He could not think that such a thing would happen through us as it would not appear to be in the German interest, while on the other hand, *Irish sympathy—especially in view of the strong, perhaps decisive influence of the American Irish against an American British alliance could not be a matter of indifference to us.* Also the disturbance of normal trade with Britain, of vital importance to Ireland for obtaining supplies of essential consumer goods, and which Ireland would have to confine to the export of agricultural produce ... (eight groups mutilated). He also expects that Britain, in view of the *American Irish*, will do everything to avoid violating Irish neutrality ... (two groups mutilated) representation with the usual proviso as to long term maintenance of neutrality.

He repeated the suggestion that in case of German acts of war against Britain involving Ireland, any suffering incurred should be kept to a minimum, and at the same time a *formal declaration should be made that* Germany has no aggressive aims in Ireland but *on the contrary has sympathy for Ireland* and *Irish National Aims—* mentioning if necessary *Northern Ireland—*that she regrets Irish suffering and will attempt to keep this to the unavoidable minimum. Avoid internment of Irish nationals in case of war.

HEMPEL

Hempel's telegram of August 26th was approved in Berlin. On August 29th Ribbentrop telegraphed instructing him to see de Valera at once. This is the text as published in Volume VII of the Department of State's *Documents on German foreign policy 1918–1945*, 422 (italics mine):

No. 428

91/100057–58

The Foreign Minister to the Legation in Eire

Telegram

No. 72   Berlin, August 29, 1939
                                                                              zu Pol. II 3053

Drafting Officer : Senior Counsellor von Rintelen.
With reference to your telegram No. 47.

In view of the deterioration in the political situation as a whole resulting from the behaviour of Poland, it appears expedient that

8

you should now make the declaration to the Irish government which you suggested. I therefore request you to call on Mr de Valera without delay and make the following statement to him, which is intended to clarify the attitude which we shall adopt toward Ireland and also which we for our part expect from Ireland, if hostilities cannot after all be avoided.

In accordance with the friendly relations between ourselves and Ireland we are determined to refrain from any hostile action against Irish territory and to respect her integrity, provided that Ireland for her part maintains unimpeachable neutrality towards us in any conflict. Only if this condition should no longer obtain, as a result of a decision of the Irish government themselves, or by pressure exerted on Ireland from other quarters, should we be compelled as a matter of course, as far as Ireland was concerned too, to safeguard our interests in the sphere of warfare, in such a way as the situation then arising might demand of us. You are requested to deliver this statement in clear yet definitely friendly terms and in doing so you can refer (*without expressly mentioning Northern Ireland*) to the wide sympathy felt in Germany for Ireland and the national *aspirations of the Irish people.*

I also request you to add that we have taken steps, whereby Irish nationals resident in Germany may remain there even in the event of war, and in this connection we naturally expect Ireland to *reciprocate in a similar way.* Furthermore, the German government would make every effort to restrict as far as possible to an absolute minimum any unavoidable repercussions which might arise for Ireland and Irish trade from Germany's conduct of the war. We are of course aware of the difficulties involved in the geographical position of Ireland. Report by telegram on action taken.

RIBBENTROP

Ribbentrop had reservations in the matter of Northern Ireland. It was the Führer's dream that after subjugating France, Germany and England should make peace and carve up Russia. Hard commitments as to Northern Ireland might later cause embarrassment. Moreover his advice from IRA agents in Berlin would not increase his confidence in Mr de Valera. Doubtless each was suspicious of the other, and not without reason.

The catch in Ribbentrop's proposal that Irish nationals be permitted to reside in Germany despite the state of war, on condition that Éire give similar permission to German nationals became apparent within a year.

For some of the German nationals had been planted as spies and agents and when they were caught, they gave Mr de Valera serious trouble. On the other hand the Irish in Germany were avowedly IRA agents and could only work against de Valera. But he accepted the Ribbentrop suggestion perhaps because Berlin acceded in principle to his proposal to keep England deceived in order to secure supply. What de Valera now most wanted was such a joint German-Éire declaration as would make it appear to the Irish electorate that Germany approved Irish neutrality and valued it above IRA belligerency, that Germany and Éire were in happy accord, and that Berlin was not taking the side of the IRA against the de Valera government. Mr de Valera explained this to the British government by insisting that unless and until Britain armed him, the IRA with German help might bring off a successful revolt, in which case Éire would be in the war as an open ally of Hitler. Since the British could not then arm him even had they wished to, there was no formal protest from London. In fact until the following June, hope if not confidence in the policy of faith still survived. The proposal for a joint announcement was made toward the close of the conversation which Hempel reported in his telegram No. 52, dated Dublin August 31st, 1939, 10.15 p.m. (italics mine):

No. 484

91/100060–61

The Minister in Eire to the Foreign Ministry

Telegram

MOST URGENT   Dublin, August 31, 1939—10:50 p.m.
No. 52 of August 31   Received September 1—2:30 a.m.

With reference to your telegram No. 72 of August 29.
I carried out my instructions today in the presence of Walshe. De Valera repeated the statement, previously mentioned in my report A.143 *of February 23, 1939*, that the Government's aim was to remain neutral. The final decision would have to be taken by the Irish parliament in due course. It was also his wish to maintain friendly relations with Germany. He feared an expression of unimpeachable neutrality, translated as 'non-objectionable', might easily give us cause for objections. He said that in spite of the Irish Government's sincere desire to observe neutrality, equally toward both belligerents, Ireland's dependence on Britain for trade [was] vital to Ireland on one hand, and on the other, the possibility of intervention by Britain if the independence of Ireland involved

an immediate danger for Great Britain rendered it inevitable for the Irish Government to show a *certain consideration for Britain* which in similar circumstances they would also show to Germany. Other danger points were, in particular, any violation by us of Irish territorial waters, *exploitation of the anti-British radical nationalist movement,* and finally any hostile action against the population on the other side of the Northern Ireland frontier who wanted to return to the Irish State. My general impression was one of a sincere effort to keep Ireland out of the conflict, but of great fear, which de Valera discussed in the usual doctrinaire fashion which betrays his real weakness. Nevertheless our *demarche* has made a definitely favourable impression. De Valera intends to submit my statement, of which I had to promise a brief version in writing to the Cabinet without delay, and will then, if the occasion demands give me further information. The Government *also wanted a short announcement* in the press that, in view of friendly German-Irish relations, I on behalf of the Reich government, had promised respect for Irish neutrality, and de Valera for his part also said that the maintenance of friendly relations with Germany as well as with other countries was desirable and referred again to the declaration of February 17, that the policy of the Irish Government was directed toward neutrality. The Government consider it important that our announcements be identical and simultaneous. Please telegraph whether you agree and the date of the announcement.

HEMPEL

On September 1st, 1939, Hempel again telegraphs Berlin 'most urgent' (No. 53) at 10.36 am.

No. 499

91/100062

The Minister in Eire to the Foreign Ministry

Telegram

MOST URGENT   Dublin, September 1, 1939—10:36 a.m.
No. 53 of September 1   Received September 1—12:30 p.m.

With reference to my telegram No. 52 of August 31.

I mention in order to avoid misunderstandings, that my declaration to De Valera adhered of course closely to instructions.

The draft of the proposal for a press announcement originates with Walshe. If in view of the rapid developments which have meanwhile taken place, I am compelled to make an independent decision, I shall only agree to a public statement which conforms to the text of the instructions. The wording noted by the Government would perhaps enable them to adopt a firmer attitude towards Britain.

HEMPEL

Berlin closed the correspondence relative to the mutually agreed upon press announcement with the following telegram:

No. 527

M/100063

The State Secretary to the Legation in Eire

Telegram

No. 85

Berlin, September 1, 1939
zu Pol. II 3135
3147. 2

With reference to your telegrams No. 52 of August 31 and No. 53 of September 1.

We are in agreement with a press announcement as proposed by De Valera. But when our promise is referred to, the words 'conditional on a corresponding attitude by Ireland' must be added. Publication here would take place in the morning press of September, 3.

WEISZÄCHER

That was the rainy Sunday morning on which England declared war.

In the language of the man in the street Mr Walshe was saying in the double-talk of diplomacy: 'Give us Northern Ireland and we will give you a neutrality that will not only bar the English from the ports but prevent the United States from coming into the war on the side of England'. What other interpretation can be put upon the telegrams?

Since an American-English alliance was what Hitler feared most, Mr de Valera through his 'Secretary General of Foreign Affairs' did not overstate its importance. Mr de Valera's hallucination that through the Irish in America he could control American policy did not imply bad faith in making the offer. He believed it. Thus eight days before the outbreak of World War Two de Valera had secretly repudiated recognition of the 'common Anglo-Irish interest in Trade and Defence'. The domestic political menace of the IRA made him afraid to keep his word. He was secretly in the German camp.

History was repeating itself. Here again was the old strategic pattern of Ireland, as England's vulnerable flank. In 1603 it had been Tyrone[9] and Spanish troops at Kinsale. In 1691 it had been Sarsfield and French troops at the Boyne. Again in The Ninety Eight it had been French troops and Father Murphy at Vinegar Hill. Now, in 1939, it was not German troops but the Irish 'smiler with the knife'. The ingenious mind of Eamon de Valera had perceived that if France was defeated, a neutrality barring England from the Irish ports might well prove the determining factor in British defeat. Neutrality was Éire's secret weapon. Éire had it in her power to destroy England without risk and without firing a shot and obtain Northern Ireland as well. Eight days before the Second World War began as Hempel's Dispatch of August 26th reveals, de Valera had decided to exercise that power.

This was the day after the IRA bomb outrage at Coventry had killed five innocent people.

The follow-up of this meeting of Germano-Gaelic hearts for a time appeared to be all sweetness and light. On October 8th, 1939, Hempel reported that Irish neutrality was being scrupulously observed. He advised great caution and forbearance in dealing with the blockade of England as it might affect Irish interests. He advised also *against* participating in Irish internal affairs; that is, he opposed supporting the IRA against the de Valera government. Hempel had a right to be pleased. After the Anglo-Irish 'settlement' in 1937, Berlin regarded Ireland as on the English side. Now Hempel not only had Éire on the German side, but controlled a 'perhaps decisive' influence in preventing America from coming into the war which his country had willed. But his anxieties were not at an end.

In Berlin there were two schools of thought as regards Éire. The more military minded of Hitler's advisers were for using Irish quislings and fifth columnists, as in Norway, to foment insurrection in co-operation with German forces. Hempel got wind of it and on November 14th, 1939, he again advised Berlin against German aid to the IRA or any intervention in Irish affairs at the moment. On November 30th he

[9] Hugh O'Neill (*c.* 1550–1616), Earl of Tyrone.

sounds the same note, urging special consideration for Éire in case an intensified submarine blockade of England is undertaken. On December 16th he has apparently been informed that other German agencies, such as the Fichte Bund or Propaganda Ministry, was establishing relations with the IRA. He advises the greatest caution. He is using de Valera to further German interests as de Valera is using him to further de Valera's interests.

That winter of 1939–40 no suspicion of such a Dublin-Berlin Axis existed in the American Department of State. The proclamation of Irish neutrality on September 3rd following a special meeting of the Dáil on September 2nd in which Mr de Valera 'explained the situation', and received unanimous support, was interpreted in Washington as a very understandable effort of a small nation to avoid the war. No one suspected Irish neutrality was a 'bought' neutrality, the price being Northern Ireland. No one imagined that de Valera would want the Six Counties by conquest with their 800,000 tough, die-hard Protestants, a two-to-one majority. No one suspected that Mr de Valera was contemplating a plan for 'exchange of populations' which he was later to divulge. No government could have known less about the inside workings of the Irish government than did the American government in 1939. As Cordell Hull had observed, Dublin was a 'very pleasant post', and the less one knew, the pleasanter it was.

After Hitler crushed Poland, World War Two had gone on for six months practically without bloodshed. My wife[10] and I were still in Washington. In late February after a family dinner at the White House I ventured to ask the president what he thought of the war; would it flare up or die? He answered that he was no prophet but that whatever happened his conscience was clear as to democratic Europe. He then told us of the approach to Chamberlain which failed.

He and Sumner Welles[11] had worked out a plan to exert American influence to stop Hitler. We were not members of the League of Nations and the isolationists in the Congress would have voted down any proposal for a defensive alliance with the Western powers. But it was within his power as Chief Executive to propose a conference to consider world peace. He believed that with a strong bipartisan American representation at such a conference, the true nature of Hitler's policies and aims would have been revealed to the American people. In 1937 he

[10] Maude Livingston Hall (1877–1952). Maude, Eleanor Roosevelt's aunt, was only six years her elder, and the two were raised in the same house.
[11] Benjamin Sumner Welles (1892–1961), a major foreign policy advisor to Roosevelt. Under-secretary of state from 1937 to 1943.

had cabled this proposal to Prime Minister Neville Chamberlain, but Mr Chamberlain was making his own arrangements and was not interested.

This is the plan which Sumner Welles describes in his volume *Seven great decisions*.[12] The late Duff Cooper discusses it in his reminiscences (*Old men forget*).[13] He characterises the refusal of it as one of the prime minister's gravest blunders. It appeared that Mr Chamberlain received the proposal while his foreign minister, Anthony Eden,[14] was on holiday at Cannes and declined it offhand without realising its significance. It was obvious after the event that if such a conference had been held with Americans of both parties at the table, American newspapers would have educated American opinion as to their danger, possibly soon enough to have made Hitler pause.

As it was, divided and confused, we drifted for two and a half years longer till the invasion of Scandinavia and then the Low Countries startled the Congress into approving one by one the president's successive defence measures. We had embarked upon the 'Undeclared War'. Whether that February of 1940 the president could have taken a stronger line and challenged the isolationists openly is a matter of opinion. Secretary Hull, who knew Congress perhaps better than the president, opposed it. 'Why force matters?' he said. From the quarantine speech onwards Congress approved everything the president asked for in the way of defence. Popular realisation was growing that if England as well as France went down, the tougher would be America's job. It was cheaper to provide the tools and, when it proved desirable to deliver them also, we were in the war without a declaration.

If the verdict of history were to be handed down today, the Roosevelt-haters on the jury would urge that the president's motive was not the good of the American people but his own political aggrandisement. Against this is the view of those who knew him as a person and understood something of his complex personality. They saw in him at once the patriot statesman, the practical politician and the American mystic. He was what is called a 'religious' man. Besides his professed religion, he had, as many Americans have, a personal creed. This was the naive American faith in the triumph of progress and good. He believed

[12] Benjamin Sumner Welles, *Seven major decisions* (London, 1951).
[13] Duff Cooper, *Old men forget* (London, 1953). Alfred 'Duff' Cooper (1890–1954), formerly first lord of the admiralty, resigned in 1938 from Chamberlain's Cabinet over the Munich Agreement, subsequently re-entered Winston Churchill's Cabinet as minister of information.
[14] Anthony Eden (1897–1977), eventually to become prime minister. Career blighted by the Suez crisis.

strongly, perhaps superstitiously, that the Power which orders the Universe *could* influence men's minds to produce unaccountable consequences. Thus while Reason told him that this was our war and inevitable, while he was doing all in his power to prevent it by preparing for it, until Pearl Harbor I believe he never gave up the *Hope* that miraculously we might be saved from it. No man of his type with four sons of military age who because they were his sons could not escape combatant service could have plotted a war for personal aggrandisement.

Not long before we embarked, I again broke the war taboo as regards Ireland. In the West European Division of the State Department I had met Hon. Robert Brennan, the Éire minister in Washington.[15] He was popular and always welcome there. It is as improbable that he then knew more of the Irish-German conversations beginning August 26th, 1939, than that they resulted in the proclamation of Irish neutrality on September 3rd. Presumably his instructions were to marshal Irish opinion in the United States in support of that neutrality. These instructions he was executing very efficiently. I called on him 'unofficially' and liked him. 'Unofficially' he asked us to lunch and gave us a delightful party. 'Unofficially' we asked him and his wife to lunch with us at the White House. It was our first experience in Sinn Féin revolutionary society. Mrs Brennan quite naturally spoke of the difficulties of bringing up two daughters with her husband '*away*'.

My wife asked 'Was he away on business?' 'No', interjected Mrs Brennan with a grin, 'in jail'. That broke the ice. We felt that we had been taken into what in Dublin they call the 'Gaol Aristocracy', and we asked questions freely. Mr Brennan was the first person I had met who knew Mr de Valera well. He told us interesting things about him. He said that his chief was indifferent to money. At times in that first tour of the United States they had had very little. Sometimes he and de Valera had had only one hotel room and had slept in the same bed. Little by little the background story of the Sinn Féin 'Movement' was unfolded as those who were in it later told it. It seemed to us adventurous, brave and gay, as well as right and profitable for the world. For a long time I thought of it in that light.

At that time I believed that every nation, great and small, had an inherent *right* to complete independence. I had never asked myself how a nation could be truly independent without power. I had assumed that

[15] Robert Brennan (1881–1964) was born in Wexford and worked as a surveyor, journalist and writer before joining Sinn Féin. He was the first managing editor of the *Irish Press* newspaper and was appointed by de Valera as secretary of the Irish legation and later minister in Washington (1934–7). After his return from Washington, he was director of Radio Éireann.

somehow it was the duty of strong neighbour nations to protect the small nation in her independence and that the small nation had no commensurate responsibility to co-operate with the strong protecting nations. It followed from this that in a time of crisis the small nation had the 'right' to jeopardise the survival of the strong protector, yet all the time be entitled to protection. It was a concept that made no sense when analysed. But I had not analysed it. Furthermore I believed strongly that now that Éire was independent Mr de Valera would realise the menace to Irish Freedom of the Axis dictatorship, and in his own time and in the purely Irish interest would co-operate in a common defence.

I had asked Mr Brennan many questions about Partition and he had explained the problem to me very reasonably from the Sinn Féin point of view. He made me realise that the South attached great importance to a united Ireland. It seemed obvious then that the war was likely to offer opportunities for uniting Ireland which might never again occur. If there could be a common island defence, eventual union would logically follow. This was an Anglo-Irish problem yet there was an American angle to it. Some of the strongest opposition to the president's programme of preparedness came from the Irish-American political pressure groups which fomented Anglophobe sentiment in the United States. Any gesture of co-operation between North and South Ireland for a common defence would obviously weaken, if not silence, this opposition. I asked Mr Brennan if he thought his government would resent my exploring the Partition question with reference to its effect on the American political situation. He said Mr de Valera would welcome any objective inquiry into the facts since they had confidence in the merits of their case.

I knew I was on delicate ground but I caught the president [Roosevelt] alone and blurted out what was on my mind. The memorandum of the conversation that I made reads as follows:

I know that Irish Partition is officially not a matter of American concern. The State Department regards it as exclusively an Anglo-Irish matter. However, you and I know that *politically* it *is* a matter of American concern. I believe that the war offers an opportunity which may never again be repeated of settling this matter by recognition of common interest. If some mutual gesture of reconciliation for purposes of a common defence could be obtained, would it not take off the pressure against your program of preparedness? I clearly understand that I have no right to suggest mediation but it is surely within the scope of my duties to ascertain the facts of the situation and report them to my superiors in Washington. For if the war continues, it will be obvious that the survival of Northern Ireland, Éire and Great Britain are tied up in the same package. It seems impossible that this will not be recognised by the three parties interested.

The President laughed and said something about rushing in where angels fear to tread. Then he added, 'Go ahead, but if you get into trouble your blood is on your own head. I won't help you'.

His only positive instructions as to my mission were to write him a personal 'background' letter at least once a fortnight in addition to my reports to the secretary of state. He also gave me a sealed personal letter to deliver to Mr de Valera, and a short verbal message which I wrote down and memorised. The president had invited the Irish leader to Washington the preceding year when the New York World's Fair was in progress and was disappointed that the war and its problems had made the visit impossible. I gathered that he had felt that a personal talk with him might have produced important and profitable results. Mr de Valera's action at Geneva in advocating sanctions against Italy had made a deep impression in the United States. Not only had the president at this time no idea that he was possibly even then intriguing against our national security but he esteemed him as a great and right-minded liberal in a class with McKenzie King[16] and Smuts. No one in the United States of non-Irish origin then understood the true nature of the Sinn Féin Movement nor the political philosophy that Mr de Valera had developed from it.

As soon as I had had this talk with the president, I called on Mr Brennan and laid my cards on the table. I asked him again if his government would resent inquiry into the Partition question with its various implications in the existing situation. He was kind and reassuring. He repeated that Dublin would welcome investigation into the facts and that he was sure that it would give me every assistance. Mr de Valera wanted to have the facts known all over the world. I did not understand then that there were two views of what Mr de Valera called 'the facts'.

From what I could gather Mr de Valera in March 1940 stood by the position he had taken the year before in the Irish Senate while speaking to Senator MacDermot's resolution on Partition. He then had favoured a 'reasonable solution' of the problem. He had reviewed the question in

[16] William Lyon Mackenzie King (1874–1950). Dominant Canadian political leader from the 1920s through the 1940s.

a long temperate speech. He said that he believed he would be justified in using force, but that Éire had no force. They must, therefore, seek a solution through mutual goodwill and co-operation. Then he made an interesting statement; namely, that if England should attempt to coerce the North, that is force them out of the United Kingdom, he would resent it as he would resent the coercion by England of any group of Irishmen. A few months later he had reversed himself and was demanding that England should coerce Northern Ireland *into* Éire. Nevertheless, in June 1940 he was refusing British proposals to end Partition on the ground that England '*could* not deliver'.

The more I thought about the idea the better I liked it. If we could help bring about some accommodation between North and South on the basis of common interest in this time of crisis, it would be a service not only to my own country but to the democratic cause.

On March 9th, 1940, The State Department embarked us in the S.S. *Washington* for Dublin, Ireland, via Naples, Italy. About the same time things important for the British government began taking place in Berlin. The captured German papers tell us that as early as January 1940, the 'treat 'em rough' faction in the German government threatened Hempel's pro-de Valera policy with proposals for an IRA insurrection against the Irish government and open hostilities against England. The code name for the plan was 'Artus'.[17] During the winter of 1939–40 Genoa was a centre of German intrigue and a clearing house for relations between American supporters of the IRA and Berlin. On January 24th the German consul general in Genoa inquired of the foreign ministry whether the German government was prepared to assist in the return of 'Seán' Russell, the IRA leader, then in New York. Americans first heard of Russell at the time of the British sovereigns' visit to the United States in June 1939. He was then supposed to have been in Detroit, possibly organising their assassination. The police withdrew him from circulation till the King and Queen were out of the country. Now, apparently, he was ready to go back to Éire to start an Uprising. This, if successful, would have overthrown the de Valera government and brought Éire into the war on the side of Germany.

In a memorandum dated February 10th, the Director of the Political Department advised the consulate general in Genoa that it would be technically possible to transport Russell to Éire by submarine but that the time for such action had not yet arrived. By the end of March, however, the project had gained favour in spite of the opposition of the German

---

[17] Also known as Plan Kathleen. For the most recent treatment of this episode, see Maurice Walsh, *G2: in defence of Ireland, Irish military intelligence 1918–45* (Cork, 2010), 272–6.

minister in Dublin. The plan, in outline at least, had been submitted by Michael Held, a German agent, planted in Dublin before the war began, of whom more later. It was set forth in a memorandum prepared by Herr Von Rintelen Hoffman, Director of the Political Department in Berlin, for the minister for foreign affairs, Ribbentrop, and dated March 28th, 1940 (my italics):

No. 18

91/100176–77/1

MEMORANDUM BY THE DIRECTOR OF THE POLITICAL DEPARTMENT

Berlin, March 28, 1940
St.S.No.144g.R.S.

After my oral report to the Foreign Minister (Ribbentrop) today he made the following *decisions* on the Question of an *Irish rebellion*

1. The Foreign Minister is instructing Herr Veesenmeyer to deal with this matter.
2. An attempt is to be made to bring Sean Russell, in accordance with his offer, to Italy through the agency of 'MacCarthy'.
3. Herr Veesenmeyer is to discuss the matter with 'MacCarthy' when he arrives at Genoa again. 'MacCarthy' is not to be acquainted with the details of the plans we have in mind.
4. I reported to the Foreign Minister the fact that 'MacCarthy' is already in contact with the Intelligence Department (Abwehr) and indeed at our instigation. It would therefore be necessary for the Intelligence Department (Abwehr) to be notified by us if we also used 'MacCarthy' as an intermediary. The Foreign Minister then decided that the Intelligence Department (Abwehr) should not yet be acquainted with the matter at this stage. Accordingly, the following arrangements are to be made:
   1. It should be ascertained by suitable means through Herr von Heyden-Rynsch,[18] either through the agency of the Intelligence Department (Abwehr), or better still through the Consulate General at Genoa when 'MacCarthy' will be in Genoa again.
   2. Herr Vessenmeyer [sic][19] who is present on a tour of the Balkans with Minister von Killinger, is to be notified as

[18] Bernd Otto von der Heyden-Rynsch, a German noble and Dortmunder, later on the General Staff.
[19] Edmund Veesenmayer. Sentenced to twenty years at the Nuremberg Trials for his role in the extermination of Hungarian Jewry. He served only six years of this sentence.

soon as it is definitely known when 'MacCarthy' will be in Genoa again. He is then to be called to Berlin by telegram and sent to Genoa. While he is in Berlin Vessenmayer [*sic*] is to report to the Foreign Minister after the matter has been discussed with him here.

Who 'MacCarthy' was I have never found out, though thousands of people must know.[20] It has been revealed since the war that the Germans actually embarked Seán Russell, together with 'Frankie' Ryan[21] in a submarine, bound for Éire, that Russell died during the voyage and that Mr Ryan returned to Germany in the submarine. 'Frankie' Ryan was an Irish 'idealist' who got into the Spanish Civil War on the side of the nationalists. The Franco people caught him and decided to shoot him. The papal nuncio in Dublin, later on, told me that this had been represented to him as a serious political mistake. He thereupon went over to London and saw his old friend, the duke of Alba, the Spanish Ambassador. 'But this man is a nasty feller', said the duke, 'a communist. Do you want me to turn him loose?'. 'Oh, No! No! No!' said the Archbishop, 'Don't shoot him, only lock him up for thirty years'. But they turned him loose. There was no IRA insurrection, no German troops landed in Éire, 'Artus' was postponed but the preparations for it in Éire brought about the series of IRA activities and the hunger strikes which culminated in the robbing of the Park Fort[22] arsenal and forced Mr de Valera to put some seven hundred of the key men in jail. The strength of the IRA position in Berlin was that Éire was a strategic terrain, that any pro-German sentiment which they could arouse in Ireland was a German asset. None of this made things easier for Hempel nor for his 'neutral' ally de Valera.

The route via Naples was then known as 'The Safety Route to Europe'. George Earle, newly appointed minister to Bulgaria, with his wife and family were shipmates. Also Duff Cooper and his wife Lady Diana, whom Americans knew as 'The Madonna' in Rhinehardt's *Miracle*.[23] We had

[20] MacCarthy may have been Seán Russell. See John P. Duggan, *Herr Hempel at the German legation in Dublin 1937–45* (Dublin, 2003), 143.
[21] Frank Ryan (1902–44), a left-wing Irish republican. In November 1936 he organised Irishmen to fight on the Republican side in Spain. He became the senior Irish officer in the International Brigade. In fact, despite this story of Gray's, it appears that the German military experts, contacts of Ryan's since the early 1930s, had him released from jail in Spain. In June 1944 he died in Germany following a period of ill health. While still a hero to some on the Irish left, this last 'German' phase of Ryan's career has inevitably affected his historical reputation. Seán Russell was, on the other hand, utterly devoid of left-wing sympathy.
[22] The Magazine Fort in the Phoenix Park, Dublin.
[23] Max Reinhardt (1873–1943). Theatre and film director. The New York revival of *The miracle* opened on 16 January 1924. See John Julius Norwich (ed.), *The Duff Cooper diaries 1915–51* (London, 2005), 281.

met the Coopers at the White House a few days previously. Mr Cooper had been lecturing across the country explaining the British viewpoint, with more success than might have been expected. He had become a conspicuous international figure two years before, when, together with Anthony Eden, he had resigned from the Chamberlain Cabinet on the question of German appeasement. He was a man of exceptional intelligence, courage and integrity, and will be remembered as such. He was also a gifted writer. He died in 1953 as Viscount Norwich, having just published an autobiography under the title *Old men forget*, which promises to be one of the classic commentaries on his period.

With lights ablaze in contrast to the 'dark' ships that we passed, we made an uneventful voyage and landed at Naples on March 19th. The president had authorised orders directing me to stop five days in each of the capitals en route to Dublin for 'consultation' with the American Chiefs of Mission.

In Rome our Ambassador William Philips[24] gave us what proved to be an accurate summary of the Italian situation. He said that Mussolini would *not* abandon the Axis, and would declare war on the Allies but only when it suited him. The Italian people did not want war but would obey him. However, the army would not fight effectively. Italy was unprepared. The army lacked both equipment and morale. In Rome the French were unpopular, but there was strong pro-English sentiment in all classes of society.

In Rome we met the Irish minister, Michael MacWhite,[25] who had recently come from Washington. He had a charming Danish wife. It was like meeting an old friend for we found that we had many friends in common.

A diary entry for March 18th says:

From diary entry
Monday, March 18th, 1940

I liked MacWhite from the beginning and we talked frankly of Ireland and Irish problems. He said ... that if a British

---

24 William Phillips (1878–1968), a career US diplomat who served twice as an under-secretary of state. Having resigned as ambassador to Italy, following that country's invasion of Ethiopia, he served later in India and on the Anglo-American Committee in Palestine, when he opposed the British plan for Partition.

25 Michael MacWhite (1883–1958). Like Gray, MacWhite also won the Croix de Guerre (three times) when serving as a captain in the French Foreign Legion in World War One. He did not get on well with Walshe in Dublin. His wife was the Danish painter Paula Asta Gruttner Hillerod.

Government could screw its courage up to the point of trusting Southern Ireland the era of bad feeling would pass sooner than one would expect because the economic and geographic facts dictate a close association between the two islands. This is what Neville Chamberlain had done in formulating his 'Policy of Faith'. MacWhite's view of the Italian situation was much the same as that of Ambassador Philips. As with Mr Brennan in Washington, he had apparently had no instructions from Dublin regarding the Irish Partition question which superseded Mr de Valera's statement of his policy of conciliation as set forth in his 1939 speech in the Irish Senate. He thought that any study of the situation on the lines of Mr de Valera's expressed policy would be well received by him.

A superior type of American, Mr William McCauley was at that time acting as Éire's envoy to the Vatican. That an American citizen should be exercising diplomatic functions for the Irish government confirmed the general American belief that Irish and American interests in the existing crisis were substantially identical. Mr McCauley was extremely kind and frank. Like MacWhite he apparently had no intimation that Mr de Valera was to shift his policy toward Northern Ireland from conciliation to coercion.

Since I was accredited to a Catholic country, which supposedly would follow Vatican Leadership in world affairs, it seemed important that I should not only ascertain if possible the general attitude of the Vatican toward the war but its specific attitude toward Irish questions.

Although Mr de Valera's new Constitution provided for religious freedom in Éire, it also provided a *special position* for the Roman Catholic Church. In view of the intensity of Northern Protestant fears about this provision, it was probable that they would not consider any formula for union with Éire unless new safeguards were devised for Protestants. Some compromise would have to be worked out providing that the Six Counties would remain a Protestant state with full guarantees for Catholics while Éire remained a Catholic state with comparable guarantees for Protestants. If the Vatican were to disapprove such a formula in principle, there was no use seeking a solution.

His Holiness Pius XII was the one person who, if he chose, could assure me on this point. I knew of course that he could not disclose his views on the merits of the war but it was possible that he would discuss matters from which his attitude toward Hitler could be deduced. The immediate difficulty was to secure an audience. We had arrived in Holy Week and both our embassy and the American College informed me that the Pope would receive no one until after Easter. My orders were to leave for Paris on the Saturday before Easter. On Thursday I mentioned my disappointment to Myron Taylor,[26] the president's personal representative to the Pope and that very evening received word that His Holiness would receive me on Good Friday, shortly after the Services in the Sistine Chapel. The fact that Myron Taylor's intercession was immediately effective was in itself the answer to the most important questions that I had in mind. Knowing, as the Pope did, the Administration's views on Hitler and German aggression, he would not have accorded this consideration to the president's personal representative if he had not been in sympathy with the president. Not only had Myron Taylor explained the president's position but at that very time Sumner Welles, Under-Secretary of State, was in Rome as special envoy of the president on his way home from Berlin where he had bluntly warned Hitler that if he unleashed a general war the consequences would be on his own head. He had also told Mussolini the same thing. Subsequently he had had a long audience with His Holiness. The Pope, therefore, at that time was fully informed as to the views of Washington on the war.

The Pope received me with great kindness and kept me for nearly an hour asking searching questions and talking with notable friendliness. I am a Protestant with strong American prejudices against theocracy and state religious systems, but his sincerity, goodwill and right-mindedness impressed me deeply. I came away convinced that he was not only a realistic statesman, but a '*good*' man, whose politics were based on Love. The emphasis he placed on the spiritual rather than the temporal character of the Church and his enunciation of present-day Catholic principles convinced me that no arrangement voluntarily arrived at between North and South Ireland, which provided for the spiritual liberties of all concerned, would meet with opposition in Rome.

He spoke warmly of Myron Taylor. He entertained a high opinion of Sumner Welles. He asked whether the president were going to run for a third term. I told him that his close friends believed that he did not wish

---

[26] Myron Charles Taylor (1874–1989) had been one of America's leading industrialists: his modernisation strategy became known as the Taylor formula. The dominant figure in US Steel, in 1937 he agreed with John L. Lewis of the Congress of Industrial Organisations to recognise a CIO subsidiary for the purpose of collective bargaining: this ushered in an era of stable workplace relations. In July 1938 he represented the US at the Evian Conference, convened at the initiative of Franklin D. Roosevelt, to help the growing number of Jewish refugees from Nazism. In 1942 he persuaded the Pope to speak against Nazi treatment of the Jews.

to run again but that in view of the critical world situation it was likely that he would be 'drafted'.

At this time anti-Hitler American Protestants were complaining of the Pope's alleged 'neutrality' without knowledge of his difficulties. Pius XII was head not only of the Polish Roman Church but of the German Catholics as well and of course of the Italian. It was at that time impossible for him openly to oppose either Fascism or National Socialism without jeopardising the interests and possibly the lives of individual Catholics loyal to his guidance and authority. All he could do was to assert Catholic principles and let the world draw its inferences. But it became clear later on that even in early 1940 the Vatican's file on Hitler contained the basic facts on which the Pope later condemned the Hitler regime as 'The Satanic Spectre of National Socialism'. This dossier served to document the remarkable publication of the National Catholic Welfare Conference in America entitled 'The Nazi War against the Catholic Church'. It defined the issue which was dividing the world with impressive clarity: It began:

Nine days after Easter Sunday in the year 1923, a harsh voice made itself heard in the Ancient Catholic City of Munich. 'If a people is to become free', it proclaimed 'it needs pride, self-will, defiance, hate, hate and once again hate'.

Four months later this same speaker made a distinction which precisely defines, today, the gulf between the Christian faith and way of life and his way and that of his followers. On August 1st, 1923, he said, 'there are two things which can unite men: common ideals and common criminality'.

As we were to find out, Mr de Valera's tragedy was that on May 12th, 1940, he was publicly to recognise this 'decisive gulf', but next day secretly to apologise for it and suppress Irish discussion of the difference between National Socialism and the Christian Way of Life.

On March 22nd, we started for Paris. It was the twenty-first anniversary of Mussolini's entry into Rome. In Milan there was a grandiose celebration. Since we had three hours' wait for the Paris Express, we drove to the square in front of the Cathedral where grandstands had been erected and a platform for the orators. Some ten thousand people were wandering about talking to one another and ignoring the speaker who was shouting in Mussolini fashion about the glory of the Italian empire and the 'Populo Romano'. The square was wired with loudspeakers so that every word blared stridently. At every oratorical pause a claque shouted in unison, 'Duce! Duce! Duce!' like undergraduates at an American football game, but no one in the crowd joined in. Even the Fascists in black shirts, wearing daggers at their belts seemed weary of the performance and made no effort either to listen or applaud. We drove to Cooks to get our money changed. At the tables in front of the cafés thousands of Milanese were sitting sipping their vermouth, apparently unconscious of the celebration. I asked the clerk at Cooks what it meant. He smiled wearily and shrugged his shoulders. 'Fascismo had been over-advertised. Sales resistance had developed'. It was a curious sidelight on Italy about to go to war.

Arriving in Paris we found that the American Ambassador to France, Mr William Bullitt,[27] was in Washington and Robert Murphy, one of the youngest and most brilliant of our Career Officers, was 'in charge'.[28] We could at once understand the warmth with which the president had spoken of 'Bob' Murphy and the confidence the West European Division reposed in him. He had no more than Philips had in Rome as to whether the 'phoney' war would change to 'hot', or if so, when. He was certainly not too confident either as to the Maginot Line or Gamelin and the French army. He interpreted the change of ministry then taking place as meaning a more forcible war policy and a stepping up of aircraft production which was tragically in arrears.

The people of Paris seemed apathetic. Except that there was a blackout, no one would have suspected that they were again at grips with their traditional enemy. The Easter Day family crowds, with baby in perambulator, thronged the Place de La Concorde and the Bois, all as usual. The man in the street was saying, 'There will be no fighting war. It would not be logic. Hitler has got what he wants without fighting'. Besides there was the Maginot Line, Gamelin and the French army, also England with the British navy. There was the usual complaint that England was not holding 'her share of the line'. As a matter of fact at this time she had taken over but forty-five kilometres. The greater part of the expeditionary force was still undergoing intensive training in England. It was reputed to be a *corps d'elite* with the last word in equipment.

Some of the most intelligent comment on the situation we obtained from a nephew of General Douglas McArthur, Douglas McArthur II, who was one of the embassy secretaries.

[27] William Bullitt (1891–1957), Philadelphia, a radical in his youth, Bullitt moved to the right. He was US ambassador to the Soviet Union from 1933 to 1936.
[28] Robert D. Murphy (1894–1978), born in Milwaukee, began his diplomatic career as a member of the American delegation in Berne. Murphy became the State Department's France expert and in 2006 featured on a US postage stamp featuring six prominent diplomats.

One of the first things that I did in Paris was call on the Irish minister to France. This was Mr Seán Murphy.[29] He was an exceptionally intelligent and cultivated man who had married a French lady. He had a realistic appreciation of the difficulties in the way of uniting the two Irelands and apparently accepted his chief's pronouncements in the Irish Senate that union must come about by conciliation and mutual goodwill. I doubt if he had any knowledge or even suspicion at this time of the Hempel-de Valera talks and the secret understanding about Irish neutrality and Northern Ireland. The same of course was true of Michael MacWhite.

On March 28th England and France signed an agreement of first importance. They agreed that neither would make a separate peace without the consent of the other. The published text reads:

The Government of Britain and Northern Ireland mutually undertake that during the present war they will neither negotiate nor conclude an armistice or treaty of peace except by mutual agreement. They undertake not to discuss peace terms before reaching complete agreement on the conditions necessary to ensure to each of them an effective and lasting guarantee of their security.

At the time this seemed to be something that could not be treated as a 'scrap of paper'.

---

[29] Seán Murphy (1896–1964), Waterford born, was part of the Sinn Féin delegation to the Paris Peace Conference in 1919. In December 1938 Murphy returned to Paris as Irish minister to France. He did not get on well with Joseph Walshe in Dublin; Murphy was, for example, much more critical of Pétain. He remained in France during World War Two: in 1950 he became ambassador to Canada and from 1955, headed the Department of External Affairs until his retirement in 1957.

CHAPTER II

MARCH 29TH–APRIL 3RD

On March 29th we flew to London. Here was blackout as in Paris. But here everyone conscientiously carried a gas mask in a black box which the Parisians did not. The confusion attendant upon mobilisation had disappeared and life went on in an orderly British manner. What the Londoner thought about the war was not complicated with 'logic'. 'If the blighters wanted to fight, why they would get "wot was wot" '. Everybody was 'carryin' on'. They had no good reason why they should win the war but they knew they would. The presumption of this confidence misled not only Hitler but others. That the English were unprepared and overconfident were stock reasons why they should be defeated. But observers lost sight of the part which imponderables play in war. The British came through because it never occurred to them that they would not. As a boy I had laboured over a Latin prose sentence which announced '*Caesar potuit quod posse putabat*.[1] It came back to me that March in London.

I was prepared for objections by the American Ambassador, Hon. Joseph P. Kennedy,[2] to my discussing Irish affairs with members of the British government since I was not acting under instructions of the State

---

[1] Literal translation: 'Caesar could what he thought he could' or, more colloquially, 'Whatever Caesar believed he could achieve, he ended up achieving it'.

[2] Joseph Patrick Kennedy (1888–1969), a prominent Irish-American businessman and politician: father of a future president. His term as ambassador and his personal political ambitions ended abruptly during the London Blitz in November 1940, with the publication of his remark that 'Democracy is finished in England. It may be here [in the US]', *Boston Sunday Globe*, 10 November 1940. When the daylight bombing of London began, Joe Kennedy took his aide Harvey Klemmer for a walk through the gloom at Buckingham Palace. 'I'll bet you ten to one, any sum you like, that Hitler will be here within two weeks'. Klemmer had discussed Nazi treatment of the Jews with Kennedy, but his boss merely replied, 'They brought it on themselves'. *Independent*, 31 July 1992.

Department. But instead of objecting he was kind, understanding and helpful. I told him what I wanted to do and he made it plain that as long as I did not involve his embassy in any way, I had his blessing. I was impressed by his estimate of Labour Party strength. He foresaw the triumph of British Socialism at a time when few outside the Labour Party would have agreed with him. He apparently had no intimation of any change in the de Valera policy of conciliation which had resulted from the de Valera-Chamberlain talks in 1937–8. He made no reference to the 'Gentleman's Agreement' and I believe he had no suspicion of de Valera's pro-German proposals set forth in Hempel's dispatch of August 26th, 1939.

The Irish high commissioner in London was John W. Dulanty. His title was High Commissioner, not Minister, because the British government did not officially recognise Mr de Valera's unilateral modification of the clause in the Anglo-Irish Treaty which defined the Irish Free State as a *member* of the British Commonwealth. Commonwealth members, among themselves, exchanged high commissioners. Mr Dulanty was a man of ability and personal charm. He had lived most of his adult life in England and had made a success in business in London. He spoke English as an educated Englishman and without trace of 'Dublin accent'. Generally he was shrewd, wise and objective in his comment on Anglo-Irish relations, yet on occasion he could become as emotional as any professional patriot.

John Dulanty was then the most important of Éire's diplomatic representatives.[3] He was also nearest to Dublin. He crossed frequently from London for instructions and consultation. He went out of his way to show us friendliness and appeared to be entirely frank. In his discussion of the Partition issue he was realistic and sceptical of making progress with Lord Craigavon and the North of Ireland government. Yet he never let fall the suggestion either that Mr de Valera would shortly change his Partition policy from conciliation to coercion or that if there were to be wartime co-operation, the North would have to become neutral; nor yet that Éire's neutrality was not to be a subject for bargaining. On these matters, had there been a change of policy,

[3] John Whelan Dulanty (1883–1955) was born in Manchester, the son of a labouring father from Templemore, Co. Tipperary. A clever man, Dulanty graduated in law from Manchester University and was involved in constitutionalist Irish nationalist politics; in 1908 he supported Winston Churchill—then a liberal—in his campaign for the north-west Manchester seat. Churchill retained his affection for Dulanty but was suspicious of his ability to place Irish actions in World War Two in the best possible light. Nonetheless, this was Dulanty's job as Irish high commissioner in London from 1930 to 1950. As a British civil servant, Dulanty won the CBE in 1918 and the CB in 1920; as an Irish diplomat he played a decisive role in the history of Anglo-Irish relations.

Mr Dulanty might well have been briefed, but he gave no indication that there had been such change. It is unlikely that at this time he knew of or suspected Mr de Valera's proposals to the German government. It was a secret closely kept in Dublin. Since the plan involved keeping London in the dark it was probable that the high commissioner was also to be kept in the dark. His job was to obtain the utmost in benefits for Éire. In my letter report to the president I wrote:

From letter to President Roosevelt

April 1940

Dulanty was very doubtful of any success with Ulster. His idea is that it will take years, that the most that can be hoped for, in a reasonable future is a joint commission on roads or an art exhibition or even an all Irish football team. But he said, 'for Heaven's Sake explore away and if you turn up any chance, tell us'.

He advised seeing all the English I could without embarrassing 'Joe'.

Among the conservative leaders whom I met in London, except for Mr Churchill, there was apparently no apprehension as to the consequences of Irish neutrality. No one anticipated the fall of France and the urgent need for the Irish ports. Instead there was what to me was a somewhat surprising attitude of goodwill and confidence in regard to Mr de Valera. The view seemed to prevail that he had a difficult political situation to grapple with at home, but would control it and would not be found wanting in times of need. This friendly and confident opinion doubtless emanated from the prime minister and his associates. For a century Irish leaders had been complaining to English governments, 'if you would only trust us'. As we have seen, in 1938 Mr Chamberlain had trusted Mr de Valera to the extent of giving Éire what in effect was a loaded pistol pointed at England's stomach. Mr Chamberlain's return of the 'ports' reserved by the Treaty for the common defence was a gesture of supreme trust. In return he obtained the somewhat Delphic declaration from Mr de Valera that Éire would never permit its territory to be used as a base of attack against England. This, as became evident later, was important or unimportant according to the manner in which it was implemented. Mr de Valera's speech on Partition in the Senate was evidently intended to give Mr Chamberlain assurances that the North would not be coerced. But while he advocated settlement by conciliation, he made no written engagement to this effect. Mr Chamberlain's friends said that he had a personal understanding with Mr de Valera on which he relied. He believed in fact that if England should need the ports, there would be a way found to make them available. In short Mr Chamberlain and his associates believed that at long last they had won 'Irish Friendship'. They had certainly paid for it. The details of this 'policy of faith', have already been set forth. The achievement consummated, the Chamberlain government in April 1940 seemed to be enjoying that 'rainbow in the soul' said to emanate from 'the consciousness of duty done'.

In London the Duff Coopers proved the most kind and helpful friends. Duff gathered a dozen of his conservative associates who were interested in Irish affairs and invited me to meet them at dinner. In the company were Anthony Eden, Oliver Stanley,[4] secretary for war Captain Margesson,[5] the Conservative whip in the Commons, the late duke of Devonshire[6] and Harold Nicholson. There was no discussion of specific Irish questions and no mention of the ports. Instead there was manifest that notable feeling of confidence in, and goodwill toward, Mr de Valera, already commented upon. The duke of Devonshire was outspoken in that sense. His family had been great landowners in Ireland. They still retained Lismore Castle with its home farms and coverts and the duke leased the best of the Blackwater salmon water. He told me that he had called on Mr de Valera in Dublin and had very satisfactory talks with him. He had confidence in him.

I sat next to Mr Eden and asked questions about the evolution of the British empire into the Commonwealth. This was a subject of special interest to Americans. He seemed to me wise, very right-minded and gifted with long-range vision. It was easy to understand the position he had made for himself in contemporary history.

Captain Margesson kindly arranged an appointment for me with the prime minister for noon on April 3rd. Shortly after breakfast on that day, Mr Chamberlain sent me word that on consideration he had decided that it was better not to see me. He said 'If it were not unfair to Mr de Valera to discuss Irish matters with me, Mr de Valera might think it was unfair'.

Thus, on April 3rd, 1940, and in spite of Mr de Valera's announcement of neutrality on September 3rd, 1939, and reaffirmation

---

[4] Oliver Stanley (1896–1950), son of 17th earl of Derby: the last of the Stanleys to play a major role in politics. In 1917 he won the Military Cross. At this point he was in the War Office. A supporter of appeasement, he was rather contemptuously offered a job by Churchill but refused it.

[5] David Reginald Margesson (1890–1965), 1st Viscount Margesson, won the Military Cross in 1916. Margesson supported Chamberlain almost to the last, but was respected by Churchill, who retained him as chief whip.

[6] Edward Cavendish (1895–1956), 10th Duke of Devonshire. Member of parliament for West Derbyshire from 1923 to 1938 and a member of Winston Churchill's war-time government.

of that position on February 17th, 1940, the British prime minister still 'trusted' him and was, if anything, overscrupulous in discussing with the new American minister matters which might concern him. There can be only one reasonable explanation: Mr de Valera had satisfied Mr Chamberlain that in spite of appearances he was still loyal to his acceptance of common defence.

In his message, the prime minister had suggested that instead of talking with him I talk with his private secretary, Sir Horace Wilson. While I was disappointed in not seeing Mr Chamberlain, I looked forward to meeting Sir Horace. He was a man of distinction and reputed to have one of the best minds in England. He was regarded by many as the 'silent partner' of his chief, rather than as a secretary.

Downing Street is a short, shabby, dead-end street off Whitehall. In war time there was a rope stretched across the entrance but no sentries, no evidence of military might. Two London policemen were on duty. I told them my business; they dropped the rope and waved the taxi driver through.

Number 10 is a comfortable, rather shabby, big, brown town house with a polished brass street number on the front door. It has a special interest for Americans for it was built by a Harvard graduate about 1654. According to Samuel Pepys, Sir George Downing was a 'stingy fellow' and a 'perfidious rogue', but he knew how to get along. In 1731, Number 10 became the official residence of Sir Robert Walpole; since then the British prime ministers have all lived there. It has become the symbol of British Democracy under Law, the reality of power behind the Majesty of the royal establishment. I rang the bell and a manservant let me into a coat room/waiting room, smelling of wet umbrellas. While I waited, I read the great names over the coat pegs around the walls. For two and a half centuries the makers of the empire had been hanging their hats on these pegs. One wondered how in this new crisis they were going to fare.

Sir Horace Wilson[7] proved to be all that I had been led to expect. This type of Englishman is the most finished product of Western Civilisation. Its weakness as a type is its over-sureness as to what *not* to do. In times of crisis the great men who save us seem to do so not by

---

[7] Sir Horace Wilson (1882–1972). The LSE graduate's stellar career in the British civil service was about to end. A strong supporter of appeasement at the heart of Whitehall, Churchill took care to sideline him immediately upon taking over as prime minister. On the eve of the Munich conference, Chamberlain had sent Wilson to Berlin. Hitler treated Wilson with contempt and anger. Wilson feebly offered 'I will still try to make those Czechos sensible'. 'Hitler ordered the preliminaries to full mobilisation once the civil servant had left', noted Michael Burleigh with some acidity in his *Moral combat: a history of World War II* (London, 2010), 66.

accepted rules. Sir Horace was kind but tired; the strain of Munich and the war months had been great and unbroken. He entertained no immediate expectation of Northern Ireland changing its mind about Éire or of any notable change in the Irish situation. What that was he did not specify and I did not inquire. It must always be remembered that at this time few if any Englishmen contemplated the possibility of the Germans occupying the French Channel ports; as far as I know, no one in Washington did either. Thus there was no sense of emergency; the need of the Irish ports lacked reality.

Toward the end of the talk, I asked Sir Horace why, since the de Valera people baulked at 'The Crown' and kept edging out of the Commonwealth, England should not favour an Irish republic with the King as honorary president. He smiled wanly and said, 'Mr Gray, you seem not to know much about the British Constitution'.

'I know this', I answered, 'that it has never proved unequal to any situation in which British interests were involved'. He smiled again and we said goodbye. When the Republics of India and Pakistan became members of the Commonwealth, I recalled this talk and wondered if Sir Horace remembered it.

At one o'clock that day I kept the appointment which Captain Margesson had made for me, to lunch with Winston Churchill.

World War Two ended Winston Churchill's long sojourn in the political wilderness. For two decades he had played the dual role of Ishmael and Cassandra. Now what he had prophesied had come true, and immediately after the declaration of war Mr Chamberlain had installed him in his old post at the admiralty. It was more than a popular appointment. Mr Churchill was the symbol of England's will to fight and survive. The admiralty signalled the Fleet, 'Winston is back'. Mr Churchill, while accepting office in the Chamberlain government, had not accepted his chief's views as to the surrender of the Irish Treaty ports. His observations on the wisdom of surrendering the ports to the de Valera government have already been noted. But he had further advanced technical defence considerations which had prompted the reservation of the ports in the Treaty of 1921. In his speech on the Éire Bill in 1938 he had said:

> The Admiralty of those days [1921] assured me that without the use of those ports it would be very difficult, perhaps almost impossible, to feed this island in time of war. Queenstown and Berehaven shelter the flotillas which keep clear the approaches to Bristol and the English Channels, and Lough Swilly is the base

from which access to the Mersey and the Clyde is covered. In a war against an enemy possessing a numerous and powerful fleet of submarines, those are the essential bases from which the whole operation of hunting submarines and protecting incoming convoys is conducted. If we are denied the use of Lough Swilly and have to work from Lamlash,[8] we should strike two hundred miles from the effective radius of our flotillas out and home. These ports are in fact the sentinel towers of the Western Approaches, by which the 45,000,000 people in this island so enormously depend on foreign food for their daily bread and by which they carry on their trade which is equally important to their existence.[9]

These were the conditions of disadvantage under which the Allies laboured throughout the war.

In the Éire Bill speech, Mr Churchill made no mention of Mr de Valera's declaration that Éire would never be allowed to serve as a base for an attack on England. He of course knew that unless Mr de Valera co-operated with England in defensive measures, this promise was without value since Éire lacked the means to implement it, even if she wished to do so. But he called attention to the 'double-talk' in which the ports surrender was announced as '*relieving* England of the responsibility for their protection and upkeep'.[10] As was obvious, these utterances did not endear Mr Churchill to the de Valera government, yet no living English statesman had risked as much as he in his attempts to place the Anglo-Irish relation upon a sound basis. His brilliant father, Lord Randolph Churchill, whom he greatly admired, had been one of the strongest unionists of his generation. He had coined the slogan 'Ulster will fight and Ulster will be right'. And he had brought up his son as a unionist. Yet in 1910 the son had joined the Liberal Party and had taken the post of Home Secretary in Mr Asquith's Cabinet. In this capacity he presented the government's Home Rule bill to the Commons on March 21st of that year. In the course of his speech he had said: 'The new generation that has grown up in our country is not going to be frightened out of its wits by the nightmares and bugaboos of a vanished past'.[11] ... Home

---

[8] Isle of Arran, Scotland.

[9] Hansard, 5 May 1938. Gray's quotation departs from that given in Hansard in a number of ways, most notably 'two hundred miles' appears as '400 miles' in the Hansard record.

[10] This is a paraphrase. See Hansard, 5 May 1938.

[11] According to Hansard, 'bugbears' rather than 'bugaboos'. From a speech given by Churchill on 14 April 1910 on relations between the two houses and duration of parliament. See http://hansard.millbanksystems.com/commons/1910/apr/14/bills-other-than-money-bills#S5CV0016P0_19100414_HOC_369 (accessed 19 August 2011).

Rule 'would conduce enormously to the strength, unity and prosperity of the empire'.[12]

To American ears these were wise words. To the American, Home Rule is the essence of his federal system. And the federal system works not only in the United States but in Canada, Australia and Switzerland. In Switzerland it works with three distinct racial strains, each with its own tradition, historic culture and race emotions. Without it Lincoln could not have preserved the American Union for had the proposal been to subjugate the Southern states and hold them in submission to a centralised government of Northerners, the struggle would have never ended. The principle of regional autonomy was the foundation stone upon which rests the structure of co-operative union.

The British unionists could and did stress the fact that under the Act of Union the Irish were partners on the same basis as the Scots, Welsh and English, and were somewhat over-represented in the common parliament. They could show that the Irish enjoyed the same measure of freedom as the British, but as the existence of an Irish Nationalist Party proved, this partnership did not meet all the needs of the situation. There were reasons for believing that Home Rule would. But one unionist argument which the Home Rulers could not answer was the charge that the nationalists were dishonest in accepting Home Rule as the 'final' settlement. They asserted that they were using Home Rule as a half-way house, not to a federal system but to Separatism and that their true aim was to destroy Britain and the empire. Since only the event could decide whether or not these allegations were well founded the Home Rulers brushed them aside. They would always say we will cross that bridge when we come to it. After all Mr Lincoln had prevented the secession of a group of states almost equal in power to that upholding union. England's power in relation to Ireland was absolute. To the American, therefore, Home Rule seemed to involve no risk of secession, no danger to British survival. But what no English statesman then understood— and no American either—was the pathological nature of the forces animating Irish Separatism. No one realised that it was a medical impossibility for an Irish schizophrenic to keep faith on matters involving the 'God Given Rights' of the Irish patriot or his ancient 'wrongs'. No one realised that it was not the British but the Princes and the Irish way of life which had made the Irish peasant what he was and that the present day Irish politician was in essence a continuation or reincarnation of the prince.

[12] Also from the Hansard record for 14 April 1910.

Mr Churchill preserved his faith in Home Rule perhaps because it had never had a trial and without realising that in any immediate future in Southern Ireland it never could have a trial in good faith, conditions being what they were. His conviction that the principle was sound was unshaken on the assumption that the Southern Irish would react to normal self-interest, which they did not. At all events after the suppression of the Sinn Féin terrorists, he accepted appointment as one of the British negotiators of what became the Anglo-Irish Treaty. Its fundamental defect proved to be that it recognised Ireland not as a political unit of the British United Kingdom with liberties and responsibilities analogous to those of an American state or Canadian Province but as a 'dominion'. In the nature of things Ireland could never be that, for the dominions, even before the Statute of Westminster, were regarded as having the right of self-determination and secession from the empire. The secession of Éire from the system of common defence could not be envisaged by a government at that time responsible for the security and survival of the United Kingdom. Dominion status within the Commonwealth worked only as long as it was implemented in good faith and with goodwill. The Cosgrave government so implemented it. But when the de Valera party came to power there was neither good will, good faith nor recognition of common interest. As Mr Churchill pointed out in his Éire Bill speech, the government of Ireland was in the hands of men whose rise to power had been 'proportionate to their animosity to England'. Mr de Valera's unilateral violations of the Anglo-Irish Treaty, which began shortly after he came to power in 1932, provided grounds for British repudiation of it. It would have been practicable for a British government to have taken this course at any time prior to the negotiation of the Coal-Cattle Pact in 1937–8. The Economic War had disclosed to the Irish people their economic dependence upon Britain in a forcible manner. Had a new treaty been negotiated in 1937, Mr de Valera would have had no choice. He would have had to accept not the dominion status, which he had spurned in 1922, but a Home Rule, which might have amounted in the future to the status of a federal unit, with no right of secession implied.

But what he would have had to accept and how he would have accepted it were different things. In all probability no proposals could have been framed which he would have accepted and implemented except as suited his 'Irish Heart'. It is possible that the Chamberlain policy of faith in winning 'Irish Friendship' and a 'Final Settlement', was no more ineffectual than alternative policies while it had the advantage of establishing a moral position in history. It must be remembered that it was a period in which appeasement was in the English air. To the British liberal mind and conscience, which we inherit and which is doubtless responsible for our recurrent millenarianism, the surrender of rights in order to invoke goodwill seemed not only reasonable but practicable. Appeasement was a 'noble experiment', similar to American prohibition. After Éire declared her neutrality in 1939, all the English government could do, short of invoking the paramount Law of Necessity, was to hope that Mr Chamberlain had not 'bought a pup' and that the Treaty ports would not be required. Although Mr Churchill differed with Mr Chamberlain on many points of his Irish policy he was in agreement in regard to no coercion of the North, and it was about the North that I wanted to talk to him.

The admiralty is hardly comparable to 10 Downing Street as a background for a great man, but Mr Churchill at this time needed no background. If there was a 'Mr England' it was he, even in April 1940. I have always been a hero worshipper and unashamed. Man's earthly hope is in superior people endowed with a little more courage, honesty, vision, generosity than the rest of us. Winston Churchill had seemed to me such a person even when as a boy he came to the United States after the Boer War and lectured across the continent. As the years went by there was constantly recurrent in the news, reports of this British Churchill in some new political adventure, at times ill-fated but always colourful. He was no exotic. He could 'take it', as well as 'dish it out'. As time went on the pattern that he developed showed not only courage but vision. For years he had been in the political wilderness, a voice generally unheeded, but without undue bitterness, warning of the Wrath to Come. Now the predicted wrath had come and his promise also had fulfilled itself. That first week of April 1940 he was still in the admiralty, but everyone 'in the know' told me that he shortly would be moving to Downing Street.

On that April 3rd there were sentries at the admiralty but I had no difficulty getting in. Someone ushered me up to the First Lord's apartment and into a pleasant drawing room into which a chilly and uncertain London sunlight was streaming. The late Sir Kingsley Wood[13] was the only other guest. He was at that time leaving the air ministry and taking over privy seal. He died not long afterwards. We had a glass of sherry and then went to the dining room. Austerity had not yet taken over, with its choice between boiled skate and potatoes or boiled hake

[13] Kingsley Wood was to become Churchill's chancellor of the exchequer and became a strong, but ineffective, opponent of the Beveridge Report in 1942.

and potatoes. It was pleasant to be given plovers' eggs, which I had not eaten for thirty years. Mr Churchill was extremely civil but he evidently was 'looking me over'. Presently he roared in his quarterdeck manner 'If you have come here to offer me a bribe to sell out Ulster for any kind of American support you had better go back'.

My letter to the president reported

From letter to President Roosevelt

April 1940

He (Mr Churchill) said he was sick of them (the Irish), that the English had given them a generous settlement and that immediately they began to break their engagements and were now stabbing England in the back. I told him that might all be true but that apparently no Englishman had grasped what Ireland really wanted, that was a generous recognition that Irish sovereignty derived from the Irish people and not from the British crown.

Today, I apologise to Mr Churchill. For while it was true that the Irish wanted recognition of Irish sovereignty as inherent in the Irish people, the de Valera Sinn Féin leadership also wanted recognition of the inherent Irish right to destroy the British empire.

I told Mr Churchill that I had no authority to offer him anything, that I wanted to find out what the facts were in regard to the so-called Irish Question in the present world situation. I was primarily interested in some arrangement for a common defence of Ireland chiefly because it would relieve professional Irish pro-German pressure in the United States in the president's efforts for American defence. I also told him that this was my own idea and not the president's. He knew enough of American politics to understand the position the president was in. He did not dispute my contention that the war and the interest of common defence offered an opportunity not only for a drawing together of North and South but a redefinition of Éire's relation with the United Kingdom. Since the Economic War had disclosed Éire's economic dependence on England, the Irish people had become disillusioned about the de Valera promises of self-sufficiency. Unless de Valera were indeed a stupid man, which at that time I did not believe, he would exploit the war as an opportunity to shift his position not only without loss of face but with political and economic advantage. If the Northern Protestants wished to recover their markets in the South without accepting de Valera's Catholic

Constitution, they had only to offer a plan of Irish federation within a federated United Kingdom system.

He made no comment but went on to recall his efforts for Home Rule in 1910 and 1911, and how he had been booed in Belfast on that account. He told me that he had imperilled his political career a second time by negotiating the 'Arrangement' or Treaty with Sinn Féin. He added that he had never been aware of any notable recognition of this service to Ireland by the people of Éire. He spoke well of Michael Collins and Arthur Griffith as men whose word he trusted. He did not mention de Valera.

I then told a story which I thought exemplified the viewpoint of the Sinn Féin revolutionaries. I had been in Dublin during the summer of 1936. James Denby, an American Foreign Service officer, was in charge of the legation, the minister having suddenly died. He asked me if I would like to meet some of the political people. I said that if there was anyone of the de Valera party who would talk objectively about the Anglo-Irish relation, without flushing up and shouting about Brian Boru, I should be glad to talk to him. Denby said he knew just one like that, David Robinson, a de Valera senator.[14] He would get him that night for dinner. He then briefed me on Robinson's story. The memorandum I made of the conversation after dinner was as follows:

'Senator Robinson, I understand that you are a Protestant and that your father was the Protestant Dean of Belfast'.

'Yes, and I went to a Protestant public school[15] and Trinity College Dublin'.

'In 1914 when war broke out you volunteered, received a commission, fought all four years in the British army, part of the time in the new Tank Corps. You lost an eye, and won the DSO'.

'Yes'.

'You were demobilised, returned to Ireland where the 'Black and Tan War' was in progress and you joined the Sinn Féiners?'

'Yes'.

'Why did you do that? You had been fighting the Germans. The Sinn Féiners were their allies'.

'I could not stand by and see the rights of my country trampled on'.

'You thought of yourself always as an Irishman?'

'Naturally, that is what I am'.

---

14 David Lubbock Robinson (1882–1943). Robinson won the DSO in the British army in World War One. In January 1919 he joined the IRA company in Roundwood, Co. Wicklow. Robinson was elected in 1931 to the Senate and stayed there until its abolition in May 1936. He sat in the new Senate from 1938 to 1943 on the taoiseach's nomination.
15 St Columba's College, Dublin.

'Eventually the treaty was signed and the civil war started; why did you follow Mr de Valera into armed resistance to the majority that approved the treaty?'

'Because the treaty was signed under duress, under threats of immediate and terrible war'.

'You believed that?'

'Yes'.

He passed over the Civil War but told how, when the victorious Free State forces were finally 'mopping up', he and Erskine Childers, the English novelist, were in hiding on the Wicklow estate of Robert Barton,[16] a cousin of Childers and one of the signers of the Treaty. Mr Barton subsequently denounced his signature. At this time a general amnesty had been proclaimed by the Free State for all rebels who had laid aside their arms. Those captured with arms were to be shot. Just as day was breaking, Free State troops surrounded the Barton house and Robinson and Childers ran out through the stable yard. Robinson, as he passed a haystack tossed his revolver into the hay. Childers did not, and was later tried and shot. An ironic feature was that the pistol which cost him his life had been given to him by Michael Collins, whose government he was attempting to overthrow.

'The next thing, Senator Robinson, was that you led a hunger strike?'

'Yes, we were demanding treatment as political prisoners. For thirty-nine days I took no food, only water and occasionally lemon juice'.

'The strike was then called off, and you were carried out on a stretcher. What then?'

'As soon as I was physically able to travel I went to England to recuperate'.

'*You went to England?*'

'Why not? I stopped at Cliveden with an old friend, Lady Astor, your American, Nancy Astor'.

I said, 'I thought you hated England'.

'Not at all. I would die for England'.

'Forgive me', I said, 'I do not understand. Suppose you were almighty, what would you do?'

'I'd declare the Irish Republic today and tomorrow I'd make a treaty with England *having everything as it was before*'.

---

[16] Robert Barton (1881–1975). Barton not only renounced his signature of the Treaty but subsequently renounced the resort to violence in the Anglo-Irish struggle. See Lis Pihl, *Signe Toksvig's diaries 1926–37* (Dublin, 1994).

At this point what was there to say? Were the gods rocking with laughter or was the Angel of Compassion in tears? Was this schizophrenia, and if so what was there to do about it? Here was a decent man, apparently sane, and then this.

In the summer of 1936 I had thought that by 'having everything as it was before', Senator Robinson had meant recognition of the inevitable interdependence of the two islands but pursuant to voluntary action by the Irish people. At that time I had believed that if the Irish people only had the opportunity for *free* decision they would decide for co-operation out of self interest, whatever might be the name of the formula. Whereas within a few months I began to realise that such was not at all the programme of Sinn Féin Separatism, on that April 3rd, 1940, I was still a believer in the 'Irish Cause' as I understood it.

Mr Churchill had listened politely. When I finished, he grunted. He was not impressed and saw no general truth in the story. He had come across no Sinn Féiners who would die for England if they could help it, under any circumstances. Sir Kingsley Wood made no comment. Later on I told the same story to David Robinson's friend, Mr de Valera. He was as unimpressed as Mr Churchill, though for different reasons. As time went on and I began better to understand, I realised that David Robinson typified only the effect of the Sinn Féin Separatist illusion on the mentality of the British liberal.

When Mr Churchill had satisfied himself that at worst I was a nuisance rather than a menace, he excused Sir Kingsley Wood. Sir Kingsley was due in the House for question time. It was evident that he had come to lunch to protect our host in the event that I had proved a hostile or treacherous visitor, likely to misquote. It is a necessary practice that statesmen follow.

I had expected to leave with Sir Kingsley, but to my surprise and gratification Mr Churchill asked me to stop on. I realised then that his charm, when he wished to exert it, had not been overrated. He began to talk as if our countries were already allies. He told me with gusto of the admiralty's new radar gadget, I think he called it the 'ASDIC'.[17] With this they were no longer the hunted but the hunters. With the 'ASDIC' the patrol ships were trailing down the U-boats and scoring 'kills'. Then he took me down to the great, silent admiralty Map Room with huge maps of the seven seas stuck with pins showing the position of every British and known enemy ship. We were in the conning tower of empire at war. I realised that this mark of confidence was not a personal tribute.

[17] The first practical underwater active sound detection apparatus, developed by the Anti-Submarine Division of the British Naval Staff.

At the same time his gesture was in the grand manner and I began to understand why his friends loved him. Like Theodore Roosevelt, he used the big stick on his enemies, but bound his friends to him by giving love. Before I left, I asked him if I might send him a memorandum setting forth my understanding of his position in regard to Northern Ireland. It would prevent misunderstanding on my part. He assented and a few days later I sent him the following:

MEMORANDUM TO CHURCHILL RE. MEETING WEDNESDAY, APRIL 3RD, 1940

I want to thank you for giving me so much of your time and confidence. My understanding of your personal position as set forth in our talk on April 3rd is this:

1. Under no circumstances would you tolerate any coercion of Ulster direct or indirect by your government or any other.
2. You would not stand in the way of any settlement not inimical to the vital interests of your government, arrived at by the two parties in agreement.
3. If by mutual consent the parties in question could approach some understanding for the purpose of considering measures for their mutual welfare and safety during the duration of the war, you would not disapprove in principle.
4. On my part it was expressly understood that I was exploring this situation to the end of informing myself and my government of the facts and not assuming to propose a mediation or to conduct a negotiation.
5. Within the limits of this understanding I feel free to discuss your position with Mr de Valera from whom I hope to gather information as to his position.
6. If Mr de Valera and the American Ambassador in London should raise no objection to my seeking an interview with Lord Craigavon for the purpose of obtaining direct from him his position in the present situation, I shall write you again asking for suggestions as to the best way of meeting him.

Please accept my grateful appreciation of your courtesy and believe me sincerely yours.

I sent this on to the president. A few days later Mr Churchill wrote me approving the memorandum as it stood.

Though I did not know it, fateful events were in progress that afternoon of April 3rd. The admiralty had obtained evidence that Hitler was preparing his invasion of Norway and Mr Churchill was issuing orders for the mining of the approaches to the Norwegian ports. The operation was 'top secret' and no one but a few insiders knew that the phoney war was at an end. So the sporting public went to Liverpool on April 5th as usual for the Grand National. I went also and watched the race in bright sunshine, lost a pound on the Irish horse that led over the last fence and faded in the stretch, and that night took ship for Dublin.

CHAPTER III

Our ship sailed without lights and on a prescribed course through the mine fields, but uneventfully. At eight o'clock on the morning of April 6th, we tied up at the North Wall in Dublin. It was a chill, overcast, typical Dublin morning with a cold drizzle. Dublin does not wake up till nine, so that it seemed very early. The familiar Liffey smells greeted us and my wife and I both became emotional upon being in Ireland again. We had spent the year 1932–3 in this perplexing little country and it had got a hold upon our hearts. We realised that we felt about it as many Americans feel about France. It was our second country. It was not a profitable mood for an official charged with reporting the truth.

John MacVeagh,[1] the officer in charge of the American legation, welcomed us. With him was Mr Joseph Walshe, Mr de Valera's permanent secretary for External Affairs. Of course I had no knowledge at this time that Mr Walshe was already working harmoniously with the German minister to hamper American preparedness. He was extremely agreeable and likeable. Moreover, he brought me cordial greetings from Mr de Valera, and what especially pleased me was the invitation to meet Mr de Valera that very day at half past twelve. Mr de Valera was waiving the formalities. The presentation of my letters of credence had been set for April 15th.

While Mr MacVeagh was grasping my hand he whispered, 'Deny to the reporters that you are giving up the legation. I'll explain'. I was at a loss, for I could not understand why it should be a matter of public interest whether or not the American government changed its Dublin

[1] John MacVeagh had effectively been operating as the US representative in Ireland, taking on many of the public roles normally carried out by the ambassador. *Irish Times*, 'Reception at American legation', 5 July 1939.

habitat. However, Mr MacVeagh knew his business so I mumbled a clumsy prevarication about a 'misunderstanding'. What had happened was this: in London a newspaper man had congratulated us on having the former British chief secretary's Lodge in Dublin for a legation. This building had been handed over to the Irish government when the Free State was established. The State Department leased it.

I had replied to the newspaper man that it was indeed a delightful house but that I had been instructed to surrender the lease on the score of economy. It sounds odd today but in 1940 the State Department had a lean budget. The reporter had put this on the wire to Dublin.

It happened that the British Representative in Éire was looking for a suitable house. Such houses were scarce and the Irish government had told MacVeagh that it was highly probable that if we gave up the premises the English Representative would wish to lease it. This would 'embarrass' his government for if they let him have it their opponents would say, 'de Valera has "let the English back in the Park" again', meaning that the English were again governing the country. Under the Act of Union both the lord lieutenant who represented the king and the chief secretary, who on behalf of parliament wielded the power, lived 'in The Park'. No sensible adult in the United States would have taken such nonsense seriously, but in Éire it was not nonsense. In the end it turned out to be a stroke of luck for us. I telegraphed the facts to Washington and was promptly authorised to continue the lease. Since I was entitled to 3,000 dollars a year as housing allowance and the legation chancery was installed in the house, the rent for the chancery came to only some 1,500 dollars. I doubt if any other United States chancery even then paid as little as this for its housing. Later I was authorised to negotiate a long-term lease, but by that time our happy relation with Mr de Valera had come to an end. He refused to sanction it. However, the Costello government which succeeded him in 1948 granted George Garrett,[2] my successor, a ninety-nine year tenancy. I have always been glad that I wrote the London newspaper man an apology for my denial of his truthful statement.

Mr MacVeagh took us and Mr Walshe home to breakfast. He and his wife had a charming house just outside the park. They gave us a sumptuous Irish breakfast before a glowing fire of turf briquettes. They

[2] George Garrett, the 48-year-old investment banker born in Wisconsin and educated at Cornell and the University of Chicago, was appointed envoy to Ireland by President Truman on 10 April 1947. He has been described by one historian as a typical 'Hibernophile' Irish American. Troy D. Davis, *Dublin's American policy: Irish American diplomatic relations 1945–52* (Washington DC, 1998), 96.

were Americans that made one proud of his foreign service. There was neither silver, china, linen nor cooking utensils in the legation, and ours were somewhere on the Atlantic, together with my motor car. In 1940 I was not only obliged to provide my own car, but pay for its shipment to Ireland.

MacVeagh took me to the 12:30 p.m. appointment with Mr de Valera. It is difficult today to recapture its mood, but the memorandum written that afternoon makes it clear that I was deeply impressed by this extraordinary man.

Éire was not at war but the government building in Stephen's Green in which Mr de Valera had his offices, unlike 10 Downing Street, was guarded by armed sentries. Inside another sentry stood at the foot of the stairway. Before one was admitted to the hall out of which rose the stairway, a plain-clothes man looked you over through a little window like those in gambling houses. Yet Éire was a neutral.

The taoiseach's office (pronounced popularly 'tee shack') and surroundings were all as they had been so often described by interviewers. He himself was the tall, gaunt figure with the suggestion of Lincoln, and ironically in the corner stood the O'Connor bronze statue of Lincoln which John McCormack, the singer, had given to the Irish government.[3] The office was bare, the flat-topped desk was bare and Mr de Valera was dressed in his invariable black clerical-looking suit with black string tie. He was always neat and his linen was always fresh. His grave eye trouble excited sympathy. It was said that he suffered from glaucoma. From time to time he removed his spectacles and put his hands over his eyes, and from time to time he showed the appealing smile that I had heard about and the suggestion of his peculiar charm.

His part in the Easter Week Sinn Féin Uprising had not been exaggerated by propaganda. However stupid and fantastic had been this adventure, when he went to his post in Boland's mill that morning, the only reasonable expectation was death or imprisonment. To me who had lived safely and within the law, this made and still makes a deep appeal. His inner tragedy seems to be that after the collapse of the rebellion, when he found himself not merely surviving but by virtue of survival the titular leader of the movement, something changed inside him. He became possessed by the Neo-Gaelic Afflatus. Since that time there is

[3] Actually by Dublin-born sculptor Augustus Saint-Gaudens (1848–1907). The original, much larger statue, also by Saint-Gaudens, stands in Lincoln Park, Chicago. See www.embassyofireland .org/uploads/documents/embassy/Washington%20EM/guide%20to%20embassy%20art.pdf (accessed 19 August 2011).

no record of his ever having done what was generous or noble or wise, only what he believed served 'the Cause'. And the evidence is strong that soon he regarded himself as 'the Cause'. He was 'Mr Ireland'. What was good for de Valera became what was good for Ireland. There was no honest view other than his. There could be no honest opposition to him. So he dedicated himself to justifying his mistakes and making them stand in history as not having been mistakes. In retrospect I know that I was never at ease with him. There was never honest meeting of the eyes except when his were blazing with anger. I now know that during the seven years of our relation he was always tricking my country but I believe that there was an honest basis for the charm that he exerted and the affection he inspired. It was as if some 'Better Self' habitually kept under restraint escaped at times to the window and beckoned. One recognised good will and went forward but found the window barred and what had been behind it vanished. It was the tragedy of him who makes a god of 'Race'.

Besides his authentic role in the Uprising, his supposed devotion to the United States had influenced me strongly. His goodbye address released on January 3rd, 1921, closed as follows:

So farewell—young, fortunate, mighty land; no wish that I can express can measure the depth of my esteem for you or my desire for your welfare and glory. And farewell the many dear friends I have made and the tens of thousands who for the reason that I was the representative of a noble nation and a storied, appealing cause, gave me honours they denied to princes—you will not need to be assured that Ireland will not forget and that Ireland will not be grateful.

This is florid but contains nothing to suggest insincerity, so it seemed to me, on that April 6th that I had clasped the hand of a friend of my country, that he would see the Axis menace to democratic institutions as our more forward-looking Americans even then saw them, and would recognise that this menace threatened Éire also as a part of the free world.

He was very courteous. He inquired about our trip across Europe and I told him in some detail of my reception by the pope and of the kindness and help which his Irish ministers had shown us. I told him with whom I had talked in London and why Mr Chamberlain had refused to see me. He made no comment on this. I told him that I had talked with

Mr Churchill whom they said would be the next prime minister and that I hoped soon to have authority to quote his views on Partition.

At this point Mr de Valera opened up with what was much on his mind. He said that he was having a difficult time with the IRA. They had taken advantage of the international situation to create disorder. He had been obliged to jail some of them and they had declared a hunger strike. Now young Plunkett, the son of one of his old friends and comrades, was at the point of death.[4] If he released them it would be taken for weakness. If he let them die they would become martyrs. He was in the throes of a domestic political crisis with international implications which had not got into the newspapers nor to Washington. The only international aspect was that the IRA were anxious to get German help to depose him and presumably 'execute' him for 'war crimes'.

No one had briefed me on this. It had never occurred to me that a banned, illegal organisation 'on the run' could be a prime factor in national policy, but after he had lost his Civil War that is what he had been. He had staged a 'come-back'. He knew how he had done it, and when he became aware that the IRA were using the same methods that he had used, he was anxious.

If the Department of State had grasped this situation, they kept it in their files. No one imparted it to me. In fact the Department had interpreted the 'Gentleman's Agreement' and the Coal-Cattle Pact which settled the Economic War as a victory for Mr de Valera. The truth was, in Ireland it had laid him open to the charge of selling Ireland out, in order to get back the ports.

At this point I gave him the letter from President Roosevelt and also one from Mayor LaGuardia.[5] The Mayor had written the conventional greeting of the politician who wooed the Irish vote while I waited in his office. He had read it to me before he sealed it. What the president wrote I do not know. Mr de Valera read it and laid it on his desk without comment. I think that if it had pleased him he would have said so. No copy of this letter can be found in the president's files. This suggests not only that it was holographic but that the president did not consider it of sufficient importance to have a copy typed for the record.

I then gave him the oral message: 'The President hopes that you will be able to come and visit him this spring. He tells me to tell you that *his foreign policy is substantially the same as yours*'.

[4] John Plunkett had been convicted of usurpation of government functions on 1 March 1940. Seosamh Ó Longaigh, *Emergency law in independent Ireland* (Dublin, 2006), 245.
[5] Fiorello Henry LaGuardia (1882–1947), three-term republican Mayor of New York, served as Roosevelt's director of civil defence during the run-up to the Second World War.

Mr de Valera nodded assent and said, 'We are both neutrals'.

But at this time it was public knowledge that on January 4th, 1939, the president had broadcast his views on the rape of Austria and Czechoslovakia. 'The mere fact', he said,

> that we rightly decline to intervene with arms to prevent acts of aggression does not mean that we must act as if there were no aggression at all. Words may be futile but war is not the only means of commanding a decent respect for the opinions of mankind. There are many methods short of war.

One of these methods was to make it possible for the victims of aggression to purchase American arms. Late in 1939 the administration succeeded in getting the Neutrality Act modified to permit such sale to belligerents. This led later to the 'Arsenal of Democracy'. After the attack on Poland and the declaration of war on Germany by France and England, he had said, 'This nation will remain a neutral nation but I cannot ask every American to remain neutral in thought as well. Even a neutral has a right to take account of facts. Even a neutral cannot be asked to close his mind and conscience'.

The question was, did Mr de Valera, when he had nodded assent, mean what the president meant by neutrality. At that time I believed that he did. As I left him he said:

'You can see me at any time and you can tell *anything to Mr Walshe that you could tell me*'. This expression of confidence in Mr Walshe had more significance than at first appeared.

As I went out with Mr MacVeagh, I did not see how things could have gone better for our country.

The above is paraphrased from my diary letter to the president, dispatched on April 9th, 1940. The letter closed as follows:

From letter to President Roosevelt

Tuesday, April 9th, 1940

He was very cordial and talked frankly of the difficulties of the situation which I will summarise for you in another paragraph. As we left he spoke with a good deal of feeling of the situation he was in with the hunger strikers, one of whom is a son of Count Plunkett, whether to let them die or release them and admit defeat. He was obviously much troubled. I have a feeling that unforeseen events may begin to move rapidly before long and that it is my job to get in close touch with these people as quickly as possible. During the night I began to think about the hunger strikers and in the morning I wrote him (Mr de Valera) a note in this sense: 'If in your view it might be helpful for me to see these men and tell them that the president of the United States was endeavouring to promote the solution of all political problems by peaceful political means, and that the pope recently had spoken to me in the same vein I would gladly do so, if the thing could be kept strictly private, as at all costs I must avoid any action capable of being interpreted as meddling with their internal politics'.

The next morning (Monday, April 7th)[6] his secretary telephoned asking me to come to his office at five (which I did). He [de Valera] seemed grateful for my offer but said that he thought it would be interpreted as weakness on his part. They would not believe that he had not instigated the visit. That if they came to call on me as they doubtless would I could take this line. He was much tougher about them this time, said he was not sure they were not bluffing.[7] Boland his minister for justice on Sunday had spoken publicly to the effect that the law could not be changed because violators of it appealed to public sympathy. I think he has decided to take a firm line. He asked me to stay on and we discussed the Anglo-Irish situation. I told him that there was *no use my pretending to be personally neutral.* I was prepared to be absolutely 'correct' as representing a neutral power, but that personally I was so opposed to Hitlerism, the persecution of Jews, the rape of the small countries in violation of express and newly-made pledges that I considered the success of the Allies desirable. I said that in my opinion if Germany were at Gibraltar, Suez, Singapore, Hong Kong, she would also be at Bermuda, Nassau, Jamaica and the Windward and Leeward Islands, that she would take our South American trade from us overnight, that Australia would probably be taken by the Japanese and South Africa by the Germans, that we would be condemned to armed self-defence for generations; that much as we might resent certain practices of Britain in the past, she had policed the seas at her own expense and had given us on the whole a square deal, that I would rather go on with her than with Hitler, that if he thought this

[6] 7 April was actually a Sunday.
[7] Gerald Boland had a reputation for decisiveness. Within a year of being appointed minister for justice, he claimed, 'Mr de Valera would not try to force me to do anything'. *Irish Times*, 19 October 1968.

disqualified me as an American representative I would ask to be relieved and go home.

He said that *he felt much the same way* but that his people would not see that they were in danger until it was upon them, that the IRA had stirred up anti-British feeling again. I asked him how important numerically the movement was. He said, 'Probably not very large numerically—perhaps a couple of thousands of individuals but that they appealed to *'something very deep in the Irish Heart'*. We talked intimately about Ulster and he gave me a map showing majority sentiment in each of the Six Counties. He claims that at least two of these counties are overwhelmingly for union (with the South) and are in effect being *coerced*. That is his line. The British refuse to coerce Belfast but connive at the coercion of these two counties and elements in the others.

I asked him about seeing Craigavon. He said, 'by all means if you can arrange it correctly, that is with the consent of the British and Kennedy. I would see him myself', he said, 'but he will not see me'. Then I led the conversation to the point I was approaching. I said 'Suppose I saw Craigavon and said to him is there any price that you would pay as a friend of Britain for something useful to Britain in the present crisis that Mr de Valera might grant you?

De Valera said 'What do you mean?'

I said, 'Let us think aloud and see what would be useful to England. How about Berehaven and possibly the recall of the German Legation?'

'No', he said, *'we could never bargain with our neutrality'*.

There you have it as the impasse stands at the moment. Mr de Valera speaking as a great gentleman on the one side and Mr Churchill as a great gentleman on the other, each saying he will do without what he needs: Churchill without Berehaven, sooner than put pressure on Ulster; and de Valera without American help, sooner than bargain for Irish neutrality.

The letter continued:

Of course I have been trying to find a formula in which some even slight measure of conciliation between South and North could be generously and conspicuously blessed by the British Government putting them on record with us in the US, as favouring some solution to the end of easing pressure upon you from the professional 'anti-Lion' boys,[8] in case events should make you want to act. And that is of course the real reason I want to see Craigavon. It is evidently a hundred to one chance but it ought to be taken. It's too important all round not to be explored. I've been very lucky so far but don't think that I shall probably not end up in the ash can because this thing is like walking on the sulphur crust over a crater full of melted lava.

When I think that your day is walking over a hundred such floors I begin to understand a bit. John MacVeagh is A-1 and a great help. I present my letters next Monday. My best to Missy.[9] I think her Church friends have done us a good turn along the line'.

The picture of Mr de Valera as the 'great gentleman' resenting the suggestion of bargaining with Irish neutrality, while he had so to speak in his pocket the bill of sale not only of Irish neutrality but 'Irish influence' in America in return for Northern Ireland, is the essence of the 'Irish problem'. Even today I believe that while the pose endured Mr de Valera was sincere. It was this pathological sincerity which deceived Neville Chamberlain and the duke of Devonshire, not to mention the newly-arrived American minister. The Irish prime minister could not be called to account for it any more than could a certified lunatic, for always with each new aspect of the situation he had 'looked into his Irish Heart' and seen what was best for Ireland that day.

This new revelation replaced all previous revelations. That, as Mr O'Hegarty[10] pointed out, nothing meant anything to him unless he could win on it[. This] was, as novelists say in their prefaces, 'purely coincidental'. Diplomacy by revelation was the Sinn Féin, Irish way and until pathological psychology becomes a recognised factor of diplomacy as practised in the World's chanceries, there is little that can be done about it except be forewarned, whether it manifests in Ghana, Dublin or Moscow.

On April 8th[11] the Dublin morning papers carried this item:

---

[8] Anti-British.

[9] Mary LeHand, Roosevelt's companion and secretary.

[10] P.S. O'Hegarty (1879–1958), veteran Irish separatist and civil servant, important Irish scholar and historian. His papers are held in an important collection at the University of Kansas, Spencer Library.

[11] *Irish Independent*, 17 April 1940 contains a protest by W.J. Whelan at the Labour Party Conference against this attempt at censorship by the IRA.

The following has been issued officially for publication: The minister for justice has issued through the Government Information Bureau the following copy of a threatening letter, which was delivered to all the Dublin daily newspapers yesterday (Monday):

OGLAIGH NA hEIREANN
Irish Republican Army
Ard-Oifig
Ath Cliath
Department of Home Affairs,
Reference No.   (Yours ... .)
                                       (Mine 977 DD)
(Please quote my number and date)
General Headquarters,
Dublin
6th April, 1940

To
the Manager:
Dear Sir,
The Government of the Republic has always respected the freedom of the Press as a medium for the expression of a public opinion in the country, but the continued omission from your columns of news interesting to the majority of the people will be regarded as an abuse of privilege and will on no account be tolerated.
(Signed) S.M. O Aodha
Secretary,
(Ministry of Home Affairs.)

This extraordinary announcement mystified the American legation. It told the newspaper editors to print IRA news 'or else'. But why had Mr de Valera released it? What had inspired such a piece of swagger and exhibitionism. The possible answer to the second question came next day. About noon on April 9th, the American embassy in London telephoned that Germany had invaded Denmark and Norway. The phoney war was over. The international situation had again exploded. Had Mr h'Aodea [*sic*] had advance notice? Was the IRA preparing to take over?

I at once telephoned Mr de Valera. He said that he had not heard the news and seemed much disturbed. In view of his understanding with Hitler as set forth in the August 26th and September 3rd, 1939, telegrams, one would have thought he would have been gratified, that he would have said, 'Well this is it; it won't be long now till we are in Belfast'. But he was undoubtedly disturbed. The most plausible speculation is that it put him on the spot. On the one hand he would have to move against the IRA; on the other London would expect him to condemn the aggression and he knew that Berlin would resent it. He had made it clear to Hempel in the September talks that in view of Irish dependence on Britain for supply he should have to have freedom of action in order to keep the British government deceived. There was no better way of doing this than by publicly condemning Germany. But he also realised that it would be like going into the cage and kicking the tiger. By previous agreement he could not be sure how much 'freedom of action' Ribbentrop was likely to grant him. Moreover, it is probable that by this time his stool pigeon in the IRA had advised him of the Artus plan, which suggested that while Germany was shaking hands with one hand, in the other she carried the big stick.

Ignorant of all this, we accounted for his anxiety on the theory that in total war the survival of Éire as an independent state was at stake. If the Allies won, de Valera had nothing to fear. England had recently condoned his violations of the Treaty, embodied in his new Constitution, had given him the ports and forgiven him a hundred million pounds of annuities. What a German victory would mean he could infer from what had happened to Austria, Czechoslovakia and Poland and was now happening to Denmark and Norway. Both these small nations had been neutral. Both had relied upon German assurances as Éire was doing. What were these assurances worth? When de Valera had told me two days before that the Irish people did not 'see their danger', he could only have meant the German danger. If German strategy demanded the extension of the German right flank to the North in an encircling movement, was not Éire a part of it? If Hitler decided to close the narrows[12] between Ireland and Scotland by seizing Northern Ireland, would he not need Éire territory for the manoeuvre? Such seemed the line Mr de Valera's thinking must be taking, and on Friday morning, April 10th,[13] the leading editorial in his newspaper, the *Irish Press*, confirmed this view. The leader was entitled 'Europe in Turmoil'. It said:

[12] Gray uses 'the Narrows' to describe the north channel of the Irish Sea throughout.
[13] 10 April was a Wednesday.

IRISH PRESS

EUROPE IN TURMOIL

The events of the past twenty-four hours have left the world dumbfounded. Even a generation which has grown accustomed to political sensations which would have been unimaginable in former times has found it hard to believe that two peaceful, highly civilised nations could be robbed of their independence overnight, without warning and without the slightest pretext except that of military expediency.

Both Denmark and Norway had made it abundantly clear that their sole aim was to maintain the strictest neutrality and live at peace with all their neighbours. The statements made by Germany after the event make scarcely any attempt to justify her action on moral or legal grounds. Her case must rest on the claim that she stole a march on Britain and France who are alleged to have had the intention of invading Scandinavia themselves. And it must be noted that the only known fact advanced in support of this assertion, namely that Britain had violated Norway's neutrality by mining her territorial waters, does not apply to Denmark. Norway alone was concerned and, as we pointed out yesterday, before taking action on her own account Germany was under a legal obligation to make a formal demand on the Norwegian Government to have the minefields removed. But these things may be left for the belligerents to argue out between them. The attitude of the two countries invaded is itself sufficient to make the position perfectly clear. Denmark has accepted the German occupation under protest and because she was too weak to offer any real resistance, while Norway opposed the invader with such forces as she could command.

Did the invasion take Britain and France by surprise? Probably there was little they could do to prevent the occupation of Denmark. Owing to its land frontier that country was at the mercy of the Germans since the beginning of the war and it must have been for strategic purposes that they decided to occupy it. On the other hand the Allies have repeatedly stated that they were both willing and able to defend Scandinavia. During the Russian invasion of Finland they pressed Norway and Sweden to go openly to that country's aid or at least to allow an allied expeditionary force to pass through their territory. How then did it come about that the Germans were able to effect landings on the west coast of Norway without, apparently, encountering much opposition from the British North sea fleet? We must await developments before attempting to answer that question. Undoubtedly tremendous events are at hand. There are reports that a great naval battle is taking place and that troops are being massed on many frontiers. Holland is specifically mentioned and should that country become involved it will mean that the long threatened war in the West is about to begin.

After reading Mr de Valera's leader, I could have no doubt that he was indeed following the same line as President Roosevelt. Though neutral in deed, he was not neutral in thought or word. He was condemning Axis aggression and presumably for the reason that it constituted a menace to Éire, as it did to the United States. On April 13th, President Roosevelt issued a condemnation of the violation of Denmark and Norway which paralleled Mr de Valera's:

Force and military aggression are once more on the march against small nations, in this instance through the invasion of Denmark and Norway. These two nations have won and maintained, through a period of many generations the respect and regard not only of the American people, but of all peoples, because of their respect and observance of the highest standards of international conduct.

The Government of the United States has on the occasion of recent invasions strongly expressed its disapprobation of such unlawful exercise of force. It here reiterates, with undiminished emphasis, its point of view as expressed on these occasions. If civilisation is to survive, the rights of the smaller nations to independence, to their territorial integrity and to the unimpeded opportunity for self-government must be respected by their more powerful neighbours.

Though the president did not say so, the implication was plain that if the powerful nations did not respect the rights of the small nations, there was but one thing for the small nations to do about it, unite in time to make the great nations respect those rights. It was futile to whine about invasion of rights under international law when the complainers refused to co-operate for the maintenance of international law. I believed at that time that Mr de Valera was realist enough to see this and to see that failure to co-operate for a common defence of all Ireland was lunacy. Co-operation should not have been looked upon as a bargaining of Éire's neutrality but the recognition of a common danger. Moreover, if Éire claimed title to the North, was it not an Éire obligation to help defend it? Fifteen years after the event it is still surprising that these so logical expectations could have been so mistaken. The truth, however, was that Mr de Valera was exercising that 'freedom of action' he had stipulated in order to deceive London. He had also deceived Washington. As far as we know Berlin made no protest at his comment on Norway and Denmark.

Until a diplomat presents his credentials, officially he has no existence. The newly arrived minister is supposed to require time for establishing his domestic arrangements. In 1940 this was easier in neutral Éire than in other parts of Europe. Our trunks and packing cases arrived from Liverpool and our car was landed at Cork. We took over my predecessor's staff of servants and were a going concern. One of John Cudahy's last kind deeds before departing as minister to Belgium had been to lend the legation to the Kildare Hunt for its annual ball. An Irish Hunt Ball is an enjoyable entertainment but not good for a house, and the MacVeagh's and the staff had been engaged in operation 'spring cleaning', ever since. To the devastation of the ball had been added that of the 'great frost' of 1940, which was regarded as an Act of God. Practically all the plumbing had burst. The Irish are optimistic about plumbing. They put most of the pipes outside. Since they freeze only about twice in five years this is considered not unprofitable.

It was a house of great charm. Its length faced south with a row of tall windows and two generous bows. In winter what sun there was streamed in. The view gave across the lawn to what is called the 'Fifteen Acres', in the Phoenix Park where trainers gallop their horses and deer and cattle graze. Beyond were the spires of Chapelizod (Chapelle Iseult), where the ill-fated princess is supposed to have retired as a penitent after the Tristan escapade. Along the skyline stretched the Wicklow Hills or 'mountains' as they are generally called. The house was not only in the Phoenix Park but in its own demesne of about sixty acres, surrounded by a sunken ditch. It had escaped the pretentiousness which characterised many of the 'big' Georgian Irish houses by reason of the fact that it was the Chief Secretary's. The Parliamentary Chief Secretary under the Act of Union, exercised the political power of the government, but the Lord Lieutenant or Viceroy was invested with the pomp of Royalty. He was installed, when not in 'The Castle' in town, in the Vice Regal Lodge in the Park, a half mile to the east of us. This house was a Georgian palace with a façade of white, two-story columns resembling the entrance to our White House. In designed contrast the entrance to the Chief Secretary's Lodge was a low vestibule-like structure, stuck on the north side of the house. It functioned as the New Englander's 'storm door' vestibule functions, keeping the north winds out of the main hall, but it was studiedly unimposing. Inside, the drawing rooms and the master bedrooms upstairs all were more in scale with human life than those of many great houses. We rejoiced in five upstairs master bathrooms, made out of former dressing rooms or expanded closets. Every room had its fireplace and we had coal and menservants to carry it, but open fires alone could not maintain a temperature which Americans call 'warm'. Fortunately there was an effective steam-heating system on the ground floor and this made the upstairs habitable though not warm. In an old saddle room in the stables I found what looked like an old-fashioned American station agent's stove. This I installed in my bedroom. My wife solved the problem by moving a bed into her bathroom. With its fireplace and an electric heater she managed very well.

In addition to this there were extensive regions devoted to the subhuman accommodations to which Irish Big House servants in Ireland have been accustomed immemorially. There was a stable court with apartments for grooms and a farm court and two gate lodges, besides a gardener's house.

Finally there were seven acres of walled gardens with orchards and glass houses all in that stage of progressive decay which marks a rise in the rights of man and a fall in the rights of property.

The list of notable people who had lived in this house or had had the right to live in it was long. The duke of Wellington was one of the first. Two of the more recent tenants that I knew about were Arthur Balfour and later his friend George Wyndham, author of the revolutionary land acts. Each held the office for seven years. There was a path around the demesne, shaded by immemorial oaks and beeches. It was a path that invited the desk-weary to a brisk mile at the day's end. I used often to think of these two men of goodwill, perplexed and saddened by their difficulties, walking that path in the dark. I believe in ghosts and was always expecting to encounter one in the shadows of this historic alley, but nothing more startling ever happened than flushing a terrified woodcock asleep by the path-side.

On April 10th we lunched with the MacVeaghs *en famille* to meet the papal nuncio 'unofficially'. I told him that I had a letter of introduction to him from Archbishop Spellman, but since I would have no official existence until the fifteenth of the month I could not call upon him and deliver it.[14]

He said gravely, 'In that case we can continue to converse as strangers'. With him was his secretary a very young Monsignor Enricci.[15] He was a lovable young man, extremely intelligent, frank and generous-minded, but terribly homesick.

My journal makes no mention of discussing the Scandinavian situation. Personally I was confident that the British navy had it in hand and that the Allied expeditionary force would promptly drive the Germans out. I imprudently bet a pound on this with Jack MacVeagh, who knew much more about German might than I did.

I asked the nuncio about the IRA. He answered that many of them as individuals were 'fine fellows' and that I would like them. We did not discuss Mr h'Aodea [*sic*] nor the peril of the Dublin editors.

The story was current that IRA murderers after doing their patriotic 'executions', would bicycle at once to the nuncio, confess and get absolution. This was not true but it is true that his door was open to the 'bad' men and that he administered much sound advice.

I asked him if he did not think, in the circumstances, a national coalition government was desirable.

He said, 'Obviously, but the Leader of the Opposition (William Cosgrave) will not speak to the Leader of the government (Mr de Valera). I have tried to bring them together without success'.

I learned later that it was true that Mr Cosgrave would not speak to Mr de Valera. He believed that Mr de Valera had overstepped the bounds of political decency and put himself beyond the pale. But he was ready to stand aside, if it were in the national interest. It was not he that made a national government impossible but Mr de Valera, who mistrusted coalitions.

It was on this occasion that I first spoke to the nuncio of my belief that out of the war situation some accommodation with the North could be obtained. He encouraged me, saying: '*Cherchez toujours la formule*'. It was not his opinion that Irish neutrality was *not* a subject for bargaining.

[14] The papal nuncio to Ireland, Paschal Robinson, was born in Dublin in 1870 and died in 1948. He was professor of medieval history at the Catholic University of America from 1913 to 1925: he wrote extensively on St Francis of Assisi. He was appointed papal nuncio to Ireland in 1929.
[15] Domenico Enricci (1909–97), later to be apostolic delegate to Australia (1962) and Great Britain (1969).

On the afternoon of the 12th, James Dillon called on us. A common friend in New York had written asking him to do this.

Mr Dillon at that time was a unique figure in Irish politics and except for Mr de Valera the most colourful. We became deeply attached to him for himself, but even had we detested him, we had incurred a debt to him that, as Americans, we could never repay. As regards America, James Dillon became the 'forgotten man'.[16] Ingenious and conscienceless, official suppression of the facts prevented Americans from realising his championship of the United States during those early years of the war. He became the 'forgotten man' but he was also the Irishman who 'did not forget'. When the objective historian explores this episode in Irish history, Washington will put up a statue to him beside LaFayette.[17]

After Pearl Harbor James Dillon defied Mr de Valera in the Irish Dáil, denounced Irish neutrality and asserted that Irish interest and honour demanded that Éire declare war on Germany as the ally of the United States. In doing this he risked almost certain political extinction. Also he took a good chance of being murdered.

By birth and tradition Dillon *was* 'Irish Nationalism'. His father was John Dillon, co-leader with John Redmond of the great nationalist Party. His grandfather was John Blake Dillon,[18] a lieutenant of Daniel O'Connell. Both father and grandfather had been imprisoned for their nationalist activities and both had found asylum in the United States. All this was before the Sinn Féin Movement had been thought of. His mother was the daughter of Mr Justice Mathew, an English, Roman Catholic judge of exceptional distinction.

James was twelve when the Home Rule bill became law. He was fourteen at the time of the Sinn Féin Dublin insurrection, and twenty when the Anglo-Irish Treaty was accepted by the Irish Dáil and repudiated by the de Valera minority faction. After taking his degree at Dublin University, he read law and was called to the Irish Bar in 1931. At that time the Irish Free State under the Cosgrave regime apparently was firmly within the Commonwealth. In effect there was still a common citizenship with the English. Irishmen lived in London as of *right* and not as foreigners.

[16] James Dillon (1912–86), son of the Irish party leader John Dillon, an enemy of Hempel and friend of Gray and Maffey in this period. Became the Fine Gael leader in 1959. Maurice Manning, *James Dillon: a biography* (Dublin, 1999), 162–3.
[17] General in the American Revolutionary War and a leader of the Garde Nationale during the French Revolution.
[18] John Blake Dillon (1814–66), commanded the Young Ireland rebels at Killenaule in 1848.

James Dillon must have known that fortune and a great career at the Bar lay ahead of him if he went to London, for he was exceptionally gifted. There seemed little for him in Ireland.

Sinn Féin had destroyed his father politically together with John Redmond, their party and their political philosophy. He had no hope of preferment in this new Ireland because of his father's achievements. The nationalists were not separatists but believers in what was essentially a conception of Anglo-Irish federation to be achieved by constitutional process. Men like Redmond and Dillon fought for Irish self-determination but they were also Europeans. They did not want Ireland left alone and defenceless and they did not want Ireland to lose her right of free entry to a market of forty-five million consumers. This is what the Home Rule Agitation meant taken together with Redmond's pledge of Irish loyalty at the outbreak of World War One. It could mean nothing else to Irishmen with open and honest minds. But Sinn Féin had done away with Redmond, Dillon and Home Rule. For three centuries Irish blood strains had helped win the British empire but a small group, at best, of small-town, half-educated 'little men;' at worst, of psychopaths and gunmen, were ready to toss away Ireland's partnership rights without a thought, and in the spirit of the rabble that burns its own public buildings. In spite of this situation James Dillon made his decision to stay in this new Ireland and make a new start. Out of family loyalty he also renounced his career at the law.

A cousin had bequeathed to the Dillons what we should call a 'country store'. It was 'Monica Duff, Inc'., a profitable enterprise in the market town of Ballaghaderreen, in County Mayo, but it needed management. One of the Dillon brothers was a priest, one a brilliant doctor, the third, Myles, a Celtic scholar holding a chair in an American university.[19] The one sister was married to one of the leading junior surgeons in Dublin. No one of these was willing to sacrifice his career to run the shop in Mayo. James not only took it on but went to the United States to study merchandising. He first got himself a job with Marshall Field and Co. in Chicago, and later with Lord and Taylor in New York. He came back to Ireland and ran Monica Duff, Inc. and went into politics. As was to have been expected, he enlisted in the Cosgrave party, at this time known as 'Cumann na nGaedheal', and later as 'Fine Gael'. William Cosgrave who had been head of the Free State government till 1932 was what is called in Ireland 'a decent man'. There is no higher praise. His word was good. He was generous to those who differed with

---

[19] Myles Dillon (1900–72), historian, philologist and celticist—a brilliant scholar with a broad-minded, open disposition.

him, and he had grasped the rudiments of sound national economy. If any man could have achieved Irish unity after de Valera's Civil War, it might well have been he. In 1927 he welcomed the de Valera-ites as a Constitutional opposition. He saw the danger of a one-party state. He also welcomed the adherence of the old unionists and the 'county' people to the Free State. He built up a distinguished Senate with powers of delaying legislation for eighteen months, an ample 'cool-off time'. He saw the justice as well as the advantage of welcoming back such of the old nationalists as were still alive. Both Redmond and John Dillon had died, but he made a friend of James Dillon and helped him to win his first election to the Dáil from Donegal in 1934. In 1937 Dillon stood for a seat in Monaghan and won. Monaghan still returns him. De Valera had formed a government in 1932 and Dillon went into the Dáil as a member of the opposition. He liked and admired Mr Cosgrave and his abilities were at once apparent. In 1940, at thirty-eight, he was Deputy Leader of the Fine Gael party.

Probably no national legislative body had so many back benchers as ignorant of so much as the Irish Dáil in 1940. This was especially true of the Fianna Fáil members. They voted like sheep. Since 1932 when they came to power, no deputy had ever voted against the party line regardless of the interest of his constituents. One such case occurred during the war, but the offending deputy never did it again. Absenteeism among these members was a scandal and exploded the Sinn Féin propaganda that they had been held 'in slavery, passionately hungering for self-government'. They were hungering for the paltry salaries. One of the unhappiest features of the situation was the effect that legislating had upon their manners. Small town members who at home had the fine manners of the Irish race, in the Dáil behaved like Yahoos. It was a tough school for James Dillon but he became 'able for it'. He 'could take it as well as hand it out'. After a time the opposition speakers avoided tangling with him.

The censorship established at the outbreak of the war under the Emergency Powers Act gave the government almost unlimited power in moulding public opinion.[20] At this time it was exercised in promoting what appeared to be the de Valera party's chief objective, to prove that in every crisis de Valera had been right instead of always wrong. He had been right about Separatism, about rejecting the Treaty, about the Civil War, about defaulting on the annuities, about the Economic War, about Irish self-sufficiency, about discouraging the cattle industry, and encouraging manufacture, and about compulsory Irish. It required no

[20] Donal Ó Drisceoil, *Censorship in Ireland 1939–1945: neutrality, politics and society* (Cork, 1996).

prophet to foresee that once Mr de Valera had decided irrevocably upon neutrality that the whole power of the party apparatus would be set working to prove that he had been right about that also.

But in April, 1940, as far as was then known, he had not yet made this decision irrevocable and James Dillon was still hopeful that he would not make it. At this time Mr Dillon had no knowledge of Mr de Valera's August 26th, 1939, proposals to Ribbentrop nor of his plotting in the United States with the German Bundists. On the other hand he regarded it as highly probable that Berlin would instigate an IRA Uprising to depose de Valera in Éire, as did we foreign observers. He had a strong sense of patriotic duty and was prepared to lay aside party politics for the national emergency. He cultivated a pleasant personal relation with Mr de Valera which lasted until it became clear that Mr de Valera planned to trap the opposition in his neutrality net, a trap from which only Dillon escaped. He and I had much the same view of the world situation and of the forces that had produced it. We both saw the menace of Axis aggression to democratic countries. We agreed also that the Allied arms would successfully resist the German onslaught. Consequently the long view situation for Éire was not critical. At the same time we both believed that the war offered an opportunity for a defence arrangement with Northern Ireland that promised a solution of Partition and might never come again.

In those early days James Dillon was a delightful visitor. In intimate company he loved fun and laughter. He drank little wine and no whiskey but gallons of tea. I tried to reform him from this habit and convert him to twelve-year-old Irish whiskey, but without success. He would even demand his tea at ten o'clock in the evening according to the custom of the early nineteenth century.

The afternoon that he called we were to have tea with the MacVeaghs to meet General Brennan, the retiring chief of staff of the Irish army. I telephoned MacVeagh to ask if we could bring Dillon. The answer was 'of course, only make sure that he speaks to General Brennan'. This was a standard social precaution. Fortunately Dillon and Brennan were old friends.

General Brennan proved to be an extremely agreeable and intelligent man.[21] He had won the prestige which later made him Chief of Staff of the regular army as a guerrilla fighter against the Black and Tans. To my

[21] Michael Brennan (1896–1986), one-time revolutionary and Irish army chief of staff, born in Meelick, Co. Clare. After the Magazine Fort in the Phoenix Park was raided by the IRA (23 December 1939) and a large part of the army's ammunition resources stolen, he was replaced as chief of staff by Dan McKenna. In fact, Brennan's retirement had been decided upon *before* the Magazine Fort raid.

surprise he showed no bitterness and made excuses for them. He said he could understand them in a way. They had thought they were coming over to Ireland to loaf about at a pound a day and found they were shot at and bombed. They 'panicked, took to drink and did bad things'. Like all the Sinn Féin revolutionaries, General Brennan believed that he had a right to shoot and bomb the Black and Tans who just wished to 'loaf about'. He also told us that the 'Home Front', that is the farmers and their women and children, 'won the war' for the Sinn Féiners by giving them perfect intelligence and continually concealing them. He was quite honest in believing that Sinn Féin had won a military victory. We liked the Brennans very much and looked forward to seeing them often. On the general's retirement from the army, Mr de Valera gave him a post on the Board of Public Works. As the 'divergence' between the American viewpoint and Mr de Valera's increased, it was not a good thing for any civil servant to have close relations with the American minister. It did not mean liquidation as in Russia, but it made him 'suspect' unless he came as a spy, as some did. We therefore avoided making advances. James Dillon was in a different category. He was an elected member of parliament and was responsible only to his constituents.

We finished our first unofficial week by going racing. In doing this we left political Ireland, to which we were accredited, and adventured into 'Happy Ireland'. On that Saturday afternoon it seemed that everybody who could was travelling the same road with us except priests, who are forbidden to race, and Mr de Valera who did not enjoy it. It was rumoured that he regarded it as an 'Ascendancy sport' and treasonable. It is more likely that it bored him and that he was not politically averse to being regarded as in a class with priests and intellectuals. I once heard one racegoer say, 'Begob it would be doin' than wan good to be on a winner'. The racing was the Navan 'spring meeting'. Navan is a prosperous little town in the heart of the Meath country and twenty miles north-west of Dublin. A group of Americans in the early days of the century used to hunt from Navan with the Meath, when the famous John Watson was Master. I had heard from them about Father Phelim, the fox-hunting priest, and one of the great wits of Ireland; and of the hunting doctor who had such a gift with broken bones that 'believe it or not, I was huntin' again in a week and me leg as sound as a bell'. It was a raw, windy afternoon but four or five hundred men, women and children had motored or bicycled up from Dublin. As many more appeared from the surrounding countryside and filled the primitive stand and paddock. It is at these small, outlying country meetings that one meets the Irish people rather than at the big meetings at the Curragh or the Phoenix Park in Dublin. I had spent the best years of my life in rural, horse-loving communities in America and felt at home.

There was nothing small-town about the horses. The big trainers at the Curragh used these early country meetings for 'trials'. In one of the first jumping races I picked an animal with impressive quarters, a plain head and a mean eye, and he galloped home a twelve-to-one shot. This of course proved in the end expensive. The Irish professional layers do not often post generous odds. There was a horse named Sir Charge that stood seventeen two. He was the biggest, finest-looking, weight-carrying thoroughbred I have ever seen. He was bigger than Thomas Hitchcock's champion steeple chaser Good and Plenty, who was beaten only in his first race. Sir Charge finished second that day, but sometime later hurt himself and never did much.

Though the sport of racing is forbidden to the clergy there is always the parish priest 'on duty', in case of a broken neck and a need for on-the-spot absolution. The parish priest on duty that day was a charming man. He told me stories about Father Phelim. There were also several important Fianna Fáil politicians present. We met Mr Rutledge,[22] the former minister for justice under Mr de Valera, and his attractive wife. He owned Sir Charge. We also met Judge Evelyn Wylie, the managing genius of the Dublin Horse show;[23] Sir James Nelson, a Turf Club Steward; and the Fianna Fáil senator, Quirk, who had been in business and politics in New York. He was very friendly. One of the best women show-horse riders in Ireland, Sheilagh White, was there and Captain Harty of the Irish army. He had visited New York with the Irish International Jumping team and had married an American, the sister of Cecil Smith, the polo player.

We were also presented to a famous old sportsman, Tom Laidlaw, who had bred two Grand National winners. He was a friend of 'Brose' Clark and Plunkett Stewart and other American sportsmen. He was a gentle, lovable man. He had lost his wife recently and his interests no longer were in the things of this world, but lifelong habit took him racing when the weather was fine. If we could have kept on racing with these people and forgotten about wars and politics, life in Éire would have been pleasanter than it sometimes was.

[22] P.J. Ruttledge (1892–1952), a close de Valera confidante, nearing the end of his Cabinet career, was minister for local government at this point. A racehorse owner.
[23] W.E. Wylie (1881–1964), appointed to act as prosecuting counsel at the courts martial of the captured leaders of 1916. He played a role of orchestrating the eventual deal between Michael Collins and the British government.

CHAPTER IV

APRIL 15TH–18TH

On Saturday evening, April 13th, Captain Harty, the friendly Irish cavalry officer whom we had met at Navan races, called at the legation officially. On Monday the 15th I was to present my letters of credence and he was to command the Headquarters Troop escorting us into Dublin. He explained the programme and translated the Irish words of command which he would use and told me what to do when I heard them. Monday morning at eleven o'clock, some fifty strong, they clattered up the legation driveway in an April snow storm. They wore blue-frogged hussar tunics and were mounted on picked horses. The Dublin jokers called them the 'Blue Hussars', and said that in off hours they worked in a Hungarian band. They were as hard-bitten a lot of young riding men as ever a horse-breeding country produced.

They went off at a sharp trot, escorting our motor car the four miles to the Castle. This had been the seat of Majesty during the days of union and before. As we clattered into the great courtyard another snow storm broke, but the American minister got out of his car and in topper and striped trousers inspected the hussars, while the photographers photographed. Entering the Castle we were ushered through an impressive corridor and up a great stairway, Mr MacVeagh, in attendance, carrying the letter of credence and my speech. Presently we reached the end of a series of drawing rooms and came upon Mr de Valera flanked by officials and ladies and gentlemen of the Cabinet. Mr MacVeagh handed me the letter and speech. It is always the same speech prepared by the Department. At the correct moment I took three steps and bowed. Mr de Valera advanced three steps and bowed. I then handed Mr de Valera the Letter. I read my prepared speech in English. He replied in Irish. We shook hands and everybody had a glass of sherry. By this time I felt every inch a plenipotentiary.

When I was in Washington for consultation in 1946 I witnessed the reception of the new British Ambassador, Lord Inverchapel. I had an appointment to see President Truman at half past eleven. At noon I was still waiting in his outer office when Lord Inverchapel came in himself, carrying his credentials in a dispatch case. At twelve-ten the secretary of state, Mr Byrnes, hurried in and apologised to Lord Inverchapel for being late.

I whispered to the secretary, 'I was to see the president at eleven-thirty. Take my turn'.'

'No', said Mr Byrnes, 'We had better stick to the schedule'.

When I was ushered into the president's office I told him that the new British Ambassador was outside waiting.

'I'm sorry', said the president with regret. 'We got behind this morning'.

While I was talking with him, I was thinking how different was my official reception on the 15th of April 1940 by the Irish taoiseach.

From the viewpoint of international law the Letter of Credence which I presented that 15th of April 1940 was an interesting document. The letter signed by the president of the United States was addressed to:

To His Majesty
George VI
Of Great Britain, Ireland and the British Dominions beyond the seas, King, Emperor of India ...

and began: 'Great and Good Friend'; It was delivered to 'An Taoiseach'. (taoiseach is an Irish word meaning 'leader' and is the equivalent of 'Führer', or 'Duce', though used here instead of prime minister. The Irish had never had prime ministers.) The explanation was that Mr de Valera's External Relation Act recognised the British Sovereign as head of the British Commonwealth of Nations and proclaimed Éire as 'externally associated' with it. Although in his Constitution of 1937, Mr de Valera had unilaterally eliminated the governor general (who had taken the place of the lord lieutenant), had abolished the oath to the Crown and appeal to the Privy Council, all features of the Treaty Constitution, he voluntarily proclaimed 'association' with the

Commonwealth. He subsequently explained 'association' by saying that he wished to keep the door open for Northern Ireland. This probably is true or partly true but his enemies were saying in 1940 that he was hoping for such benefits as association might bring, while repudiating all responsibilities. This also was probably true. This 1938 Constitution declared the president to be the head of the state yet as long as Douglas Hyde was president, Mr de Valera evidently regarded himself as such and on one occasion at least told me that he was that. After Mr O'Kelly became president he received the new diplomats and insisted on his constitutional prerogative.

The inter-party coalition which came into power in 1948 declared a republic and the president continues to receive the new diplomats.

Why Mr de Valera replied to my English speech in Irish was a question not difficult to answer. Both languages are sanctioned by the new Constitution, but Mr de Valera and his Separatist group were anxious to impress on the outside world that English is only an unfortunate and temporary makeshift and that Irish is the true and natural tongue of the nation, though today only one person in six speaks it. Very few Irish politicians speak Irish except as American High School students learn to 'speak' French, but they usually begin their speeches with a paragraph in Irish, which they have memorised, and then continue in English. It is the badge of being 'Irish' Irish, like the Gaelicisation of proper names.

That afternoon I wrote the president:

From letter to President Roosevelt

Monday, April 15th, 1940

My dear Boss:

I got presented this morning, big show with the army out and all that. Mr D. kept me after the 'act' and 'plunged in', after a moment or two. He said he was terribly worried about the Norwegian situation.

I said, 'What did you think of the President's announcement concerning the rape of those countries?'

'That was very good', he said, 'but do you know anything definite as to the military situation in Norway. I am afraid they are going to take Sweden too'.

I said, 'I only know what I read in the papers'.

He said, 'We don't want to know any of the English secrets and make a point of not knowing them. Can you find out for me

69

about this Norwegian situation? They will know more in Washington than here'.

I said, 'It has been announced that communication has been cut between Norway and Washington but I will try London. I am calling up Joe (Ambassador Kennedy) in an hour or two. I will tell you about it later'.

Our American minister to Norway, Mrs J. Borden Harriman,[1] had followed the King and Queen in their flight. No one knew where they were. Mr de Valera was naturally concerned about the Scandinavian countries. They had non-aggression pacts with Hitler on which they had been relying as Éire was relying on German assurances. More than that, at any moment precedents might be established which would vitally affect Éire. Later Sweden created an embarrassing precedent for Éire since she allowed the passage through her neutral territory of Norwegian iron ore billed to Germany and, during a considerable period, German troops also. Analogous privileges accorded to Britain by the Éire government, and after Pearl Harbor, to the United States, would have been of great value to us.

The official dinner in the state apartments of the Castle that evening was as elaborate and well done as the ceremony in the morning. Food, wines, service, cigars, all were unexceptionable.

The de Valera revolution had been to a large extent a 'social movement'. It appealed to the 'common man' and repudiated the symbols of privilege. Like the 'Great Commoner', William Jennings Bryan,[2] Mr de Valera banned the 'topper' and wore the black 'cowboy' hat. He and his Cabinet constituted the surviving nucleus of 'The Sixteen'[3] and the left-wing IRA faction that had staged the Civil War. Almost every man present had been condemned to death or jail either by the British government or by the Free State government, yet only eight years after coming to power this new aristocracy had all turned out in tails and white ties in the best London tradition, I had never sat down to dine with so many people who had been 'martyred' and thrown into prison, nor with so many politicians, who after having been down and out had 'come back in' and stayed 'in'. It had its embarrassing side. It was

[1] Mrs J. Borden Harrison (1870–1967), American suffragist/socialite and social reformer: as minister to Norway, she organised evacuation efforts while hiding in a forest from the Nazi invasion.
[2] William Jennings Bryan (1860–1925), the key political leader of American populism, three times unsuccessful democratic presidential candidate, Secretary of State 1913–15.
[3] Combatants in the Easter Rising of 1916.

like dining in a house in which there has been a highly publicised domestic difficulty. Just as I would have wanted to ask my host whether he really beat his wife as alleged, I wanted to ask the questions to which every historian of the period was trying to find the answers. I wanted to ask why Mr de Valera had not abided by the majority action of his own parliament; why he appealed to the gun and started a Civil War. How he escaped being shot for rebellion, first by the British and then by the first Irish government ever to be recognised by the comity of nations. I wanted to ask him whether Michael Collins had been the chance victim of an ambush or the designed victim of an assassination; and if he knew who murdered Kevin O'Higgins. Of course I asked none of these questions.

As we met these people, they all seemed to be exemplary parents, churchgoers, good citizens and those that we came to know well, were the kind of people we were glad to have as friends. I never felt the difference of religion to be any bar between us. We encountered no bigotry or intolerance. But politics was a different matter. This was a barrier subject which we tried to avoid. Our Irish friends had better manners than most of the American Roosevelt-haters that one met in American society but their emotions were as strong.

The dinner was jolly like all Irish parties. There were only two speeches. Mr de Valera said a few words extending us a cordial welcome and I read the following: it was not very successful but it was short:

Your Excellency, Ladies and Gentlemen,
No American need feel a stranger in Ireland. In no other country does a little goodwill bring so immediate and generous response as here. But beyond that, we have grown up with twenty million of people with Irish blood. Even if we have none ourselves we have had continuous association with Irish character and mentality.

The type which the American melting pot is evolving is not yet established but it is already evident that Irish traits will characterise it in a measure beyond the proportion of Irish blood. So when we come to Ireland we are not perplexed by your ways of thinking and feeling because these ways are largely ours.

We are amazed by one thing and that is the greenness and cleanness and fertility of Ireland and the beautiful farming of the land. Many of the wisest friends I have in America are like me farm-minded. We feel that we have made a tragic error in pressing forward so fast on the road of industrial development with its resulting black countries and industrial slums. We feel that general well-being is wrapped up in life upon the land and that there are more important things than machines and money. Greece and Rome were agricultural civilisations with small capital cities devoted to the culture of the mind and spirit. And we have not yet improved upon that culture.

Some compromise with this ideal is of course necessary both for you and for us but I am grateful that I know an Ireland that is still as beautiful as when Patrick came to it and where people still have sound roots in the soil.

This was politely received but I could see that the latter part did not make a hit. Mr de Valera at that time was more interested in industrialising Ireland than in making it an ideal rural civilisation. He was not having too much success.

That sentence, 'So when we come to Ireland, we are not perplexed by your ways of thinking and feeling because these ways are largely ours', I still believe to be true. The controlling political minority however, under the influence of the Neo-Gaelic Afflatus is something else, just as the population in mental institutions is something else. The average American visitor never knows either.

At dinner I was placed at Mrs de Valera's right and had an interesting talk. It appeared that she refused to go into society except on rare occasions. She had a delightful and ingenious mind and reminded me of Maude Adams[4] who in old days I had known and still loved. Mrs de Valera as a girl had been one of the pioneers of the Gaelic revival and had met her husband through teaching him Irish. She devoted herself to her children, her house and to writing Irish plays for young amateurs. I looked forward to seeing much of this interesting woman. But it did not work out. Even before Pearl Harbor and the landing of American troops in Northern Ireland, her husband had decided on a course bound to alienate him from the United States. Naturally he could not afford to have his wife on informal terms with the American minister and his wife.

After the dessert the women did not 'withdraw' but in the manner of the Continent everybody left the table at the same time and gathered in small groups for coffee and liqueurs. The room was a great banqueting hall and the part of it in which we sat after dinner was arranged with comfortable chairs and little tables. First, however, Mr de Valera guided

---

[4] Maude Adams (1872–1953), American stage actress, the highest paid performer of her day; famous in the role of Peter Pan.

us through portions of the Castle which we had not seen and showed us the chapel of the Knights of Saint Patrick. This was the order instituted primarily for Irish Peers, intended to be the equivalent of the Knights of the Garter in England. Each Knight had his stall in the chapel and displayed his arms and his banner. Mr de Valera explained that he hoped that succeeding governments would preserve this pageantry as part of Irish history. There have been no new knights appointed since the Irish government came into power. It does not recognise British honours or patents of nobility bestowed on Irish citizens.

During my talk with Mr de Valera he kept recurring [referring] to the problem of Northern Ireland, insisting, as I wrote next day to the president, that the British are making a 'terrible' mistake in not settling it. It seemed to me then, as it does now, that for the British to give up control of their lifeline through the narrows without a satisfactory arrangement with Éire would have been the second step toward national suicide.

From letter to President Roosevelt continued

Monday, April 15th, 1940

I told him that he might be making a bad mistake not taking advantage of the international situation to do something bold and original such as he loved to do with his own people; that this was obviously the time to convince Ulster of the South's friendliness and that he could obviously do it by taking some steps to aid Ulster in the war. Then he could get his concessions. He knows this is true but it is a hard pill to swallow in his present state of mind. I am making a study of his speech on Partition delivered a few months ago, a copy of which he recently gave me together with the debates on Partition in 1927.

I ended my letter to the president: 'Your Pan American announcement came out this morning and was the big headline. You have, I believe, the support of at least eighty per cent of the people here as I believe you must have the support of that percentage at home'. Fifteen years later I still think this was essentially true. The Irish mind left to itself reacted normally not only to enlightened self-interest but to what was just and generous. At that time Mr de Valera could have led it in any direction he saw fit. I believed then that he was going to lead it to recognition of Éire's place among the democracies.

In the circle to which we came back after seeing the chapel were two couples with whom an especially happy relation developed. These were the Seán T. O'Kellys and Seán MacEntees. Mr O'Kelly, 'Seán T.' as he was generally called by friends, was then minister for finance and vice premier or 'an tánaiste'. His wife was Phyllis Ryan, sister of the minister of agriculture and of Mrs Mulcahy, wife of General Mulcahy, one of the leaders of the opposition party. She was a woman of unusual character and intelligence. She had taken a university degree in chemistry and had become 'City Analyst' with her own laboratory. In 1945 her husband was elected president in succession to Douglas Hyde.

Seán MacEntee was minister at that time for industry and commerce and later on for local government. He was one of the ablest men in the Cabinet. He had cultivated tastes in English literature and an unusual degree of intellectual integrity for a politician in any country. You could talk to him realistically and he took no offence. His wife, like Mrs O'Kelly, had taken a university degree and was a lecturer on Irish in the National University. She was one of the wittiest women in Ireland and one of the kindest. A friend of hers told us 'Margaret has a sharp tongue, a hard head, but a soft heart'.

Before I left for Ireland, my old friend and Harvard classmate, Cameron Forbes,[5] who had been Ambassador to Japan as well as Governor of the Philippines, gave me this advice: 'cultivate two or three men in the government; get to know them. They will tell you no secrets but you will get a true background picture of their government'.

We found the O'Kellys and MacEntees, as it were, made to order for us. Later I realised that undoubtedly Mr de Valera had already thought of this in reverse and had assigned them to the analogous job of getting an inside picture of the American legation. Others had been assigned to the Axis Missions. We Americans never had any secrets to keep and could and did talk freely.

After dinner I asked Mr O'Kelly what had been his role in the revolution.

'He was the Achilles of the movement', put in Mrs MacEntee. 'He was shot in the foot'.

Mr O'Kelly was one of the best raconteurs in Ireland and very lovable. I asked him if he had ever been in the Castle before he came as a Cabinet minister.

'Downstairs', he said, 'in the dungeon, but not in the dining room'.

This started stories of life in various English jails which they all said

5 Cameron Forbes (1870–1959), former investment banker, Ambassador to Japan 1930–2.

were more comfortable than the Irish jails. Then Mr O'Kelly began describing the night before Mr de Valera was to have been executed in April 1916. According to his story they told him he was a 'goner' and entertained him by holding a mock trial. He was charged with being 'Pretender' to some group of rocks in Dublin Bay and condemned to death. They cut buttons off his coat for souvenirs and Seán T. got his fountain pen.

Mr de Valera was standing by listening and confirmed the circumstance that someone got his pen and that he never got it back. I was deeply interested at the time and felt that I had been dining with such a group as spent the last evening with Socrates. Later on, however, I checked the narrative with others who should have been among 'those present' and they knew nothing of it. One had to suspect that our hosts had been putting on an entertainment for us.

In the old days of the Irish Kings the 'life of the party' was a character called in Gaelic a 'file'. He made wisecracks and poems and told stories. If Mr O'Kelly had not become president of the Irish republic, he might have been a noted 'file'.

Mr de Valera neither drinks nor smokes but he does not frown on cakes and ale for others. That evening I was introduced to 'twenty-year-old John Jameson'. Ireland is divided into Sectarian supporters of 'Locke', 'Jameson', 'Tullamore Dew', and 'Paddy'. At twenty years old they are all good. Taken in moderation for 'the stomach's sake' Irish whiskey is prescribed by the best Irish physicians as the 'wine of the country'. One of the first times that the O'Kellys dined with us I asked 'Seán T.' how he would take his whiskey. 'Half and half' he said, 'but plenty of water'.

It was difficult at the time to see these pleasant, kindly people as characters in Irish history. Yet they are credited with accomplishing what no Irish revolutionary movement had been able to accomplish. They had changed a basic European relation, established for seven hundred years. And they were shortly to achieve a place in World History by endangering the survival of England and all democratic Europe by refusing to join in the common defence against Axis aggression. They had no military power but they had strategically important ports which they withheld. Fifteen years after the event it seems probable that in 1940 they did not understand what they were doing, for their own Irish survival was wrapped up with that of Free Europe. Even if one is vexed with his neighbour he does not commit suicide in order to destroy him. Today it seems more probable that they had come to believe the Sinn Féin propaganda they had preached. In destroying the Nationalist Party they had maintained that they had the power to drive the English out of Ireland by arms. They did not need constitutional process. They did not need England or her markets. When unexpectedly England withdrew and they came into possession of the 'plant' and palaces of a government that had gone out of business, they began to believe that they had really driven out the English by force of arms, that the palaces were spoils of war. They began a make-believe life in them. Like the Medicean Pope who said, 'Since God hath given us this Papacy, let us enjoy it', they began to enjoy the symbols of power even though the power had not been theirs. Hence, the 'Blue Hussars', the impressive receptions in the lord lieutenant's great drawing rooms, the elaborate state dinners. In the same spirit of make-believe our kindly friend, Seán T. O'Kelly, when he became president, drove to the Royal Dublin Horse Show in a vice regal landau drawn by four horses, himself arrayed in topper, morning coat, 'striped pants' and white gloves. In the same spirit he went to Punchestown Races on a coach and four and was photographed on the box seat with the Lady Rugby[6] on his right and the American Countess of Dunraven on his left. All this was make-believe, but it was happy, constructive make-believe. It was a gesture of conciliation to the remains of the old ascendancy unionist regime. It said in effect, we have murdered your people and burned your Big Houses but that is over. We are really one people. Let us get together. Unfortunately for all concerned Mr O'Kelly was not speaking for the Irish government.

Mr de Valera had no interest in driving behind four horses, whether at horse shows or Punchestown. His conformity to 'imperialism' stopped with evening tails and a white necktie, but he had his own make-believe and it was not conciliatory and useful like that of Mr O'Kelly. He believed not only that he could make his own rules of political right and wrong, of justice and injustice by 'revelation', but that he could declare what was fact and what was not. He was like the Admiral who makes it eight bells by decree regardless of the clock. The caricaturists of those days used to cartoon him as 'Dev in his Ivory Tower'. But the dreams he dreamed made for disorder, confusion, bloodshed and economic decay. In April 1940 he also hopefully believed that a victorious Hitler would give him Northern Ireland.

I had no suspicion that such was the truth at this time. I find that in a letter to my friend Honoré Palmer,[7] dated April 14th, 1940, I wrote

---

[6] Wife of Sir John Loder Maffey, United Kingdom Representative to Ireland, who became Lord Rugby in 1947. This event took place in 1946.

[7] Honoré Palmer, born in 1874, was the son of Potter Palmer, the wealthy Chicago businessman. Honoré Palmer's son was Potter Palmer III.

regarding him: 'I like him very much and feel implicit confidence in his integrity. He is a man of honour'.

After the Irish government, the Irish president was the new minister's concern. The Irish Constitution was modelled after the British and French Constitutions rather than the American. The Executive was a symbol, without political power; like the British Monarch he was 'above politics'. The legation had been informed by the Irish government that a state dinner given by President Hyde was to be the next item on our programme, but there seemed uncertainty as to the date. Moreover we had received no appointment to call on the president and pay our respects. Finally we received notice that the president was confined to bed by a 'bad cold' but that his sister and official 'hostess', Mrs Cambreth Kane, would be pleased to receive us at tea on April 18th. She was a woman of character and distinction. She gave us no hint that her brother was gravely ill, but the next day Joe Walshe got me on the telephone and told me in confidence that the president, sometime before, had suffered a severe paralytic stroke. The doctors now believed that he would make at least a partial recovery but for the immediate future at least he would not be able to receive callers.

The truth about his condition was concealed from the public because of the critical international situation and its repercussion on the Irish internal situation.

Politically Dr Hyde's position was peculiar. Mr de Valera was in power when the first election to choose a president was held under the new Constitution. Mr de Valera nominated Seán T. O'Kelly. The Cosgrave opposition said 'No', and proposed the Rt. Hon. Alfred Byrne, Lord Mayor of Dublin. Fianna Fáil would not accept him. Mr de Valera, however, believed that it was important to install the first president without controversy. So there followed an inter-party conference which finally agreed on Douglas Hyde. It was a case of the candidate who had no enemies. He was a 'decent' man who had no strong convictions about politics or about anything except the Irish language, which was 'standard equipment' for all patriots. So it came about that this first president of Mr de Valera's Catholic, independent Éire was a Protestant, a member of the landowning Ascendancy class, who by the standards of the Sinn Féin group in power was not an Irishman at all. Douglas Hyde was the son of a Church of Ireland Protestant canon, the Reverend Arthur Hyde of Tibohine, French Park, County Roscommon. He was born in 1860. He was educated at Trinity College Dublin, and was (as I have been told) in sympathy with Irish rationalist aspirations, as expressed in Home Rule, but as they say in Ireland '*took no interest in politics*', meaning that he was not a revolutionist, but a loyal subject of the Crown. He was an Anglo-Irish gentleman and sportsman, being renowned 'in the West' as a wing shot, and especially brilliant in the woodcock coverts. He and the late Lord Kingston were reputed to be the best men in Ireland 'at the cock'.

Most Anglo-Irish families trace back to ancestors who settled in Ireland about the time the Mayflower settlers came to Massachusetts. They usually call themselves Irish, especially when in England, but this is not enough to support the claim in the view of the 'hundred per cent patriots'. One must be both a Gael and loyal to the 'old religion'. Unfortunately for the 'Sea Green' group the outstanding martyrs and patriots between 'The Ninety Eight' and 'The Sixteen'[8] with the exception of Daniel O'Connell whom they now repudiate, and Redmond whom they destroyed, had all been Protestants of English blood, to wit: Grattan, Wolfe Tone, Robert Emmet, Lord Edward Fitzgerald, Isaac Butt, Davis, Mitchell, Charles Parnell and Arthur Griffith. Though not English, Mr de Valera himself is not Irish, having been born a Spanish subject in New York of a Cuban father. To take care of such personages the Extremists invest them with a sort of honorary status of 'Irish Irishman'. The qualifying formula appears to make anyone eligible who has contributed notably to the downfall of the British empire. Douglas Hyde's contribution was unquestionably incidental and unpremeditated. He probably had no realisation of the political consequences of his part in the Gaelic revival and the establishment of the Gaelic League. Yet these things eventually produced Sinn Féin and Irish Separatism. Without the Irish 'literary revival' of the eighties and nineties, it is unlikely that Mr de Valera's Éire would have come into being. Dr Hyde was not only one of the members of the 'Language Movement' but one of its most effective. In his boyhood in Roscommon, Irish was still the language of the old people and he learned it from them. He became a 'speaker'. Moreover when he went to Dublin he did not forget it. However, the Professional Irishman may have regarded him at the time, he looked upon himself as Irish. He was fired with a passion, both as scholar and Irishman, to preserve the lyrics, legends and language of the Gaelic past. The great names of the movement which the outside world celebrates were Synge, Yeats and Lady Gregory, but it was Dr Hyde

[8] The 1798 Rebellion and the Easter Rising of 1916.

who knew the Irish and did the spade work. From 1893 to 1915 he was president of the Gaelic League. From 1919 to 1932 he was Professor of Modern Irish at the National University, Dublin.

I asked him once which of the bearers of the great literary names had helped him most to revive the language when he was president of the Gaelic League. I added that I knew that Synge had no Irish.

'He had not', said the president.

'How about Yeats?'

'Willie Yeats, a dear fellow, a very fine man, but he had no Irish'.

'Then it must have been Lady Gregory. She tells us she gathered the legends from the cottage folk in the west'.

The president shook with laughter.

'Augusta Gregory knew no Irish. She wrote a curious kind of English that we used to call Kiltartanese. (Kiltartan was the name of her father's country place). She got the legends out of a book. A very nice woman but knew no Irish'.

So it appeared that the Big Three of the Gaelic revival knew no Irish. It was an Anglo-Irish show.

Dr Hyde never took an interest in politics but in recognition of his distinguished work as a scholar, he was appointed to the first Irish Senate under the Treaty Constitution, 1925–1926, and again by Mr de Valera in 1938.

During the arrangements and counter arrangements for our reception between Mr de Valera's ministry of external affairs and the president's organisation at the president's mansion, it became apparent that emancipated Gaels were not that one happy family which we were told would follow liberation from the British yoke. What in Washington they call 'The Palace Guard', in Dublin was Mr Michael McDunphy. External Affaires referred to him as 'the President's secretary', that is a civil servant, like the stenographer.[9] Mr McDunphy however styled himself 'Secretary to the President', that is the incumbent of an office prescribed by the Constitution. Once he wrote me a letter on behalf of President Hyde and signed it 'McDunphy', as if he had been a peer. However, we had no part in this internecine controversy and no complaints of Mr McDunphy except when he called my wife on the telephone and then was not on the

[9] Michael McDunphy (1890–1971), civil servant and excellent linguist, appointed secretary to the president of Ireland on 29 December 1937. In Janet Egleson Dunleavy and Gareth W. Dunleavy, *Douglas Hyde: a maker of modern Ireland* (California, 1991), 423, the authors note that Gray consistently spelled the secretary's name 'McDumphy'.

line when she replied. This was merely a case of bad manners. A more serious incident was when, without authorisation from his master, he had made a call of condolence on the German minister when Hitler's suicide was announced, although he had made no call of condolence on the American legation on the occasion of President Roosevelt's death. But the point of the McDunphy episode was, as Dublin gossip had it, that he exercised a sort of 'keeperage' over the president which after his illness became absolute.

Douglas Hyde was a little man with an enormous walrus-like moustache. The Dublin cartoonists exaggerated this. Oliver St. George Gogarty, thereupon referred to Mr McDunphy as 'Keeper of the Great Seal'. The late James Montgomery, a rival wit and for a long time Irish film censor told me that it was he, who had said it first. 'Oliver is very naughty', he added, 'he only takes my good ones.'

The last thing that Mr de Valera wanted with the 'hot war' flaring up again and the IRA on his hands, was the death of Douglas Hyde and the opportunities for rebellion provided by a general election. Fortunately President Hyde convalesced to such a degree that he could receive visitors in bed and dispense sweet Manhattan cocktails to Americans. He liked them himself. To the end of his term he worked at translations from the Irish poets which were scholarly and interesting if one were interested in a dying language and a literature which had never matured. He was a kindly, gentle, pathetic figure whom chance brought into this Irish scene of make-believe and pose and play-acting, of sinister conspiracy against the forces of democratic civilisation, of futility and failure, a figure ineffective even for Irishness.

Formal calls upon the Diplomatic Corps was the final duty in the new minister's induction to his job. Of the foreign nations which had representations in Dublin that spring of 1940, only England, France and Germany had what is called a 'vital interest' in Irish policy. The rest by this time were captive nations or neutrals, or nations which accepted Éire's neutrality at Mr de Valera's appraisal of it. The representatives in Dublin of these nations were generally professionals whose major concern was to get their pay checks and avoid trouble. They all went on leading their drab, humdrum, futile, diplomatic lives as if the world were not in flames. No one discussed doing anything about it. No one seemed to realise that it was the disunity of Europe that had made the catastrophe inevitable.

No one seemed to realise that it was all primarily due to the illusion of an inherent Right to Independence without the power to maintain it and to resistance to the Evolutionary Forces counselling security through co-operation. No one discussed the necessity of taking measures to the end that it should not happen again. They all hoped somehow sometime that someone would rescue them so that they might go on again in disunity as before. Those with whom I talked of the need for collective security said, 'but you Americans do not understand our history', as if that justified unwillingness to cope with the facts. So they covered their weakness and shame with the tattered rags of national pride. From the American view-point they were simply too stupid to make the sacrifices of sovereignty which each of the American states had made to create the United States of America.

One of the good deeds that must be credited to Mr de Valera was his humanity to the stranded representatives of Poland, Czechoslovakia, Denmark, and later to those of Holland and Belgium. He was as stupid as their statesmen had been in refusing adequate defence precautions in time, but he was luckier. British and United States power saved him. Nevertheless, his consideration for these humiliated diplomats was kind and courageous. The Germans had taken over the Czech Consulate in Dublin when they swallowed Czechoslovakia but the Irish government continued to treat Dr Kostal,[10] the consul general, as if he had a measure at least of diplomatic standing. This unhappy man went back behind the Iron Curtain at the end of the war. He was a friend of Jan Masaryk. In 1948 my wife and I were at a picnic lunch, which Mrs Roosevelt gave at Hyde Park for delegates to the United Nations. Two sinister characters, one the Czech delegate, the other his 'keeper' and chauffeur, arrived about three. All the food had been eaten. My wife got a table for them, robbed the family icebox, and gave them a better lunch than the rest of us got. Then she told them how much we liked Dr Kostal in Dublin and asked where he was now. They gave her a stony look and said that he had a job 'in the country', presumably in the Uranium mines. No one hears from him.

The Irish government similarly recognised M. Dobrzynski,[11] the

[10] Dr Karel Kostal, the former member of the Czech Philharmonic Orchestra, arrived in Dublin on 6 October 1936. He had previously worked in Paris and Copenhagen. He spoke on Czech films at meeting of the Irish Film Society in 1937, and the Karel Kostal string quartet gave concerts on RTÉ. His moving Dublin speech on Czech democracy on 13 November 1939 is worthy of note. Returned to Prague in 1947 to work for Masaryk, and was later fired by the communists.

[11] M. Dobrzynski (1883–1962), a man of independent means, was appointed consul-general in 1940. He refused to work for the communist government of Poland after the war, and died in Ireland in 1962. His daughter's memoir states that, while neutrality was the only rational course for Dublin, his daughter found Irish disbelief in Nazi atrocities hurtful: 'Only when the first pictures were released from Belsen and Dachau much later, did they acknowledge their mistake'. Krystyna Dobrzynska-Cantwell, *An unusual diplomat* (London, 1998).

Polish minister, as representing the Polish government in exile in London. These diplomats of submerged countries, however, were all on sufferance and had no influence.

'Liberated' Dublin was not the background for a 'brilliant' diplomatic society. The glories of the eighteenth century and of the first decade of the nineteenth had passed. The town-houses in the great squares had become doctors' offices or lodging houses. The late earl of Granard, who had married the American Beatrice Mills, told me that he had been born at 15 Merrion Square, the house which in 1940 was our consulate general. The family seat was Castle Forbes on the Shannon and the Grand Canal near Longford. His grandfather had a light canal boat which a trotting horse could pull. With two spare horses and riding grooms the family would go aboard after dinner and to bed. By ten the next morning they would have made the sixty miles to Dublin. Now that was all past. Lord Iveagh, head of the Guinness family, had given his great house to the Irish government to house the Department of External Affairs. There was no longer a 'season', there were no more private balls. From the diplomats' viewpoint Dublin socially was a 'small town' assignment. Rich and social-minded diplomats did not seek designation to Éire. Moreover, the war had made general diplomatic parties impossible. You could not mix Allies and Axis people. My wife and I therefore gave only small, intimate parties at lunch and dinner, which we always tried to lighten up with a few government people.

The papal nuncio was first on my list of calls after the president. He was dean of the corps. He would have been that under the usual rule of seniority but Irish protocol decrees that since Éire is a Catholic country the papal nuncio should ipso facto always be dean. Archbishop Paschal Robinson was Irish born, a cousin of the late Sir James Nugent, and British educated. He came to New York in early manhood. His father had been an executive for Peter Fenelon (Pat) Collier who had made a fortune in New York publishing religious books and then had started *Colliers Weekly*. Before taking orders he had been managing editor of the old *North American Review* when it belonged to Lloyd Bryce. After joining the Franciscan Brotherhood he taught history at the Catholic University in Washington. Then the Vatican drafted him for its diplomatic service. He had been its trouble-shooter in Palestine and Malta before coming to Ireland. He told me that he was the first papal nuncio to Ireland since, I think, the twelfth century. Common report had it that the Irish Bishops having got along for seven hundred years without a nuncio believed they could get along for sometime longer. Obviously he had encountered a good deal of 'sales resistance', but as far as we could find out had surmounted it by patience, forbearance, tact and fairness. In principle a papal nuncio selects candidates for vacant bishoprics and sends them to the Pope. The Irish bishops had been doing this themselves and if our information was correct, Paschal Robinson forwarded no names which the bishops had not first approved. There was a story current that someone had asked him soon after his arrival what he thought of the Irish bishops. He had a trick of pretending to be deaf when it suited his purpose. 'Irish bishops', he repeated, 'I have met no Irish bishops. I have met twenty-six popes'.

After we became friends, I asked him if the story were true. 'No! No!!! No!!!' he shouted, 'The idea is unthinkable'. So I knew the story was true.

He lived in what had been the under secretary's lodge, about half a mile from us in the Park. This was the house which Winston Churchill and his parents had lived in when Lord Randolph Churchill was private secretary to his father, the duke of Marlborough.[12] The duke was lord lieutenant. There was a room that one passed through on the way to the dining room furnished with one great gilt chair set on a dais, a portrait of Pius XII, and nothing else. 'It is the custom of Nuncios', Archbishop Robinson said, 'always to have such a room ready for his Holiness, in case he should unexpectedly drop in'.

He liked fun. Though we had lunched together only a few days before, when I called on him officially, he said, 'Excellency, I am glad to make your acquaintance, and welcome you to Ireland. Your face is strangely familiar'.

We were within a few months of the same age. He had lived a dedicated life and was frail and often ill. I had loved fox hunting and polo and still was overfond of shooting, fishing and golf. I was still able to shoot all day or play eighteen holes. He died soon after we left Dublin, but at eighty-nine I still shoot.

Once when he was ill I said to him, 'Excellency, isn't it time that you turned over a new leaf and began a bad life? Look how I flourish'. His eyes twinkled and he shook his head sadly, 'Too late', he said, 'Too late'.

He was one of the few Christians I have known who practised Christianity.

[12] Celia Lee and John Lee, *The Churchills*, 12–18.

At the time I was one of those who believed Neville Chamberlain had done the right thing in going to Munich. No avenue of escape from total war could be left unexplored without assuming a frightening responsibility. But, since Munich, the Germans had demonstrated that they had willed war. No reasonable course was left but to fight and destroy this evil power. Feeling as I did about Hitler, to call on his minister and shake his hand was not a happy business. As Mr de Valera had told me, Dr Eduard Hempel was a career diplomat, a man with European manners, an amateur of music and the arts.[13] His press attaché, an unsavoury character named Petersen, circulated the legend that he was not a Nazi nor even supporter of Hitler and that he suffered from party line 'keeperage' by his first secretary, Herr Henning Thomsen.[14] This story was pure invention.[15] In the first place, Hempel brought with him through the customs, under diplomatic privilege, a radio sending set in a suitcase. This he could only have done under instructions from a Foreign Office which trusted him. Mr de Valera's fiction that he was not in sympathy with Hitler was baseless. No German at that time was getting a diplomatic job who was 'out of line'. As Mr de Valera well knew before Hempel's arrival, the then German minister Herr von Dehn had been snapped by an *Irish Times* photographer at a garden party, kissing the nuncio's ring. With a dispatch which left no doubt as to the reason for his recall, Her Von Dehn went back to Germany. After this, Ribbentrop would never have sent a minister to Dublin who was not in close sympathy with the government. The captured documents show that Hempel was up to his neck in the net of German espionage, and Petersen's story that Hempel and Thomsen did not get along, was later branded by the Italian minister as 'hokum'.[16] When Italy made a separate peace the Italian minister, who disliked the Germans, told me that Hempel and Petersen had many laughs over the story of their quarrelling. Petersen was a bad type. He was reputed to be living in sin with an Irish girl in a flat in Stephen's Green. He was the centre of an afternoon circle at the Buttery Bar. Here he 'picked up' the checks and was the 'good, honest, German friend' of Éire. When France

---

[13] Hempel is described by his most recent Irish biographer as a conservative career diplomat who was only a nominal member of the Nazi party. Duggan, *Herr Hempel*.

[14] Henning Thomsen, an enthusiastic Nazi, was appointed first secretary to Dublin on 20 November 1938. After the war, Thomsen made a point of disputing articles in the press which downplayed Hempel's role in espionage, while playing up his own. Duggan, *Herr Hempel*, 228.

[15] The details of this story are slightly different. Dr von Dehn was already in his new post in Bucharest before Hitler saw the offensive photograph: he was then dismissed and his career ended. Duggan, *Herr Hempel*, 21.

[16] For Petersen's 'drunken indiscretions' and IRA sympathies, see Duggan, *Herr Hempel*, 132.

was undergoing her crucifixion in June, Petersen had a considerable following of Irish barfly 'patriots', 'geniuses', frustrated artists, tarts, all the riff-raff that calls itself the 'intelligentsia' of a 'small-town Greenwich Village'. Here they played at spying and 'in confidence', telling Petersen the servants' hall gossip that was going the rounds. They looked forward to the new 'liberation' by the Führer, much as the highbrow wing of the Sinn Féiners had done twenty-five years before. Later on Petersen disappeared. The Irish government did not regard his Continental morals with approval.

The First Secretary Thomsen was an outsized Prussian Nazi, reputed to be a member of the Gestapo. He was said to be a cousin of the Thomsen in the German embassy in Washington. He had Prussian manners but he also had Prussian guts. After the War, while poor Hempel struggled to make a living peddling cakes,[17] Thomsen started laying brick and became, I believe, a successful contractor. He also became an Irish citizen.

There was a curious story current at this time in the English and American newspapers that the German legation in Dublin had a staff of eighty and consumed ten gallons of milk a day. Who invented the milk, I could never find out. The German Mission enrolled at this time some fifteen or sixteen and the accredited agents, planted before the war, were far short of forty unless the IRA and the corps of ardent German sympathisers were taken into account.

Herr Hempel had a charming house and garden at Blackrock, a suburb on Dublin harbour. His chancery was an ugly, modern red brick house in Northumberland Road. It was here that, accompanied by Mr MacVeagh, I called upon him. Herr Thomsen was with his chief. Herr Dr Hempel received us with great courtesy. He was somewhat over-civil and did not ring true. He spoke fluent English with little accent. I was conscious of being ill at ease. Hempel might be doing his duty as he saw it but he was serving a Führer whose hands were red with the blood of Jews, Poles and Norwegians, on whose conscience was the annihilation of Austria and Czechoslovakia. I was naive enough at seventy to be shocked by these things. I had seen something of German-waged war at first hand in 1917–19. I had seen the evacuation of French civil populations. I had gone into Laon the day the Germans left it, after four years of occupation. I had visited Longwy the day after the armistice. Moreover, the conviction was strong that once Dr Hempel's chief had conquered and organised Europe, this great barbarian force, armed by modern science, would be aimed at the Americas.

[17] His wife, Eva, ran a confectionery business. See Duggan, *Herr Hempel*, 225.

We exchanged pleasant commonplaces while Thomsen looked on and then we took our leave. I was not to re-enter the German legation at 58 Northumberland Road till I took possession of it in the name of the United Nations at the end of the war and found the wires of a radio sending set and other interesting items. The Irish government had seen to it that we did not gain admittance until the files had been destroyed.

Vincenzo Berardis,[18] the Italian minister at this time, was a career man who had served a long period in Moscow and was intensely interested in Muscovite art. His wife was a distinguished-looking woman, daughter of a Milan banker and frankly pro-Ally. She was ill and homesick and lonely and we felt very sorry for her. They had a big house belonging to the Hon. Mrs Eileen Plunkett who was then in the United States. Mrs Plunkett was one of the three notable Guinness sisters. Lady Oranmore and Browne was another and the Marchioness of Dufferin the third. Berardis was a highly-strung, erratic personality, anxious for understanding and sympathy, but uncertain how to obtain them. After Italy had made a separate peace, he told me that he had been on bad terms with the German Mission since Italy had entered the war. Hitler taking no chances with his great and good friend, the Duce, had sent a German division to Rome as a 'compliment', which amounted to 'protective custody'. This, Berardis and other Italians, who disliked Germans, resented. Berardis was one of those people who disliked almost everybody. He always spoke of Hempel as 'Mickey Mouse'. He seemed to have had no instructions looking toward a special relation with Éire before Italy entered the war. This seemed strange in view of the common bond of religion and of Mr de Valera's leanings toward totalitarianism. Apparently Mussolini, interested as he was at this time in anti-British intrigue, had never considered the strategic possibilities of Éire and the IRA. Ciano in his diaries mentions Mr de Valera but once and that in a perfunctory manner.[19]

One conversed with Berardis in French. He spoke this language volubly with a strong Italian accent and apparently without opening his mouth. He was noted for this. The late Valentine Castlerosse[20] told me that he had known him in London. Once he asked him why he did not learn English. Berardis replied that he did not like English and did not

[18] Vincenzo Berardis, author of *Italy and Ireland in the Middle Ages* (Dublin, 1950). Paola Ottonello, 'Irish/Italian diplomatic relations in World War Two', *Irish Studies in International Affairs* 10 (1999), 91–113.
[19] *The Ciano diaries 1939–1943: the complete, unabridged diaries of Count Galeazzo Ciano, Italian Minister of Foreign Affairs, 1936–1943* (Garden City, New York, 1946).
[20] Browne, Valentine Charles Edward (1891–1943), Viscount Castlerosse, 6th Earl of Kenmare. He wrote 'Londoner's Log', a gossip column for the *Sunday Express*.

wish to learn it. 'Then', said Lord Castlerosse, 'I said to him, "In that case, my dear fellow, why don't you learn French?"'

The French Mission, which one might have expected to exert a strong pro-Ally influence in Éire, was in charge of George Cauvet-Duhamel.[21] He was a grave, capable, young man who stayed on as first secretary after the new minister, M. de Laforcade,[22] who arrived just as his country was being overrun. M. de Laforcade and his mission accepted Vichy out of loyalty to the diplomatic career tradition and tried to believe that Pétain was 'fooling' the Germans, but their hearts were not in it. They had nothing to do with the Axis missions. They gathered with the Allied representatives at the ceremony on Armistice Day, which the de Valera government did not forbid, but did not officially recognise. They sat with the Allied delegations at the various official church services in the Catholic Pro-Cathedral which we all attended out of respect to the Irish government, regardless of our religious affiliations. Vichy forbade them to join with the Allied powers in representations to the Irish government and they seemed to exert little or no influence with Mr de Valera.

The Spanish minister was Don Juan Garcia Ontiveros,[23] a middle-aged gentleman with the friendly manners that come from a kind heart. He had a very nice wife and two pretty daughters. He had been Spanish consul-general at an important South American post. He spoke little English and appeared to take little interest in Irish affairs. With Mr de Valera's pro-Franco orientation he had no difficult problems in Dublin. It was in the early spring, I think, of 1944 that he invited the Allied diplomatic corps to a requiem mass in memory of the late King Alphonso. He did not deny that this forecast a re-establishment of the Spanish monarchy in the near future. Franco was to announce himself as regent during the infancy of Alphonso's son. But nothing came of it.

One of our best friends in the diplomatic corps was the Belgian minister, Maurice Goor.[24] When Belgium was overrun and the government fled to London, Éire continued to recognise it, but M. Goor

---

[21] George Cauvet-Duhamel was a literary diplomat, lover of the arts and patron of the Royal Hibernian Academy. Arrived in Dublin at the end of October 1937. A fluent Russian speaker. A student of the Irish language and a friend of the Gate Theatre. A close Gaullist confidante who continued to work under Vichy for tactical reasons.

[22] F.X. de Laforcade was particularly interested in religious art.

[23] Don Juan Garcia Ontiveros joined the French services in 1911 and arrived in Dublin on 2 May 1939. He was the first Spanish minister to be appointed by Franco, and was previously consul-general in Hamburg. A professional Spanish diplomat, he later served in Buenos Aires.

[24] Maurice Goor (1877–1959), most important previous posting was Belgian consul-general in Canada up to 1922. Goor had been in Ireland since 1923 and stayed until 1957. He is buried in Ireland.

was under instructions to take no active part in Allied conversations with Mr de Valera. He spoke perfect English, knew Ireland well, hunted with Irish fox hounds, played golf and had many Irish friends.

Holland was represented by a consul general, Mynheer I.R.A.W. Weenink.[25] He was a stout, kindly, timid, middle-aged, burgher who might have come out of a 'Franz Hals'. After Hitler had crushed France and we were expecting a landing in Éire, a young, renegade Dutchman, who had refused to respond to his country's call to the colours, allied himself with the German Mission and terrified poor Weenink with threats of the Gestapo and concentration camps.

The Swiss representative, Acting minister Charles J. Benziger,[26] had been consul general in Dublin for many years. He was a straight, right-minded, competent man unquestionably pro-Ally in his convictions; but like the representatives of other small powers, he could not afford the luxury of expressing his views.

Sweden was represented by a consul-general. His wife was a Finnish lady and his sympathies, if not his loyalties, shifted as events unrolled.

One of the most intelligent diplomatic representatives in Dublin at this time was the Danish consul, Mr Osteberg.[27] He was also the head of the Danish Cement Trust plant in Ireland and was primarily concerned in preventing the confiscation of this Danish property by Germany.

Canadian policy during the war was never wholly clear to our legation. Until the spring of 1940 a trade commissioner had looked after Canadian interests. Not long after our arrival, Mr Hall Kelly, a Quebec lawyer, arrived as high commissioner. He died unfortunately after a short tenure of office, and was succeeded by another lawyer, John D. Kearney.[28] Mr Kearney was very likeable and popular. Rightly or wrongly, after Pearl Harbor, we received the impression that while Canada had been in the fight from the beginning, they were taking a special line as regards Éire. There was the suggestion that they were acting on the theory of keeping a 'door open' for Mr de Valera in case he wished

[25] I.R.A.W. Weenick (1875–1953). A former soldier, believed to have been influenced by de Valera's condemnation of the Nazi invasion of Holland.
[26] Charles J. Benziger. Worked formerly with the League of Nations.
[27] Harald A.V. Osterberg (1884–1969), an engineer who lectured periodically at Trinity College, Dublin and was a co-founder and director of Irish Cement Ltd. A former industrial attaché in the Danish embassy in Washington, and a keen sailor, he remained consul-general after the war; he was presented with copies of an Irish translation of Danish fairy-tales in 1955. He resigned in January 1959.
[28] An Irish Canadian, John D. Kearney, 'a compactly-built man with humorous eyes', *Irish Times*, 28 August 1941. His later report on the British offer of 1940 has attracted the attention of historians like Robert Fisk and T. Ryle Dwyer.

to come back into the Commonwealth. Mr de Valera strengthened this impression when at a farewell dinner which he gave for Mr Kearney he thanked him warmly for always having 'understood and sympathised' with the Irish viewpoint.

Russia at this time had no Irish representative. The two governments had been quarrelling over the title to some Latvian ships which had been brought into an Irish harbour about the time Russia swallowed up the Baltic states. Prior to this, however, there seems to have been a considerable degree of co-operation as well as sympathy between the Soviets and revolutionary Ireland. Mr de Valera had loaned the Soviets some twenty thousand pounds of the fund he had just collected in the United States. The security was a packet of the Tsar's jewels. Moscow redeemed these after the war. Connolly, the Dublin Labour Leader and 'Martyr of The Sixteen',[29] was a communist. With his 'Citizens' Army' he had played a conspicuous role in the Easter Week Sinn Féin rebellion. Even before Lenin's Bolshevik putsch, during the de Valera Civil War, the de Valera troops had flown the red flag from various buildings in Cork, notably from the Heffernan flour mills. However, this pro-Russian orientation had passed away. During the war the only combatant which the Irish Censor permitted the Irish editors to abuse openly was our Russian ally.

Brazil had an agreeable consul general, whom we liked very much. Chile's representative, though neutral, was at first pro-German. Later Chile adopted a pro-Ally policy. During the summer of 1940 a Japanese consul-general appeared. He and his problems became one of our minor headaches during and after the war.

There was in Dublin during the war crisis only one experienced, high-class, trouble-shooting, diplomat. This was the English representative, at that time Sir John Loder Maffey, KCB, GCMG. Later he was made Lord Rugby. His official title was 'United Kingdom Representative', but Éire accorded him the rank of minister. As I have explained, the Colonial Office did not recognise Éire except as a member of the Commonwealth and the Commonwealth states appoint high commissioners. Mr de Valera would not accept a high commissioner from England and the compromise of a UK representative was worked out. Sir John was a professional servant of the empire in the Cromer tradition. His story had been a success story. From Rugby school to Christ Church, Oxford, to the India Service by competitive examination. A Greek and Latin scholar, he also knew modern languages; he was a fine cricketer, a fine shot and

---

[29] The Easter Rising of 1916.

a renowned fisherman. Before he was forty-five he had become chief commissioner on the staff of the viceroy, the duke of Connaught, and after that became chief commissioner of the North Eastern Frontier Province. As such he was custodian of the Khyber and proconsul of India's No Man's Land. This marked him as one of England's picked men. In 1923 he was shifted to another 'trouble' job, and made governor general of the Sudan. In 1926 he was made permanent under-secretary of state for the Colonies and ran the Colonial Office till 1933. By this time he was Sir John Maffey, KCB, with the Grand Cross of Michael and George. For six years he lived the outdoor English life in Norfolk that Indian civil servants look forward to. But when the war came, Neville Chamberlain sent him to Dublin on his third trouble-shooting mission and the most important of the three.

In the long-term evolution of the Anglo-Irish relation, his nine years' work in Éire must inevitably assume an historic significance. My own appraisal of it, after seven years of close association with him, is that but for his amazing patience and tenacity to the 'long view', the Anglo-Irish relation during the war would have been very different. It might well have been better for Éire to have been brought face to face with the realities while the crisis was on, but there can be no doubt that Britain's position today is the stronger morally for her forbearance. She appears to have taken a calculated risk. During this period, England over-expiated such sins as earlier governments may have committed against the Irish people.

When I went to call on him, I was prepared to find him 'ensconced in imperial splendour'. England as a matter of policy has always given her representatives impressive backgrounds. It was a cold morning with the habitual Dublin grey sky and icy drizzle. Fifty Upper Mount Street proved to be a respectable but rather shabby house in a respectable but shabby street. Opposite was the headquarters of Mr de Valera's Fianna Fáil party. An Irish policeman stood on the sidewalk. There was no UK flag on the staff.

The temperature of the representative's private office was around fifty. There were some comfortable leather chairs, a desk, a table and lithographs of the king and queen. Beneath the table was his Labrador retriever, Dido. There was a fireplace, but since the calendar proclaimed spring, no fire. Sir John was a spare, broad-shouldered man, nearly six feet six, with a greying, distinguished head. We talked about nothing of importance for fifteen minutes. I left with the impression that he was the hard-boiled, stony-eyed, British official. Later, I came to know him as friend and ally and to trust his wisdom as I came to rely upon his friendship. In fair weather and foul for seven years we carried on as 'partners' in the world struggle, often with heated argument but without misunderstanding or rift.

Sir John Maffey returned my official call promptly and I told him what was in my mind regarding the North. Mr Churchill had written me on April 15th approving my memorandum of our conversation in regard to Ulster. I had at once shown this to Mr de Valera, who was polite but by his attitude suggested that it was only what he expected. However, it left me free with his knowledge and consent to explore. I told this to Sir John who was friendly but somewhat non-committal as it would be necessary to consult the Dominions Office (DO). He not only received the 'green light' as to my going to Belfast but undertook to arrange my introduction to the governor general of Northern Ireland, at that time the duke of Abercorn. The duke had held this office since the establishment of Northern Ireland as a political unit within the United Kingdom. He was on excellent terms with Craigavon and the Northern Ireland government. Sir John Maffey and the DO thought it best to arrange the expedition unofficially through the duke of Devonshire who was a cousin of the Abercorns. Devonshire at this time held one of the under-secretary posts in the government. The British attitude seemed to be that I could do no harm in Belfast. In the case that later on they needed Craigavon's help in getting the ports, it might weigh with him that Washington was interested. I think no one believed me when I explained that I was not acting under instructions but merely making a routine report on conditions within the scope of my mission. But Sir John warned me that the arrangements would take time. Bureaucrats move cautiously. It was an unusual proposal and to some extent involved considerations of policy. With the design for 'Operation Belfast' underway there was nothing to do but wait for word from the duke of Abercorn.

CHAPTER V

APRIL 18TH-28TH

The first IRA hunger striker to die, died during the night of April 17th–18th. Here was the triumph of emotion over sanity. Hunger-striking had been a weapon of de Valera when in minority in 1922. Now it was turned against him. On the morning of the 18th there was an organised procession of sympathisers. On the way to town I overtook them on the Liffey quay[s] near the main entrance to the Phoenix Park. In my report to the president I wrote,

From letter to President Roosevelt

April 1940

It was led by a detachment of ladies in Sam Browne belts looking like our lady Red Cross officers in the first world war, then a squad of boy scouts (the Catholic organisation) in green shorts, very cold looking in the raw morning; then about a thousand down-and-outs, presumably the unemployed of the dock workers union who turn out for these things as a matter of course. No one seemed to be paying any attention to them.

If we had known that the German government was then arranging to get Seán Russell to Berlin to arrange an Irish uprising backed by German troops to overthrow the de Valera government, we should have taken a more alarmist view of the demonstration. There was no doubt about the general disinterest of the public in Dublin on that April 18th.

Reports indicating a similar popular apathy came from Cork, a strong IRA centre, where we had an energetic and well-informed consul, William A. Smale. He had sent us a graphic report of an IRA attack on the radio station on the preceding Saturday night, followed by a procession demonstrating in sympathy with the hunger strikers. He reported the impression that the crowd was merely curious, not stirred. This suggested that the organisation had lost its hold on the popular imagination or was losing it. It was difficult even for observers who knew Ireland to pronounce with confidence what was happening. Mr de Valera was obviously anxious but whether because he saw his hope of winning back the IRA was withering or because he anticipated an armed Uprising with German assistance it was impossible to say. A considerable amount of money from the United States was still finding its way to IRA headquarters. As long as they had money there would be disorder.

Mr de Valera had predicted truly when he told me that the IRA people would be coming to see me. Just before lunch on April 19th, the Countess Plunkett called me on the telephone and asked if I would see her.[1] She said that her son was on the 55th day of his hunger strike.[2] I made an appointment for three o'clock. She arrived with her husband, a distinguished figure with a grey beard and very deaf. He was a papal count and had been a member of the first Irish republican Cabinet.[3] There was also her daughter-in-law, wife of the hunger striker. The diary memorandum which I typed out that afternoon states that an hour's conversation ensued in this sense:

From diary entry

Friday, April 19th, 1940

I expressed my sorrow at the plight her son was in and asked her why she did not urge him to break the strike and live for his country instead of dying for it. That he would be far more useful to his cause if he were alive. From her answer I guessed that she had suggested that to him but that he has turned it down.

She said, 'If only this government would put them in custody of the soldiers, that is all they ask'. (The point of this was to secure recognition as prisoners of war instead of members of an illegal organisation). I said, 'They are charged with breaking the law of the land. If we four were the Government, and my son broke our

---

[1] Née Mary Josephine Cranny (1858–1944).

[2] John 'Jack' Plunkett (1897–1960), fought in Easter week and was arrested in 1936 following a police raid on an IRA broadcasting station. While interned in the Curragh, he survived a 40-day hunger strike.

[3] George Noble Plunkett (1851–1948), Parnellite and then republican; papal count.

law and then went on a hunger strike, what could we do? We would have to maintain the law when challenged'. 'It's not the law of the land', was the answer. '*It's the law of this government which does not represent the people of Ireland*'. I said it was my understanding that this government had won a clear majority in the last elections and that the constitutional opposition also recognised the validity of the government and that these two bodies of the electorate could not represent less than 80 per cent of the people and probably more. She said that was a mistake; it represented only a minority, that the IRA sympathisers kept away from the polls. I said you don't really believe that? She said, 'It is God's truth'. Most of the time I was shouting into Count Plunkett's ear trumpet and holding his wife's hand in an effort to be sympathetic, for after all this woman's son was dying and was a brave though deluded man.

From time to time as seems always to happen in Ireland on any sombre occasion everybody had a good laugh and speculated how long the 'byes' could last.[4]

I said I thought it very unfortunate for Ireland that there were those who wanted to start a new civil war; that we had had one and that that was enough for America. She said, 'This government is not an Irish government; it is controlled by England'. I said, 'Hasn't Mr de Valera got the British, not only out of Cobh, but out of Berehaven?' 'Well', she said, 'there was that Somerville who was shot, for recruiting for the British Navy'.[5] I got angry at this and said. 'That man happens to have been a dear friend of mine. He was one of the best friends Ireland has had since the Treaty. He never recruited for the navy. He told some boys who wanted to enlist where to go, but he sent more boys to the Irish army than to the British Navy. He was a very saintly man'. At this the daughter-in-law agreed. She came from west Cork and had heard about him. I went on, 'You people are worse than the Americans who have been hiding their heads in the sand like ostriches and not looking at the danger that faces them. If I was an Irishman, I would fight on the side of the English till Germany is beaten, then if I wanted to fight the English, well and good'.

Count Plunkett said, 'I would take a chance myself with the Germans. We are friendly with them'.

[4] A reference to the Irish pronunciation of 'boys'.
[5] Admiral Boyle Somerville (1863–1936), murdered by the IRA on 24 March 1936. Gray published a tribute to him in the *Irish Press* at the time.

I said, 'What about Denmark and Norway? Have you been more friendly than these countries?' He had nothing to say to that. I spoke then of the terrible position in which these boys were putting the government, Plunkett at least being a son of an old comrade. I asked him if he had not been in jail with Mr de Valera, Mr Seán T. O'Kelly and others, the night before Mr de Valera was to have been executed by the British, the night they held a mock trial over him. He recalled that he had been. I said, 'Do you think these men like to do this to your son?' 'They have betrayed us', he said, and he went on with the story of the continuous republic which for six years had functioned.

Finally I said, 'What do you want me to do? I cannot in conscience ask the government to weaken, because my government would not countenance such a request, and personally I feel that they are doing only what they must do'. We parted very good friends. They did not seem to resent my attitude but thanked me for receiving them.

About an hour later on thinking the matter over and feeling that I might have done more, I telephoned Countess Plunkett and said this, 'You may tell your son from me that if he will give over the strike I will sit on a platform, on which *as a civilian citizen* of Ireland and *not* an IRA member he may plead his cause in a constitutional manner although I disagree with everything he says. If he is willing to do this I will be willing to resign so as to keep my word'. She said, 'But if he breaks the strike on this condition he gives way. That is the whole point'.

I said, 'That *is* the whole point. But that is all I can do'. An hour later she telephoned that the strike was off. I wrote this note to her: 'Dear Madam: I hope fervently that medical care will restore your son to you and enable him to live for his country and serve it with as much wisdom as he has courage. Make my respects to Count Plunkett and believe me, with great sympathy, Yours very sincerely'.

The mentality disclosed in the quoted conversation, so incomprehensible to the American, was the practical expression of the 'doctrine of the second Dáil', which has been set forth, as explained by Seán O'Faoláin.[6]

The government did not disclose what, if any, terms it had made with the hunger strikers. Following this announcement of its ending came

[6] Seán O'Faoláin, *Sunday Independent*, 25 April 1943.

96

news of the death of a second striker. That evening there was another IRA demonstration in Dublin. My wife and I encountered the procession as we drove in to the movies. In a postscript to my letter to the president, dated April 19th, I described it as follows:

From letter to President Roosevelt

Friday, April 19th, 1940

... we were stopped by a long IRA procession escorting the body of the man who died after the hunger strike was broken. This was far more impressive and sinister than the one in the morning of the day before. There were at least three companies of fifty or sixty men each, of IRA who marched as soldiers, very smartly though not in uniform and unarmed, and were determined-looking lads and not the bums of the other procession. There was a long halt and they all stood impassively in the rain. It was very grim, a dedication not to love of country but to hate of the established order, whatever that might be. I believe there is something like a college secret society psychology in this problem. The young join it largely because it is banned.

The following day I returned Count and Countess Plunkett's call. They were people of means and lived in a big, Victorian house crammed with excellent furniture, dusty paintings, and Victorian bric-a-brac. According to my diary:

From diary entry

Saturday, April 20th, 1940

He was sitting with a book before the fire and she reclining with furs about on a sofa opposite him. She apologised for not rising, said she was ill. I said she had had enough to make anyone ill. She said the news of the son was good, that he was taking nourishment and gaining. One of the men had a very bad time. He could not at first retain any nourishment. She thanked me for what I had done and I said that I understood that she had done a great deal, and a neighbour of mine, the Nuncio, a great deal too. She agreed to that. Then we talked no more about hunger strikers and the explosion was never mentioned. We discussed Patrick's purgatory on Loch Derg (which she said, incorrectly, the

English had closed), the American Indian and his fate, India and the Indians. I told them the story that Harold Nicolson had told me about the heckler in Kansas City who had shouted, 'How about the Indians?' to whom he had replied, 'whose Indians, yours whom you exterminated, or ours whom we over-educated?' There was a good laugh. It was thought very good for an Englishman.

The Count told me that he had gone into one of the Northern Counties as a Republican and stood for a seat in the Northern Parliament. He put up at a pub and heard there was a meeting of some kind being held in an upper room. He put a table out, set a chair on it and was prepared to address those who were at the meeting as they came out. It turned out to be a Primrose League[7] meeting but they stayed politely to listen. He talked the Irish Republic to them and finally they suggested a bigger and better pub down the street and all adjourned thither.

If one understood the pathological psychology revealed in this episode, one would understand Sinn Féin and the political Irish. I did not understand it, Not till long afterwards did I suspect its pathological nature. I was trying to learn but there was little to be learned about Ireland at diplomatic lunch parties. An Irish friend hinted that the answer to my question was not in what the Irish people say or think but in what they feel and that is locked in the Heart of the Countryside, which is not vocal. It is something that eludes the pollster. And what this feels on Monday is not necessarily what it feels on Tuesday.

It was the problem of a 'common people' always and habitually underprivileged and oppressed. Their own pagan system had been an aristocracy based on slavery and they had been the slaves. From the beginning their own kings and princes had of right oppressed them down to the Tudor era when the foreign landlord with his title deeds and the sheriff superseded the prince.

The solution of the problem was not 'Nationalism' or 'Independence' or glorification of Irishness, but social and economic evolution, what is loosely called 'social justice'. And it was on the way. The now aristocratic way of life was disintegrating in the fires of new social forces. The Big House was on the way out, for the power to tax was the power to destroy. But there was nothing prepared to replace it but racialist and nationalist nostrums. At a time when the Irish people needed ever closer co-operation with The Neighbour the politicians offered them Separatist

---

[7] The Primrose League, founded in 1883, aimed to spread conservative principles in Great Britain.

Independence, whatever that might be. Some even ordered the Irish language as an economic cure-all.

The peasant masses had no formulated programme of their own. They might *feel* deeply but they could only *be* for or against the local leader who to them was *in loco principis*. Generally speaking as far as the Big House provided protection, prestige, employment, opportunity for poaching and petty larceny, they accepted it and in their way were loyal to it. When it failed to offer those things or to offer them graciously they were bitter. Very possibly the local leader was an ally of the Big House as might be the priest. If so the people also were allies. If not, the situation became bad. If they burned the Big House there would be no more employment. But habitually the peasant mind did not *think* about consequences. It only 'felt'.

What the Irish mind 'felt' about America was the one thing which it was important for the American legation to find out and this could not be done by ringing non-existent doorbells or asking questions. However, there is one disguise in which the foreigner can travel Ireland without exciting suspicion and that is in the role of sportsman, as one of Seán O'Faoláin's 'Happy Irelanders'.

So much had happened to the world and to us during our first official fortnight in Ireland that I was event-weary. I wanted to 'go fishin'.' Maude also wanted to get away to some place where nothing happened.

After my meeting with Devonshire at Duff Cooper's dinner in London, he had written telling me that I would always be welcome at Careysville, his fishing lodge on the Blackwater. His factotum in charge of the establishment also wrote me. English people when they are kind mean it. So on April 21st my wife and I set off for the Blackwater.

A spot of fine weather blessed us. As soon as we were clear of Dublin and headed South, we entered a country outside of Time. No one hurried. It was also outside Reality. Hitler was fighting in Norway, the world was tumbling down, but this Irish peasant life went on as usual and not much changed through the centuries. The same was true of the 'Country' people. Their sons were in the British army but the older generation went on as with their routine lives. That Sunday afternoon we saw the Irish countryside under blue sky and sun. The furze was in yellow bloom. I quoted ostentatiously to my wife, 'and furze unprofitably gay'. It was all I could remember of the 'Deserted Village'. I remembered it because as a little boy I thought it was 'furs', which did not make sense. I discovered later that Mr de Valera disclaims Goldsmith as an Irish poet, together with Swift, Moore and Sheridan. They are 'foreign' writers.

Besides the furze, the hawthorn—'The May'—was beginning to show white. The pastures were turning green and the winter grain was up. Even under these happy conditions it was a lonely country. One rarely saw men working in the fields. There was little traffic on the roads. If we stopped the car there was only the sound of the wind. Under gale and rain it was a sad countryside, but under the sun it seemed even lonelier. The castles which every few miles had once been proudly silhouetted against the sky were now only ruined towers, but the pattern of life which they implied was still evident. A diary entry reads:

From diary entry

Sunday, April 21st, 1940

Stopped at the hotel in Cahir and was given a drink by the lady manageress as a tribute to my predecessor; John Cudahy. Left Maude at the 'Grand Hotel' at Fermoy. (This was the village from which the 'American peer', Maurice Roche, takes his title.) Went on to Careysville to see about the fishing. Found the river was very high. (No fishing.) Went on to Lismore and delivered a package for Adele Cavendish (Fred Astaire's sister) who was in London. Charlie was there but I did not go in.

What was regarded by many as the best salmon water in Ireland was this two miles of the Blackwater at Careysville. It was then leased by the duke of Devonshire. Later he bought it.

From diary entry

Monday, April 22nd, 1940

Drove back to Careysville with Maude and found Thomas B. Ponsonby of Kilcooley Abbey, Major Bertram Bell of Fota and Captain Gough Cobden, a very nice chap from Tipperary, lamenting that the river was too high and too roiled with peat water for sport. The high price of coal had caused the reopening of old turf bogs and the drains being cleaned out brought the brown water down to the river. Major Bell had married the late Lady Barrymore's daughter, Dorothy. Thereupon occurred another 'small world' experience. Lady Barrymore had been a daughter of General James Wadsworth of Geneseo, New York, killed in 'The Wilderness' in the Civil War. She was thus the aunt of Congressman and former Senator James W. Wadsworth. Tom Ponsonby as well as the Bells had visited him at Geneseo.

For twenty years I had hunted in Geneseo with Major Austin Wadsworth's hounds. He was a cousin of the late congressman who with his wife, Alice Hay, had been our friends for forty years.

The fishermen were very kind and invited us to stop to lunch. To invite ladies was against the Duke's rules, so we thanked them and went back to Dublin.

The only grievance that I brought back from Ireland was against the Irish salmon. Boy and man I had killed the fish of the American and Canadian lakes and rivers. I had killed Florida tarpon and sailfish and other sporting fish of the Gulf Stream. I had taken a few autumn salmon in Scotland, but the Irish salmon defeated me. He comes into the Irish rivers, in a not-normal state of mind. He is 'on the tiles' as they say and his mentality is as twisted as that of the average Irish adolescent on sex. He is sour and mean and unpredictable. This had won him a high place in druid eschatology, a thousand years before Columbus. He was the symbol of the ultimate, the unpredictable, unrevealable wisdom.

I was unused to casting a fly with a two-handed rod and I decided that what the fawning 'gillies' called my 'bad luck' was bad fishing. I concluded that until I could lay a long, straight line into the wind and 'present' the fly properly, there was no use my fishing. About this time I met Colonel MacGillicuddy, the 'MacGillicuddy of the Reeks', (pronounced Mackdecuddy).[8] He told me that casting a good fly had nothing to do with it. The Irish salmon made his rendezvous with fate for his own reasons. He said that his stretch of river at 'Beaufort', near Killarney was so bad that for years he had given up fishing it. He kept no fishing gillies. One morning an Englishman and his wire arrived with letters of introduction and he asked them to lunch. The Englishman asked if his wife might fish as she had never caught a salmon. The MacGillicuddy sent them off with the garden boy. They returned shortly with a twenty-two pound fish. The boy reported privately that the lady 'could not at all fish, but threw the fly into the water as if she was emptying her apron'.

[8] Colonel MacGillicuddy had won a DSO in World War One and later served in the Irish Senate.

Unfortunately this influenced me to keep on. But it was clear that something was 'wrong'. The telephone would bring the news that 'the fish are lepping out, come quick'. I would rush off but when I got to the river the fish 'were no more taking'. Whatever it was that had been 'put on me' worked also on anyone with me. Sir John Maffey, who threw a beautiful line, used at first to take me with him, but while I was fishing he caught no more than I. He would sometimes work after union hours (teatime) and come in late with a fish but never while in competition with me.

As a rule when I did catch a fish it was a 'slat' which is the spent cock fish that in England they call a 'kelt'. They must be returned to the river. I came to take an unfavourable view of all uncooked salmon.

There was a tragic occurrence recorded in the news which aroused my sympathy. A sportsman in the Irish army stationed at Limerick way had wrongfully taken high explosives from the army stores and blown a pool. Unfortunately he destroyed himself and not the fish. I could understand what had happened. He had watched the fish weaving in the current and ignoring him, and he could not take it. Often I wished for dynamite. When I read of a small farmer arrested for pitchforking a salmon on the spawning beds, I would have wished to subscribe for his defence.

There were, however, notable people as lucky as I was unlucky. Conor Maguire,[9] Chief Justice of Ireland, was such a man. He was above suspicion of using explosives. He was too good a Christian to traffic with the 'old influences', yet he would fish a flat piece of the Liffey just above Dublin known to be without fish and pull out a fine salmon every time. He always stopped on his way home and left us a piece of his fish. Thus in a way we came to profit by his having 'on him' the opposite of what was 'on me'. The Liffey salmon has a peculiarly rich flavour. Those who fish other rivers say it is due to the sewage from the Guinness brewery.

When it got around that I had been 'jinxed' I had many invitations to fish, for the Irish sportsman is very kind. Everyone wanted to get the unfortunate American 'into a fish'. The late Major Johnny O'Rorke had the fine Slane water on the Boyne; the late Colonel Quinn some famous pools on the Slaney. The Charlie Cavendishes invited me to the Lismore water and Colonel Richard Charteris to his stretch of the Suir which produces exceptionally heavy fish. Sir George Colthurst of Blarney invited me to the Lee; the Guy Crosses had me to their famous Galway water and also to Costello. The Paddy Cullinanes, when they took 'Inver', had me there. But it was all practically fruitless. In the end my

---

[9] Conor Maguire (1889–1971), lawyer, revolutionary and judge.

favourite river became one that for several years had something 'on it' like what was 'on me'. This was the Maigue where it runs through the park of Adare Manor. It was said that the earl of Dunraven soon after he had inherited the place from his cousin, the international yachtsman, went out with a rod and killed five fish in a morning. It seemed to him too easy and an overrated sport and he never fished again but he invited me to fish whenever I would.

He regarded me with a kindly but cynical interest. From his easy chair he could look through a 'picture window', and watch me struggling with the rain squalls on his river bank, while his log fire burned cheerfully. Occasionally he would come out on his terrace and call to me to come in and have something warm. Finally I explained to him that principle was at stake. I had no hope of beating the salmon but I had to keep on and if I was going to fish and not catch fish I would rather do it at Adare than at other places for it seemed to me one of the most beautiful spots in the world.

The most famous gillie in Ireland was Willie Flynn at Careysville. He was an expert fisherman, but it was his conversation which made him famous. I wrote down some of his stories. One was this: he was going home in the dark across the stepping stones of a ford and found the water had risen suddenly. 'I stood on the first stone', he said, 'and put me foot down here, and it was up to me knee. And I put it down here, and it was up to me knee. And I put it down here, and it was up to me knee'. (All with pantomime) '"Glory be to God!" I said, "I am destroyed" and at that I ran so fast across the river, God help me I was wet only to me ankles'.

He told me that at four-thirty that afternoon, there would be a fresh run of fish in the pool that I was fishing. It was a Tuesday and he said that since they lift the nets at Lismore, sixteen miles down the river on Saturday night, and it takes forty-eight hours to come up, there would certainly be one there at the time he said. I fished till five and no fish. At tea I taxed him for breaking his promise. 'Ah, God', he said, 'it's all my fault. The fish they know only God's time and when I said four-thirty it was that "summer time" and it will be one hour and twenty-five minutes later that they come to that pool'.

Some of Willie's kinsmen had gone to the United States and prospered. At the close of the war one of them came back and took the fishing just above that at Careysville and brought a party of American friends. I was told he made a great deal of Willie. This is not uncommon in Ireland. A fellow with only a few shillings in his pocket may be brother or cousin to one who had gone to the Land of Opportunity and 'made good'. It is rare that there is any 'brush off' of the poor relation. The outstanding virtue of the Irish as a people is loyalty to their parents and old people, something too rare in America.

The bulk of salmon in the Irish market is caught in nets or fish traps. Usually professional fishermen under license can draw nets in tidal water. Above tidewater the rod fishing belongs to the owners of the abutting lands. The Irish government, in order to make rod fishing available to the public, has taken over some of the lakes and streams in the West where brown trout and the famous white sea trout are to be caught as well as salmon. I had hoped to plant our small-mouthed black bass in some of the Irish lakes but the war made it impracticable just as it defeated my scheme for planting hard and soft clams in the Irish estuaries which seem made for that purpose. The salmon rivers open at different times of the year though geographically not far distant one from the other. The first January fish in the public market sometimes sells for a pound a pound.

It is curious that though we passed through Cashel shortly before stopping at the Cahir Arms, the diary makes no mention of the most impressive man-made thing in Ireland. On the castellated rock jutting up from the Tipperary plain stands the Irish Romanesque chapel of Cormac and the Gothic Cathedral of his successors. In the eighteenth century a Protestant Bishop took the roof off, and unless the Irish government puts on a new one the frosts will reduce it soon or late to a pile of stones.

The afternoon of that Sunday that we drove back from the Blackwater, I walked across the park to the nunciature. This became a Sunday afternoon practice. The nuncio would give me a cup of tea or old Jameson, or both, and enlightening talk. As I walked back to the legation I wondered what was the meaning of what we had seen during our trip to the Blackwater. No one had mentioned the war. For all intents and purposes it was as far away as the 'floods in China'. We had met only kindness and were not conscious of exciting aversion. Perhaps this meant that the Irish masses were well disposed to the United States, that as James Dillon had told us, it only needed 'leadership' to rally them to the cause of democracy which Washington was upholding. But the pro-democratic leadership never was exerted.

On Tuesday, April 23rd, was our first 'Punchestown'. Punchestown is the annual two-day steeplechase meeting of the Kildare Hunt. The Hunt controls the adjoining land and from its stands one watches the horses going over a full-length natural steeplechase course. During the old Regime, Punchestown had become a national institution as well as a sporting event. The Lord Lieutenant used to attend in state with his vice-regal entourage. The Kildare Street Club and the various county clubs all over Ireland had their tents and served lunch to their members. The Kildare Hunt Committee gave lunch to the VIPs in the club house. It was an 'Ascendancy hosting'.

But in 1940 it was more than this. If there was any basis for Irish unity, Punchestown was the symbol of it. It was the Irish Olympia where a truce between the warring Greek states prevailed while the games were in progress. We were told that Mr de Valera strongly disapproved of Punchestown as the symbol of 'ascendancy' and 'foreign sports'. But he was advised to make no attempt to abolish it, lest he incite popular revolution, not by the Big House people but the voting 'peasantry'. And When Seán T. O'Kelly as president of Ireland attended in coach and four, crowned with a grey topper and was cheered, the battle was over. Sport had defeated 'sea-green incorruptibility'. It was one of the subjects I never discussed with Mr de Valera, though I advised him on occasions to go racing for the fresh air.

In an article in the Dublin *Sunday Independent* of April 25th, 1943, just after Mr de Valera was beaten by the inter-party coalition, Seán O'Faoláin apostrophised Punchestown:

This is the Happy Ireland. This is the Happy Irishman. You will find him in other places, such as the Horse Show, the Bloodstock Sales, a Point-to-Point, the Dogs, playing cards on a raincoat in a train, at a Harvest Home, out rough-shooting on the hills, hammering a handball fast and furiously on a Sunday afternoon as you drive through some little village, but he is always the same, easily recognisable happy man, roguish, argumentative, hot-headed, warm-hearted, amiable, and supremely sane and sensible. The world knows him and the world loves him. And when I stand among thousands of his like next Tuesday or Wednesday I know that I shall feel content that here is a place and an occasion where Ireland is tops.

He continues:

And I know well that when I am driving back from Punchestown next Tuesday or Wednesday evening, drunk with air, and as the car crosses the bumpy bridge of the Canal and the streets of Dublin begin, within ten minutes I shall see some damfool poster or some paragraph in the evening paper that will shatter that blissful emotion.

I will say to myself, as I have said a dozen times and more before, after a day out with The Happy Man:

'Why is it that this utter sanity of the Irishman at sport does not carry over with anything like the same voltage into private and public life? Take any five hundred of those blokes at Punchestown, corral them into a city square, set some passionate politician talking at them about Partition, or Gaelic, or Great Britain, or The Republic (God help us!), and I swear that a third of them will go raving mad, a third will get a dim glaze in their eyes like men who feel they ought to go a bit mad, but have too much sense to do it, and only about a third will have enough sanity to slip quietly away to a pub or to their homes for a sane *gosther* about the August meet at Tramore'.

This from Ireland's premier essayist, historian and man of letters, who in 1922 had himself with 'glazed eyes' followed the idealistic Mr de Valera in his armed rejection of majority rule.

I have been told by Irish friends that in 1948 when the inter-party coalition 'came in' there was a general sense of relief, not on political grounds but because the era of bleak restraints and hatreds seemed to be over. People again could have a good time. An Irish friend wrote me, 'It is like what takes place in a schoolroom when teacher steps out'. The spirit of the Restoration was manifesting in Éire.

On Punchestown Tuesday in April 1940, it rained so hard that at the last moment Maude refused to go. I drove off alone, thinking that the attendance would be small. By the time we were within two miles of the place, the roads were blocked with bicycles, ass carts, motor cars, pony carts. All the 'Tinkers' in Ireland seemed to be there. Some sportsmen came riding on farm horses. I saw nothing of the racing, only a vast acreage of open umbrellas. I also saw with interest and for the first time the then greatest living English lyric poet, Lord Dunsany. He had bought a race card from a gypsy woman who had defrauded him in the matter of change and was futilely appealing for justice. I came to know him after his return from Greece and discovered that besides being a great poet he was one of the best snipe shots in Ireland. In later years I attended very enjoyable Punchestowns but that afternoon I was glad to get back to a hot bath and a medicinal potation.

On April 25th we lunched with the nuncio. He was in a mood for anecdote and started off by telling us about 'Patrick's Purgatory' on the little Isle in Lough Derg. It is a popular objective for pilgrims. 'They say', he said, 'that there is a deep hole that goes straight down to where the bad people are. I correct myself. There are no bad people, only some not as good as others'.

The food was elaborate and my wife asked him how he kept house so well. According to my diary he answered:

From diary entry

Thursday, April 25th, 1940

'When I was appointed Nuncio ten years ago by the former Pope, I said to him, "Holy Father, I wonder how I am going to keep house in Ireland. The house is in the Park, out of town and inconvenient for the sisters who usually do that."

"I will tell you", said the Pope, "I have two lay brothers from Poland who look after me and I have no trouble. My sister came to see me soon after they were installed. She thinks no man can keep house. She put her finger on the mantelpiece looking for dust and fortunately one of my brothers had wiped it off that morning. After that she had nothing to say. You go to the Monsignor who has charge of the Bureau that supplies the brothers and you will have no difficulties."

I went there and they said, "There are no brothers available. There are nine applications ahead of yours." I told that to Cardinal X and he said you must tell the Holy Father. I said I cannot bother the Head of The Church with my housekeeping in Dublin. He said, "You must. He likes that kind of thing." So I told the Pope my troubles. He said that is very easily arranged and he gave me a note to the bureau, commanding them to supply me with four, one who could speak English, another French and the other two—it made no difference what they spoke, and now I have no troubles'.

Of the serious talk I wrote the president;

From letter to President Roosevelt

Thursday, April 25th, 1940

He (the Nuncio) tells me in confidence that the Censorship is drying up the sinews of war for the IRA. It pinches the cash and checks from America. In his view without funds they will rapidly lose effectiveness. He has found out that a number of the toughest IRA characters have recently joined the British army. He thinks the whole movement is very largely a matter of unemployment. If they could get jobs that suited them the movement would soon fade out ... . We are asking him and the de Valeras and Granard to lunch next Thursday. The Nuncio says that Granard is the most popular man in his county (Longford) with all three parties, that is including the IRA.

That afternoon (April 25th) I called on Mr Cosgrave. While Mr de Valera was opposed to 'foreign sports' and the Irish 'kulaks', Mr Cosgrave, leader of the Fine Gael opposition, believed that horse sports were as Irish as English. Above everything he wanted to achieve Irish unity and recognised that the old unionists were an essential element of the community, though their open political support might not be an asset.

It was 'correct' for a newly accredited Chief of Mission to call on the leader of the opposition and Mr Cosgrave received me by appointment. My diary records:

From diary entry

Thursday, April 25th, 1940

I called on Mr Cosgrave at his house in the country. Mrs Cosgrave was there and gave us tea, a very alert, kind and intelligent woman. I told him what I hoped to do by exploring the situation in the North and how it affected our home politics and foreign policy. He was very sympathetic. He said James Dillon had given a good report of us. I asked him if there were no chance for a national government. He said, 'unfortunately no', that he could not trust Mr de Valera. He could not work with him. He could not forgive him for having plunged the country into civil war in 1922. At that time he had tried to get de Valera to go to London with the plenipotentiaries but that he always refused. I asked him if it would not help if the Anglo-Irish went into politics. He said he would welcome them. I stayed for an hour and a half and he promised to see me whenever I desired. I found him in favour of close co-operation with England and of assisting them as much as is politically possible.

He had made it clear, however, that he would not discuss Irish foreign policy with me. That was the government's affair. As time passed I found that when Mr Cosgrave made a statement, it was true. At this time he was living comfortably but modestly as a country gentleman at 'Beech Park' ten miles out of Dublin near Templeogue. Here he farmed something less than a hundred acres, grazed beef cattle, raised his quota of grain and kept a couple of hunters. Once or twice a week he was out with the Ward Union.

Soon after our arrival Roderick More O'Ferrall[10] had called on us and in his mother's name invited us to lunch and go racing to the Curragh. On April 26th,[11] as we were getting in the car to start there was an explosion that rattled the windows. Someone telephoned the police and found out that a bomb had exploded in the Castle. What that might mean we had no idea but I arranged to be advised if the IRA were starting a Civil War. On arriving at Kildangan we announced the bomb outrage but no one seemed to think it more than an incident in local politics. Our hosts suggested that we did not discuss the subject before the servants. Their kinsman, Colonel More O'Ferrall, although a Catholic and of the 'ould stock' had been murdered about the time the IRA had murdered Vice Admiral Boyle Somerville of Castle Townshend. Servants may be loyal and well-intentioned, but they were terrified of the local IRA leader to whom they were under obligation to report what went on in the house. The More O'Ferralls were one of the old county families still able to carry on more or less in the old tradition. There were three brothers in this branch: Roderick, the heir, Francis and Rory. The latter two at this time were in the British army. Their mother was an English lady, still very handsome. Roderick was a trainer. Training race horses was one of the professions which had become possible for Irish country gentlemen. Fifty years earlier the Hon. George Lambton,

[10] Roderick More O'Ferrall (1903–90), horsebreeder and farmer. Horses bred by O'Ferrall at Kildangan won eleven classic races: in this venture, he had a partner, the British diplomat Sir Percy Loraine.

[11] This explosion happened on 25 April.

brother to the earl of Durham and one of the most popular men on the English turf, had turned professional trainer. 'Atty' Persse, a lovable Irishman, had followed suit. In 1940 one of the most charming men in Ireland, Cecil Boyd Rochfort, was the King's trainer, while Charles Moore, another Irishman, was manager of the King's stud. At the Curragh the brothers Blake, Hubert Hartigan, Darby Rogers and 'Bob' Fetherstonhaugh were all famous and popular 'gentlemen' trainers. Roderick More O'Ferrall was notably successful. Kildangan was a big comfortable Victorian house with extensive stables, some three miles from the Curragh. The estate comprised about a thousand acres of the best land in Kildare. The red clover cut six tons to the acre.

There were some twenty people to lunch. Curragh days, Mrs More O'Ferrall never knew how many were coming. People telephoned at the last moment proposing themselves. One of the distinctions of the house was a really dry, well-shaken American Martini. It is of course deplorable, but this seems to be the one product of American culture that excites no nationalistic resentments.

The British ambassador to Italy, Sir Percy Lorraine, was a fellow guest. He was back for a short holiday. He told me that no one knew what Mussolini would do in the end, but he, Lorraine, was confident that the Italian people would not fight very hard.[12] This was much what William Philips had told us. Ciano in his Diaries reveals that he held Sir Percy in great esteem. Sir Percy perplexed him. He was intelligent (like Ciano) yet he did not lie. He was a new type to the Italian. He had bred some high-class horses which he kept at Kildangan and raced successfully.

Another guest was Mrs Kevin O'Higgins. Her husband had been one of the 'strong' men in the Cosgrave government. He was said to have had the keenest mind in Ireland. After the Civil War someone shot him in the back of the head as he was coming home from church. As one of the Cosgrave-Collins government, he had been instrumental in executing seventy-seven of Mr de Valera's followers who had violated the amnesty provisions and had been arrested with arms. It was generally supposed that one of the de Valera faction had murdered him, but no one was arrested for the crime. Mrs O'Higgins had great beauty and charm. Later she married Arthur Cox, the outstanding solicitor and office lawyer of Ireland.

[12] Sir Percy Lytham Loraine, 12th Baronet (1880–1961), diplomatist, a strong supporter of appeasement in the British foreign service: on his return to England in 1940, Churchill snubbed him. He became a keen racehorse owner, keeping horses with Roderick Moore O'Ferrall at Kildangan.

We also met the Evelyn Shirleys. Colonel Shirley had inherited a place in Ireland, Lough Fea, but the family seat was in Warwickshire. This had been in the Shirley family since the Norman conquest and was recorded in the Doomsday Book. It was there in a kitchen dresser that Shane Leslie found a priceless bundle of Swift's letters to Stella.

We did not know it at this time but Mr de Valera and his left-wing Sinn Féiners in principle regarded all Big House people much as Stalin regarded the kulaks. They were enemies or potential enemies of the Fianna Fáil 'party line' state. But while they deviated politically, they were an economic asset. An establishment like that of Roderick More O'Ferrall's employed a deal of labour. The sale for export of Irish horses brought money into the country and reduced the adverse trade balance. The conditions prevailing in the eighteenth century had reversed themselves. Then, many of the great landowners were absentee and the rents from the Irish estates were spent out of Ireland. Today under the land laws passed while Ireland was in the United Kingdom the tenants had become owners of their farms. The Big House owners retained only their unproductive demesnes and small home farms worked by hired labour. The incomes on which they lived largely came from England and were spent in Ireland. If the government took their houses and liquidated them as a class, it would create a serious unemployment problem. Thus as long as the Big House did not meddle with politics it was unmolested. Some Big House people contributed to both parties. It was a serious matter to get in wrong with the local Fianna Fáil leaders. One might not be able to get diesel oil for his tractor and lighting plant. If he raised seed wheat it might not be 'approved'. His rates might go up. If he wished to cut down a tree on his own property the permit might never come. He might get tangled in one of a dozen ways in the paperwork of a welfare state, administered by unfriendly and not very competent bureaucrats.

What we had looked forward to as a restful week where nothing happened closed with a weekend with Lady Leslie, Winston Churchill's famous American aunt. We had never met Lady Leslie but we had common friends and Sir John Leslie[13] was a friend of Maude's sister and of her husband, the late Stanley Mortimer. He had married Leonie Jerome,[14] one of the three remarkable daughters of the remarkable

[13] Sir John Leslie (1857–1944), educated at Eton and Cambridge. An opponent of Irish Home Rule.
[14] Leonie, the youngest of the three Jerome sisters, married 'Jack' Leslie in 1883. Her sister Jennie married Randolph Churchill and was Winston Churchill's mother.

American Mr Leonard Jerome. I had always been told that Stanley Mortimer had been Sir John's best man at the wedding in New York, but his grand-daughter Anita Leslie, who should know, says in her book about her American grandfather that it was Frank Gray Griswold. He was one of the great sportsmen and 'men of fashion' in New York in the eighties and nineties. If I remember correctly, he acted as racing representative in England for his cousin, Pierre Lorilard, at the time when Iroquois won the Derby. This was the first time that an American-bred horse had won this classic. Frank Griswold had been very kind to me when I was young. He had been my ideal of a sportsman. I had known Lady Leslie's daughter-in-law, Mrs Shane Leslie, when she was Marjorie Ide, in Manila in 1903. Her father was then one of the Philippine commissioners. Later he became governor. Before the Philippine assignment he had been our Commissioner in Samoa. Marjorie's sister, Anne, who married Burke Cochran, was the 'little American girl' in Apia to whom Robert Louis Stevenson deeded his birthday by formal conveyance. Hers was lost three years out of four because it came on February 29.

Soon after we had arrived in Dublin, my wife got a note of invitation from Mrs Shane Leslie, writing in her mother-in-law's name. It was so kind that we were glad to accept it. Motoring down with us on the Saturday afternoon was Mrs Josephine MacNeill, whose brother-in-law had been Professor James MacNeill, the first governor general of Ireland under the Treaty. It was he who as head of the Irish Volunteers had tried to stop the Uprising of Easter Week 1916. Mrs MacNeill was a woman of distinction and character. She was ignored by the de Valera government, but the Costello government sent her to Holland as Irish minister.

On arriving late Saturday afternoon, we found that Mrs Shane Leslie, my old friend, had been suddenly called to London to say goodbye to her oldest son, Jack, who was embarking with his regiment for France. We were further disturbed to find that Lady Leslie, 'Leonie' as everybody called her, had had a severe fall and was very 'low from shock'. The doctor would not predict her recovery. We decided that we should immediately go back to Dublin, but Sir John's sister, Mrs Murray Guthrie, of Torosay Castle, Mull, was acting as hostess and would not hear of it. She was a forceful woman and intimated that to leave an Irish house at such a time would be a breach of manners. So we stopped on, as did Mrs MacNeill.

A new conception of the Irish landlord was revealed to us. While it was a good thing for the Irish economy to have the Big House maintained by income that came from England, this income since the land acts had been steadily shrinking while taxation and the costs of maintenance had steadily risen. A crisis was fast approaching which Big House owners did not attempt to ignore but which they were in general helpless to meet. The American way would have been to shut up the houses and discharge the servants. But the 'right type' of Big House people would not think of doing this, except as a last step before bankruptcy. The social stability of the system depended on this responsibility of the owners for their people. Wages, pensions, cottage maintenance costs had become a first charge on the family income. As a matter of fact in many cases the whole place was being run for what in New England we call 'the help'. 'The help' generally regarded this as their 'right', and may or may not have rendered loyalty in return. Some undoubtedly did. Others did not. There was current a story about a pantry boy who helped 'free Ireland' by leading the IRA to the Big House, where he was employed. They burned the house and murdered the master. The boy finding that he had no job went to his widowed mistress and demanded a 'character', for, as he pointed out, he could get no employment unless she gave him one.

Sir John Leslie at eighty-three was very deaf but erect, urbane and charming. He was regarded almost as the last surviving Irish Victorian country gentleman. He told us that during his marriage ceremony in New York, as he knelt before the altar, he remembered that the porter at the Holland House where he was stopping chalked his room number on the soles of his shoes. He realised that the people in the front pews must be reading the number and was embarrassed.

Sir John had been one of the Signers of the Covenant when in 1910 Ulster was preparing to resist Home Rule by force. The Protestants in Monaghan, however, were not numerous enough to hold the county so they were reluctantly abandoned by Carson and Sir James Craig. This was an especially bitter pill for Sir John, for Glaslough was literally on the border. His lands marched with those of the earl of Caledon, elder brother of Field Marshal Alexander, in County Tyrone. If he had been two miles to the north he would have been in Northern Ireland. This abandonment, as southern loyalists saw it at the time of the Treaty, created deep resentment among the southern unionists. A unionist nobleman who I knew, with a show place near Dublin, always spoke of it as 'The Great Betrayal'. It accounted for much of the apathy which many of the old unionist residents in Éire manifested toward Irish neutrality. They felt that England was getting what she deserved. Their sons, however, all joined up with the British forces.

As in other Anglo-Irish families there were differences at Glaslough in religion and politics. Sir John's oldest son and heir had become a Catholic, changed his name from John to Shane, and besides being a brilliant writer, was a strong nationalist. However, like Senator David Robinson, he was friendly to England and throughout the war was in London serving in the Home Guard.[15] Like General Hubert Gough, Henry Harrison, the Hon. Frank Pakenham, now Lord Pakenham, and others, he was an apologist for Irish neutrality, but worked for better relations.

Sunday morning at Glaslough, Lady Leslie was reported 'very low'. We again debated packing up, but were again persuaded not to and instead went off to church with the Protestant contingent. Sunday church-going is the prescribed thing in the Protestant houses as well as in the Catholic. As a rule the Big House supports a small Church of Ireland church to which the few Protestant gentry in the neighbourhood and the exceptional Protestant farmer, retainer, or shopkeeper worship. The Catholic attend their regular parish church. These small but select Church of Ireland congregations once were symbols of English pride and ascendancy. Now they are dwindling remnants of the old regime and without hope of resurgence. If and when there is another schism in the Roman Church in Ireland, it is not likely that Anglo-Catholicism will gain from it. It is rather probable that Communism, as in Catholic Italy, or some other economic religion promising a more abundant life in this world will win converts among the Irish 'have nots'.

At lunch there was no better news from Lady Leslie. In the afternoon after 'the naps' we took the regulation walk around the lake. The weather was happy and Glaslough, the 'Black Lake'[16] looked Mediterranean blue. The hillside pastures were yellow with primroses. At tea-time word came from the sick room that Lady Leslie had suddenly become much better, and wished to see me. As the nurse took me into the shaded room, Lady Leslie was lying on a chaise-longue under a coverlet of old lace. It was the common saying that this American woman without beauty or wealth had for half a century been a great figure in European society, but it seemed to me that she *had* great beauty. As she lay there she seemed

[15] Shane Leslie (1885–1971) never publicly criticised neutrality but privately believed that Irish policy was mistaken. See Otto Rauchbauer, *Shane Leslie: sublime failure* (Dublin, 2009), 85, note 41.
[16] Literal translation is the 'green lake'.

infused by some inner light of personality that transfigured her. She asked me had I seen her nephew, 'Winston' as I came through London. I said yes, and that he had been very kind. I also told her what she must have known, that he was shortly to be the new prime minister.

Then we talked about our common friend who had just died, Frank Griswold. Her magic, whatever it was, to me seemed undiminished. Like Theodore Roosevelt and his sister Corinne, she made the person she was talking with seem more than he was. I left her, fragile, faded, near the border, yet with the moving sense that these twenty minutes constituted a friendship. Fortunately, Lady Leslie recovered and we went several times more to Glaslough. She and her sister, Lady Randolph Churchill, and Mrs Moreton Frewen were great figures in the Edwardian era and live on in the pages of her grand-daughter Anita's *The remarkable Mr Jerome*.[17]

---

[17] Elizabeth Kehoe, *Fortune's daughters: Jennie Churchill, Clare Frewen and Leonie Leslie* (London, 2004); Anita Leslie, *The remarkable Mr Jerome* (New York, 1954).

CHAPTER VI

MAY 1ST-20TH

The bomb explosion at the Castle on April 25th had caused material damage but no loss of life. There were no clues.

On May 1st our Cork Consulate telephoned that Vice Consul Patterson was coming to Dublin with information that he could not give us over the telephone. It proved to be a series of alarmist items obtained from a high police official who was his friend. Patterson was an engaging young American of independent means who had obtained the consular appointment because he liked the country and had married an attractive Irish woman. There was no doubt that he had been told these things. It was only a question whether they were true. One was the report that the German legation in Dublin was nightly receiving messages from Berlin which they acknowledged by jamming the 240 watt local current. Another was the report of a wireless sending station maintained by the IRA in the German interest. It was supposed to be in the Wicklow Mountains and the police had not been able to find it. Third, that a German submarine had recently put in at the mouth of the Shannon. Fourth, that a landing of German troops by submarine was shortly to take place to act in conjunction with an IRA Uprising. Finally, that the Irish government was alarmed over the possibility of a seizure of the ports by the British.

In the afternoon I walked across the Park to the nuncio's and told what I had heard. He had already heard it. He said that it had been reported to him that the submarine at Shannon Mouth had not received a friendly welcome from the local inhabitants. How much truth there was in the other reports he was not prepared to say. In the light of the captured German papers it is evident that the German expedition was not merely Irish imagining but that Artus was being discussed in IRA circles.

Mr de Valera had pledged his word to Neville Chamberlain that Éire would never be used as a base of attack against England. One was forced to ask whether these things constituted an attack, and if so what was the pledge worth?

On May 2nd, Mr de Valera lunched with us informally, although he had a rule against lunching out. Moreover he brought Mrs de Valera with him although she too had a rule against lunching out. In the little diplomatic world of Dublin every party had a meaning and the meaning of this was taken as indicating a 'firm Irish-American understanding'. Since the American president and his secretary of state were daily denouncing Hitler, de Valera was evidently in agreement with them. This had been forecast by the condemnation of the German invasion of Norway and Denmark by Mr de Valera's newspaper in April. All this seemed to indicate that the logical first step toward ending Partition by participation in a common island defence was likely soon to take place. Whether or not it actually ended Partition at once, it would certainly relieve the pressure of the Irish-American Anglophobes on the president's defence measures. I wrote the president about the lunch party:

From letter to President Roosevelt

Thursday, May 2nd, 1940

Food pretty bad and Maude in despair about the chickens. In Ireland a 'green goose' is one fed on grass. Our chickens generally seemed to be 'green-fattened'. De Valera told us about his eyes. He has had one operated but the other is now getting worse. He wanted to have it attended to in America, but was unable to get away last spring. He has no time to read even if he had the eyes. He seemed very much interested in education, even more than in foreign affairs.

After lunch I got him aside and asked him if the government had been anxious of late over the possibility of the seizure of the Irish ports, by the British. (This question was suggested by Patterson's report from Cork). He said no, no specific anxiety, only the disquietude of the general possibility. He feels it would set back the reconciliation a generation at least.

I asked him if he did not think that an attack or raid by the Germans on the Irish coast would cause a crystallisation of pro-Ally sentiment that would welcome aid in repelling the attack.

He suggested that it *should* but was not positive now it *would* work out. It might be seized upon by the IRA to start an insurrection. He is very solicitous about these people; shuns thinking in terms of ruthless majority action against them. I told him that if he had any information that would make him dread the seizure of the ports to let me know at once, and I would telephone the President who I knew would be deeply concerned. He said he would.

This period between our arrival early in April and the invasion of Belgium we believed to be the honeymoon of our relations with Mr de Valera. Later the captured German papers made it clear that instead of honeymooning we had been buying a 'bill of goods'. My pro-Irish sympathies had made me a 'sitting duck' for the Great Idealist. He had sold us the same 'pup' that he had sold Prime Minister Chamberlain and for the same reasons. He needed American supply and good will as he needed those things from Britain and he had been giving us the 'English Treatment'. (Hempel in his telegram to Ribbentrop of August 31st, 1939, had stated that de Valera in view of Ireland's dependence on Britain for supply demanded permission to exercise 'a *certain* consideration for Britain'.)

On May 5th, in that spirit of simple, German good faith characteristic of the Hitler regime, Ribbentrop was giving de Valera the runaround, as he was giving it to us. While Hempel and Walshe were calling each other 'Joe' and 'Eduard', Ribbentrop parachuted his agent, Herr Captain Hermann Goertz, into the Dublin area. His mission was to create 'Umdeckung Sympathie'[1] between the IRA and the Fatherland, to liquidate the de Valera government when and if the Artus plan were implemented and to organise a German spy system distinct from Hempel's. The chief item of his equipment was 20,000 dollars in American small bills. This was four days before the invasion of Belgium and the Netherlands.

On Friday, May 10th, our London embassy telephoned that Germany had attacked Belgium and Holland. Again Germany's solemn assurances were 'scraps of paper'. Czechoslovakia, Poland and Scandinavia had been only curtain-raisers. Now the show had begun.

Jim Seymour, speaking for Ambassador Kennedy, has asked us to plan for the care of American refugees passing through Ireland to embark for home at some Irish port. Seymour was arriving in Dublin that evening.[2]

---

[1] One possible translation of this phrase is 'covert understanding'.
[2] Jim Seymour (1895–1976), secretary, private attaché to Joe Kennedy senior, and former Hollywood screenwriter. Personal papers in the Kennedy Library.

I at once wrote Mr Kennedy putting the resources of our Mission at his disposal and offered some comment on the situation as it might affect Britain. I said:

From letter to Ambassador Kennedy

Friday, May 10th, 1940

There is one point which I did not touch on in my last letter to you. That is the possibility of the Germans making a decoy landing which would send the British off at half cock and induce them to seize one or more (Irish) ports. In the view of the people here who know best, it would be better to let the Germans take half of Southern Ireland than have the British come in before the Government asks them. Of course, what has just happened may produce an effect on public opinion that will have important results, especially if Louvain is bombed or church property destroyed. But don't be too sure that it will express itself in any modification of Irish neutrality in the immediate future.

Last night I talked with the British Military Attaché in Denmark, who has just got out. He told us that they reported to his Government, about a week before it happened, that some sixty troopships would be going up the west coast but no effort was made to intercept them. He is terribly troubled. If he speaks out in meeting they will break him.

Early on May 11th, Sir John Maffey called on Mr de Valera and gave him the substance of the British reports from Belgium. The bombing of Amsterdam and Louvain, the machine-gunning of civilian refugees on the roads, made a grim picture of Hitler's 'New Order', which had captivated Irish-separatist imagination. He asked him what he now thought of the value of German assurances. There was a definite parallel between Belgium and Éire. Both had declined defensive co-operation with the Allies and had chosen to rely on German promises. Mr de Valera told Sir John that the next day (Sunday) he was making a speech in Galway, and would have 'something to say on the subject'.

On May 11th, Neville Chamberlain resigned and the king asked Winston Churchill to form a government. Mr de Valera could not have liked this. Mr Chamberlain had saved him once and had appeared to believe in him. He knew what Mr Churchill had said about 'the men now in power' in Ireland. He knew also how important to British survival Mr Churchill regarded the ports, and he knew Mr Churchill was no 'appeaser'.

In Washington on that same 11th, the president condemned the new German aggression in no uncertain terms. He warned the nations to prepare since the dictators were seeking world conquest. He sympathised with Queen Wilhelmina's fruitless protest to Hitler. There was nothing neutral in his utterances.

On the 11th, Goebbels's broadcast boasted that German paratroops were triumphant 'in three countries'. This might portend that Ireland was to be the fourth. It would be, if Hitler proceeded with encircling movement and crushed England by cutting her supply line at the Irish Narrows.

On Sunday, May 12th, Mr de Valera said what he had to say in Galway, and on Monday morning, May 13th, the Dublin newspapers reported portions of it as follows (italics mine):

Today, these two small nations are fighting for their lives, and I think I would be unworthy of this small nation if, on an occasion like this, I did not utter our *protest against the cruel wrong which has been done them.* We have to see to it that they will find us a united people ready to resist.

Again:

You know that we have declared our neutrality and proclaimed our desire and intention to save our people from the horror of this war. Small countries like ours had the same desire. Some of these small countries had no greater wish than not to be involved in the war. They have been involved against their will, not having done anything as far as we can see to deserve what has happened to them.

He added

The fact that we want to keep out of this war may not be sufficient to save us. The one thing that is going to help to save us is the determination that *any invader of any sort* that comes into this country will be resisted with all our might.

From the Allied viewpoint he could not have said more. Unquestionably he was on our side.

On May 13th, the Argentine foreign minister stated that 'neutrality was a dead conception'. He urged Argentine belligerency.

On May 13th, I telegraphed the president a brief summary of what I thought was the Irish reaction to events. On the same day the president addressed the Congress, bespeaking a united front and reminding the nation that 'these modern conquerors were seeking to dominate *every mile of the earth's surface*'. That meant the United States and Ireland as well as Belgium.

On May 14th, Holland was cut in half. Wilhelmina fled to England. That night Sedan fell. May 15th, Holland capitulated. Indian nationalist leaders condemned the German invasion. Secretary Hull in a speech said, 'we cannot close our eyes to the orgy of destruction ... . The anarchy of the Dark Ages menaces the world'.

On May 15th, I wrote the president amplifying the telegram which I had dispatched on the 13th:

From letter to President Roosevelt

Wednesday, May 15th, 1940

The reaction here to your statements and policy in regard to the invasion of Belgium and Holland seems to be very favourable. I think it has had a good deal to do with Mr de Valera's first condemnation of Germany made Sunday, May 12th, in a speech to a Galway party meeting. The Government has been afraid to take this stand up to now. Of course the Pope's attitude must also have been a factor.

If I had then had any doubts about Mr de Valera's orientation, the Galway Pronouncement would have removed them. Believing in him as I did, he had said only what I had expected. I took it so much for granted that I missed its importance in my reports. I wrote him a short personal letter congratulating him on his courage and wisdom. This he never acknowledged. Later when we found out what had happened, we could understand why.

On its face the Galway speech was a statement of first importance. It was brave and explicit. It nailed the Irish flag to the masthead of Western democracy. Yet it excited little comment. The *Irish Times* printed a perfunctory leader about it and that was all. We did not know then that the Censor had operated on Smyllie's leader.

If America slept with three thousand miles of ocean between Hitler and New York, Dublin with only the North Sea between, appeared to be blind and deaf. Two days after the onslaught on the Low Countries I attended a dinner of the PEN Club (Poets, Essayists, Novelists), the elite of the Irish intelligentsia, given in honour of Smyllie, Editor of the *Irish Times*, the leading Irish opposition newspaper. In my letter to the president, begun May 15th, I said: 'They (the speakers) were bitter against the Irish censorship but no one dared openly to condemn Germany, though they honoured the Czechoslovak envoy (Dr Kostal, the former consul general) and his wife, who are still here. Smyllie had the last decoration conferred by Dr Beneš'.[3]

(The dinner guests had not yet heard of Mr de Valera's Galway proclamation). The letter continued:

From letter to President Roosevelt continued

Wednesday, May 15th, 1940

They gave me a big hand before I made my speech and dead silence afterwards. Draw your own conclusions, I didn't say anything except that the Irish were nice people and had good newspapers. They probably resented it. One speaker quoted Doctor Johnson's remark. 'The Irish are a just people. They never speak good of one another'. It took me some time to appreciate that nothing excites more instant contempt than the foreigner who attempts to make a pleasant impression. There is only one Blarney stone and it belongs to Ireland.

When the ladies left the dining room, I joined a group at which Maurice Walsh was presiding.[4] I told him that millions of Americans were regretting that he was doing no more 'Thomasheen James' stories for the *Saturday Evening Post*. He said that he wanted to introduce me to a well-known Irishman, John Jameson, Inc. It was all very pleasant.

It was also unreal like most things in Separatist Ireland. I went on reporting to the president the daily trivia noted in my diary:

You probably know, but I only got it from the Nuncio the other day, that the Vatican had forbidden its Nuncios for the past two

---

[3] Edvard Beneš (1884–1948), led Czechoslovak independence movement, and was later minister for foreign affairs and president of Czechoslovakia. He was forced to resign as a result of German pressure following the German military occupation of the Sudetenland.

[4] Maurice Walsh (1879–1964), popular novelist, best remembered as the author of the short story that became the basis of the John Ford/John Wayne film *The quiet man*. His humorous stories about a feckless servant were collected as *Thomasheen James: man-of-no-work* (London, 1941).

years to accept the hospitality of German diplomats. I have to go to lunch with the German minister in the near future and the job of getting Maude there is one that I despair of. She will probably be taken with lockjaw on the fateful day.

Yesterday we had the O'Kellys (Seán T., the Vice-premier, an admirer of yours) to lunch; the Nuncio also and Sir John and Lady Maffey, as well as Belle Roosevelt and her sister. It went off very well.

We had lunched with Belle and Kermit as we passed through London. Kermit, though in bad health, was indomitable as ever and was leading a detachment of volunteers into Norway. I saw him last in Lord Derby's box at the Grand National. Belle and her sister, the Hon. Mrs Herbert, came over to visit us.

I am pretty sure that the British Government appreciates the folly of attempting any kind of a coup against the Irish ports, whether executed by the French navy or their own. I get nothing from Vatican sources that makes me suspect the Duce is going to war. The Italian Minister and wife here are very anti-German but they get no news from Italy. The Nuncio has the only news, whatever that may be. (Mr de Valera divulged no reports from his Ministers in Rome.)

All this while the fate of civilisation trembled in the balance. On May 16th, the Germans pierced the Maginot Line and blasted Louvain.

On May 16th, I had what appears to have been the most important conversation that I had thus far had with Mr de Valera. I saw him at his office at noon and in the afternoon I wrote to the president:

From letter to President Roosevelt

Thursday, May 16th, 1940

We heard you on the radio last night giving your message to Congress on emergency preparedness. I think it was generally understood here, as the passage urging the Congress to put no obstacle in the way of airplane delivery was emphasised in the Irish newspapers. At last this government is waking up to its danger, though doing nothing. I had an hour's talk this noon with Mr de Valera. I asked him first if he had any objection to my sending for one of our military attachés from London to inspect the Irish dispositions for protection of airports in case of a parachute raid in conjunction with the IRA. As a diversion, it is not unreasonable to expect it, as, with a thousand men, they could stir up trouble here for weeks.

Goebbels had already forecast such a possibility.

He (de Valera) said that if he showed our attaché the dispositions the Germans might ask for the same privilege. It did not occur to him that the Germans already knew them. He is trying to get five or six hundred machine guns in England but it is doubtful if they can be spared just now.

I believed that if I had a strong report from an American officer I could urge the president to send Ireland what was needed.

The most that could be expected of the Irish army at present is to cope with parachute troops on a small scale and possibly to intercept arms landed by submarines for the IRA. I commented upon his condemnation (in Galway) of the German invasion of Holland and Belgium and asked him if he did not think it got a good reception from press and public. He said, 'On the whole, yes'. He then spoke of your message to Congress. He said that a year ago he thought you were going too fast but he now saw that you had been right.

I suggested that the time had come for him to take a definite position, as you had, that his neutrality was not going to save him, and that he had to consider his situation from the viewpoint of assisting in the defeat of Germany.

He said that this was true but how fast he could go he could not be sure. He was waiting further on events. I asked him if that was not what the Low Countries and Scandinavia had done to their cost. He said yes, but he had to be very cautious. I asked him if he had not had staff consultations and an agreed-upon plan with the Allied Command. He said no, that he was afraid to do that, not because it would increase the danger of German invasion but because it would tend to divide public sentiment at home. I told him that of course he must be the best judge of that, but he must weigh that danger against being caught defenceless. He said that he had something on his mind that he wished to talk about. He then asked, could I confidentially enquire of you whether in view of the fact that *Ireland and Irish bases command the North Atlantic trade routes both by sea and air* you could proclaim that the United States was vitally interested in the maintenance of the status quo as regards Ireland. I said, 'What you would like would be an American guarantee of your independence'.

He admitted that it was, but saw that it was out of the question to ask that. He said if I received a favourable reply to this enquiry he would consult his Dáil and Ministers and make a formal approach. He said a pronouncement would strengthen his leadership very much.

There were two noteworthy points in this proposal. First, that he recognised the strategic importance of Éire in any crisis of the Atlantic Powers, an importance which later he soft-pedalled, if he did not actually deny; and, second, he showed a realisation of Éire's dependence on outside support to maintain her independence. Personally I should have been glad to have had the United States guarantee Irish independence in return for assurance that if and when we should enter the war, bases would be put at our disposal. But in 1940 I believed that the political situation in Washington made such a suggestion impossible. I could only transmit Mr de Valera's inquiry to the president as he requested and without holding out hope of favourable action.

Cordell reveals the state of mind of the administration at this time. On May 15th Ambassador Kennedy had telegraphed him from London depicting the heroic attitude of prime minister Churchill, despite the desperate situation of the Allied Cause. Kennedy suggested that 'if we had to fight to protect our lives we should do better fighting in our own back yard'. Mr Hull comments, 'The President and I were asking each other the same question in those fateful days, but we reached a different conclusion from Kennedy's. It seemed to us that we should do better to keep the fighting away from our own back yard. This we could do by helping Britain and France remain on their feet. Then came the question, exactly what could we do to help them? On the political side we had to bear in mind that although the American people were seeing ever more clearly where their interests lay in the European War there was still a strong isolationist sentiment in and out of Congress. Many of the isolations maintained that the United States could go peacefully on her way whoever won the war in Europe. On the material side stood the question: Exactly what war supplies could we sell Britain and France, and how quickly could we get them to the theatre of war?

'On one point the president and I had not the slightest doubt; namely that an Allied victory was essential to the security of the United States'.[5]

What Mr Hull did not mention and probably did not know was that Mr de Valera's organisation 'The Friends of Irish Neutrality' were marshalling communists, Bundists, fascists and honest isolationists to resist what the president and he regarded as essential to American security.

My report continued:

From letter to President Roosevelt continued

Thursday, May 16th, 1940

He (de Valera) is frightened by this situation but not prepared to cope with it. His interest even now, is in the foundation of an Institute for Advanced Studies. I like him and admire him but he is not the man for a war. He went to America while Collins was making the decisions (in Ireland). The trouble is he has no slogan except a United Ireland and that is not for the present. The IRA has the affirmative position and he is on the defensive as far as popular appeal is concerned.

I am spending the weekend (Sunday, May 19th) with Seán T. O'Kelly and the Nuncio at Granard's and I will find out if there is a chance of the church calling 'A Holy War' (it had been talked of), but that would mean abandonment of neutrality.

On May 17th, the Germans pushed deep into France.

On May 17th, came the long-awaited message from Belfast.

Commander Oscar Henderson RN DSO, as secretary to the governor general, wrote me that the duke and duchess of Abercorn would be glad to have me and my wife as their guests the night of May 22nd. On May 17th, I wrote thanking them and explaining that my wife was indisposed. (She refused to go.) But that I would come with pleasure and hoped to see Lord Craigavon also. To make it sure that there would be no misunderstanding I also wrote in my reply, 'I am, so to speak, *exploring* a situation in which my government is deeply interested and in no sense am an embassy from the South. However, if anything mutually helpful should be suggested it would be a pleasure to proffer assistance if requested'.

[5] Cordell Hull, *The memoirs of Cordell Hull* (2nd edn, London, 1948), 766.

My report to the president records that on May 18th, the day Brussels fell, I advised Mr de Valera of this as follows:

From letter to President Roosevelt

Saturday, May 18th, 1940

I told him I had made arrangement to see Craigavon next Wednesday, (May 22nd) and asked him if he had any line of compromise in mind to assure a measure of co-operation at least. *His suggestion was that Ulster join them in Neutrality and in return he would reaffirm publicly* their adherence and loyalty to external association with the British Commonwealth. He said that he got that expression and conception from Mr Wilson. I said that from a military viewpoint in the present crisis Britain could not afford to give up control of both sides of the Narrows of the Irish Channel: was he prepared to lease the necessary ports? This had not occurred to him. I asked him if he did not think that some concerted action with the North were possible, say a common examination of the situation by a committee of public safety. He said he thought not, that it would be easier to deal directly with Westminster. *I asked him if he did not think that the crisis was the time to make progress toward union, that a compromise now might produce results that would otherwise be impossible (to bring about) for years to come: assuming the Allies won.* If they did not win, Irish freedom was a vanished dream. He agreed in principle, but could devise no line of compromise. I fear that the common view of him is true; that he is incapable of compromise. He has got out on a limb and is lonely there, but does not know how to get back.

I did not put it in my letter to the president but I asked Mr de Valera at the time how the North, which was a belligerent, even if it wished to join the South, could by proclamation become neutral again. Obviously a truce and a separate peace treaty with Germany would be necessary. He said he thought not, that it could all be managed. It is this kind of fantastic day-dreaming by the man entrusted with the destiny of the Irish people which reveals his calibre as a statesman.

May 20th, Weygand[6] was put in command. The letter continued: 'We are lunching with the German minister on the 28th', and then was interrupted till after our return from Castle Forbes, when it went on:

[6] General Maxime Weygand (1867–1965), in May 1940 recalled from Syria to become French commander-in-chief.

From letter to President Roosevelt continued

Monday, May 20th, 1940

Had interesting talks on the situation with Seán T. O'Kelly and with Cosgrave, who was there Saturday night but left when O'Kelly came Sunday noon. He will not speak to either him or de Valera. You can be sure that neither the Government nor Opposition will do anything like stabbing Britain in the back but neither will they go farther than a beneficent neutrality unless the Germans attack.

I am going to Ulster tomorrow to see the powers that be there. It is also arranged that I am to call on the Cardinal first.[7] I talked to him on the telephone this morning and arranged it with the Nuncio, who was with us at Castle Forbes.

I have just sent a telegram asking to have reasons, spoken of as 'obvious', for not sending an American repatriation ship to either Cobh or Galway explained. There are objections to Bantry Bay as there are no satisfactory tenders and very limited accommodations.

Our consular force, which dealt with the embarkation problem, strongly recommended the use of Cobh, that is Queenstown, which was equipped with modern facilities for embarking passengers in a big ship and for watering her. Washington, however, in yielding on Bantry Bay insisted on Galway as second choice. Galway could be used only on certain tides and was able only to maintain the daily water usage of big ships but not to increase the supply. Later the president explained to me what the 'obvious reasons' were. He did not want an American ship mined or torpedoed on the way to Cobh in the Irish channel. He believed it more than possible that the Germans would sink our ship and then charge the British with the offence, all of which would have increased the political confusion in America. The letter went on:

From letter to President Roosevelt continued

Monday, May 20th, 1940

J.K. Davis, the US Consul, who evacuated Nanking and recently Warsaw, is on the job here (as Consul General) and doing it swell. I doubt if there are more than five or six hundred people from Ireland proper who will want to go or who will be able to, unless they are transported free.

[7] Cardinal Joseph MacRory, Archbishop of Armagh, 1861–1945.

The MacEntees (Minister for Commerce) are lunching with us today. Last night we had Desmond FitzGerald, an opposition Senator, and member of the Cosgrave Government. These little parties work out very well.

There was also a postscript:

At the Nuncio's an hour ago I had an interesting talk with Father Sylvester, rector of the Franciscans at Louvain. The story of his escape was about as bad as could be. They (the Germans) machine-gunned and bombed refugees systematically to add to the confusion. We hear this morning that the library at Louvain is burned again. '*Furor Teutonicus redivivus*'.

No word of Father Sylvester's experiences was permitted to appear in the Dublin newspapers. It was hard to realise that in a country that spoke our language, with people like so many we knew at home, there could be this general assent to the suppression of the most important news in the world; essentially for the reason that publication of it would work to create public opinion favourable to France and Britain. I made every effort through our embassy in London to obtain for Father Sylvester information as to his Franciscan College, probably without success.

While we were reporting Mr de Valera as gallantly condemning the aggression of Germany, an event occurred which should have aroused our suspicions if it did not alert us to the fact that he was double-crossing us, that his condemnation of Germany, like his protestations of undying gratitude to the United States, were not worth the idle breath that uttered them. Either on the Monday that I got back from Castle Forbes or on the following day, May 21st, a friend of Senator Frank MacDermot told me this curious story about the censorship.[8] Mr MacDermot was then writing a weekly letter of comment on Irish affairs for the London *Sunday Times*. (This is not a Sunday edition of *The Times* but a separate newspaper.)

Mr MacDermot had submitted his 'copy' for the issue of May 19th on the preceding Tuesday or Wednesday. His deadline was Thursday, May 16th. To his surprise the paragraphs devoted to praising Mr de Valera for his Galway utterances were excised. There was no explanation. Here was the Irish censorship under Mr Aiken banning on Wednesday

---

[8] Frank MacDermot, Irish senator, former TD of the Centre Party. Unsuccessfully contested in West Belfast as a nationalist in 1929. For his role in the debate on the Irish Constitution, see Angela Clifford, *The constitutional history of Éire/Ireland* (Belfast, 1985), 120–3.

what it had passed on Monday. Moreover, it was censoring the head of the Irish government.

We could not believe that it meant what it seemed to mean, but we noted, as time passed, that the Censor never again permitted reference to Mr de Valera's Galway speech. It was expunged from the record.

While we were digesting these perplexing facts the Dublin grapevine brought us the following: The German minister on that Sunday afternoon had been advised by telephone from Galway as to the de Valera pronouncement. He lost no time in lodging a protest. 'Friend Joe', had disappeared but Hempel got hold of Fred Boland. Then it appeared that next day Frank Aiken, 'Minister for the Coordination of Defensive Measures' upheld Hempel. He told de Valera that if that was to be his line toward Germany, he (Aiken) was through. Germany was sure to win the war. Why affront the traditional friend to pull out chestnuts for the traditional enemy? What Mr de Valera said to Mr Aiken, the grapevine did not say. At that time Dublin opinion regarded Mr Aiken as being useful to Mr de Valera in holding the 'left wingers', but as 'not very bright'.

What in fact had happened? We did not know until the captured German files became available. And then came out the story which if it had not been true would have been unbelievable. The truth was that de Valera's Galway speech condemning Germany was 'eyewash' intended to deceive the Allied world. No sooner had it been publicly delivered than it was secretly withdrawn and apologised for.

Let us suspend the narrative at this point and consider the evidence now available and the conclusions which it compels. Only by doing so can the reader appraise the measure of difference between what we were reporting to Washington, believing it to be true, and what actually was the truth.

Hempel begins the revelation in his telegram, No. 239, to Berlin, dated May 14th, 1940, supplementing telegram No. 234 sent on May 13th, the day on which the *Irish Press* printed de Valera's Galway speech. Up to a point Hempel undoubtedly was in de Valera's confidence. Up to a point they had a common interest in Irish neutrality. In Hempel's view the advantage to Germany of keeping the Allies out of the Irish ports outweighed the IRA alliance. He upheld this view in his reports to Berlin. He upheld de Valera as against what he called the 'Nationalists'. But Berlin was not yet convinced that Hempel was right. While ready to profit by Irish neutrality, the Wilhelmstrasse had not yet abandoned the IRA and their Uprising. The advice of the IRA agents in Berlin was certainly to the effect that de Valera had sold out to Chamberlain and was not to be trusted. Accordingly, the Artus plan was still on the agenda and involved the liquidation of Mr de Valera. Hempel was in a difficult position until he could 'sell' his conclusions to his chiefs. Therefore, in reporting to Berlin on 14th May 1940 he gives the Foreign Office the impression that he was protesting vigorously, while at the same time attempting to mollify Foreign Office indignation. In this purpose he could rely for assistance on the Irish chargé in Berlin who was avowedly Pro-German. He makes it clear at the outset that he had made a protest. His telegram No. 239 reads (italics mine):

The Minister in Eire to the Foreign Ministry

In answer to the protest, which in the absence of Walshe I made to Boland, he replied (without rejecting it) that Ireland was the only small (country) in Northern Europe with the exception of Sweden, which under difficult circumstances had so far been able to maintain neutrality, and which in view of the threatening danger would have to maintain (the) fundamental point of view of a small nation which would not want to be drawn into a war of the great powers.

Further de Valera in his unprepared speech (said Boland) had not mentioned Germany and had not wanted to commit himself on the question of guilt. In addition he had established extensive and good political connections with small Northern nations as had been made known to him (Hempel) in 'sympathetic understanding'.

In reply (said Hempel) I emphasised our protests to Belgium and Holland for their non-neutral status. Boland indicated that he would talk to de Valera himself, presumably as suggested by de Valera since Boland had advised de Valera already on Sunday (after his return from Galway) in view of my request to talk to him at an early date in regard to the utterance referred to, that a protest could be expected. I may file a supplementary report after their discussion. Boland presumably will also inform Warnock (Irish Charge d'Affaires in Berlin). I gained the impression that they consider it *very important* not to let any unfavourable opinion come up with us in regard to Irish Neutrality.

HEMPEL

In Berlin's telegram of May 16th, referring to Dublin's telegrams No. 230 of May 10th and No. 234 of May 13th, Under-Secretary Weiszäcker, acting for Ribbentrop, instructed Hempel (italics mine):

If it has not been done already please make serious representations to Walshe against statements by de Valera and to Prime Minister in discussion planned with him and submit approximately the following:

The protest speech made by the Prime Minister (de Valera) would have to be rejected by us unequivocally, and we would have to express our great surprise since he comes from a country which for centuries has suffered under the yoke of our enemies. The weighty reasons for our justified interference in Belgium and Holland have been set forth in our memorandum made available to the whole world for publication.

Also that we regret that the Irish Government has made itself less familiar with our memorandum than with the utterances of enemy propaganda and has become its tool.

(*The following crossed out*) In view of such attitude it would be made difficult for us to maintain in future our traditional community of feelings for Ireland.

Note ✗ It (The German Foreign Office) already furnished incontestable proof of English and French intentions to attack the Ruhr District through Belgium and Holland as well as complicity of both countries. Additional irrefutable proofs which in the meantime fell into the hands of German troops will be published in the near future.

Between the receipt of these instructions, sent on May 16th and May 21st, Mr Walshe had apparently apologised in Dublin and had instructed Mr Warnock, Irish attaché in Berlin, to apologise there also. A dispatch to Hempel, signed by Under-Secretary Woermann, dated May 21st, informs him that Warnock had apologised and apparently not with the resentful dignity of a diplomat under compulsion (italics mine):

No. 291
_____

91/100204

MEMORANDUM BY THE DIRECTOR OF THE POLITICAL DEPARTMENT

Berlin, May 21, 1940

I mentioned to the Eirean Charge d'Affaires today the protest which our minister in Dublin had made (Telegram No. 239 from Dublin) respecting the speech of de Valera. Mr Warnock had already been informed by his government and *expressed himself in a similar apologetic manner as the Deputy of the Eirean Foreign Minister (Walshe) had to our Minister.* (in Dublin.)

The Chargé d'Affaires (Mr Warnock) added the remark that Eire wished to maintain neutrality toward all powers and said *personally* that Eire in the last war against Britain, *had started the attack too early.* This mistake would not be repeated. In view of the German successes, (Woermann observed) the question, however, was whether Eire *would not come in too late.*

WOERMANN

What Hempel's telegram to Berlin of May 10th said, we do not know. May 10th was the day Germany attacked the Low Countries and it may well have reported merely the conventional notification to the Irish government of the 'defensive' operation.

But Woermann's telegram to Hempel, dated May 21st, reporting Warnock's apology, indicates that the apology was made in an atmosphere of friendliness and mutual understanding. Otherwise Warnock could not have ventured his personal view that in the last war against Britain Ireland had started the attack too early, thus prompting the rejoinder that in view of German successes the question was, in this present war would not Éire come in too late? Obviously it was a good-tempered exchange between officials who on the basic question, the defeat of Britain, were in agreement. Presumably Mr Warnock was only expressing the view of his superiors in Dublin. I had recently told Mr de Valera that personally I was not neutral but at the time I knew that my president was as convinced as I that Hitler menaced American vital interest.

One thing is certain. No responsible statesman without good reason makes a major pronouncement of policy on a Sunday, only to withdraw it on Monday. Yet this is what Mr de Valera did. Either he did it willingly, pursuant to an undisclosed design, or he did it under compulsion. As of May 12th and 13th, 1940, there was nothing to suggest compulsion in the military situation. The Allied outlook in the Low Countries was bad, but Germany was not in a position to force Eamon de Valera to eat brave words still fresh in his mouth. Debacle followed swiftly but on May 13th the French armies were undefeated, the Maginot Line was intact. A powerful British expeditionary force was in France and the British navy still ruled the seas. The United States whose belated entry into the First World War had proved the deciding factor, was still an ostensible neutral but the utterances of the Roosevelt administration made it clear that American opinion strongly condemned Hitler's Germany. Hitler at best could expect no aid from America, and at worst, what in fact he got. Therefore, it is reasonable to believe that if the German minister had threatened Mr de Valera, Mr de Valera would have told him to go to hell and joined up with the English.

Unless Mr Aiken was the actual power in the Fianna Fáil government, which I never heard anyone suggest, he was in no position to tell his chief that he must withdraw the Galway speech and apologise for it. Mr de Valera had defied Arthur Griffith, Kevin O'Higgins, even Michael Collins. No politician had ever given him orders. The powerful Irish leaders in the United States had tried it in 1920 and failed. Any kind of pressure roused his anger and invoked reliance on what he called 'Our Christian Fatalism'. His legend as the 'Irish Idealist' rested on the assumption that he always did the *right* thing regardless of consequences. His supporters constantly repeated the story of his doing *the right thing* in Geneva where he presided over the League during the Abyssinian crisis and advocated sanctions against Italy.

Equally unaccountable on the theory of compulsion was the spirit of sympathetic understanding, 'Umdeckung Sympathie', existing between the German mission in Dublin and the Irish ministry of external affairs. Joe Walshe was hypersensitive to the suggestion of pressure. He would get red and explode like a firework. But as I personally knew, at this time he and the Germans were on affectionate terms.

If it was not pressure which produced the apology it must have been design. The evidence indicates that Mr de Valera at this time was walking not one tight rope but two. He believed that Germans would win the war. He wanted Northern Ireland without strings. In payment he had secretly offered an Irish neutrality which would bar the Allies from the Irish ports, also Irish influence in America to prevent American intervention in the war. He could not avow this position because four families out of five in Greater Dublin cooked with gas. Ireland had no gas coal. Dublin was dependent on England for gas coal as for gasoline and fuel oils, for binder twine, for consumer goods. It was necessary that London regard him as a secret ally and keep him supplied. There were other cogent reasons for being regarded by London as a friend. If the Artus plan were put into execution he would have to call in the English troops in Northern Ireland to save his government from being liquidated. Hempel was doing his best to block Artus, but he had not yet persuaded Berlin to abandon it. The situation was therefore what diplomats call 'fluid'. Anything might happen. As May began Mr de Valera certainly knew about Artus and Hempel could not reassure him. By May 6th he knew that Germany had dropped a parachute agent near Dublin the night before. When therefore on May 10th Germany entered Belgium and Holland there was ample reason to expect a German landing and an IRA Uprising. If such a thing happened Hempel could do him no good. He would have to turn to Westminster. When therefore on May 10th Sir John Maffey gave him the news from the Continent and urged him to take a stand he saw his opportunity and grasped it. By condemning Germany he could receive London, thus insuring supply and armed help in the event of Artus. It is unlikely that he confided this thought to Hempel, but he must have explained to him that this was a case for, according to Britain, that 'certain (special) treatment' in order to get supply. It was obviously in the German interest that London suspect nothing as to the 'Dublin-Berlin Axis'. How could he deceive London better than by condemning Germany? How could Berlin better further German interest than by sanctioning the deception? It was a '*ruse de guerre*' and he was ready to make full apology for the record to satisfy German 'face'.

No other explanation fits the known facts and as a 'plan' it is no more fantastic than other of Mr de Valera's policy conceptions. Moreover if he had not misjudged the power of his influence in the United States to keep America out of the war, if Germany had not lost the war instead of winning it, and if the German Foreign Office files had not fallen into Allied hands, he might well have 'got away with it'.

Mr Warnock came into the American news again when he was withdrawing his mission from Berlin to Switzerland as the war ended. Not far from the Swiss border he posted a notice on the great house of a German prince that the property was under the protection of the Irish government, which was in occupation of the premises for diplomatic purposes. The area was in the American zone, and the American commander who had expected to use the schloss for headquarters was vexed when he had to make do with sheds and pig pens.

An interesting question is what, if any, was the relation between the Galway speech incident and Mr de Valera's request on May 16th that I feel out the president on the possibility of guaranteeing Irish neutrality. Was it a precautionary measure, in case Berlin let him down? Or was it the outcome of conspiracy with Hempel? If the United States undertook to keep the British out of the Irish ports for Hitler, the Wilhelmstrasse boys would have had a laugh.

Whatever Berlin may have had in mind Hempel never weakened in his support of de Valera as against the IRA.

Mr de Valera's conviction that Hitler would win the war was stupid in view of the opportunities he enjoyed for obtaining authoritative information as to what was going on in the United States. It was doubtless due to the fact that he knew few if any *Americans*, only 'Irish in America'. As a matter of fact he himself never told me that Hitler would win, though he scoffed at the suggestion that the United States would become involved. But his deputy Joe Walshe told me. Further, Mr Walshe was confident that at the worst, Hitler would not lose. Cardinal MacRory told me that Hitler would win. Count Plunkett, the patriarch of the IRA, expressed the same opinion. We know from the German papers that one of Mr de Valera's generals was collaborating with Hempel. Belief in German victory was in the Dublin air. At the end of the war a former Lord Mayor of Dublin, 'Paddy' Doyle, a very 'decent' man, said to me 'You know, at the beginning we were all sure Germany was going to win'.

One of the strangest things that ever happened in Ireland was that this secret apology story never leaked out. In one of my early talks with Mr de Valera I had asked him if he had had secret defence talks with the British General Staff. He said no because in Ireland everybody would know the secret. He referred to the story current in Dublin about the Royal Commission, appointed in the 'old days' to inquire into the state of Ireland. After three years it submitted its report as follows:

1. Everything in Ireland is secret.
2. Everybody knows the secret.
3. The best whiskey has never left Ireland.

Not only was the apology for the Galway speech kept secret but so was the definite offer which the British government made de Valera six weeks later, which would have ended Partition. If the opposition leaders, especially James Dillon, had known of these things the course of Irish history would in all likelihood have been different, and happier. They would have told the people.

CHAPTER VII

MAY 22ND-31ST

In spite of the discouraging talk with Mr de Valera on May 16th, regarding a common defence with the North, I set out for Belfast on May 22nd with a considerable degree of confidence. I interpreted what he had said about the necessity of Ulster 'becoming neutral' if she were to join with Éire as 'cow-trading talk'. Knowing nothing of the secret apology for the Galway speech, his condemnation of Germany had convinced me that he appreciated the menace of Hitler's national socialist dictatorship to free institutions everywhere. I was convinced that he was waiting on the course of events for the opportune moment to take appropriate action with those who were resisting the aggressor. Moreover, I could not believe that an intelligent man would pass by this opportunity to achieve the unity of Ireland which he proclaimed as his great aim. And I had no suspicion that he might be counting on German victory to achieve it.

Moreover, while opportunity was knocking at de Valera's door, the pressure of impending calamity was knocking at Lord Craigavon's. Only four days before, Mr Churchill had broadcast his memorable words, 'The hour is grave but the cause is far from lost'. For the North I believed it was to be an hour for sacrifice. Craigavon was a 'big' man and capable of sacrifice.

Finally, there were two inescapable facts which I believed would influence Mr de Valera if he really wanted to end Partition: one was the unifying influence of common danger and comradeship in arms, the other was the circumstance that he had it wholly within his own power to avail himself of this unifying influence, and that clearly in the interest of Éire's survival. No politician ever had a stronger case with which to mould public opinion. All this, of course, assumed that he was not secretly on the German side.

Immediately after lunch, therefore, on May 22nd I set out by motor car for Armagh where I left cards on Cardinal MacRory.[1] I had been advised by telephone that he would not be at home but that he would welcome my courtesy call. From Armagh we went on to government House at Hillsborough some ten miles south of Belfast. This was a noble, Georgian mansion set in a walled demesne. It overlooked a picturesque lake. The Abercorns proved exceptionally sympathetic and friendly but Lord Craigavon, whom I had come to see, had unexpectedly flown to London. As Mr Churchill had said, 'the hour was grave'. This was at once a disappointment and a factor of encouragement. In London he would learn how grave the situation was and how great the need for sacrifice of his preferences.

The duke made his apologies and said that the Right Hon. John M. Andrews, Minister for Finance, was dining with them together with other members of the Cabinet. The governor general's position made him avoid politics but he was naturally a strong loyalist and the duchess an exceptionally capable, outspoken woman. At tea she told me I knew nothing of the 'racial differences' which made division of the island a logical and necessary arrangement. It was refreshing to be told things which I did not want to hear. In Dublin they tell you only what you want to hear.

I told her that from the American viewpoint such ideas were uncivilised, that she must believe in the 'melting pot' instead of a parochial nationalism. She was a formidable debater but proved a staunch friend to the United States when our troops arrived in Northern Ireland. Her friendship once given never weakened or 'was withdrawn'.

In the absence of his chief, Mr Andrews could make no commitments nor even entertain the possibility of their being made. He was obviously sincere and motivated by what I have since come to suspect was the same persecution complex that affects many of Éire's separatists. Like them he seemed more apprehensive of his Irish opponents than of Hitler. He

---

[1] Cardinal Joseph McRory, Archbishop of Armagh (1861–1945), born Ballygawley, Co Tyrone, educated Armagh and Maynooth. Professor Oscott College Birmingham 1887–9, Maynooth 1889–1915, Bishop of Down and Connor 1915–28. Supporter of Michael Collins but opposed Collins's decision to call off republican boycott of Belfast goods in January 1922. An opponent of Dublin recognition of Northern Ireland. Refused to take in person an honorary degree offered by Queen's University Belfast. In 1931 he declared that the Protestant Church in Ireland was 'not even a part of the Church of Christ'. Professor J.J. Lee, drawing from the German archives, shows that the Germans believed in 1940 that McRory was 'in favour of possible German action to end partition', *Ireland 1912–85: politics and society* (Cambridge, 1989), 267.

repeated the duchess's statement that the people of Ulster were of a different racial stock, and like her insisted that they wished to continue as part of England. If self-determination were to be invoked he was in a strong position.

I then took up (with Mr Andrews and his colleagues) the question of some emergency co-operation with the South but at that time got no response. Their position was, 'We are part of Britain. What happens south of the border is no affair of ours'.

I then said, 'You are like a man in the bow of a boat. In the stern is another man and there is a hole in the middle of the boat. You say to the man in the stern, that is your hole. It is no concern of mine. Meanwhile the boat is sinking'.

I thought highly of the British admiral king who is on duty in Belfast. (He gave me some helpful data on the fifth columnist methods in Holland and Belgium.) Personally I liked the Northern ministers very much and sympathised with their feelings only I doubt if this is a time for feelings.

This government (Éire) which has been talking against them for ten years had no idea that the Ulster people had any feelings to hurt. They don't realise what they have built up on top of antipathies already there.

On the drive back to Dublin I asked James Murphy, the legation chauffeur and a Catholic, if he had enjoyed his visit. He said he had been treated 'wonderful, room with fire, seated at the right hand of the butler at meals but he could not understand why the secret service detective had locked him in his room when he went to bed. I asked had he spoken about it. 'I did', he said, 'the next morning. They said, "Why do you all down there, want to come up here and murder us all in our beds?" and I said, "It's the other way around. We are terrified of you coming down with the British army and navy"'.

There it was, in the proverbial nutshell, ignorance of each other and a handful of trouble-makers on each side preventing knowledge and fomenting hostility. The spirit of Sinn Féin worked on both sides of the border.

I asked James Murphy had he noticed any difference as we crossed the border. He said he had. It was distinctly noticeable to me. It struck me as much the same difference that before World War One we used to note in crossing the state line from South to North Carolina. North of the Irish border the towns seemed busier and more prosperous though perhaps even uglier. They were like the stark, forbidding, busy towns of Scotland. The farming seemed tidier and more energetic but to an

American these hardly seemed to warrant establishing North and South as 'foreign' to each other. If Germans, Irish, Scandinavians, Italians, Greeks, Poles, Jews, Negroes, could combine with the British colonial stock to form the American people, surely the Scots-Irish, originally Irish Gaels, could unite with the Southern Irish who were a mixture of prehistoric peoples, together with Gaels, Danes, Normans and British. It was the common occupation of a strategic region, considerations of common defence and common economic interests that inevitably make a common ideology and hence a nation. The duchess's reasons against federating with the South seemed no better than Mr de Valera's against federating with England, Scotland and Wales.

On arriving back in Dublin (May 23rd) I immediately arranged an appointment with Mr de Valera. I told him that Craigavon was in London but as he doubtless anticipated the chances for a co-operative arrangement with the North did not seem good. I said that it put him on the spot as well as the North.

'Well', he said, 'there are a *hundred thousand British troops up there*', the implication being that if the Germans attacked Éire, he would ask them down.

I replied, 'There are less than one division, mostly green troops, recruits in training, probably not more than 8,500 of all ranks. Anyone with a bicycle and a sheep counter can go about and verify this for himself'.

'Good God!' he said, 'I had no idea of that'.

This showed what his military intelligence was. The menace of an IRA Uprising without formidable German help had never frightened him while, as he believed, there was a strong force of British troops over the border which he could summon to his aid. The discovery that there were no such troops in the North stirred him to immediate action.

On May 23rd, when de Valera talked to me about the hundred thousand British troops in Northern Ireland which he could summon if the Artus plan were put in operation, Hempel telegraphed to Berlin a survey of the Irish situation and a skilful build-up of de Valera as against the IRA. Hempel said truly that de Valera's main objective was getting Northern Ireland, but he refrained from telling Berlin that de Valera did not want it till the end of the war as payment for Irish neutrality. He did not want an IRA insurrection either with or without the help of German troops. Hempel obviously understood the situation but was obliged to support de Valera by indirection. Various agencies in the German government favoured the Artus plan and backed the IRA. In consequence Hempel had to sell the idea that Irish neutrality, which involved no risk and which could be violated at any time if desirable, was the best policy for Germany. Here is the text (italics mine):

No. 310

91/100208–9

The Minister in Eire to the Foreign Ministry

Telegram

Secret   Dublin, May 23, 1940
No. 261 of May 23   Received May 24—3.05 p.m.

The feeling here under the influence of our march into Belgium-Holland, apart from expressly nationalistic Eirean elements is noticeably worse at present, especially in Church circles, which without this have been strongly influenced against Germany by the recent attitude of the Pope, at least amongst the higher clergy. The impact of our victories has (group mutilated), as far as I could observe, given Eirean nationalism up to the present no real impetus. (Hempel usually refers to the IRA as the 'Nationalists'.)

I have found no indication of any imminent British attack on Eire. I assume that the serious difficulties expected here in the case of an attack and the political reaction in the USA are particularly feared by Britain at present, and that therefore only in an emergency, e.g. suspicion of being forestalled by Germany, would she attack.

De Valera, in my judgement is still the only recognised political leader of great stature who has the nationals firmly in hand. He will maintain the line of friendly understanding with Britain as far as ever possible on account of *geographical and economic dependence which will continue even on Britain's defeat,* as well as his democratic principles, even in face of the threatening danger of Eire becoming involved in war. Voluntary political concessions which would violate neutrality have not been likely up to the present. In the case of an attack by Britain, de Valera would indeed hardly be able to do other than call on national unity to offer resistance the strength of which would be largely determined by the strength of the reaction in Eirean nationalism.

On the other hand he would not call on the hitherto restricted circles of Eirean nationalism who hope for German assistance, but would rather attempt to localise the conflict and set all wheels in motion in the USA. Wide circles of people, and particularly the Church would support him in this resistance. The danger of internal disturbances on the part of the I(rish) R(epublican) A(rmy), which might obtain a large increase in members, would not be sufficient against the strong resistance of de Valera.

Continuation follows.

HEMPEL

No. 310

91/100211–12

The Minister in Eire to the Foreign Ministry

Telegram

URGENT   Dublin, May 25, 1940

Continuation of No. 261 of May 23

Received May 25—11.30 a.m.

Any German assistance, especially simultaneous proclamation of the liberation of Northern Ireland, on which in itself there is, in my opinion, *no German interest* would as a German war aim, probably give the anti-British national movement (IRA) a powerful impetus.

At the present time the possibility of German intervention in Eire before Britain intervenes is widely discussed here. Such action would in my opinion and if *necessary* after the best political-diplomatic preparations, meet with strong resistance as de Valera would with spontaneous (group missing) organise wide masses of the people. I believe that he would then, supported by automatically forthcoming British assistance, proceed ruthlessly against the opposing radical nationalists. I would further expect, in such a case, strong reaction in USA including the majority of the Irish element there.

In the present situation, we must, in my opinion, bear in mind the possibility that de Valera, exploiting Britain's dangerous position, will take up again more strongly the realisation of his main aim, namely the return of Northern Ireland. He has been working in the USA for a long time for support to this end. Pressure on Britain might be considered in the first place on the line that he pointed out to Britain that there was again a new danger in Eire being involved in war as long as no decisive step has been taken in the Northern Ireland question. I think that it is conceivable to interest the French Government. Any successes would greatly strengthen de Valera's position in the case of future difficulties, and could strongly, and perhaps decisively, influence conditions in Britain's favour and probably bring Britain political advantage in the USA who perhaps have a hand in the game.

I shall report again if there are concrete signs of such a development. Up to the present there are only a few facts which call for increased attention.

In the Eirean Army, which is partly made up of elements in close contact with the I(rish) R(epublican) A(rmy)—it is said especially amongst the volunteers—that feelings are clearly divided. I recently heard from a reliable source that the Army, together with the nationalist population, would be prepared to carry on strong resistance in the form of guerrilla warfare against a British attack. I assume at the same time, however, especially in the case of any intervention by Germany before Britain, that, apart from *sections of the volunteers* they would be on the whole, a reliable tool in the hand of the Government and would obey their orders.

HEMPEL

Hempel's reference to 'interesting the French government', seems to be a warning to Berlin that de Valera might get the French government to advise England to give him Northern Ireland in return for the ports and a common defence. By the time England acutely needed the ports, however, France had ceased to be a factor.

Hempel's reference to de Valera's activities in the United States is interesting but unclear. Hempel evidently accepted de Valera's belief that Irish-American politicians controlled American policy as regards supporting the Allies.

On May 24th the answer to Mr de Valera's inquiry about an American guarantee came from Secretary Hull. I at once called on Mr de Valera and read him a paraphrase of the telegram. It regretted that the American government would be unable to take the requested action, although anxious to assist Ireland in any way possible. Such action would constitute a departure from traditional American policy and likely lead to confusion and misunderstanding not only in Europe but in the United

States. I was further instructed to explain that Ireland held a very special position in the hearts of the American people and that the secretary of state hoped and prayed that Ireland would be spared from the tragic conflagration.

Mr de Valera then stated that he had hoped that in 1922 the United States might have joined with other powers to guarantee the neutrality of Ireland. I told him that I thought that no United States Senate at that time would have approved such a measure. He said the British had probably blocked it.

He made no mention of the fact that in 1922 he was leading an armed rebellion against the newly established Irish government.

It is possible that we missed an opportunity in refusing Mr de Valera's request. We might have offered him such a mutual defence pact as we were shortly to conclude with Canada. This would have silenced the opposition of Senator David Walsh of Massachusetts and his Anglophobe followers to the administration's defence measures, and after Pearl Harbor it would have automatically provided us with Éire bases, but in view of Mr de Valera's understanding with Hempel it is very doubtful if he would have accepted any agreement that implied reciprocal obligations.

When Mr de Valera came to power in 1932 he had accepted the Cosgrave defence organisation. This called for a standing army of five thousand. There was no navy. Such an army, in Mr Cosgrave's opinion, was large enough to crush any new de Valera insurrection. It was not large enough to burden the taxpayers. For those who enjoyed self-deception it was a token of Irish sovereignty and power. Cosgrave, who was a realist, relied upon England for protection. De Valera, while denying dependence on England, also relied on her for defence.

In 1937–8 he had promised Chamberlain that Éire would never allow her territory to be used as a base for attack on England. This implied either the power to make the promise good or co-operation with England or both. When the war began, however, he refused co-operation yet for over a year did nothing to increase Irish defensive power, which was negligible. As he knew, the IRA had declared themselves an ally of Germany in January 1939. In the early spring of 1940 they raided the Fort Arsenal in Phoenix Park. It was such a raid as they made on Omagh in Northern Ireland in 1954, and in 1955 on various military depots in England. There was however one essential and disquieting difference: Phoenix Park was an 'inside job'. It proved that there were IRA members and German sympathisers in the Irish army. No one in the army knew certainly where his fellows stood. The result was demoralisation. Moreover the army was short in numbers, lacking in material and slack in discipline. The army knew it was ineffective. It had no combat planes. It had no modern arms. There were a few batteries of obsolescent field guns, a few obsolete armoured cars, practically no machine guns, no anti-aircraft artillery, no tanks, few land mines. There were hardly enough old rifles and not enough ammunition for one day's general engagement. But even after the Fort Arsenal raid de Valera did nothing. The Chief of Staff, General Brennan, finished out his term and was succeeded by General McKenna.

On May 6th, 1940, de Valera knew that Germany had dropped the spy Goertz by parachute the day before. He knew that he was at large and protected by the IRA. From the time the IRA knew of the Artus plan, Mr de Valera must have known of it and the presence of Goertz in Ireland must have meant to him that the plan was shortly to be implemented.

His design therefore was to strengthen his position with the British by tricking them with the Galway speech, secretly withdrawn, and by tricking Hempel with the suggestion that it served the German interest to deceive the British. In the event of Artus he relied on inviting down the British troops in Ulster. And then by chance I had let drop that there were less than a division of British troops in the North, and he had said, 'My God! I thought there were a hundred thousand'. That was on May 23rd. On May 24th I communicated to him the American refusal to guarantee Irish neutrality.

Then came the alarming realisation that having tricked both 'friends' he had only himself to rely on. And on May 27th he launched his grandiose 'defence programme'. He was a quick worker when de Valera's interests were at stake. This called for a political party truce and united defence measures under his leadership and control. He refused to agree to a national government but set up a Defence Council comprised of members of the three important parties.

The military programme provided for a regular army of fifty thousand, that is two divisions, an armed 'Local Defence Force' or militia and an unarmed 'Local Security Force'. This latter was designed to establish a nationwide intelligence service similar to that improvised by the Sinn Féiners during the Black and Tan fighting.

The arms-bearing manpower of Éire at this time was between two hundred and fifty and three hundred thousand. Of this something over two hundred thousand were enrolled in one of the new service categories. About forty-five thousand served in the British services, representing roughly the unionist Protestant population and their sympathisers. These figures invalidate the post-war Sinn Féin propaganda claim that one hundred and sixty-five thousand Southern Irishmen fought under British colours.

In May 1940 Mr de Valera had only the odds and ends of obsolescent armament already in the army depots. He had not yet even received the promise of the twenty thousand rifles which President Roosevelt was shortly to allocate to him. He had only the prospect of what the English government might be able and deem prudent to allow him. Since to all intents and purposes he was engaged in a conspiracy to destroy England, his confidence in a British arms supply could not have been great. What the Germans may have promised him we do not know. It is unlikely that they promised him anything since the IRA as allies had first call on German supply. Having an army without arms, however, seemed not to trouble him except as the inability to obtain arms impaired his prestige.

It soon became apparent that the de Valera defence programme was not a defence programme but a political enterprise. It was designed to tie the hands of his political opposition, to control the military manpower of the nation and by identifying neutrality with independence to pull the rug from under the IRA. All these things it did effectively.

With the entire arms-bearing manpower of Ireland under his supervision, de Valera soon ceased to take the Defence Council into his confidence and it became a rubber stamp for his decisions. A few Irishmen saw the fraud in this. But they were few and as a rule they were not politicians. One of the few was the late Desmond FitzGerald. He lunched with us about this time. He was a gifted young man of enormous charm. He was generous, brave, gay, erudite, brilliant. Moreover he was intellectually honest. He had been one of the young idealist leaders in Sinn Féin. He had been minister for defence in the first republican regime. Later he retired from politics but was still in the Irish Senate. I asked him how Mr de Valera's recruiting was getting on.

'Not well', he said. 'The Irish people are not unintelligent and their religion forbids suicide. If there is any landing of foreign troops, those who are not lunatic will hide their rifles in the thatch and be discovered digging as peaceful peasants'.

At this time I differed with him about Mr de Valera. He said that he knew him well. He had been in the same English jail with him. When they exercised, he was chained to the same iron bar. I asked him, 'Did you not come to have a great affection and admiration for him?'

He said, 'No, every time I saw him I liked him less'.

Even without the German papers, Desmond FitzGerald and some others saw that the defence programme was make-believe. But they could do nothing about it. Under the Emergency Powers legislation the government could jail people for such views. Although neutral and at peace, Éire was a police state.

Once Mr de Valera's great defence programme was launched, public interest in it waned. During the initial period there was feverish government activity. They planted railway ties in Phoenix Park to prevent airplane landings. They issued orders to take down signposts. They erected road blocks.

Six months later some counties had still ignored the order about the sign posts. As for the road blocks, I saw one concrete post pushed down by the mudguard of a light touring car. It had been set less than a foot in the road bed. Like the rest it was make-believe.

Government speakers began to explain the defence policy and recruit the new forces. Probably the ablest of these 'keynote' speeches and the one which most effectually set forth the government's plan was that which Dr James Ryan, minister for Agriculture, delivered to his Wexford constituents.[2]

Dr Ryan began by saying that Éire was faced by perhaps the most serious situation which had arisen in their time. Great Powers were in a death struggle for supremacy and as a consequence the rights of small nations and neutrals were not likely to be respected (italics mine):

> This country may be looked upon by one of the belligerents as a good point from which to attack the other. It may be looked upon by the other as a menace for that reason. You will see therefore that the danger of invasion is real and immediate. If an invader were to come in for a limited time, it might be tolerable. But that is not likely. *A vital position* during war would be equally important to the victors when peace comes.

It is interesting to note that Dr Ryan very honestly stressed the strategic position and importance of Éire in the world situation, as did Mr de Valera in his request for an American guarantee. However, when Washington later pointed out this fact in its proposals for co-operation, the Irish government always brushed the point aside.

The policy expounded by Dr Ryan was unquestionably trickery, but was astute. To say to England and Germany, 'if the coat of the aggressor fits put it on', was too neat a half-truth not to be applauded.

[2] James Ryan (1891–1970), doctor and businessman, senior Fianna Fáil politician and Cabinet minister.

A telling paragraph was, 'Beware of the false patriot who tells you that such a foreign power will come as a friend and not as a foe. A friend does not break into your home at night. He waits until he is invited'.

As a matter of fact if a 'home' is in danger of fire, flood or violence and the inmates are asleep, to break in is exactly what a friend does. But there was no political group in Éire to expose Dr Ryan's sophistry. The extremist elements asserted that England was a more dangerous enemy than Germany. One of them said to me, 'In 1649 the Protestant Cromwell massacred thirty-five hundred Catholic men, women and children in Ulster'. That was to prove the British menace. Few intelligent Irish people still were citing Cromwell in political argument, but almost everybody enjoyed Dr Ryan putting a 'fast one' over on the 'traditional enemy'.

No political group echoed the hope which Mr de Valera had shortly before expressed to Neville Chamberlain of a friendship which would make possible whole-hearted co-operation in '*all matters of common interest*', of which defence and trade were the most important.

One reason for the popular approval of the de Valera defence policy as expounded by Dr Ryan was the general recognition of what it really meant. The Irish masses grasped the point that Irish neutrality in depriving England of the ports was in the German interest. They could thus enjoy weakening the 'traditional enemy' without incurring the danger of reprisal. It was their 'secret weapon'. Thus he created his backfire against the IRA.

On the other hand if England should unexpectedly win, he would not have to make explanations. England was used to 'Irish politics'. Moreover as long as the United States was neutral, Irish neutrality was respectable.

In the dark days of May and June 1940, having no suspicion of Mr de Valera's trickery, I was a believer in the probability of a German attack in conjunction with an IRA Uprising. If Hitler could hold Ireland for four months and close the Irish channel at the Narrows, hunger would have defeated England. I was anxious to help in any measure which would work for the safety of Éire, for a common island defence, for obtaining arms from the USA and for helping Irish recruiting and training.

On May 28th, we lunched with the German minister, Herr Hempel. This was fifteen days after Mr de Valera had condemned German aggression in his Galway speech. It was one day after the Irish government had launched its defence programme, aimed at 'any aggressor'. At the lunch party there was no mention of either subject.

We had gone to lunch with the Germans reluctantly as an official duty. My wife and I both felt strongly about the unprovoked invasion of the Low Countries. I had served in our army in France during the First World War and I knew what German invasion meant to the invaded. No high official serving a regime which committed such crimes, as Hitler committed against the Jews, could pretend that he had no personal responsibility for them.

The Hempels had the manners of the 'great world' and entertained with grace and courtesy. Their first secretary, Herr Thomsen, however, was an outsized, boorish Prussian with a wife to match. They might have been cinema types for Gestapo officials. On this occasion they were on their good behaviour but it was obvious that the success of German arms had intensified their arrogance.

Everything was well done and for weather we had an Irish 'pet day'. The glassed loggia where cocktails were served was flooded with sunshine and we looked out upon a charming garden in bloom. The Hempel children appeared for a few minutes before lunch and made their manners to the guests. What struck us especially was that they addressed Mr Walshe as 'Uncle Joe', indicating his status as a family friend. He had a charming way with children though he had none. He had been educated for the Jesuit Priesthood and though he never took final vows neither did he ever marry. Another interesting thing was that Hempel had seated Mr Walshe on Madame Hempel's right, though according to Éire protocol he was a civil servant and ranked after all foreign diplomats. This must have been a calculated affront to the United States and a compliment to the Éire government though two weeks before it had condemned the invasion of Belgium.

It confirmed the revelation of the German dispatches that the 'condemnation', like the secret apology, had been what the Irish call 'cod' and arranged for purposes of deception. As far as Éire was concerned that German lunch party was the climax of 'Umdeckung Sympathie' for it was not long before this beautiful friendship was to be put under strain. Ribbentrop, like the Irish Idealist, was walking two tight ropes.

I confess it with shame, but it was not for several days after the event that I realised that I and my country had been 'insulted'. At the same time I grasped the reason for Joe's embarrassment when Fräu Hempel herded him around to her right. At the moment I had been absorbed in relief that my wife on Hempel's right appeared to be chatting happily with him.

On that May 28th, Mr Reynaud broadcast from Paris his comment on the Belgian King's surrender. He said:

It is this Belgian army which has suddenly capitulated, without conditions *en rase campagne*, on the order of its King, without warning his comrades, France and Britain, opening the Dunkirk road to the German divisions.

Thus in the middle of a battle, King Leopold III of Belgium without warning General Blanchard, without a look, without a word for the British and French soldiers who at his agonised appeal, had come to the rescue of his country, King Leopold III of Belgium threw down his arms.

This is an event without precedent in history.

It drew no comment from Mr de Valera's newspaper.

The tempo of catastrophe in France continued to quicken, with repercussions in Dublin. On May 31st I wrote the president:

From letter to President Roosevelt

Friday, May 31st, 1940

Things are getting pretty tough. I have put most of the latest phase of things in two dispatches to the Secretary. The important thing, however, of which I dare not write except most confidentially is the possibility of events shaping so that the British have to occupy Berehaven to combat the submarine menace when it starts up again. After the *Roosevelt* comes in tomorrow and on the assumption, which is fair, that I have received instructions from the Secretary of State, I am going to ask to be informed what the Irish government will do in the event that due to submarine warfare Britain is obliged to cancel Irish allotments of coal, grain, petrol, and other staples that have been very generously made thus far. Also that in the event of an appeal to the good faith shown by the British two years ago in giving up the ports their understanding that in the event of danger, assistance would be rendered, what they (the Irish government) intends to do. If you could hit on a message it would be a great help. If the Irish-American Church could send some message that appealed to Ireland to aid Democracy it would be a great help.

Washington never authorised us to make the inquiry in question and it was never made.

My report to the president continued: 'I have been talking very intimately with James Dillon, Cosgrave's lieutenant who is on the new National Council of Safety'.

Mr Dillon was deeply concerned for his country's safety. He had no suspicion of the secret apology for the Galway speech. Like us he believed that Mr de Valera was honestly taking measures against German aggression and not merely against the IRA. He discussed with me various expedients for obtaining American arms, not driblets for political ends, but an armament adequate for realistic defence. As deputy leader of Fine Gael he was ready to back Mr de Valera in any such programme. But he had no illusions as to Éire's ability to defend herself against a German onslaught with the old rifles and guerrilla tactics used against the auxiliary police. If they meant to undertake a defence the only logical course was to throw in with England and the North. This would compel England and England's friends to give them their share of armament.

James Dillon's father and grandfather had been in English jails for their Irish nationalist activities before Sinn Féin had been thought of. He had no inherited affection for any British government but he was a realist. On the record, England since 1922 had lived up to the Anglo-Irish Treaty, even when Mr de Valera had violated it. He believed that England was acting in good faith, and as between England and Fascist Germany, he put his trust, as a Catholic and an Irish leader, in England. Most important of all he recognised the fact that if anything would end Partition it would be companionship in arms for the defence of all Ireland.

His party had charged de Valera with bad faith on the Partition issue. They said that de Valera wanted the issue more than union. If union were achieved the North would come into the Dáil with a block of thirty-six Protestant votes which, acting with the opposition, would put de Valera out of office. It was a political situation not unlike that in Washington which for years made one party or the other oppose the admission of Hawaii and Alaska to statehood.

I was able to give Mr Dillon the newspaper reports banned in Éire that I received from the United States indicating that the more intelligent elements of the American people had awakened to the significance of the German menace. The American Press had with unanimity condemned the invasion of the Low Countries as had the president. I told him I believed that the pattern of 1914 was repeating itself, and that our policy of aid for Hitler's enemies would inevitably bring us into the war.

Mr Dillon in his advocacy of the Allied cause as being also the Irish cause sometimes showed more courage than prudence. There were times after hot interchanges in the Irish parliament with Fianna Fáil characters from the Irish underworld that I opened the morning newspaper with apprehension lest I should read of his murder.

He had no personal quarrel with Mr de Valera. He was prepared to work with him and under him during the emergency. He never underrated his great political talent and he was frankly admiring of his charm. He told me once after a day spent with Mr de Valera on a defence inspection trip that it was one of the most delightful experiences of his life.

It will eventually be placed in the historical record that Mr Dillon and his Fine Gael associates in fact approached Mr de Valera with *a plan for a realistic defence of Ireland, in conjunction with the North and with England and the Commonwealth, that Mr de Valera admitted that it was the logical thing to do but stated that the country was not prepared for it* and would not follow it, if it were enunciated. The implication was that Mr Aiken strongly opposed it. Mr Dillon at this time refused to take any action without Mr de Valera's approval and support. He, of course, had no knowledge of the secret apology for the Galway speech.

Mr de Valera made it clear later on that he resented my friendship with Dillon but in view of the extra-diplomatic activities of his minister in Washington there were no grounds on which he could protest. It was my duty in Éire, as it was Mr Brennan's in Washington, to ascertain and appraise the forces of opposition.

There was however a material difference between my relation with Mr Dillon and the relation of the Irish minister in Washington with 'The Friends of Irish Neutrality'. Mr Dillon was always working in the interest of his own country and in co-operation with its government. 'The Friends of Irish Neutrality' on the other hand was a subversive pressure group working in the interest of Germany, and opposing the defence preparations of their own—the American—government. The day after Pearl Harbor they disbanded.

Continuing to the president in regard to Mr Dillon, I wrote:

From letter to President Roosevelt, continued

May 31st, 1940

He is for throwing in with England at once as the lesser of two dangers. He believes Ireland will become the battlefield if the Irish cannot keep the Germans from making a landing. I don't think they can stop them, unless they (the Germans) intend merely a strategic diversion with a small column. The situation needs drum beating and a slogan. Perhaps de Valera will hit on it.

CHAPTER VIII

MAY 31ST-JUNE 8TH

On Friday night, May 31st, the old, reliable United States liner *Roosevelt* anchored in Galway Bay. She was to embark Americans still in Europe and anxious to get home. Lord Castlerosse came up from Killarney to report for the *London Express*. He called it the ' "Now or Never" Ship'.

Our records showed between three and four thousand American citizens, mostly of Irish birth, as residents in Éire. Most of them were Irish in feeling. They were Americans for what there was in it. Most of them used their American citizenship to escape Irish taxes and financial regulations. However, Washington offered them all facilities for repatriation. They were circularised and warned that this might be the last opportunity to return in an American ship. Only a small percentage responded. Provision was made for loans to the needy but even this did not produce the anticipated flood of applications until it was too late to process them. Our London embassy told us to prepare for any number of American passengers coming from England, up to a thousand, which was more than the ship could accommodate. They would be leaving England by the regular means of transportation. This meant arriving in Dublin in the morning, catching the train to the west, and arriving in Galway about noon. They might come the day before and spend one night in Galway. This seemed a simple proceeding except that there was only one modern hotel in Galway which could not take care of more than a third of the Americans who might appear. Furthermore, if everybody arrived on the morning of embarkation, train accommodations between Dublin and Galway would have to be doubled or trebled. It was only a hundred and twenty-five mile journey, but it was war time and no buses were for hire.

We discovered that while on the map Galway looked like a great port, there was no pier at which a sizeable ship could lie. The fact was that in the whole of Éire only Dublin had a quay or jetty which would accommodate a loaded ship of eight to ten thousand tons. In Galway such ships had to anchor three miles off shore in the outer bay. There was lighter service but the pier to which the lighter tied was in a tidal dock which could only be used when the tide served. There was no freshwater tender, and we had to tow one around the south coast from Cork. Even so, it could only maintain the ship's daily usage. It could not increase its supply. Finally we discovered that there was no motor boat for hire in Galway harbour. The harbour master had one, but he was a busy man and not under our control. What we would have done, had not our vice consul in Cork, Bob Patterson, towed his own motor launch across the island on a trailer, nobody ever found out. The only helpful factor in the situation was that the Irish officials were, without exception, extraordinarily kind. The Irish people are at their best in an emergency of this kind. They enjoyed cutting red tape and winked at technical irregularities. They endeared themselves to all of us.

Our consul general, Mr J.K. Davis, had acquired renown for having successfully evacuated Americans under fire in China during the Japanese invasion. He had been let down a wall in a basket. Later in Warsaw with Tony Biddle he had lived for weeks in a cellar while the Germans were bombing the city. He had become the No. 1 consular expert in evacuating Americans under war conditions. It was not surprising that his health had suffered. The Department had sent him to Dublin as a quiet, salubrious post to recuperate. And now he was evacuating Americans again. It looked as if the jinx was still on him.

American law and departmental regulations were as inadequate for improvised repatriations as Irish facilities. Americans were arriving from London with irregularities in their papers which left our consular officers aghast. Joe Kennedy was a businessman and his consul general, John Erhardt, for a career officer, was unbelievably efficient. Their idea was to get the people home and settle the red tape later. The result was they passed on all the doubtful cases and left them on our doorstep.

I was all for getting people home, but ignorant of the law. At a point Stephen Kendrick, who was in charge of our visa section, baulked. I said to him, 'I'll take full responsibility for this writing. Only push them along'.

'Look', said Steve, 'read the law. You *can't* take the responsibility. It's Steve Kendrick who has to pay the ten thousand dollar fine and go to jail for ten years'. He showed me the book and it was all there. At the same time we could not leave a six months' old American baby on the Galway quay while its parents went to New York. Eventually, Mr Kendrick, who was a very superior officer, found a formula he was willing to take a chance on, and later Congress passed legislation legalising all infractions of the regulations.

The entry in my journal for Saturday, June 2nd, reads:

From diary entry

Saturday, June 2nd, 1940

I started at seven a.m. with Belle Roosevelt (Mrs Kermit), Mrs Robert Montgomery, and Frederick Palmer.[1] They were all on their way home. Frederic Palmer was the Dean of American War Correspondents. He had made a great name reporting the Russian-Japanese war in 1904–5, and had been one of Pershing's aides in World War One. He was an old friend, and had stopped the night with us as had the ladies.

It was raining when we started and promised to be a bad day for embarkation, but by the time we were half way over the island it cleared and when we reached Galway about ten-thirty it was fair and became bright with sunshine later in the day. The first news on arriving was that a telegram had been received from the New York office of the US Lines forbidding the embarkation of the 76 persons who had paid for cot accommodation in the hold. It was a horrible place to put human beings but it was better than nothing if one had to get to America. A party of Rhodes Scholars had booked in it. They accosted me with the tale that they *had* to be in America for their examinations. This seemed rather comic with England *in extremis*, but I got hold of Harvey Klemmer, whom Ambassador Kennedy had sent over, and he got Truitt of the Maritime Commission on the telephone. It was five a.m. for Truitt (in Washington) but he behaved well, and by three-thirty we got an answer permitting the passengers to go aboard. It would have been bad otherwise as some had their baggage in the hold, some had wives and children already on board, and none of them had any money.

[1] Frederick Palmer (1873–1958), born in Pleasantville, Pennsylvania. Fifty years experience as war correspondent. Nathan A. Haverstock published a biography, *Fifty years at the front: the life of war correspondent Frederick Palmer* (Washington DC, 1996).

I went out to the ship about two in Patterson's speed boat and met the Captain and the Irish Government's port surveyor who impressed me as a competent and straight fellow. He certified the 813 passengers on the score of safety and permitted seventy-odd between decks. This was the point I wanted to drive home in the presence of witnesses so that the Company could not say the surveyor had forbidden carrying passengers between decks.

In a previous letter to the president (dated May 31st) I had written:

From letter to President Roosevelt

Friday, May 31st, 1940

I am insisting on a personal check by our consuls of the Captain's report on life-saving apparatus. We are working in conjunction with the Irish Government's survey officer. I shall refuse to allow the issue of the emergency certificate unless there is full equipment of life rafts and life preservers to supplement the deficiency in lifeboat capacity. I don't want to get caught on that score if there should be an accident.

Castlerosse wrote,

There was one American lady who was doubtful whether, for lack of space, there was any chance of the passengers arriving in America alive. She came from New York so I was able to reassure her. Anybody who has been trained in the New York subway during the rush hours can challenge any ordinary sardine when it is simply a question of nestling tight.

The memo of June 1st continues:

From letter to President Roosevelt continued

Saturday, June 1st, 1940

Belle and Mrs Robert Montgomery had a cabin on the top deck so small that no cot could be put in it. Very lucky for them. Fred Palmer was complaining that he had only a cot when he thought he had a bed. He had been telling us the day before how he had to sleep on the floor after being in Alaska because the beds were so soft. Went ashore about four-thirty. (I had taken Hall-Kelly, the Canadian High Commissioner, out with me.) Said goodbye to him, finished up my business and started back about five. I took Flory of the UP.[2] with me. Very nice fellow. He spent the night with us and went off Sunday night, all of us dining first with the Frank MacDermots at the Royal Irish Yacht Club.

My report continued:

We got through the *Roosevelt* embarkation better than I had dared hope and I have been writing personal letters of appreciation to half the population of Ireland, besides inserting a card in the press. But no more Galway, 'Uncle Franklin', unless reasons that are unknown to us and to the Irish Government make it imperative that Cork Harbour be not used. At Cobh they have all the facilities and enough water for lightering at any tide.

The president's objections to Queenstown (Cobh) had proved timely. Goebbels at that very time was broadcasting that the German Intelligence had reliable information to the effect that Churchill was to sink the *Roosevelt* and accuse Hitler. The only time I was ever grateful to the Irish Censor was for his suppression of this report in the Dublin newspapers.

The letter to the president ended: 'If we are caught in a war we have plenty of "Jameson" but no soap'.

The kindly helpfulness of the Irish people, officials and private persons during this trying episode undoubtedly had political significance. There could not have been manifested more good will toward the United States. The attitude of the people was as James Dillon had represented it. If de Valera had recognised it and mobilised it, he could have instituted a pro-American policy which would have put him on 'the pig's back'.

On June 3rd he asked me to come and see him. Without preliminary talk about the weather, he asked me to help him get arms from Washington. Mr Brennan, his minister, was making a formal request and he hoped that I would back him up. I told him that I would, and at once dispatched a telegram to the president urging a favourable response to Mr Brennan's representations.

My diary for June 3rd records a memorandum of the conversation and notes that on leaving Mr de Valera's office I went to the shop of Mr Kelly the wine merchant. Mr Kelly told me that the police had been

2 *United Press.*

rounding up IRA members and had just arrested two on the premises next door. At last Mr de Valera had begun taking strong measures against the 'enemy within'.

On June 4th, the Hempels lunched with us. Since May 28th when we lunched with them the Allied situation had become so desperate that there were not many diplomats left that we could ask to meet them. Italy was not yet in the war, but the Italian minister had expressed so strong a dislike of Germans that he was not to be considered. The papal nuncio could accept no invitation to meet a representative of Hitler. It was hardly tactful to ask the Swiss chargé, for his country was preparing feverishly against German violation and most of the other countries, represented by missions in Dublin, were at war or already Hitler's victims.

We, of course, asked Joe Walshe, but he side-stepped. He was 'unable' to come. He suggested the Fred Bolands to represent Mr de Valera. Mr Boland was the number two career man in External Affairs at this time. His wife, an extremely attractive woman and a talented painter, was strongly anti-British and pro-German. Thus she fitted in very well. For the rest we had the Spanish minister and his wife, the Thomsens, the MacVeaghs and Mrs Crocker of New York who was stopping with us.

'Outwardly', as they say, 'all was harmonious', but with obvious effort on the part of the Hempels as well as ourselves. It was not a situation which it was profitable to repeat. The recent utterances of the president, Secretary Hull and the American Press made it clear that at least a breach of relations with Hitler was near. So when Madame Hempel gave me an opening, it seemed kind for all our sakes to take advantage of it. She had expressed the hope of seeing us soon again. As I wrote the president, I replied:

From letter to President Roosevelt

Tuesday, June 4th, 1940

These are very tragic times (all Northern France just lost), but whatever happens I hope you will always believe that it has been a privilege for me to know you'.

'But what could happen?' she said.

I said, 'But suppose my country enters the war? You remember the last war'.

'But why should she?' she said and her face fell—below zero.

She was so completely taken aback with dismay that it was evident that the possibility of American participation had never occurred to her or to her husband. This struck me as showing bad intelligence at the Wilhelmstrasse.

The report to the president went on.

> The German Minister is a very decent fellow and we got together after lunch. I said with subtle diplomatic approach,
> 'Do you trust Mussolini?'
> 'I think Hitler and he have complete understanding', he said.
> 'I hope so for your sake', I said, 'but how about Stalin?'
> He shrugged his shoulders sadly and smiled.
> I said, 'He is the lad who is going to win the war. Europe will go Bolshevik'.
> 'No', he said, 'our middle class is already deflated. National Socialism is already doing for them all that Bolshevism could promise'.
> Then I said to him, 'You missed Bill Bullitt by a hair. You ought to have better marksmanship'. We both laughed in a silly way and he said, 'Wouldn't it have been awful!' This had reference to the German air bomb that a few days previously had dropped without exploding through the dining room when Ambassador Bullitt was a guest at an official French air ministry luncheon.

I recall telling Hempel what I had just said to his wife and my report continues

> Then we agreed that we must be *civilised* whatever happened and remain personal friends which I thought was a good idea if the Germans come in here and I am in a coop like John Cudahy (Ambassador to Belgium).

In parting I suggested to Dr Hempel that American attacks on his Führer, like German attacks on my president, made social relations uncomfortable for both of us, that we should therefore each remain scrupulously 'correct' and friendly when we met in public but not attempt further parties. He agreed with relief, clicked his heels and said goodbye. This mutual suspension of social relations did not anticipate very much the official breaking of diplomatic relations.

As I went out with the Bolands to their car, Mr Boland said something to the effect, 'Well, you are well out of it in any event'. I replied, 'I don't see that. The Gallup poll on the question of selling munitions to the Allies on credit shows a change in the last few weeks from 35 per cent for and 65 per cent against to 51 per cent for and 49 per cent against. I think this shows the trend that will bring us in'. This obviously surprised him. He said, 'You don't mean that?' I said, 'I do and I believe it'.

After the War ended, an American officer in Berlin who had been handling the captured papers of the German Foreign Office wrote me that he had come across a complaint from Hempel about the 'unneutral attitude of the American minister in Dublin'.

On June 6th I wrote the president setting forth the background reasons for my telegram of June 3rd supporting Mr de Valera's request through Brennan for arms. We had just received long-delayed official mail from Washington in which were two letters for me from the president. They made me feel that I was working on lines approved by him. I, therefore, began my letter:

From letter to President Roosevelt

Thursday, June 6th, 1940

I can understand why people 'go down the line' for you if you write them letters like that. Two days ago Mr de Valera asked me to come to see him and as a result I sent the telegram which requested you to give your personal help to Brennan, the Irish Minister in Washington, in his effort to get certain equipment. I suggested that if the exact things could not be obtained, might not General Marshall delegate some good man to study the problem and outline an alternative programme of material based on what was available, always remembering that the Irish defence forces must rely upon small arms, guerrilla tactics and swift action against invading parties, not giving them time to co-ordinate.

The general situation as regards (Irish) morale has improved very much in the past week. There is at last a definite leadership apparent. They have rounded up a lot more IRA lads and last night, Aiken, about whom a good many of the Opposition had doubts (as to his being pro-German) came out strongly and without reservation for defence.

This as later became obvious was 'defence' against the IRA.

After Mr de Valera finished talking arms, he said in substance: 'What terrifies me is this'. He went to the map and pointed to a spot at the head of Donegal Bay where Lough Eske extends north of the border, and another point also north of the border fifty miles to the northeast, the head of Lough Swilly. 'If I were the Germans', he said, 'I would land at these points and proclaim myself a liberator. If they should do that, what I could do I do not know'. Then he added, 'Please don't mention that to anybody. It might get around'.

I said to him, 'I think the people up North ought to know that. Would you want me to go up again and tell it to Craigavon, also other things pertaining to the situation?' He said he would be grateful if I would. I said I would have to think it over and if I could get a legitimate reason for going, that is, to 'explore' the situation for my government, I would let him know.

After considering the matter on the drive back to the legation, it seemed so clearly in the American interest to secure, if possible, a common defence of North and South against Germany that I decided to go if only Craigavon would see me.

My letter continued:

I immediately wrote Abercorn's Comptroller and Secretary (Commander Oscar Henderson, RN, DSO) saying that I was ready to come up and further explore the situation in Ulster for my government if Lord Craigavon would care to see me.

On June 5th, I received a favourable reply to my letter to the duke. He invited me to come on the 7th, and I at once accepted the invitation by telegram. At this juncture confidential information from London threw new light on the situation in the North. My letter to the president went on to say that Downing Street had sent for Craigavon and had given him '*merry hell*', all but ordering him to make up with de Valera and end Partition on the best terms he could.

From letter to President Roosevelt continued

Thursday, June 6th, 1940

They found him very tough, blaming the South for this and that just as de Valera keeps blaming the North. They told him to forget it, that Ireland had to defend itself as a unit and he must take his medicine. Of course they are not telling this to de Valera just yet as he will be stubborn enough without knowledge of this advantage, but he will have his chance and my private guess is that he will get his point and give away nothing as he always has in the past.

This was the first intimation that reached us of the 'firm offer' from London to be made to the Irish government regarding lease of the ports. The reason was the upswing in U-boat sinkings which manifested during the last week in May, as the Germans menaced the French Channel ports and forced withdrawal of British naval units. The contingency had arrived which Mr Churchill foresaw in 1938 when he protested the surrender of the Irish Treaty ports. The total tonnage sunk in May had been 273,000 tons; for June it was to be 471,000. This included Allied tonnage.

No instructions or advices came to us from Washington in regard to the matter of the ports although the Department of State must have been informed by London. Presumably this was a 'hot potato' which neither the president nor Secretary Hull wished to handle. Senator David I. Walsh of Massachusetts was still a power 'on the Hill'. The first reference to the Irish ports recorded in Secretary Hull's *Memoirs* is under date of November 25th, 1940. Hull writes:

> Lord Lothian, the British Ambassador,[3] explaining conditions in Britain said, 'the first consideration was to secure permission to occupy Irish harbours'. Undoubtedly he would have liked our diplomatic assistance but I interrupted him by saying: 'In my opinion de Valera and his associates will not agree to anything at present'. Any aid from us therefore seems virtually impossible just now.[4]

My prediction that Mr de Valera would make no concession was verified, but I had never ceased to *hope*. The reasonableness and long-term profit of common defence, if Partition were to be ended, seemed obvious. It was the *sure* way. It seemed impossible that Mr de Valera would not understand it, as it seemed impossible to us that he would

[3] Lord Lothian (1882–1940). As Philip Henry Kerr was Lloyd George's private secretary in 1920–1 and a key player behind the scenes in establishing dialogue with Sinn Féin. See Carl Ackerman, 'Ireland from a Scotland Yard Notebook', *Atlantic Monthly,* April 1922. Lothian was appointed British ambassador to the United States in April 1939.
[4] Hull, *The memoirs of Cordell Hull,* 872.

not see that long-term Irish interest lay in being on the side of the United States. We did not understand that he wanted to *dominate* the North, to obtain control without constitutional obligations to the Protestant majority, and that he believed that Hitler would give him what he wanted. Thus he embarked upon his adventure in trickery, and Craigavon, nailing his flag to the mast outjockeyed him, for it was de Valera who first definitely rejected the British proposals and thus must bear primary responsibility for the continuance of Partition.

We had the new French minister and his wife to lunch on June 6th, two days after the party for the Germans. M. de Laforcade had arrived just as his country's resistance was disintegrating. I waived protocol, called on him immediately, and asked him to lunch. His position was tragic and he appeared stunned by the suddenness of it. I offered him all the facilities of our Mission. He was grateful but observed hopelessly that it took *three years* to learn anything about a post in a new country. He and his wife, a superior woman, conducted themselves with dignity and courage through the years when Pétain's Vichy represented their France.

For the French lunch party, Joe Walshe was 'available'. My report to the president ended: 'The Granards were also here. Beatrice Mills, the Countess of Granard, sat on my left with Joe Walshe, the Fenian, on her left and we were all very jolly. Can you believe it?'

On this same June 6th the Irish police arrested Michael Held. Hitherto unknown, he became the key figure in what overnight became an international 'incident'. The Germans had planted him in Dublin before the war as an agent and 'cover' for German spies. Before his exposure he was the respected 'Michael Held and Son, Sheet Metal Works, 72 Francis Street, Dublin, residence "Konstanz", Templeogue'. At 'Konstanz' the police found evidence that identified the parachutist dropped on May 5th in Meath as the Captain Herr Doctor, Herman Goertz, a regular officer in the Abwehr, a person of some consequence. He was a remarkable little man, dedicated to National Socialism and the New Order. He had been sent as a spy to England in 1935 to report on English military aviation. The English caught him in March 1936, sentenced him to four years at hard labour, but released him in February 1939. The whole story of his Irish mission we shall never know, but he was undoubtedly a political agent to the IRA as well as a spymaster. The Irish government in 1947 announced that he had swallowed prussic acid as he was about to be put aboard an American plane bound for the American zone in Germany. American intelligence never had the chance to interrogate him. Goertz left a statement which he had prepared for publication. It is important because of its omissions and misstatements. Apparently he expected to be allowed to live in Éire after the war and his document undertook to prove that neither he nor the high command had ever contemplated an attack on the de Valera government or had co-operated with the IRA, assertions refuted by Hempel's dispatches to Berlin.

There is no reason to doubt his statement that at daybreak on May 5th, 1940, he landed safely in County Meath, in the vicinity of Trim. He was not at the time aware of it, but he landed on the estate of Captain Harry Fowler, a renowned Irish sportsman and former Master of Hounds. By chance, I was sitting in a Dublin club and heard Captain Fowler tell part of the story before it became public knowledge. He said that his cowherd had reported to him that morning (May 5th) that he had discovered 'a great sheet' stuffed in the 'well' or spring from which the cattle drank. He brought this to Captain Fowler, who reported the matter to the local police. Thus within a few minutes the Gardaí would have telephoned Dublin and de Valera would have been put on the alert. But until Held's arrest he could not have known who had been dropped or why. The evidence found at 'Konstanz' was the trump card that he so badly needed. It proved that Ribbentrop was double-crossing him with Artus. It gave him a grievance against Berlin that strengthened his hand with Hempel. It also strengthened Hempel's support of de Valera in the Wilhelmstrasse. Most important of all it gave de Valera the chance to employ the formula 'Neutrality is the equivalent of Independence' against the IRA. Since they who proclaimed belligerence and denounced neutrality were 'Enemies of Independence'. It is probable that by June 3rd, Mr de Valera had enough on Held and Goertz to warrant him in beginning the IRA roundup. Hence the arrests on that day next door to Mr Kelly the wine merchant. The German files show that Hempel was aware of the situation as early as June 4th, for he sent telegrams to Berlin on the subject on that date and on June 7th and 8th.

Further to the president under the date of June 6th:

From letter to President Roosevelt continued

Thursday, June 6th, 1940

I am going up tomorrow morning, lunch with the Abercorns and come back tomorrow night if possible. I will go on with this then. I think I have mentioned to you that de Valera always maintains such a dead pan—no meeting of the eye—that the idea comes back to me that I am taking a big personal responsibility in giving my English friends and you the picture of him as out and out anti-Nazi. Well a little thing occurred at our last session which really assured me. He has a German (Jew), a Nobel Prize Winner who fled Germany, engaged for his Institute for Advanced Studies, Professor Schrödinger.[5] This man is now in abject terror in Ireland, fearing that the Gestapo is going to get him, and de Valera is more concerned over him than many much more important matters. In asking me if I could help in getting him to America, he spoke of the Germans in a way that left no doubt as to his feelings.

This protection of Professor Schrödinger, like his exposition of the tactics to be employed by the IRA forces that might implement the 'Artus' plan, will always perplex those who deliver the final verdict on Eamon de Valera. At the present time I can only interpret them as another example of that 'specious frankness' which was his most effective technique of deception.

On June 7th I went to Northern Ireland for the second time, returning the morning of the 8th, and reporting to the president as follows:

From letter to President Roosevelt

Friday, June 7th, 1940

I got off about ten-thirty for Government House, Hillsborough, Ulster, and arrived for lunch. There were just the Abercorns and myself and I had a chance to make it clear that I was not trying to butt in on other people's business but that the US was interested in the settlement of the Irish problem and although Craigavon's Ministers had told me that they were not interested, if it was agreeable to him I wanted to hear it from the Premier himself. I also said that if he, Craigavon, were to ask me, I would give him my impression of things in the South. The Duke said that he understood perfectly my position and was grateful to me for taking a helpful interest that Craigavon had been to London and was coming at 3.30 to report to him, and afterwards would see me. So I went to my room and waited till they sent for me, wondering how I was going to talk to a 'crushed' statesman. I decided of course I could never let on that I knew what had gone on in London.

[5] Professor Erwin Schrödinger (1887–1961), distinguished physicist, Nobel Prize winner in 1933.

Craigavon is a red-faced, hard-bitten fellow of seventy-one with fishy grey-blue eyes set on an angle. He had a pleasant smile for a face cut out of a granite rock. However, I liked him from the start and we got along fine. We talked till tea, that is till five, about an hour, and I never would have known that he had been 'crushed' by the Downing Street steamroller. We went over the same ground that I had gone over with Mr Andrews, his finance minister. The Ulster people were a different race, were part of Britain, and were not interested in Southern Ireland, which had been disloyal, had pulled down and burned the Union Jack. I told him what the South was doing in absolute good faith. He seemed surprised to hear it and said he was pleased. I asked him what would happen if the Germans landed in Ulster and proclaimed themselves 'liberators'?

'Oh, we will take care of them', he said.

I then asked him if he did not think it well to co-operate with the South for the defence of the Island. He said that he thought it would be fine but that of course it was a matter for the general staff in London. He absolutely refused to take any step that would recognise the South in any way that differentiated Ulster from Britain.

Finally we had tea with the Abercorns.

He has diabetes (Craigavon). He brought out a packet from his pocket that contained a piece of diabetic bread and a slice of plum cake made of diabetic flour.

At dinner that night Mr X. (a prominent member of the Stormont group) was present. He is manager and part owner of a big linen mill. After dinner he talked very freely and took a different line (from Lord Craigavon). He said that if the South had followed the line which Cosgrave set out on, by this time they (Ulster) would have been in. They could not have kept out. But now, union was set back for a generation at least. They could not join with a country that had walked out of the Dominion status.

I said I thought that stuff (Separatism) was for home consumption, that they (the South) wanted very close ties with Britain as long as they had the power to choose and didn't have the relation imposed upon them. He said that was probably true.

I never saw Lord Craigavon again. He died November 25th, 1940. He was a remarkable and in many ways a great man. John Andrews succeeded him. Craigavon was probably the only man on the Allied side who could cope with Mr de Valera in negotiation and win. In the light of what the captured German papers have revealed I owe an apology to his memory. Fortunately he knew Mr de Valera better than I did.

The letter continued:

From letter to President Roosevelt continued

Friday, June 7th, 1940

I got up early next morning and was back at my desk at ten-thirty. The legation's *Secret Service*, Mr James Murphy, also doubling as legation chauffeur and cow milker, tells me that at Government House, Ulster, the guards and servants were amazed at the reports he gave of preparations here to resist the foe. 'God', they said, 'we thought you was going to join the Germans and march up and massacre us all'.

CHAPTER IX

JUNE 8TH-12TH

Returning from Belfast to Dublin the morning of June 8th, we found that Mr de Valera had carried his offensive against the IRA to New York and Boston. It was the 'exiles' who contributed the dollars that financed the IRA.

One of the star reporters of the *United Press*, Mr Reuel S. (Dinty) Moore[1], was in Dublin covering the embarkation of returning Americans. He asked Mr de Valera for an interview and Mr de Valera gave him a manifesto. It began by repeating what he had been saying in his recent speeches:

> In a conflict such as is now raging—when powerful belligerents are locked in a deadly struggle—the rights of small nations count for little. Small nations have but one course to follow: to build up their own strength and rely on their own spirit.

He emphasised the 'Neutrality equals Independence' formula and warned patriotic Irishmen not to rock the boat. He addressed his manifesto to 'those of our race outside Ireland and to our friends everywhere, particularly in the United States'. The usual form of address was to 'Our Exiles' or to 'Our People Overseas' but he had begun to realise that Americans did not like the assumption that American citizens owed loyalty to any country but their own.

[1] Reuel S. (Dinty) Moore, University of Oregon graduate, class of 1921. The nickname arrives from the popular American beef stew products created in 1935 by the Hormel Corporation. A UPI correspondent in 1933, he was author of the later popular song 'She thinks she's hot, but she's not'. Moore corresponded with Frank Gallagher later in the war.

The manifesto was also a warning to Berlin to lay off Artus. Otherwise they would lose the support of that 'Irish influence in the United States, probably decisive', and provoke American intervention.

Generally speaking Irish America at the first had been more anti-British and pro-IRA than the people of Éire. They knew less about the facts. They were inclined to believe the IRA charge that de Valera had sold out to Chamberlain and had made peace with England, as in fact he had done. His aim at this juncture was to convince Irish America that he was just as anti-British as ever. This he proceeded to do. He said:

> Today in four-fifths of Ireland we are free. After long and bitter years of struggle we have regained our independence in these twenty-six of *our* thirty-two counties, and it was in the exercise of that independence that we asserted our neutrality when this war began. we have since maintained this neutrality scrupulously.

In June 1940 he never expected the dispatches of his friend the German minister would be published.

He then went on to describe the national mobilisation, ignoring the fact that his new forces had no weapons, and finally reached the substance of his message, which, as was his habit, he put at the end.

> Should there be any of our old friends (the IRA) who are foolish enough to lend themselves now to any action to weaken the elected government here, I would ask them to halt and to remember that what they are contemplating is nothing less than a betrayal of the dead generations. The bitter fruit of their interference may be the turning of our country into a cockpit for the belligerents, the bringing of the horrors of war upon our people, and perhaps in the end throwing us back into a bondage as hateful as that broken so recently after seven centuries of sublime sacrifice.

The reader could take his choice whether the bondage was to be under England, which had recently turned them loose to achieve their own unhappy destiny under Separatism, or under Hitler.

It is interesting to recall that, when Tyrone seemed victorious in the only Irish rebellion that was ever formidable, he and his associates could think of nothing more Irish or *sublime* than inviting an Austrian archduke to rule them. The point however that Mr de Valera was making with the American exiles was that *he* was carrying the anti-British banner while the IRA were rocking the boat.

After reading his proclamation, I walked the half mile across the Park to the nuncio's. I wanted to hear what he would say about it. He said nothing about the statement but he did say: 'I wish that you had got here a half hour ago. Mary MacSwiney was here. She left some papers that she wanted you to have. A very remarkable woman'. Miss MacSwiney had produced a counter manifesto.

At this time she might have been described as the last of the 'Old Bolsheviks'. Vitriol still ran in her veins, but more slowly. She was still the Direct Actionist who had preached Mr de Valera's doctrine; 'The Majority must not be allowed to do wrong'. She had been the member of the Sinn Féin Dáil in 1922, whom the historian P.S. O'Hegarty describes as precipitating the Split and the Civil War. It was of her that he wrote:

> … of all the impostures of which the anti-treaty party is made up, perhaps the most shameless and loathsome (after that of de Valera) is that which Miss Mary MacSwiney has so sedulously foisted on the country—the imposture of herself as a 'Sea-green Incorruptible'.

And again,

> To the whole Split and Civil War, Miss MacSwiney contributed nothing but bitterness and hatred and malignancy. On the night the vote was taken I heard Mick Collins, after the vote, make an appeal to the other side to co-operate with him in keeping peace and order in Ireland. I have always believed that if Mr de Valera had answered that appeal he would have answered it in the spirit in which it was made; but he did not get the opportunity. Before he or anybody else could draw a breath, Miss MacSwiney was on her feet, hatred and passion in her face And in her Voice. 'No', said she, 'we will not co-operate with you, nor help you in any way. You are worse than Castlereagh'. She had only one policy now, and that is—to make trouble for the Government of the Irish people, in the name of that Republic which she and her friends have dishonoured.

In another passage Mr O'Hegarty comments generally on the ladies in the movement. 'The long period of the truce', he says, 'had upon them an effect even more deplorable than that which it had upon the Volunteers.

> They took not to drink but to war ... . To them the truce was nothing but a trick played upon the British, and to them peace was a loveless thing, and no life so good as the life of war. They became practically unsexed, their mother's milk blackened to make gunpowder; their minds working on nothing save hate and blood ... . The suffragettes used to tell us that with women in political power there would be no more war. We know better now. We know that with women in political power, there would be no more peace.[2]

In 1940 Mary MacSwiney entertained a less favourable opinion of Mr de Valera than in the 'war days'. She now looked upon him as a liar, traitor, coward and renegade, but she understood his point that Irish neutrality would injure England. What she could never forgive him was his acceptance of majority rule in order to win office.[3]

The significance of Miss MacSwiney's utterances is largely in the light which they throw on the Sinn Féin patriot mind. De Valera once had been their 'fair-haired boy', had taught them their patter about the Second Dáil and the nonsense about Irish Rights on which he nourished his 'Movement'. What the IRA were *now*, he and General Aiken had been but a decade before.

Mary MacSwiney's home was Cork. What she was doing in Dublin with a manifesto the nuncio did not explain. Her document was headed 'The Crisis' and was pre-dated June 10th, 1940, though it was but the 8th. It began:

> Various wild rumours are afloat, owing to the vague somewhat panicky speeches of Fianna Fáil Ministers. There has been a call for a united front against a possible invader; vague talk of Fifth Columnists; a general roundup of the loyal citizens of the Republic of Ireland as a preliminary to getting the united front. Then there is a defence conference, made up of Home Rulers of

---

[2] P.S. O'Hegarty, *The victory of Sinn Féin* (Dublin, 1998), 72.
[3] Mary MacSwiney (1872–1942), republican, believed that 'no compromise is the only sane policy in Ireland'. (Richard English, *Radicals and the republic: socialist republicanism in the Irish Free State* (Oxford, 1994), 270). She had, however, broken with de Valera while the latter took a strong anti-IRA line after the murder of Admiral Boyle Somerville.

various shades, but all accepting the British connection, and a security Corps into which all the pro-Britishers of the Country are flooding, whether they call themselves Unionists, Nationalists, Catholics or Freemasons, with the one idea that they are meant to spy on Republicans, those pro-German Fifth Columnists who must above all be watched.

As she intuitively understood de Valera's neutrality strategy, she also divined the primary purpose of the mobilisation, 'to spy on Republicans'. In another paragraph she propounded her solution for the Crisis.

Now what is the real solution for Ireland in the present crisis? First, let all parties stand straight for the Republic, and declare every link with England broken; the minority who would object to that course 'on principle', and not merely through fear, is so small as to be negligible. Let those who prefer to be British citizens be facilitated in every way to leave the country. If that is not feasible at the moment let them be registered as aliens and care be taken that they do no mischief to the neutrality of the Republic.

Our chief danger, however, is not Germany but England. England no doubt would wish to make our country the battlefield instead of her own. But does any sane person believe that Germany will pass over the country of her Number One enemy to convenience that enemy by attacking minor British objectives in Ireland?

Presumably Miss MacSwiney expected that I would transmit her document to the United States for publication. I might have passed it on to Mr Moore who would have been glad, as a good newspaper man, to print the 'other side'. But at that time I had too much sympathy for Mr de Valera and his difficulties.

As far as we know Goertz's instructions at this time were to foment IRA activity, organise espionage and sabotage but not to promise a precise date for the German landing. Berlin had postponed Artus. But when Mr de Valera struck, the IRA struck back.

That night of June 8th someone dropped through the legation letter slot a publication which appeared to be an answering blast to the de Valera statement. It was contained in a publication known as *War News*, and announced to be the resumption of the official news organ which the 'Republic' had issued when Mr de Valera was its president and was conducting his Civil War against Collins, Griffith, Cosgrave and their Irish Free State government.

War News resumed with an introductory proclamation, ostensibly denouncing England, but in reality an indictment of de Valera.

WAR NEWS
ISSUED BY THE IRISH REPUBLICAN PUBLICITY BUREAU

IRELAND'S CLAIM

The doom of the British Empire, the foulest and most infamous institution the world has ever known is at last at hand.

The subject peoples, 'the natives' are at last coming into their own.

Where does Ireland stand?

Are we to be meek, subservient slaves?

Are we to be neutral?

'Ireland, her own from the centre to the sea', said Fintan Lalor. As long as any part of Ireland is under the heel of the invader there is only one honourable stand an Irishman can take, that is armed revolt.

The Robber Empire still rules us, still holds our territory. Rise Irishmen, and make your claim now.

De Valera, damn your neutrality—we claim our country. Every inch of it, North and South'.

The appearance of the de Valera statement just before the reappearance of *War News* suggests that a stool pigeon in the IRA had tipped Mr de Valera to the publication date. Later the IRA charged their then Chief of Staff with being an informer. However that may be, Mr de Valera had beaten them to the draw.

War News carried the legend: 'Issued by the Republican Publicity Department'. It was a miniature newspaper in format—seven and a half by ten inches. Under the title, 'Rise Again', the leading article ran as follows;

The lamps of Truth have been extinguished over Europe, indeed all over the world, yet *War News* reappears to keep alive the sacred flame in Ireland. There is nothing very unusual in this. Ireland shed the lustre of her spirit and culture over a darkened world in past centuries, and today we are proud to play our part in the preservation of that great tradition, … .

The second article on page 1 was headed, 'The Prisoners'. On June 5th, according to the IRA report, they had arrested three-hundred and ninety. Eventually the government locked up some seven hundred. The article began:

> There is one test by which we shall know that Mr de Valera is sincere when he speaks of the defence of Ireland. The test will be the opening of the prison gates. The men in jail will be needed when the time comes to repel the English. If Mr de Valera has any sincerity left he will release all Republican prisoners now. He knows, the Country knows, that the only object of the IRA is to secure and maintain the Republic of Ireland.
>
> Every day during which the prisoners are held is a day on which the country knows that England and not the will of the Irish people is dominant in Government Buildings.
>
> Will Maffey always have his way?

There was a article entitled 'National Defence'. In it Seán T. O'Kelly is quoted as saying that the millions expended on the Irish army were spent in the confidence that they secured 'a modest insurance against attack'. The writer comments: 'How any sane being could hold such opinion with the examples of contemporary history before him utterly taxes human credulity'. He concludes by exhorting all Irishmen to arm themselves and rally to the defence of the Irish republic. It is interesting to note that the IRA writer does not dignify de Valera's promise never to let Éire become the base of an attack on England by mentioning it. This has the flavour of Miss MacSwiney's composition and asks the same rhetorical question, 'how any sane being … ?' Although she disagreed with the IRA policy on neutrality, it is quite possible that she had come up from Cork to help with this resumption of *War News*. She was a privileged character—she shared too many of Mr de Valera's early secrets to be locked up.

The issue contained a page of 'newsy items', mostly reports of police raids, which the Censor had banned from the daily newspapers. As an example, 'raids have been carried out lately upon the following: An Stad Restaurant, 30 Hollybank Road; 2 Butterfield Avenue; 31 Gardiner's Place; Elliott Hotel; Belgrave Square area, Fitzgerald Street; Harold's Cross'.

Another item was: 'A big number of detectives have been hanging about Moss Twomey's', (Maurice Twomey was then chief of staff of the IRA).

There was also a crack at our friend, Seán MacEntee:

MacEntee, known as 'the banker's friend' when Finance Minister, presently in Industry and Commerce, admits the fact that ours is a dependent economy; they would have to get out of the habit of thinking it was the Government's job to put bread in every man's mouth, and give him jam along with it.

Obviously that happy state of affairs is reserved for traitors, jobbers, and, shall we say, superannuated Police and Army Chiefs.

Coercion is good enough for the people.

War News attacked Mr de Valera in a thoughtful piece entitled 'The Voter's Predicament'. This too has the MacSwiney style.

Can any man or woman, not a pro-Britisher, who cast a vote for Fianna Fáil in any election since the party was first returned to power, say that what they voted for has come to pass?

The People voted Fianna Fáil in order to open Cosgrave's Jails.

The same jails are now full again.

The people voted Fianna Fáil to do away with pensions.

Thousands of new pensions were granted.

The people voted Fianna Fáil because de Valera said he could win the Republic bloodlessly if given a chance.

De Valera has given them an English King.

De Valera's censor does not allow the word Republic to be mentioned in the Press. The only place where it is allowed to appear is on the Fianna Fáil notepaper, where it is kept for a decoy for fools.

The People gave de Valera the job of abolishing coercion.

Instead of doing that he raised his own salary and those of T.D'.s. He has multiplied jobs and made the cost of government so heavy that the people are ground down with taxes.

De Valera promised a Republican constitution. By false pretences he obtained a minority vote which has made democratic advance to the Republic impossible.

De Valera promised a free Press.

Never was the Press in Ireland so censored as it is now. The people are allowed to know only what de Valera wants them to know. The people are given no correct information on which to base a decision regarding their vote in the impending elections.

When de Valera says the elections are open to all he lies.

No Republican could be nominated. In order to do so he would have to be as dishonest as the rest of the junta that rules this country; he would have to sign a form signifying his acceptance of the Twenty-Six County Parliament as it stands.

Recently the voters of Dublin made the only protest in their power. They stayed away from the polls.

Gerald Boland gave his word to Darcy's comrades and broke it. Can you count the times de Valera has broken his word?

The voters of Galway showed what they think. What man or woman who votes can possibly know what way his vote may be interpreted in the future?

These things only are certain. Every vote for Fianna Fáil will be a vote for coercion and jailings.

It will be a vote to let Craigavon have his way in Belfast.

Voters! de Valera has a load of treachery on his conscience. Our advice is to you that you keep your hands clean of the blood of any more Irishmen.

What value are the promises of a liar?

At this time, neither the IRA nor Miss MacSwiney suspected that the German minister had sold them down the river and was backing de Valera and neutrality. Nor did they suspect that Hempel was keeping them as insurance, in case that de Valera double-crossed him. But the IRA views of Mr de Valera expressed in *War News* could not have reassured him.

What perplexed and worried us most at that time was not Mr de Valera but Irish mass opinion. This was a difficult thing for foreigners to find out. Our Anglo-Irish friends who had lived their lives in Ireland were divided in their views. The Dublin Irish people that we saw did not seem to have strong opinions. They were vexed about shortages of coal and gas but they seemed to have no apprehensions as to what German victory would mean. France was supposed to be the traditional friend of republican Ireland but France's agony brought no expression of sympathy for France or indignation at the aggressor. If these feelings existed, the Censor suppressed their expression.

Sinn Féinism was probably responsible for this. For a generation Sinn Féin had indoctrinated them with its philosophy of selfishness, its sham history and its belief in words and phrases rather than facts. This had been so successful that even some of the politicians had come to believe in what they told the people. They were, therefore, up to a point sincere. Now they all seemed to believe that enlarging the army to fifty thousand and establishing a Local Defence Force provided for Irish security.

I had become pleasantly acquainted with Mr J.J. Horgan of Cork. He was a leading citizen and lawyer. Moreover, for some years he had been contributing an essay on current Irish affairs to the *Round Table* quarterly. It was the one objective and penetrating appraisal of contemporary Ireland that appeared. I asked him what the Irish people were thinking.

He said that he had gone out among the farm people to find out. An old farmer in west Cork had given him the answer. 'We would like to see the English *nearly* bate'. That 'nearly' expressed the realisation that in spite of all, Irish eggs were in the same basket with England's.

There was a story current in Dublin to the same effect. Two 'shawleens' were riding on a bus. Said one, 'Glory be to God! Thim Germans are bating the English'.

'Glory be to God!' said the other. Then, after a pause, 'Would thim Germans be coomin' here?'

'Coomin' here?' said the first. 'What would the British navy be doin'?'

I believed then and I believe it more strongly now, that had de Valera given the Irish people a brave and honest guidance, told them the truth about the Axis, they would have supported him as they supported James Dillon in Monaghan against de Valera's bitter opposition. He would not have had to worry about the IRA and the anti-British issue. But his political harp had only the one string, hatred of England. So his golden opportunity slipped away.

When the news of the evacuation from Dunkirk reached Dublin it was taken as the end of England. But as far as I know, there was no outburst of jubilation from the pro-German Irish similar to their outburst of resentment on European Victory day. There began to stir a sobering suspicion of the truth which they denied. Yet it was difficult for the Irish to understand how Dunkirk had raised English morale instead of lowering it. For that matter it was hard for us to understand. Yet it was the astounding fact.

Sir John Maffey had gone over to England to see his badly wounded son who had been brought over from the Dunkirk beaches. I saw him when he got back. I asked him how things were in London.

'Pretty grim', he said. Then he laughed, '*Everybody is saying "Thank God! Now we are on our own"*'.

Mr Churchill reminded parliament that wars are not won by evacuations but he told the epic story with exaltation. The British navy with a volunteer fleet of yachtsmen, some 861 recorded craft of all kinds, had accomplished the impossible. They had suffered terrible losses. The Germans had sunk 243, more than one in four. But they brought back 220,000 British and 115,000 French soldiers. Of the total ships in the armada 168 were Allied craft. Lord Gort, the Commander in Chief, was the last to leave.

Mr Churchill not only told the story of the evacuation but he spoke of winning the war as a matter of course. England had only begun to fight.

The Sinn Féin Irish could not understand this. They resented it the way the Vichy French did. England ought to know when she was beaten. Why prolong the war and inconvenience everybody? The traditional Irish attitude toward defeat glorified it as something noble. When Sarsfield or Hugh O'Neill was 'bested at the game', as the ballad has it, they became heroes. The Sinn Féin Irish never understood Churchill. They never understood the civilisation which the Normans had brought to them. They never grasped the meaning of Magna Carta, or the first parliament. They had nothing to rally about but leaders; no central idea except tribal loyalty to a person, no appreciation of 'Civility', of government by law.

When France broke her written agreement not to make a separate peace and refused to send her fleet to English or North African ports, these Irish sympathised with France. When Churchill damaged the great ships to keep them from falling in German hands, they attacked him.

After the publication of Mr de Valera's Galway speech on May 12th, the Irish censorship allowed no condemnation of Hitler or Mussolini, nor any generous word in praise of the Allies whose wheat was feeding half the Irish people and whose coal was supplying Dublin with the gas to bake the bread. If that June was England's finest hour, it was not Éire's.

Neither was it one of the finest hours of my own country, though in the United States men were at least free to speak their minds. And Americans were biting no hand that fed them. To us in Dublin it was not a happy experience to sit, as it were, in safety in a diplomatic stage box and witness the murder of Europe. On the Continent there was no longer law. What was left of the forces of Law and Morality had been thrown back to the British island. Could they rally and rearm in time or was the millennium of German dictatorship, predicted by Hitler, about to begin? To play no part in this drama, save pass the ammunition from the rear, seemed not only ignoble but stupid. This our isolationists were shortly to discover. As the days passed it became always clearer that in situations where there is a moral issue, to be neutral not only indicates a disease of the spirit but of the intelligence. No one has ever outwitted the 'moral order'. I looked up the passage in Revelations having to do with the neutrality of the Laodicean Church: 'So then because thou art lukewarm and neither cold nor hot, I will spue thee out of my mouth'.[4]

Over the weekend (June 8th–10th) my wife and I were glad to slip off to Castletownshend. It was, we thought, over the rim of the war-torn world and for us it was a place of happy memories. We had gone there in June 1933 for the summer. We had planned the winter in Italy. In the autumn we got as far on our way to Italy as London then were drawn back to that Irish village to abide till the next June. This June we arrived at half past seven. Nothing had changed. Nothing fundamental had changed for two thousand years. The sun was still high, the air was golden still, and before changing for dinner we walked in the garden and looked over the harbour to the promontory where the Spanish admiral and the eighteen sailors of the Armada lie buried. The peaceful scene recalled 'far off forgotten things and battles long ago', and then our hosts told us that a cousin evacuated from Dunkirk and his brother, a sailor, survivor of a mine disaster, had just arrived. So the war was with us after all.

My letter to the president, dated June 10th, reports:

From letter to President Roosevelt

Monday, June 10th, 1940

Maude and I stopped with Admiral Hugh Somerville and his wife. He is a brother of Boyle, who was murdered by the IRA. Katherine Crocker stayed at Drishane House with Edith (the senior partner of 'Somerville and Ross') and Cameron (her brother). I went to church the next morning. Two or three pews in front there was an old man (Major Chavasse) with two red-headed sons, Paul and Kendall. Paul, (a naval Lieut. Commander) about ten days ago was in a mine layer that struck a mine. He was caught in his stateroom and had to dive and swim under water till he got to a companionway. Pretty close thing. The other boy, Kendall, (a major in the Guards) had been one of the last to be evacuated from Dunkirk a few days before. They both talked

---

[4] Revelations 3:16, King James version.

freely about it all, had their tails up, and were looking forward to 'going back'. (We got no impression that the war was lost.)

During the service my eyes wandered to the memorial tablets which covered the walls. They commemorated military and naval Townshends, Somervilles and Coghills. As Dicky Adare told us, 'The memorials in these little Anglo-Irish churches record the story of the British Empire'. Today there is a new tablet in memory of Vice Admiral Hugh Somerville's son, Philip, a destroyer Captain with three DSOs.

The letter goes on:

This is Monday, June 10. We are back in Dublin. Kendall has just gone over on the night boat to England to reform his battalion. His wife is stopping the night with us, a game girl if ever there was one. These people don't seem to know when they are licked. An hour ago, at nine o'clock, we heard Duff Cooper announce Mussolini's entrance into the war in a speech that is probably the bitterest ever made over the radio. Perhaps at midnight we shall hear something as scathing from you. I shall wait to hear you at twelve fifteen.

It was the following day that the president spoke at the University of Virginia.

From letter to President Roosevelt continued

Monday, June 10th, 1940

Things may move pretty fast now. People at home, at last seem to be waking up to the fact that it will be less expensive to do this job while France and Britain are afloat than to do it single-handed afterwards. This is tougher than when the Germans were at the gates of Paris in '14 and again in March 1918. Well, we've all got to keep our tails up.

No sooner, so it seemed, had we loaded the S.S. *Roosevelt* than we were advised that the *Washington* was coming to Galway to pick up those who had been left behind. She was due to load on June 12th and sail that night or the next. I wrote the president:

It looks at present writing as if we were going to embark about 950 people from Galway, Thursday and Friday (June 12, 13th).

We are looking out for some of the things that we slipped up on last time but the fact remains that Galway at most has beds for about 700 visitors. This week there are four hundred members of a teachers' convention there and unless we can hold a lot of the *Washington*'s passengers back in Dublin and Cork till Thursday and Friday, there will be no beds for them. The local steamship people keep insisting that they must get over to Galway because it takes so long to examine baggage and passports, all of which is true. I wanted to have a lot of baggage examined here when it arrives from England and then sent across in bond but I have no authority to insist upon it and nobody takes the suggestion very seriously. They (the top officials) don't care how long Americans mill around in a freight shed with no place to sit down. The local steamship agents are weak brothers.

There was no announcement in Berlin this week that the British would sink the *Washington* and try to blame the Germans, as there had been the week before about the *Roosevelt*, but there was very nearly an actual 'incident', as we later found out.

The night before the embarkation, June 11th, we dined with Mr Meade and his wife in Dublin. As I reported it,

From letter to President Roosevelt continued

Tuesday, June 11th, 1940

Meade is the leading surgeon here and the party were all authentic Dublin Irish people except for the Swedish Consul and his wife (and ourselves). There was the Minister for Industry and Commerce and his wife, a sister of the famous Father 'Paddy' Brown, the aforesaid Swedes, the Provost of the National University, Patrick Rooney, Esq., a leading barrister, father of Mrs Meade, and a sweet Limerick lady, Mrs 'Tommy' MacLoughlin, wife of the engineer of the Shannon works. I have not laughed like that since we got over here. Well, at a dramatic pause I was called to the telephone. I tried to look important because I thought Maude had planted the call, so she could rat about 9.45 and go home. I got to the phone expecting Mr Flynn, our trusty butler, to whisper, 'It's me, Flynn. It's a quarter to ten'. Instead he said, 'Liverpool and London has just been calling you. The *Washington* has just been torpedoed and the passengers is all in the boats'. Till I got home a few minutes later there was quite a 'state of mind' on. Then I found out that the story was false. There had only been a scare. Then I had to telephone Meade that there had been overstatement. The *Washington* was afloat.

Later we found out what had started the false report and how close it had come to being a true one. Early that morning the *Washington* on her way from Lisbon had exchanged the following blinker messages with a German submarine:

June 11th, 1940. Latitude 42° 12′ North - Longitude 12° 50′ West.

Sub:	Stop ship
Sub:	Heave to ship
Sub:	Torpedo the ship
Ship:	American ship
Sub:	Captain ten minutes to leave ship
Ship:	American ship
Sub:	Ten minutes
Ship:	Washington American, Washington, Washington American (continuously)
Sub:	Silent
Sub:	Thought you were another ship, please go on.
Ship:	Thanks

Resumed for half hour in direction of sun to get away from submarine.

0630:	Secured stations
0653:	Sighted another unknown submarine several miles off port side; course altered into sun with submarine dead astern.

No exchange of messages between submarine and ship.

0751:	Resumed course; submarine out of sight.

Commander expresses his appreciation of conduct of passengers and crew.

If that submarine commander had been only a little more 'trigger happy', he could have made Pearl Harbor unnecessary. America would have been in the war.

The night of the Meade's party I heard on the radio the president make his University of Virginia speech and utter the historic sentence, 'The hand that held the dagger struck his neighbour in the back'. The next morning I wrote him:

From letter to President Roosevelt continued

Tuesday, June 11th, 1940

I kept awake for the midnight news and then heard you. I could feel the whole atmosphere of the quadrangle at Charlottesville and hear the cheering. It was very different from what we have here.

It was a swell speech. They are afraid here to play up the dagger phrase, which was the dramatic note. The *Irish Press*, de Valera's organ, carries it this morning but in *small type* and without comment. The *Irish Times* does not print it and that is the pro-English paper.

The *Irish Times* dared not print it. It had been especially persecuted by Mr Aiken's censorship.

The letter went on:

From letter to President Roosevelt continued

Tuesday, June 11th, 1940

This morning, June 11, the Belgian Minister called on us to thank me for your remarks upon Il Duce. He is a bit cut up about his King. He has an idea that he (the King) talked with Weygand on the 26th May and told him they couldn't hold out and that probably Weygand told him he would bloody well have to. There are people here who criticise Duff Cooper's 'dispassionate' comment upon Il Duce. But they are the people who are always defeatist. What Cooper had to do was to buck up his own people and the French. It was a large order for everybody had his tail down over the French situation. You had to get fighting mad or give up. I think it was a fine speech and a useful one. Cooper and Churchill are keeping things going.

The next day we began our second embarkation. Again Harvey Klemmer, the Maritime Commission representative, came over from London, arriving at the crack of dawn. He breakfasted with me and again we set out by motor for Galway. We arrived in time to lunch at the Galway Railway Hotel with Commander Hitchcock and the attractive Tania Long, the newspaper feature writer. The hotel dining room was a madhouse. Besides the Americans bound for the *Washington*, there was a convention of 400 Irish school-teachers in Galway city, not to speak of some forty of America's leading newspaper reporters. My diary records: 'Went out with Klemmer in harbour master's launch. Found Captain Manning up in the air about the newspaper men'.

Since at that time I did not know how nearly he and his passengers had been to constituting an 'incident', I could only advise him on general principles to 'meet the press'. He eventually talked to a delegation chosen by themselves and no sensational story came out.

From diary entry

Wednesday, June 12th, 1940

Going back with the harbour master, found that a purser's clerk had just been drowned. Pitched out of a launch returning from shore. Met the (Ray) Athertons on board and gave him the telegram from Leland Harrison (US Minister to Switzerland) which came in my care. Got back to shore about six-thirty, called up the Bishop of Galway but found he was in Dublin. Bought some cakes (instead of dinner) and got home about ten-thirty, a lovely, cloudless evening; still light.

CHAPTER X

JUNE 12TH-22ND

The second week in June political Dublin was convulsed with repercussions of the 'affair Goertz', and the arrest of Michael Held on June 6th. Here was Ireland's traditional friend dropping parachute spies on neutral Ireland! What could it mean?

According to his own story Herr Captain Doctor Hermann Goertz on landing near Trim in County Meath on May 5th had set out for a 'contact' in County Wicklow. Dressed in German uniform and boots, he swam the Boyne, walked two nights and part of two days and arrived safely at the 'friendly house' which was his destination. Here he tells us an Irish lady hid him and purchased civilian clothing for him. Sometime prior to June 6th he moved to Michael Held's house in Templeogue, Dublin. Goertz makes no mention of this but it is the point at which the story given out by the Irish government begins.

It appeared that the Helds' Irish servant girl shortly before June 6th reported to the police that she had been dismissed under what she considered suspicious circumstances. Her employer told her that his plans had changed unexpectedly and that he and his wife had no further need for her services. In lieu of notice he paid her generously in cash. It was this which aroused her suspicions. He also saw to it that she left the premises without delay. We do not know what day Goertz arrived at the Held house but the government announced that the police searched it on June 6th. In a locked guest room they found Goertz's uniform as a German regular with insignia of rank, his Iron Cross with Oak Leaf cluster, his military 'papers', and 20,000 American dollars in small bills. There was, moreover, something even more incriminating. This was a suit of new civilian clothes and some shirts marked with the tab of a

Dublin merchant. The police had no difficulty with the merchant. He knew the lady who had purchased the suits and haberdashery. She was the beautiful Mrs Francis Stuart, born Ynez [Iseult] MacBride. Her mother was the beautiful Maud Gonne who, with Countess Markievicz and the American, Mrs Erskine Childers, Senior, had been the heroines of the Sinn Féin republican movement.[1] Maud Gonne was reputed to have been the great love of William Butler Yeats' life and is immortalised in his poems. She was also the mother of Seán MacBride, the brilliant, unsmiling young Dublin barrister who was defiantly defending such members of the IRA as the de Valera police had taken into custody. In 1948, in the first inter-party government he was to be minister for external affairs.

Before coming to Ireland officially, I had read a novel of young Mr Stuart's *Try the sky*.[2] I thought it promised a great deal and I looked forward to meeting him in Ireland. It appeared, however, that he was in Berlin as an agent of the IRA. Why Mrs Stuart should be buying men's clothing while her husband was in Berlin was difficult to explain, and the police arrested her.

Goertz, in landing during the emergency in the uniform of a belligerent without permission, had violated Irish neutrality. Mrs Stuart, an Éire national, in abetting him was chargeable with treason.

Held was tried as a German agent planted in Ireland before the war and given a prison sentence. The government held Mrs Stuart in custody for a time, then quietly convicted her on a minor count, and soon afterwards released her. The government 'inspired rumour' had it that it was a 'cat and mouse' release, planned to trap Goertz. More probably it was to propitiate old friends and especially to muzzle her formidable brother Seán MacBride.

The Goertz affair proved a heaven-sent opportunity for Mr de Valera and he exploited it with skill. Its first effect on Irish opinion was to excite anti-German feeling. Germany had violated Irish neutrality which had been announced as the equivalent of Irish Independence. Henceforth de Valera could say to Hempel: 'Here we are trying to control anti-German feeling, keep England out of the ports and work with you in good faith, and you do this to us. You can see that it forces me to become more pro-English in order not to give away our secret understanding'. Goertz's illegal landing also strengthened de Valera against the IRA. Here was an 'enemy' of Ireland who had violated Irish neutrality, affronted Irish

---

[1] Maud Gonne MacBride (1886–1953). Her autobiography *A servant of the queen* was published in 1938.
[2] *Try the sky* was published by Gollancz in London in 1933.

independence yet the IRA were hiding and protecting him. There is a strong probability that de Valera's police could have picked Goertz up any day they wished. Goertz confirms this when he tells how he took a furnished house in Dalkey and was visited by a series of prominent Irishmen yet was never disturbed. A year and a half went by before Mr de Valera found it profitable to have him under lock and key.

While the Irish government gave the newspapers a free hand in printing the details of Held's arrest and trial, no editor was allowed to comment on the significance of the facts. Furthermore the Censor suppressed the list of prominent Irish people to whom Goertz might turn for help, that was found among his effects in the Held house. We know of this list through Hempel's reports.

The publicity given to the Held arrest misled the American legation. We believed that de Valera was inciting anti-German feeling to the end of gaining popular support for acceptance of the British proposals and the announcement of the common defence which would end Partition. We did not realise that at this time Mr de Valera's primary anxiety was the IRA and Artus.

Our private news from London made it clear that my 'exploring' of the Northern Island situation was at an end. The English government had taken over. The U-boat pressure had forced their hands. They were formulating concrete proposals. If de Valera accepted them, not only the use of the ports would be obtained, which was of first importance, but Mr de Valera's acquiescence would ease Irish-American pressure on the Roosevelt administration. Since both the greater and lesser objectives were in my view American concerns, I felt I should do what I could to urge Irish acceptance. I firmly believed that it was the wise thing for Mr de Valera to do in the Irish interest.

I had established a personal relation with him. I liked him. I had been in Dublin only two months but twice he had asked me to do him important favours and I had done my best to serve him. Now I could at least tender him my advice for what it was worth.

It seemed wise to feel out the situation first. He had told me that I could tell anything to Mr Walshe that I could tell him. My second Belfast visit gave me the opportunity to talk things over with Mr Walshe before seeing his chief.

In a portion of the letter to the president dated June 11th but finished several days later, I gave the account of this conversation:

From letter to President Roosevelt

Tuesday, June 11th, 1940

I told him (Walshe) in complete detail of my trip to Belfast and suggested that he and some of the younger men get busy, working out in their heads some sort of compromise union solution of partition in the case that events suddenly make co-operation for the duration of the war inevitable. 'Dev' is sure not to compromise and they have got to put pressure on him from within his own party if they are going to act quick. Then he opened up what I had really gone to him to explore but hesitated to suggest he said,

'If by any chance you should come into the war, how would that affect us?'

'That is just it', I said, 'If we did come in, We would need ports in the south and west, Cobh and Berehaven at least, also landing fields for transatlantic flights. How about it?'

Of course he meant with the US *in*, the Irish Government could take the chance they dare not take now.

The letter ended: 'I am having my picture taken on Friday morning with 'Dev' for *Life*. They are getting up an Irish number.'

I could not have asked for help in influencing Mr de Valera to co-operate with Northern Ireland from anyone more opposed to the idea than Joe Walshe. But I did not then know it.

At eleven o'clock in the forenoon of Friday, June 14th, I called on Mr de Valera. The *Life* photographer arrived promptly and 'took' us shaking hands. Mr de Valera's bronze statue of Lincoln dominated the background. The irony of the great American unionist in the Separatist headquarters never seemed to occur to the taoiseach. After the photographer left, I stopped on, to talk. I expected Mr de Valera to make some reference to my conversation with Mr Walshe the day I got back from the North, but he made none.

Hempel's reports to Berlin reveal that both Joe Walshe and Frederick Boland were urging Mr de Valera *not* to accept the British proposals for a common island defence. They believed Hitler's New Order was on the horizon.

My report to the president reads:

From letter to President Roosevelt

Friday, June 14th, 1940

We discussed the situation, which is very grave, as the French armies are being driven steadily back. I promised again to try to hurry rifles for him. He talks very frankly. Went home and began a letter to the duke of Abercorn in which I thanked him for his kindness and told him I thought Craigavon must make a gesture to the South, otherwise the island was indefensible. James Dillon came in in the afternoon and I read him a portion of the letter. He was afraid that it might encourage de Valera to ask too much and refuse such compromise as would save the face of the North. We discussed the constitutional questions involved and how to get around recognition of the King. He had devised a federal body, some sort of senate or council whose sole function would be the channel through which External Affairs would be conducted and which would conduct necessary relations with the King. Then one federal Dáil and Senate and a county council with home rule for Ulster. Violation of the new constitutional pact would produce reversion to status quo. Not very good but a beginning.

The letter that I wrote the duke of Abercorn was dated June 14th, This was the day the Germans entered Paris. It records our views at that time;

Dear Abercorn

It is impossible to obey your injunction not to thank you for your hospitality and it is especially impossible not to thank you for the large measure of confidence you have accorded me.

As I have told you, my position has been that of exploring first hand the attitude of Northern Ireland toward Partition and my warrant for it has been the substantial interest of my Government in some final settlement of what is called the Irish Question. Beyond this and without instructions from my Government my personal concern over the situation had led me to attempt to convey to you and Lord Craigavon my impression of the unquestionable good faith of the Government of Éire in preparing to meet the present emergency. It is of course obvious to you as to me that without the closest military co-operation and without mutual trust and good will the defence of this island would be impossible.

My personal habits of belief and hope are in co-operation everywhere. I should like to see the whole thirty-two counties of Ireland united by free choice. I should like to see this united Ireland bound by free choice to Great Britain. I should like to see the two islands in the same way united with the British Commonwealth of Nations, and I should like to see all the democracies of the Western Hemisphere partners in this same enterprise. I am a unionist on a large scale because I see no other way in which Christian democratic civilisation may hope to survive.

On this fourteenth day of June the situation is already critical if not desperate. As I see it there are two possibilities: one that Britain fights on alone the other that Britain and a remnant of France fight on with the assistance of the United States. If the United States should intervene and the outcome be the defeat of Germany I think it a fair assumption that the United States would hope for a permanent solution of the Irish question, which apparently is some solution of Partition. If the United States does not intervene it would of course have no say in the matter. In the case that Britain fights on alone, more than ever the need for military co-operation and united action seems to be imperative. You of course personally will understand that the difficulties of the government of Éire increase with each successive disaster to the Allied arms. There are evidences that the Nationalists on your side of the border are resentful of the government's attitude here and will exert increasing pressure on it.

Middle of the road opinion always drifts toward the victor and fears to back a losing horse. If this situation be allowed to drift, even for another week, in my opinion it will very likely be too late to do anything. In my opinion, unless at the least some immediate and striking gesture is made by Lord Craigavon in the direction of Geographical Unity for the purpose of Island defence, the consequences will be grave. I believe his apprehension of such a step as involving him in the political surrender of his position to be justified, but I fear the choice that confronts him is between that and a break-down of Irish defence with the consequence of opening Britain to attack from the rear, which might well prove fatal.

Forgive me for writing so frankly, but I am very apprehensive. Every day, every hour counts. You must weld this Island['s] opinion into a mind devoted to repelling the invader or go down.

God grant that vision and mutual forbearance will prevail.
Faithfully yours,
His Grace,
The Duke of Abercorn,
Governor of Northern Ireland,
Government House,
Hillsborough, Northern Ireland.

The report to the president continued:

From letter to President Roosevelt continued

June 1940

Saturday, June 15th, we lunched at the MacEntees' and met Father 'Paddy' Brown[3] of Maynooth who charmed us all. He is Mrs MacEntee's brother. The Seán T. O'Kellys, the former Chancellor of the National University and his wife and Mrs P.J. Rutledge (wife of the former minister for justice and very attractive). Very jolly, with far too much excellent food and wine.

Marjorie Leslie (Mrs Shane Leslie) came to us on Wednesday and is ill in bed. At the MacEntees' I had a little talk with O'Kelly about de Valera. (O'Kelly was then Vice-Premier.) I told him I had written Abercorn urging him to urge Craigavon to make a gesture (to Éire) and warned him that he (O'Kelly) must sit on Dev's head to make a compromise settlement possible in case the gesture was made. S.T. was very understanding. I said, 'You and Lord Craigavon could come to an agreement. We (Americans and Irish) are used to making deals'. He laughed and said that was so.

On June 15th Hempel received instructions from Berlin regarding the Held affair. He had evidently sent telegrams to Ribbentrop on June 4th, 7th and 8th, reporting the situation, and explaining the mischief which the incident had done, presumably with 'I told you so' insinuations. Ribbentrop's reply, signed by Woermann, reads (italics mine):

---

[3] Son of a Parnellite national teacher, a gifted professor of mathematics who had been taught maths by de Valera, created a lifelong bond.

No. 437

91/100237–38/1

The Director of the Political Department to the Legation in Eire

Telegram

No. 320   Berlin, June 15, 1940, 2.30 p.m.

zu Pol. II 1372g

In accordance with your suggestion you are empowered to get in touch with the Eirean Government in a confidential way regarding the case against Held-Stuart before the action starts and, in connection with reports on this case, make the following statement on the German Government's attitude:

The Eirean Government must be clearly aware that the struggle between the German Reich and Britain was now entering upon its decisive stage. We were conscious of the fact that the measures we had to take for carrying out this struggle against Britain *which had been forced upon us,* might also affect Eirean interests. Just because of this, however, we considered it important *to inform the Eirean Government once again that our sole objective was Britain.* We believed that Eire whose enemy through history was known to be *Britain,* was fully aware that the outcome of this struggle would also be of decisive importance for the Eirean Nation and the *final* realisation of its national demands. (This is certainly a promise that Eire would get Northern Ireland.) Given this situation, we believed that we could also count on the *greatest possible understanding from the Eirean* Government, despite their neutral attitude, even if Eire may in some ways be affected by our measures.

If your communications meet with ready response you will be able to follow them up with the warning that matters such as the charge against Held should also be *treated in a correspondingly careful manner by the Eirean Government, and above all, in the press.*

On Sunday, June 16th, there was a large and important all-party defence meeting in College Green. The letter to the president continues:

Went to the big mass meeting in the morning. About 10 a.m. J.J. Horgan came to see us. He had been stopping with General Brennan.

He had told me the stories about Irish opinion regarding England that are set down in the preceding chapter. If England was really 'bate' Ireland was too.

From letter to President Roosevelt continued

Sunday, June 16th, 1940

Father 'Paddy' Brown came and we all went together to the big meeting in College Green. De V., Cosgrave and Norton[4] the Labourite, all spoke from the same platform. I stood on the edge of the crowd not wishing to get in too deeply as I was lunching with Maffey and playing golf at Portmarnock. What struck me was the apathetic, rather perplexed attitude of the crowd. Not much enthusiasm.

However, it could be called a success. Later Gilroy, the political reporter of the *Irish Press*, told me that he had asked Cosgrave after the meeting if he had spoken to de Valera. He replied, 'I have not spoken to him for twenty years and it will probably be twenty years more before I do'.

Other leaders of the opposition parties spoke to him and shook hands but they entertained much of Mr Cosgrave's aversion and distrust. It soon became evident that Mr de Valera's plan of 'uniting the Irish people' was by shrewd but unprincipled political subjugation of the opposition leaders rather than by compromise and a meeting of minds. In effect he was always saying, 'If you don't agree with me you are a traitor to Ireland and a British agent'.

My memorandum goes on:

Lunched with Maffey alone at Farm Hill. His house was surrounded by armed guards as we drove in.

Sir John was a noted sportsman and extremely popular with all classes of Irish people. However, if some patriot had shot him it would have seriously embarrassed the Irish government. The IRA was bent on embarrassing the government and doubtless Mr de Valera was justified in taking elaborate precautions. At the same time the escorting was

---

[4] Bill Norton (1900–63), started working life as a post office clerk, trade unionist and labour politician, was to serve in post-war Irish coalition Cabinets 1948–51, 1954–7.

always done in a manner that suggested that there was justification for assassination. It was another variation on the 'hate' theme.

From diary entry

Sunday, June 16th, 1940

After lunch we played golf at Portmarnock. Lovely afternoon. Beat him four up. (Usually he beat me.) He was very down with the French news. I said, 'I feel ashamed, having a country which for the present is safe, and a home in it'.

Then I turned the conversation into pleasanter channels and asked him if the story about the Duke of Windsor slipping off when he was at Peshawar and going alone into the Bazaar was true. Maffey, who was the British Political Agent, was supposed to have told him that if he would give his word that this would not happen again, nothing would be said about it. Otherwise he was under arrest.

Maffey said this was not true. What happened was that the tour was not going well and that the Prince knew it. They all tried to pretend that it was going well and routed him through places where there was a minimum of danger. The Prince got on to that and blew out at Maffey. Whereupon Maffey, who knew his father well, told him some things. For some years afterwards, whenever Maffey was a guest of the King and the Prince was present, Edward would look at him with resentment, but one day several years later he came and held out his hand and said, 'I think you were right about that'.

All very handsome.

Maffey came back with me to tea and we found Father Brown still there. Maude had asked him back to lunch and he had stopped on for tea. Granard[5] came to dinner with his boy, John Forbes. Also Desmond Leslie. Granard was on his way to London for a week. I told him to tell them they needed a gesture from the North very badly. (The earl of Granard had been Master of Horse to three British kings, was member of the Privy Council, and at this time Controller of Ascot.)

---

[5] Bernard Forbes, 8th Earl of Granard (1874–1948), Anglo-Irish soldier and liberal politician.

From diary entry
Monday, June 17th, 1940

A little weary after 18 holes yesterday. Wrote a lot of letters and worked on a draft of a letter to de Valera. Sent a telegram to the President asking him to hurry up the 20,000 rifles for de Valera.

James Dillon came to dinner. He was deeply exercised over the danger to his country and the lack of realistic measures to meet it. He would do nothing however except in agreement with de Valera as he did not want to rock the boat. My memorandum reads:

FROM MEMORANDUM ON MEETING ON NATIONAL DEFENCE BETWEEN JAMES DILLON AND EAMON DE VALERA

After dinner he told me of his showing de Valera a scheme for ending partition, the one we had talked over. He said he would be willing to fly it as a kite and be disavowed. Dev said he would have to study it. Dillon said most of the Defence Council except Aiken were for inviting England to come in at once. I doubt the wisdom of making any overtures to the North at present. At nine o'clock we heard Churchill's great speech over the wireless in which he said Britain would go on alone.

In retrospect James Dillon stands out as the only politician in Éire who had the courage to be guided by the realities of the situation. Others saw through the Sinn Féin make-believe, but feared to speak up in the meeting and oppose de Valera in a situation in which he could and surely would use the anti-British issue against them. None of them of course had any knowledge of the apology for the Galway speech and the implications pointing to a German entente.

Mr Dillon had worked out a scheme for getting around the obstacle of anti-British sentiment. It envisaged primary co-operation with the French. The 115,000 French Dunkirk evacuees would be sent over to Éire for reforming and rearming. Other French units as they fell back to the south and west would be transported to Éire with such equipment as they had salvaged. These together with the Irish forces would be placed under the command of picked French officers, and the resulting Anglo-Franco-Irish combination would be in a position to ask for arms from the United States as a belligerent on the democratic side.

I asked Mr Dillon to prepare a memorandum of his ideas on this subject that I might send to President Roosevelt. This he did, making it clear that the memorandum was only a first study of the problem subject to amendment and development. It reads:

MEMORANDUM FROM JAMES DILLON FOR PRESIDENT ROOSEVELT

If the result of our defence preparations transpires to be that an invading force penetrates deeply into our country and is subsequently driven back and exterminated, the material loss to the country will be crippling and the personal sufferings of the residents in the area devastated will be of a character to appal our people who are quite unfamiliar with the nature of wartime suffering for civilians. The death and maiming of civilians will shake the morale of our people and the sufferings of women are likely to be of a character calculated to break that morale completely, with the consequent possibility of civilian collapse to the possible vital embarrassment of such armed forces as we would have in the field.

To avert this suffering for our people and the possible collapse of morale (which if it touched the Army might degenerate into demoralisation) it appears to us that invasion must be prevented and that to do this unified command for the defence of this whole island of 32 counties is vital now and that with such unified command the defences of the Island should be entrusted to combined Allied forces consisting of French, British and Irish troops, drawing supplies from the United States of America on the personal request of the Irish Government to President Roosevelt for material wherewith to protect our country from attack by a foreign enemy.

Fully appreciating the political difficulties that such a decision might create we feel that our joint undertaking to ensure that the most effective measures for the protection of our people as well as of our country demands that we should not allow any question of political embarrassment to deter us from pursuing any course which we are convinced is essential to secure the main objective of immunity for our people and country from the horrors of total war.

It might appear that a proper preliminary to this departure would be the introduction of Conscription in Ireland. We feel that this course is not to be recommended because (l) we have not the material or the resources to equip a larger Army than the voluntary system appears capable of producing, (2) because the introduction of conscription at this time would be the equivalent of planting a banner around which every potential 5th Columnist in Ireland could rally without revealing to the people his true purpose and at the same time provide the protagonists of internal division with an ideal cloak for their subversive activities. It is of course true that our problem would be greatly simplified if America were to declare war but at the present time with America in a state of non-belligerency and morally at war with the Axis Powers it appears to us that the radical consequences of unified command for the defence of all Ireland, i.e., the subsequent impossibility of survival for the anachronism of Northern Ireland would correct the undesirable aspects of our proposal for such elements in the country who might suspect in it a suggestion that it represented the reconquest of this country by the British. This corrective would be further fortified by the fact that with the progressive retreat of the French armies in France it might become not only practicable from the Allied point of view but desirable also that a substantial part of the Land, Sea and Air Forces incorporated in our defences would be French forces under the command of French officers and it might even be provided that the Supreme Command of this Western Defence would be committed to a French General Officer thus establishing beyond all doubt that with the passage of the emergency foreign troops would be withdrawn under the direction of the Government of the French Republic acting through officers of the French Army.

This proposal to co-ordinate Irish defence with French defence was the logical corollary of Mr Dillon's proposal for ending Partition. When Mr de Valera disapproved the former it followed that he also disapproved the latter.

From diary entry

Tuesday, June 18th, 1940

The news of the French break-down came this morning. Gilroy came to see me at ten. Heavenly day. He told me the story of Cosgrave not speaking to de Valera. He said he felt Dev had been slipping but was getting up again on the defence issue.

Mr Gilroy was a sound, fair-minded, and objective political reporter or 'correspondent' for Mr de Valera's newspaper. We were never treated unfairly or unkindly by him or by the reporters of any of the Dublin newspapers. I believe he had at this time no knowledge or suspicion of de Valera's secret bargain with the Germans.

Two days before, on June 17th, Hempel had replied to Woermann's instructions directing him to warn the Irish government to handle the Held-Stuart case in a careful manner. This telegram, if it exists, is not available. But in his telegram to Berlin dated June 19th, Hempel says (italics mine):

No. 506

91/100247–51

Telegram

TOP SECRET

No. 324 of June 19   Dublin, June 2, 1940
                                              Received June 21—11.30 a.m.

With reference to my telegram No. 320 of June 17, de Valera requested me yesterday to call on him for a lengthy conversation which was held in the presence of Walshe in a *forthright and pleasant manner*. I reiterated what I had told Walshe. As to the case of Held, I had the opportunity of expressing, without displaying too great an interest and by keeping to the line pursued heretofore, our wishes for careful treatment especially in public, which Walshe tacitly supported. De Valera listened to my statements with interest but obviously attached importance, above all to assuring me of Eire's further adherence to strict neutrality. He explained that at the beginning of the war anxiety about British intervention had been uppermost in his mind but Eirean neutrality had so far been respected by the British, which could of course change. Without any reference to the case of Held he admitted that with Germany's approach anxiety had, as was understandable, grown about possible German intentions to use Eire as a base for attacks on Britain by exploiting '*the weak minority* (The IRA) *which was working against the Government's policy*'. He had repeatedly declared publicly and *had only in that way succeeded in obtaining the* return of Eirean ports from Britain, that Eire would *not* become an assembly base against Britain. To this he would adhere. As he could assure me however, he had explained to the British just as definitely that any British intervention on Eirean territory would meet with the same determined resistance. Except for the minimum of loose connection with the British Empire laid down in the Constitution which was *exclusively intended to facilitate the future return of Northern Ireland to Eire*, and to the *strong economic dependence of Eire on Britain*, Eire stands in exactly the same position towards us as towards Britain. With regard to the solution of the Northern Irish question he must, in view of the British-Irish balance of power, adhere to a peaceful solution, (de Valera wanted no 'Artus' Plan operation) as only so could a permanent and tenable position be reached. If it came to an invasion then Eire would inevitably become a battlefield for the belligerents. In a British invasion we would fight with Irishmen against Britons. In a German invasion, against these with Irishmen. He was carrying out a completely realistic policy and saw, in determination to resist any attacker to the uttermost, the only possibility to reduce the danger.

In a discussion today on another subject Boland referred to yesterday's conversation with de Valera and told me in *strict confidence* that British pressure for the abandonment of Eirean neutrality—apparently accompanied by the bait of future concessions in respect of Northern Ireland—had recently increased again but that de Valera had rejected all advances 'most vehemently'. As I recently heard from another source, de Valera is supposed to have made a similar statement to a prominent representative of the Irish Nationalists (IRA) and also to have given *this as a reason for the army increase*.

Hempel was aware of de Valera's two-way formula: for British consumption the new Defence Programme was protection against Germany and the IRA, for German and IRA consumption it was 'modest insurance' against England. What Hempel always saw was the value of Éire neutrality in barring England from the ports (italics mine):

Continuation of Telegram No. 324 (Pol. 11) of June 19.

It is therefore very possible that de Valera is, in his usual clever way, exploiting incidents such as the case of Held which brought out the German danger, so as to be better armed also against

British intentions and to strengthen his position against the largely anti-German Cosgrave opposition.

Compared with the unmistakable signs of panic after the case of Held, I am of opinion that my conversations with Walshe and de Valera have at least had a somewhat relaxing and reassuring effect and in pursuance of the *exhortation I expressed some weeks ago for* the continuance of their *understanding neutral attitude,* and were an encouraging influence. *I have the impression that at any rate Walshe and Boland are discerning more and more the trenchant and significant effects which the changed world situation is having on Eire and the obvious weakness of the democracies.* It remains 'to be seen what repercussions this will have on the future handling of the case against Held-Stuart. According to reliable information I have just received, the material found is said to incriminate seriously a number of reputable Irishmen whose political activities have so far been irreproachable, because of their connections with Germany; there is, at all events, a continued danger of further serious consequences and, as de Valera's statements also clearly indicate, grave anxiety about German intentions to use Eire as a base for operations against Britain. This anxiety is constantly growing through alarming reports recently received from the Irish element in America.

In my opinion the recent efforts of groups working for Britain in Northern Ireland to undermine Eire's neutrality by a gradual rapprochement at first especially in the field of co-ordination of defence measures have, at present, no prospect of success. Lord Craigavon, whose position is indeed under attack by his own rank and file, is said, furthermore, to have rejected all advances for a rapprochement with Eire. In these circumstances the influence of the United States for a settlement of the Northern Ireland question, said to have been exerted by Roosevelt in a moderate degree solely for the self-seeking purpose of securing the Irish-American vote, is probably no longer being felt. In view of German strength, it seems to me that the idea of possible German action for *the return of Northern Ireland* would now also find acceptance in non-radical nationalist circles, amongst others, allegedly with the *far-seeing influential Irish Cardinal MacRory.*[6] The defence forces of Northern Ireland are said to have been

---

[6] Cardinal Joseph MacRory, Archbishop of Armagh, 1861–1945. He may have been concerned that it would become known that his closest political allies formally placed the northern nationalist community under the protection of the Third Reich.

substantially strengthened, amongst other things, by the recruitment of Ulster Defence Volunteers.

Recruitment (in Éire) was progressing. 50,000 applications have allegedly been received, particularly from groups of old liberation fighters. Despite the few reports I have received of growing pro-German feeling in the country and ostensibly also in the army, my general impression is that the case of Held has, on the whole, also turned feeling against us.

From here onwards telegram very mutilated.

. Repeat has been requested.

Continuation of Telegram No. 324 (Pol. 11) of June 19

The mutilated part at the end of the above telegram on page 2 reads as follows:

The fear of invasion, now primarily a German one, with tragic consequences for the strength of the Irish nation weakened by centuries of struggle and also for the liberty which had been gained at great effort has, above all, shaken responsible thinking persons suitable for leading positions, while on the other hand, radical nationalism (IRA) has *no recognised leader and seems to be losing in esteem.* Despite the continuation of the unstable situation with elements of surprise (two groups mutilated) and as a result of the recent call for the army increase and the internment of political suspects the creation of a parliamentary united front for the defence of liberty and neutrality has been furthered. The wishes of anti-German circles in the Cosgrave opposition which were recently expressed again, for setting up a National Cabinet in which the opposition would be represented have so far been rejected by the Government.

HEMPEL

It is important to note that in his exposition of this theme to Hempel, de Valera explains that only by proclaiming that he would never allow Éire to become the base of attack against England had he obtained the ports. He also explained that the proclamation of Association with the Commonwealth in the new Irish Constitution was put there to facilitate the *acquisition of Northern Ireland.* It meant nothing in itself. England was in the same position to Éire as Germany. This was also Lord Craigavon's view.

In the last paragraph of this section of the telegram there is an interesting reference to Boland, presumably Frederick. Apparently Mr Boland 'leaked' to Hempel in 'strictest confidence' that the British were making proposals in regard to Northern Ireland. He also tells him that Mr de Valera had rejected the proposals 'most vehemently'.

Hempel makes it clear that he felt that he had coped successfully with the situation considering its difficulties. He says, 'Compared with the unmistakable signs of panic after the case of Held, I am of opinion that my conversations with Walshe and de Valera have at least had a somewhat relaxing and reassuring effect and in pursuance of the *exhortation I expressed some weeks ago* for *the continuance of their understanding neutral attitude* and were an encouraging influence'.

Since this telegram was dated June 19th, the 'exhortation of some weeks ago' might well have been the consequence of de Valera's reaction to the parachute landing of Goertz on May 5th and his Galway speech of condemnation on May 12th.

My diary notes:

From diary entry
Wednesday, June 19th, 1940

Lovely warm, bright day again. Went to see Maffey at 11.30 a.m. He told me had nothing further about the North and agreed that something must be done at once. He said that he thought that if there could be some sort of concrete proposal to put up to Churchill it would do good. I told him that I had been discussing that with James Dillon last night. He asked me if I could get it and would Dillon stand for it. I said that Dillon had told me that he would be the goat if de Valera wanted it. My own feeling is that something ought first to come from Craigavon but I have put in a call for Dillon.

Maffey told me he had been having talks with the Irish Government over defensive measures and a good deal was arranged as to airplanes and naval support but that when it came to offering him torpedo nets for some port on the west coast to be used in case of a hasty embarkation, de Valera baulked and said he would be charged with selling out to the British. Very difficult.

Marjorie Leslie went off after lunch. Castlerosse is coming at five and Dillon for dinner early.

Mrs Shane Leslie had received messages by automatic writing through her husband's cousin, Claire Sheridan[7] the sculptor, that her son 'Jackie', who had gone to France with his regiment, had been killed. The news had made her ill. Later it appeared that 'Jackie' was not dead but a prisoner. Since he was a cousin of Winston Churchill, the Germans held him in special custody somewhat in the nature of a hostage.

It was encouraging that Mr de Valera was arranging with the British for air and naval support, but discouraging that, at a time when we were cutting red tape, doing irregular things and sticking out our official necks in the effort to save a desperate situation, he should make fish of airplanes and fowl of torpedo nets. The torpedo nets might have helped Sir John Maffey's staff with their women and children to escape.

Besides giving a copy of the letter to Abercorn to Sir John Maffey, I sent it on to Ambassador Kennedy in London with the following:

From letter to Ambassador Kennedy

Wednesday June 19th, 1940

Dear Joe:

I am pounding this out with my own two fingers. There is a bird over here named X——, an American (of Irish descent). He telephoned me about two weeks ago saying he was a friend of Colonel Scanlan. I had him to lunch and thought he was all right but in a week I began getting some reports on him from Irish sources to the effect he was phoney and what did I know about him. I wired Scanlan and he telephoned me that as far as he knew X was all right; that he had had the Blank agency in London for thirteen years but that now there was no more business and he supposed that he was at loose ends. Last night an Irish friend of mine told me that X had been checked as stopping with at least one person on the secret service list as a Fifth Columnist. Will you have him looked up by the British?

Later we got Mr X embarked for the United States. Whether he was disloyal I never certainly knew.

Klemmer was grand again getting the *Washington* off.

[7] For Clare Sheridan (née Frewen) see Rauchbauer, *Shane Leslie: sublime failure*, 13, 65–6.

The big College Green unity defence meeting was a success but in a sense only a moderate one. The crowd apparently didn't believe in the reality of the situation pictured, suspected perhaps it was some political shell game.[8] De Valera is undoubtedly gaining strength from taking a positive and energetic position but there is a lot of slack water which he hasn't got moving yet and there is a formidable fifth column movement moving in the other direction. The only thing that I can see that would save the situation is a gesture from Ulster, at the least recognising the geographical unity of the island for defence. From what I get from the inside I believe if Ulster made some real compromise Éire would throw in with them immediately and give the ports and airfields which will be so urgently needed when Gibraltar goes down.

Of course I am sending the letter to Abercorn, to the Boss (the President) but haven't got it off yet. I have given a copy of it to Maffey, who asked for it.

If you get inside dope from the British intelligence about something starting this way, send me a wire in clear as follows: 'We hear Cudahy is all right'. (My predecessor who was Ambassador of Belgium had not been heard from for several days) I want to have notice to protect or burn the codes and some of the telegrams. Good luck,

Aff.

Am sending this over through Maffey's pouch

A declaration from Craigavon at this juncture probably would not have influenced Mr de Valera, but it would have made it more difficult for him to have refused co-operation.

That same June 19th, I began a letter to the president:

From letter to President Roosevelt continued

Wednesday, June 19th, 1940

Dear Boss

This is a lovely hot afternoon and the Irish are complaining of the heat. We have had three weeks of this weather broken by only one day's rain. There is a before the battle atmosphere on. People are settling down to the reality of probable and imminent invasion. It can hardly be doubted that if the Germans attempt a landing

---

[8] Sleight-of-hand swindling game in which a small object is concealed under a walnut shell or the like, and bets are made as to which shell the object is under.

on England they will make an effort via this undefended country with its unmined coastal waters.

The great Park meadow that I am looking out on is studded with railway ties set in the ground and four feet in the air to stop airplane landings and the rattle of machine gun practice comes from a post a mile away (Chapelizod). Somebody let off an anti-aircraft gun a few minutes ago and I did what I have been putting off for two weeks, that is examine the wine cellar as an air raid shelter. We could retire there with a corkscrew and be very brave.

I have been telegraphing frantically to you for rifles for the volunteers the past few days, first, because they are needed here, and second, because the time may come soon when the most useful thing I can do for you is strongly to urge compromise with Ulster on Mr de Valera, and I want to be thought of as helpful to them and well disposed. The Government needs the rifles even more to establish confidence in its power to obtain them than for actual defence.

They had their big defence meeting Sunday noon on College Green. The speakers all take the line of demanding preparedness against *any* invader. No one specified. Privately and confidentially they admit they only fear Germany and are making preparations with Britain for Irish defence. In recent talks with de Valera, and Seán T. O'Kelly, MacEntee, and Joe Walshe, I have suggested that if Germany crushes Britain and permits her resurgence as a third-class power she will of necessity keep Ireland as a Gibraltar, to watch Britain and house a German garrison, also to develop the ports which control the traffic of the western Atlantic, both air and maritime; also as 'lebensraum' for four or five million German farmers who could very easily increase productivity of the island about eight times. No one in the Government has differed from this view, but of course the man in the street does not visualise it. Accepting this premise, the Government can only choose between making such a result less likely by joining up with Britain at once, or pursuing neutrality without hope that it will be respected, or by joining the Germans. In no one of the alternatives can she hope to escape being a battlefield.

As you see, it adds up as a little better total in favour of throwing in with Britain, with the chance (if England holds off Germany) of preserving the liberty she enjoys and very possibly of bringing Partition to a close.

As is apparent now, but not then, Mr de Valera was primarily interested in undercutting the IRA with Germany. How far he took his 'team' into his confidence we do not know. If any one of them was fully in his confidence it probably would have been Frank Aiken. The strength of his position was that he could always assert that he was trying to get assurances from Germany to respect Irish neutrality and save the Irish people from invasion. Since the whole anti-British element in Éire did not want to believe that German assurances were worth nothing, he could take this line with safety. All our analyses of the situation were necessarily based on patent facts and probabilities. As we had no suspicion of what he actually was trying to do, they were erroneous. We were predicting what a normal, right-minded man would do in given circumstances. As we found out later he was neither normal nor right-minded.

The letter continues:

One thing that would strengthen the Government politically and enable them to carry the lag pro-British public sentiment would be a gesture of at least military unity for the duration of the war by Craigavon. But he knows that if he made this, it cuts the ground from under his political position as being part of Britain. De Valera knows it also and that is why he should accept it as an entering wedge.

When I was up at Government House in Ulster on June 7th and 8th and saw Craigavon, as I wrote you, I became satisfied that he intended to do nothing or learn anything. He was the perfect Bourbon but very pleasant. A week later I wrote the enclosed letter as a bread and butter letter to the Duke of Abercorn. The situation was drifting so fast and in such a bad direction down here (I mean by that up till that time no very definite stand in regard to defence had been taken, although the National Defence Council had been formed from the three Parties) that I took the chance. I showed it (the letter) to Sir John Maffey and he advised me to send it and asked for a copy to send to Downing Street. After all, if it does no good it can do no harm except to Gray, and somebody has got to speak out in meeting. Maffey, who is better informed than I am, agrees a hundred per cent with the view I have unfolded. I had a talk with him this morning enquiring whether Downing Street had followed up its 'talking to' Craigavon the week before. He said no. He was convinced the Colonial Office would only go on talking and would do nothing, that he, Maffey, would have to go over their heads to Churchill, but he wondered if someone could not give him a tentative, unbinding draft of the south's present ideas as to Ulster, maximum and minimum. Well, it happens that last night, June 18th, James Dillon was here to dinner and told me that he had shown de Valera exactly such a draft, that very afternoon and he offered to be the goat and sponsor it if de Valera said the word. He is coming to dine again tonight and we will go over it. We fixed it up last week, but it seemed to me that it was not the time to trot it out: better wait until the North makes an advance. Of course if de Valera approves the idea, I shall have nothing to do with it unless he asks me to transmit it to Maffey as a kite.

The letter continued the next day, June 20th. It recounts the talk with Sir John Maffey on Sunday, June 16th, on the Portmarnock links and goes on:

Castlerosse has just left with a pint of scotch under his ninety-inch belt. He told me one good one: 'A Scotchman was talking with an Australian and trying to impress him with the fact that he was a Scotchman. "Have you got many Scotchmen in Australia?" he asked. "Oh, yes," said the Australian, "but our trouble is rabbits".'

Castlerosse, talking of airplane production, said Lord Nuffield had been the recent devil in the plot. He said Nuffield claimed that he could do all these things that Henry Ford says he can do, and then he didn't do them. He said his boss, Beaverbrook, had doubled production since he went in.

Dillon dined here again last night, June 19th, and tells me that de Valera does not want him to make any trial proposition to Ulster, so I shall have to get hold of Maffey and tell him it is all off. It is heartbreaking when so much depends on making this island impregnable to have petty jealousies and hates making a united stand impossible.

My report to the president under date of June 22nd continued:

The drought was broken last night by rain. Yesterday I got a letter from Abercorn thanking me for mine (the enclosed) saying I was always welcome at Government House and adding that as I had not marked my letter private he had sent it on to Craigavon. So far so good. In the past week there have been two resignations of Parliamentary secretaries in the Ulster government in protest against Craigavon's ineffective defence measures. (These were Mr E. Warnock, K.C., Parliamentary Secretary to the Minister for Home Affairs, and Colonel A.R. Gordon, Financial Secretary to the Minister for Finance). Just what it means I don't know, but it is probably, in part, a movement for an understanding with the South.

A message came from Mr de Valera at noon today, Saturday, June 22nd, asking if I could come to his office at 3.30. (This was four days after he had sent for Hempel). He looked very white and drawn and was off later in the day to address meetings at Tralee and elsewhere. He asked what I thought of the American situation and whether I had any late or especial news. I said I thought our position was that of being *morally at war with Germany now*, that if Germany had the power she would treat us as an enemy and destroy us, that the new Cabinet appointments were exactly as you stated them to be, an evidence of the country's increasing solidarity for defence but that it was evident that the fact they were both announced interventionalists was significant. I said that neither Stimson[9] nor Knox[10] could have taken this step except after consultation with other Republican leaders, and that personally I could only regard it as a step toward more active assistance to the allied cause in the interest of American defence.

I told him that I thought he was doing everything he could do and doing it very well and asked him if any word had come from Craigavon. He said no.

I said, 'if I were you I would sit tight and wait for it but when it comes I think you would do well to make compromises and meet them more than half way'.

He said, 'There is only one solution of this thing and that is for the North to join us in our neutrality until we are invaded. We could be more useful that way'.

I said that I still thought that was absolutely out of the question; that Britain must control the Narrows on both sides and have access to the Northern Ireland ports. I should have asked him how a portion of country at war *undeclares* itself and becomes

---

[9] Henry Lewis Stimson (1867–1950), republican secretary of war 1911–13. Appointed secretary of war under Roosevelt, 20 June 1940.
[10] William Franklin Knox (1874–1944). Appointed US secretary of the navy, 20 June 1940.

neutral, and whether this can be done without the consent of the enemy.

He asked me whether, if Ulster joined the South in neutrality, the United States could not guarantee that combined neutrality.

I told him that the Secretary of State's reply to his enquiry on the possibility of guaranteeing Éire's status quo would in my opinion be the answer to a new enquiry, namely that it was impossible.

I told him that in my thinking about the situation, as if I were an Irishman, I always had to come back to the proposition that if England went down, Ireland would of a certainty be occupied as a citadel guarding her and controlling the Atlantic.

He said, 'Years ago Ireland's neutrality should have been guaranteed for that very reason. When President Wilson was talking about the "freedom of the seas" Ireland should have been the Switzerland of the proposition'.

I said, 'Look at Switzerland now'.

He said, 'Of course *if America came in, it would alter our situation overnight.* But as it is I can't throw in with the British *now. I can't ask unarmed men to face an enemy in coats of mail,* even if I were sure the people would follow me.

I said, 'Perhaps if you would throw in *now* England would share her arms with you'. 'Why doesn't she do it now?' he asked. 'When the Germans land', he went on, 'they are going to announce themselves as liberators and call on us to help them free Ulster'.

I couldn't say that I did not think this was so. Instead I said, 'I think you are doing everything that can be done at present. I haven't met a single person of any school of political opinion who does not applaud you and say that you are the only man for this terrible job'.

It was certainly true at this time that Mr de Valera was receiving general approval regardless of party lines. The indecision and futility which I had earlier reported seemed to have been replaced by energetic leadership. The fact was that Hempel had accepted the thesis that it was Germany's interest to back de Valera and neutrality rather than the IRA. Thus de Valera could proceed against the IRA without fear of German retaliation. As he also clearly saw, and doubtless had intended, he would regain control of the anti-British issue.

The memorandum of the conversation continued.

From letter to President Roosevelt continued

Saturday, June 22nd, 1940

I said 'Of course I do not know it officially, and I never mention it to anyone, but I know you have complete understanding with the British about sending powerful assistance the moment you are attacked and what more can you do at this moment?'

'They ought to let us have anti-aircraft guns, for one thing', he said. 'A few tanks, if landed Wicklow way, or on the West could roam about Ireland unmolested, except by land mines and it would only be chance that we could mine the right roads'.

I said England must shortly be putting a strong motorised force into Ulster with tanks enough to cope with anything but a major expeditionary force.

He thought that was likely.

I then asked him if he had received from me the message that had come from Under Secretary Welles yesterday and of which I had transmitted a paraphrase at once to the Secretary of External Affairs (Mr Walshe).

He said no and seemed very pleased that he would get in part at least what he had asked for, thanks to your intervention.

This was the telegram announcing that twenty thousand rifles had been earmarked for him to be delivered through the British. The only lie I told the president in my long correspondence was misrepresenting Mr de Valera's attitude on receipt of this news. What he actually said was, 'I wish they could have sent them directly to us and not through the British'. He looked very sour. I didn't want the president to know this as it would not have improved our chances of getting more arms.

From letter to President Roosevelt continued

June 22nd, 1940

I am writing Sumner (Welles)[11] that anything that we can do just now to put him under obligations to us will help very much when this Ulster situation comes to a head, as it is very likely to do soon. If he baulks at a reasonable compromise which will save Ulster's face, we'll have to tell him that American public opinion will not stand for it, that the left wing IRA which he used to rely on to put

---

[11] Sumner Welles (1892–1961), educated at Groton and Harvard, major foreign policy adviser to Franklin D. Roosevelt and served as under-secretary of state (the second ranking position) from 1943 to 1973.

American political pressure on in his behalf, is now denouncing him as having sold out to Britain and, besides that, is discredited with us as allied with the Nazi Fifth Columnists; that while we have twenty million Catholics, we have forty million fundamentalist Methodists and Baptists who are well organised politically and who are inclined to sympathise with Ulster if coerced especially now when American sympathy is turning in favour of England.

I am working on the draft of a memorandum on this line which if the emergency arose I would pass on to him in the form of a friendly suggestion of what might be the American reaction. His mind works in queer ways but I like him the more I see him and we are getting used to each other. When I left him today I told him he must get some diversion, something to take his mind off this problem. I asked him if he had anyone read to him.

'I'm all right', he said. 'My work is a diversion'.

He told me one other thing. He said Dublin had no defence but could not be proclaimed an open town, because the Government offices could not well be moved nor the barracks that are all around it.

He thinks England is due for a tremendous air attack, not by hundreds of planes but by thousands. He is probably right. I told him the story of the Irish farmer who when asked what he thought of things said 'I'd like to see England nearly bate'.

He laughed and said, 'That's it, "*nearly.*" But that has never been my idea. As soon as I was confident that we were going to be let alone *I have wanted a very strong England*.

It is bright light here this week till nearly eleven. When I take late walks around the little park and look over into the sunken ditch outside I see things which are not for your young ears to hear, things which cause me to slink back into the bushes to hide my blushes. Nature seems to be much the same in Holy Ireland as elsewhere.

If this 'interview' with Mr de Valera had been cabled to the United States as a 'follow up' of his statement issued through the *United Press*, it would have doubtless borne the headlines: '*De Valera wants Very Strong England. Ready to join her now if armed*'. It would have given Mr Hempel a somewhat different view of Mr de Valera from that which he records in his report of his talk with him four days earlier.

It was interesting that both he and Mr Walshe on separate occasions should have spoken of American entry into the war as '*changing everything for us overnight*'.

Until after Pearl Harbor Mr de Valera always told me that his American advices were to the effect that under *no* circumstances would the United States enter the war.

CHAPTER XI

In June 1940, the British government, unaware of Mr de Valera's secret arrangement with Germany, offered to end Partition in return for permission to use the Irish ports and establish an all-Ireland defence. Mr de Valera refused the offer, thus twice within a year without informing the Irish people or obtaining their mandate he ranged himself on the side of the dictators and against democracy.

The story of the British proposals came to the American legation bit by bit. My diary letter to the president under date of June 24th, states,

From letter to President Roosevelt

Monday, June 24th, 1940

Yesterday, which was Sunday, June 23rd, we got the French Armistice terms. I put in the day with Father ('Paddy') Browne. He came to lunch, then we played golf and came back for dinner. He is the brother of Mrs MacEntee whose husband is Secretary of Industry and Commerce and close friend of Seán T. O'Kelly. He is pretty well 'in the know' and gave me the low-down on the Cabinet line-up. I asked him if he did not think a gesture of friendliness and help from the North was the most important thing at present to hold the South in line with the bad French news. He said 'yes'.

He was a man of honour as well as high intelligence and notable in any company of scholars. I have never believed that he was party to Mr de Valera's German adventure.

On June 11th, Winston Churchill had just said, 'the hour is grave'. It was so grave that it seemed immaterial whether control of the defence forces was in London or Belfast. From our viewpoint the important thing was unity in co-operation with the Allies. The political consequences in the United States of common defence would have been considerable.

My letter to the president continued under date of Monday, June 24th:

From letter to President Roosevelt continued

Monday, June 24th, 1940

Maffey telephoned me just as I was about to telephone him. He stopped in on his way downtown. I told him ten days had passed since I had written Abercorn and that it might now be too late, but had anything been done up there? He thereupon took me into his confidence and told me things that I had better not put down on paper but which you could probably get from Lothian (British Ambassador in Washington) if you asked for them.

Generally the idea was that they had been working hard on de Valera but had not yet got him to recede from his position of neutrality. They were afraid that if Ulster made gestures now it would be looked upon here as a palpable trap to get them into the war. That of course is all so, but undercover stuff (secret diplomatic exchanges) get nowhere in bucking up morale in the South. I finally made this suggestion: 'Let someone important in Ulster say, "We respect your neutrality. We hope you can stay out of it, but if you are invaded in spite of our political differences we are all Irishmen, and we will back you up to the last man and the last gun."' Let's see how that goes.

In the light of the unknown facts it is unlikely that it would have 'gone at all!'

What Maffey is chiefly concerned about is the possibility of intensified submarine war, making the need of a protected port in Southern Ireland essential. I warned him again against forcible action on the score of its effect upon American opinion, and the opportunity it would give enemies of Britain in the United States to score. He asked me if I could think of some way of approaching this. Thus far I can't. I wish I had your head for these things.

Maude has the Nuncio and his Secretary to lunch today with Beatrice Granard, Lady Powerscourt, the Frank MacDermots and Granard's brother, the Pasha, and sister. I wish you were here.

On June 24th Sir John Maffey told me that Malcolm MacDonald, British minister for Health, was secretly in Dublin.

From letter to President Roosevelt continued

Tuesday, June 25th, 1940

This is Tuesday morning, June 25th and the pouch is to be closed shortly. We are expecting any outward-bound mail may be the last for an indefinite period. To me it seems possible that the major German landing might be made here though the difficulty of petrol supplies would be a serious one (meaning there was little in Éire to seize). The whole of Ireland uses just about the amount used by the London Bus Company. I enclose a postal item which you may not have.

During that morning of June 25th, the most interesting and intelligent young man in political Ireland called on me. This was Erskine Childers, Jr. His father, the English novelist, had been executed by the Cosgrave party at the close of the Civil War. His mother was Miss Osgood, daughter of the Boston publisher. At this time he was the youngest member of the Dáil and a member of Fianna Fáil. His wife also was an American. He came to talk Irish-American trade, a matter in which I was acutely interested. We did not mention the war. My letter to the president reports:

From letter to President Roosevelt continued

Tuesday, June 25th, 1940

I told him that I had already urged on Seán MacEntee the development of exports of ground peat (the Germans and Belgians before the war had supplied the American market), of hand-made tweeds, the popularisation of Irish whiskey in the USA and Limerick bacon for an American luxury market. In my opinion it was then the best in the world. (Government control afterwards ruined it.) I said that I had heard a lot of talk about these enterprises but nothing was ever done. He said that unfortunately that was so, that he couldn't get Irish exporters to combine and spend money in exporting and marketing in the US. He was very discouraged about Irish economics, said the new industries, with few exceptions, were not succeeding. He said— and this was significant—that Irish wealth is indicated in the cattle census. It has not changed but a few per cent since 1913.

This means that the Irish national income has not materially increased. Yet since his party 'went in' (in 1932) the national debt has increased from thirty to seventy million pounds (now over four hundred million) and the national annual budget from about twenty to over thirty (now in 1959 over a hundred and twenty-five). The Hospitals Sweep, with the income from English securities and remittances of American and British origin used to compensate for the adverse trade balance but now (because of the war) the sweep income is out. He thought they ought to make an American loan for purchase in America of essential commodities. I told him that was fine, and that no doubt the First National Bank of New York would arrange it but that the pound was certain to go down and they would have a bad time repaying a dollar loan. Moreover, they probably would be unable to make a sterling loan in New York but if they did not make it at once and got into the war they could make no American loan at all unless Congress passed new legislation. With all you have on your mind this must seem childish prattle but you asked for it.

We had dinner last night with a Dr Collis[1] interested in Dublin slum clearance and housing. There was a charming Jesuit (Father Canavan)[2] as the other guest. He told us this one: An Englishman was watching the annual football game in Ulster between Linfield, the Orange institution, and the Celtics, the great Catholic team. He applauded good plays impartially. A dour Orangeman observed him and asked, 'Are ye for Linfield?' 'No', said the Englishman. 'Are ye for the Celtics'? 'No. I am just applauding the good plays'. 'Then ye must be a bluidy atheist'.

Love to all in which Maude joins.

In a letter to the president, dated June 28th, I wrote:

From letter to President Roosevelt continued

Friday, June 28th, 1940

Yesterday, Thursday, (June 27th) was quite a day. Sir John Maffey arrived early on his way to his office and finally said that he had been authorised by his Government to take me into his confidence and tell me that a proposal for a complete ending of

[1] Dr Bob Collis (1900–75) paediatrician, author and rugby player. He was to be among the first group of physicians to treat the survivors of Belsen concentration camp.
[2] Father Canavan was a Jesuit and philosophy professor, who had advised de Valera on the 1937 Constitution.

Partition had been made to the Irish Government in return for the *ending of neutrality*. He said that it had been communicated to Joe, (Ambassador Kennedy) and that Joe had passed it on to you. He, Maffey, hoped that I could see my way clear to see de Valera who was supposed to be discussing the matter in full Cabinet. I told him I would have to wait for instructions. I therefore sent a telegram secret and confidential, saying in effect I have been privately informed of a situation of which I believe you have been informed by London. Shall I enquire attitude of Irish Government? Believe advisable to make enquiry before decision is taken. Then I called Joe (Ambassador Kennedy in London) and asked him if he had transmitted a certain proposal yesterday to you. He said he had and suggested that I do nothing till I heard from you. No answer has thus far come, 12.30 p.m., Friday (June 28th).

There never was an answer. I took it to mean that the White House had enough anxieties without stirring up Anglophobe Irish opposition in the United States. It is unlikely at this time in view of what we now know that had I been instructed to present American hopes that a formula for common defence would be found, it would have made a difference. The Irish decision had been made. The letter continued:

From letter to President Roosevelt continued

Friday, June 28th, 1940

I told Maffey (during the talk on Thursday, June 27th) that I thought it a mistake to go at it this way, that in my opinion there should have been preliminary gestures of goodwill from Ulster and a preparation in the Press of some kind of emergency programme which could get the South committed and then lead to the inevitable precaution of getting ready together, whether it violated neutrality or not. The move the British have taken in promising a complete and immediate ending of partition I am afraid now (with France crushed) will look like a trap. The opposition (have) told me that a month ago *such a move would have been jumped at by de Valera*, but it was not considered. And yet it is a wonderful thing for this Government if they had the guts to accept it and I believe that with the right kind of leadership they could put it over. They naturally feel very timid these days and wishfully think that by not plumping with England they are going to make their lot easier in the event of a crushing German victory.

The truth was, by *not* 'plumping' with England, de Valera expected to get Northern Ireland 'without strings'.

Maffey showed me the draft of the original proposals made by Malcolm MacDonald for the Cabinet to de Valera. *It guaranteed the whole works, lock, stock and barrel, providing for the immediate* setting up of a commission to draft a new all Ireland constitution but insisting on a declaration of war by Éire. De Valera countered with his favourite proposal that Ulster should withdraw from the war and become neutral, though how this could be done he did not say.

Chamberlain who (as Lord President of the Council) is directing the negotiation for the Cabinet came back, waiving the war declaration and proposing that Éire go ahead and arm with British arms (which as a matter of fact they are already doing), invite English troops to come in and put the ports at the disposal of the Allies.

He further *guaranteed* consent of the North to Union, though this morning (Sunday, June 30th) the papers carry a proposal made yesterday by Craigavon in which he says he will never consent to political union though willing to combine for military ends. He doesn't realise what they are intending behind his back yet.

Mr de Valera rejected the proposals and at once began building an alibi and a propaganda of justification. He alleged that had he accepted the proposals British *could not have 'delivered the goods'*. He cited Craigavon's public statements to support his assertion. But the fact is that Craigavon never stated that he would *never* consider constitutional changes in the North's relation with Éire until *after* de Valera had rejected the proposals. This put the responsibility back on de Valera. Craigavon outjockeyed de Valera. The British never told me the date on which they regarded the negotiation as terminated but the evidence indicates that it was certainly before June 29th. It is not improbable that the negotiation formally terminated on July 26th or July 27th when Malcolm MacDonald was secretly in Dublin.

Hempel, in his telegram to Berlin dated June 19th, reports that 'today' Boland had told him that de Valera had 'rejected all advances (for the abandonment of neutrality) most vehemently'. If that be so Mr de Valera had made his decision ten days before Lord Craigavon had refused political union with Éire, which is the important point.

The British proposals were the last Irish negotiation that Neville Chamberlain directed. They ended in tragedy like his 'Gentleman's Agreement'. His biographer, writing of Mr Chamberlain and the fall of France, says: 'from Ireland came not a word to reward his policy of faith'.

Again he quotes Mr Chamberlain's diary for June 28th: 'The de Valera people are afraid we are going to lose and don't want to be involved with us'.

This was the day before Lord Craigavon issued his manifesto in the Kirkistown speech. It is probable that Mr Chamberlain had just communicated to him the failure of the negotiation.

Speaking of the various decisions which confronted Mr Chamberlain at the close of his career, he mentions as one of them, 'to urge on the unyielding Irish, North and South alike; that neither neutrality nor Partition could weigh in the scales against a German occupation of their country'.

The King accepted Mr Chamberlain's resignation on September 30th, 1940. Among those who sent tributes to him was Eamon de Valera. He appears to have been the sole beneficiary of 'the policy of faith'. Mr Chamberlain died on November 9th.

After the war former senator Frank MacDermot told me that Mr de Valera had decided to say 'no' before the British made their offer. When the first 'rumour', reached Mr MacDermot, he went to Belfast to find out what reception the proposals would get at Stormont. The Northern minister with whom he conferred told him that there was division of opinion in the North; that there were strong doubts as to de Valera's good faith but that in view of the gravity of the situation and the acute need for the Éire ports, he himself would probably resign if Craigavon refused to co-operate with Westminster. On Mr MacDermot's return to Dublin, Mr de Valera was unable immediately to see him. He then called upon the minister for the Coordination of Defensive Measures, Mr Frank Aiken.

Mr Aiken cut him short. 'MacDermot', he said, 'get this clear, we are never going to abandon our neutrality'. If anyone knew Irish policy at that time, it was Mr Aiken.

On Saturday, June 29th, at 3 p.m., Craigavon made the speech at the celebration of Kirkistown Royal Orange Lodge 1412 in which he said:

We have been criticised in some quarters on the ground that we are relying on regiments from Great Britain for the defence of our shores. It seems to be forgotten however, that we are a part of the United Kingdom and that the distribution of his Majesty's Forces is a matter for the military authorities ... .

My task, as your leader, has been made more difficult during the past few weeks by certain speeches, by letters in the public press, and by expressions in Parliament vaguely suggesting that Ulster should agree to a united Ireland. The supreme consideration for all of us within our beleaguered Islands is the safety of the whole United Kingdom, and I am glad to think that our firm attitude in the past has literally saved the situation. If an all-Ireland Parliament (in which, by representation, Ulster loyalists would have been in a hopeless minority) had been in existence at the outbreak of hostilities, I am persuaded that Great Britain would have been faced with an all-Ireland neutrality today and British troops would have been unable to land on Irish soil except by force.

The situation created by this campaign for a United Ireland, intensified since the outbreak of war, has been made immeasurably more difficult by recent declarations of Mr de Valera and also by the speech of Mr Seán T. O'Kelly, Vice-Premier of Éire, in the Dáil on Wednesday (June 27th) when he said:

'If anybody can get rid of Partition it will be this Government, and I am hopeful that we will. The matter is receiving attention. Those who run may read. It would not be wise to give any further information on this matter'.

Later, Mr O'Kelly said: 'I believe that de Valera will yet succeed ...'

That speech clearly indicates that Mr de Valera is once again blackmailing the British government to end Partition—and this at the very moment when the enemy is at our gates. It is sinister evidence that something serious is afoot.

I wish, therefore, to declare that I will be no party, directly or indirectly, to any change in the Constitution conferred upon Northern Ireland, which assures us of full partnership in the United Kingdom and the British empire.

Nevertheless, in the interests of both North and South, I am prepared to enter into the closest co-operation with Mr de Valera on matters of defence, provided he takes his stand, as we are doing, on the side of, Britain and the Empire, clears out the German and Italian representatives from Éire, and undertakes not to raise any issue of a constitutional nature.

I have never been a stumbling block, but I will never put my hand to any plan that would imperil the United Kingdom and the Empire. The world well knows the colours under which I have served my King and Country throughout a prolonged political career.

You and I have worked shoulder to shoulder for almost half a century: your faith in me has never been betrayed, my faith in you has never wavered … .To the end, then, let us maintain that priceless bond, so that in the trials that confront the Empire, Ulster may play a worthy part and vindicate her siege of Derry battle cry—'No Surrender'.

The 'criticism' to which Craigavon referred in opening his Kirkistown speech was not restricted to the parliamentary secretaries, Mr Warnock and Colonel Gordon, who had resigned in protest at their chief's policy. There was a widely held opinion in the North that a gesture of island unity in a common defence was at the moment highly important. It was the view which I had been pressing for American reasons. Its unsoundness derived from the fact, which we did not know that Mr de Valera had already sold Ulster to the Germans. Probably Lord Craigavon did not know this either but he believed that de Valera was capable of it and he was certain that he would never honestly contribute to a common defence.

On June 29th vox populi was expressing itself vociferously in Belfast through the columns of the *Northern Whig*. The Marchioness of Londonderry, whose husband was high in Conservative government circles, upheld Craigavon. She wrote:

The responsibility for this critical state of affairs rests entirely on the British Government … . Lord Craigavon and the Ulster Government have no control of the armed forces of the Crown. What then is the use of upbraiding him and them for not doing anything? … Ulster is a part of the United Kingdom and is governed by the Imperial Parliament in all matters affecting defence and must therefore fall into line … . Will therefore the British Government, even at the eleventh hour, assume the

225

responsibility which belongs to it and approach the president [*sic*] of Éire and ask him if he desires protection. They should ask him if he will invite the British Navy and British troops into Éire to defend Irish soil; if he will declare war on Germany and remove the enemy German minister immediately. On Mr de Valera's reply may depend the future of the whole of Ireland North and South.

The earl of Antrim[3] took issue with the Marchioness. He wrote:

I would like to support Lord Dufferin[4] in his plea for an Ireland united to defend herself against the Nazis. Lord Dufferin's critics have not understood his argument, although I should have thought it simple enough.

Surely the facts are these: the quarrels and disagreements of Ireland become parochial and unimportant beside the position in which Ireland finds herself today. Ireland is in danger of invasion by Germany. To most of us the thought of any part of this island under Nazi rule is unbearable.

When that horror is combined with the fact that a conquered Ireland would be a terrible menace to England, it must be the duty of Northern Ireland to forget the past in the present danger, by making every possible effort, and, if necessary, concession to bring Dublin into active co-operation with England in the war against Hitler.

A contributor signing himself, 'Exile from Éire', rebuts Lord Antrim and excoriates Lord Dufferin. He says:

Sir,
Two bright young Ulster men, Lord Dufferin and Mr Ed. Ward,[5] are advocating union with Éire for the duration.

Mr Ward's dream that it is 'horribly clear' to him Éire's neutrality will not save her is not a very momentous revelation, for even Ulster children are aware of it.

Éire realises it too, but inexplicable though it be, she would immeasurably prefer German domination than the detached association as now with the Commonwealth.

[3] The 8th earl (1911–77).
[4] Appointed under-secretary of state for the Colonies in 1937 before he resigned from the government in 1940 to join the British army, refusing a post in the war-time coalition government of Winston Churchill.
[5] Edward Henry Harold Ward (1905–93), became 7th viscount Bangor in 1950. Father-in-law of author Richard Dawkins.

Éire declarations that the border is a handicap for defence of the 32 is clever propaganda—an attempt to convey to Britain what a danger the border is.

Nationalist Ireland is not pro-Ally any more than she was in the last war. Take a cross section of a day's public utterances. Cardinal MacRory in a 'War address' made the middle cut a plea for the abolition of the border, adding a litany of alleged grievances his flock suffers here, though they continue to increase. A priest at Newry proposed last week a resolution of congratulation to Pétain whilst a Munster mayor stated the War was no concern of theirs.

A month ago a Roman Catholic bishop proposed the toast at a gathering of influential Nationalists—'An Ireland Catholic, Gaelic and free!' What loyal helpful allies for defence of the Empire!

Even de Valera has said he will oppose the entry of 'both' belligerents: is it unfair to suggest he was referring to Britain and Germany?

Lord Dufferin holds we should go hat in hand to Éire begging reunion. Was there ever a more contemptible proposal? Shades of the great Viceroy Dufferin!

Éire's stand cut from Britain is her own concern and her own funeral. Lord Dufferin makes reference to Quisling, I merely mark that, and add nothing.

Yours truly,
EXILE FROM EIRE.

Mr Beresford Richards of Craigavad, Co. Down, rebukes Lord Dufferin and Mr Ward while his fellow townsman, Mr Shillington, equally an Ulster patriot, applauds Mr Ward, as also does Mr J.C. Lyle, CVO of Portrush.

And so it went. Men of principle were concerned over principle, tempers were rising, and all because they did not know that Eamon de Valera had sold out to Germany. Such situations constitute the ironies of history and provoke the laughter of the gods.

The letter to the president dated June 28th continued:

From letter to President Roosevelt continued

Friday, June 28th, 1940

My own hunch is that if de Valera pushes them too hard, Churchill will say, 'to hell with you', and strike. That was why I felt it might be a good thing to let de Valera know you knew of the offer at once. However, the more I think of it, the more I think it is better to wait a bit and not give the impression that we are helping Britain get them into a trap. They have *got to see and feel for* themselves that nothing is going to save them if Britain goes down. MacEntee (Minister for Industry and Commerce) made a speech to that effect last night but he is not taken into the conference. De Valera had with him Aiken and Lemass only. Lemass is reported to be clever. Aiken, as I wrote you has been suspect as a Fifth Columnist but on the best authority I can get, this is untrue. X. as I wrote you characterised him as a 'dud'. Apparently the Premier never lets them talk in meeting. Once or twice Lemass began to show interest but was 'shushed'. Before this reaches you (it will go by the *Washington* about July 7th) the situation may have crystallised. Of course if Éire is attacked before the negotiation is broken off, de Valera will take the British offer, if it is still open, as it probably will be. If they should crush Britain without attacking Éire, he will look on if he can. You cannot blame him for thinking that he will fare better if he does not dip in. In all this it must be remembered that while the Government wants Britain to win there are enough people whose hatred of Britain has been kept alive by the present regime for political purposes, to make it difficult for the Government to throw in with Britain before being attacked by Germany. Of course the Germans must have made the Government promises but what they are I haven't yet been able to find out. *If I ever find out it will not be by asking questions.*

Further under date of June 28th,

Granard came to lunch and was very chatty. He had just come back from a few days in England.

At three o'clock I had *another* lunch with the Papal Nuncio to meet the Cardinal, Primate Archbishop MacRory. There was also the Italian Minister Berardis, Seán T. O'Kelly (Minister for Finance) and the Nuncio's Secretary, Monsignor Enrici. I got along fine with the Cardinal, who is a spry little man. We agreed that Irish whiskey was the noblest work of man and a very desirable gift of God.

Berardis, (the Italian Minister) who sat opposite me, began explaining in his almost incomprehensible, but fluent, French what the Mediterranean System required, and how the British never would understand it. Then I turned to the Cardinal again with my stock opening, 'We need a little more Christianity; don't you think so? And then, if that is so and you believe in conciliation why are you harping on the wrong of partition?' (At this particular time.) In his address at Maynooth the day before he had got loose on that line and had to be soft-pedalled by the Government. The banquet became more and more like an Oppenheim stage diplomatic function with Berardis holding his hand before his face, but so I could hear him, in stage whispers, telling Seán T. O'Kelly that he mustn't be beguiled by the British and Seán T., understanding very little of it (though he knew French well), kept saying, 'Oui, oui', at intervals and looking sourer and sourer. And the dear old Nuncio at the head of the table, like an old bird with a parrot's eye, smiling benignly and missing nothing. Along about six the primate was ready to leave and I took him back to his hotel. In the car I said, 'You feel partition to be the great crime against Ireland. What price should Éire pay to end it if they had a chance?'

'No price at all', he shot back. '*It is ours by right*'.

'What are you going to do with eight hundred thousand black Protestants?' I said, 'if you try to coerce them?'

'I don't know', he said.

'Don't you think that's got to be thought out?' I said. 'I wasn't joking about what you said yesterday at Maynooth. I don't know any of the details, but it is clear that North and South are trying to reach an understanding and everybody that stirs up feeling is going to make it harder'.

He agreed that if that were so, the less said the better. He promised to come to lunch with me the next time he came to Dublin.

Whether or not the cardinal had been consulted by Mr de Valera in regard to the British proposals I do not know. It is probable that he had been. Mr de Valera at times worked with him very closely but it was reported that they did not always see eye to eye. Mr de Valera insisted on Daniel O'Connell's proposition: 'We take our religion from Rome but not our politics'. This is not exactly what O'Connell said, but it currently passes for it.

I came to like the cardinal. He was one of the few Irishmen that I met in high places who said openly what he thought.

My letter to the president continued under date of July 1:

From letter to President Roosevelt continued

Monday, July 1st, 1940

… a party, and it was very jolly. She [Phyllis Ryan, wife of Seán T. O'Kelly] is a chemist and has a government job (City Analyst), does the water analysing. Maude asked her, 'Will you analyse my water?' meaning the legation well in case the city water supply was stopped. When there was quiet, Seán T. told this one: A Dublin white woman produced a black baby, 'Well', she says to her husband, 'this is what comes of your drinking all that dirty black Guinness stout'.

After lunch I had a private talk with O'Kelly and he told me what the British proposals were, substantially as I had read them in Chamberlain's memorandum. He felt that the British government without meaning to deceive would find that they could not implement their promises 'just as in '14 and again in '16 [*sic*]? The Irish government must reject the proposals and accept only *an accomplished fact of union before abandoning neutrality.*'

What Mr O'Kelly said about the British in 1914 and again in 1916 was at the least controversial. The North refused Home Rule in 1914, largely because as they asserted, the South was accepting it *not* as a final solution but as a stepping stone to Separation. In 1916, after the Sinn Féin rebellion, they said, 'See, we told you so'. It is undeniable that until the Dublin Uprising there was always hope for Home Rule for the whole of Ireland. The Sinn Féiners who opposed Home Rule and destroyed Redmond and the Nationalist Party extinguished the last hope of a united Ireland in any appreciable future.

From letter to President Roosevelt continued

Monday, July 1st, 1940

Craigavon in the morning paper is quoted as saying that while he will accept island unity for the duration of the war he will not be a party to any infringement of the constitution. O'Kelly believed that Chamberlain could not get him coerced.

I said, 'What if we are invaded?'

"We'll fight', he said, 'and get English help'.

And then I said, 'And get partition ended if you can?'

"Yes', he said.

Had there been honest doubt as to the ability of Westminster to implement its promise to end Partition, Mr de Valera could easily have obtained undertakings from Canada and Australia. Moreover the thesis that England *could not deliver the North* collapsed as a reason for refusing the British proposals when Mr de Valera subsequently took the position that Britain *was* coercing Ulster and holding her against her will. This was tantamount to asserting not merely that England *could* deliver the North but *should*. Although it was notorious that Northern Ireland opposed union with Éire by a two-to-one majority, no one in the South challenged the Fianna Fáil 'coercion' propaganda.

The letter to the president goes on:

From letter to President Roosevelt continued

Tuesday, July 2nd, 1940

James Dillon, deputy leader of the Opposition, came to see me. He and Cosgrave had been informed (officially) of the situation; so I could talk with him. He backs de Valera's position, says that if de Valera tried to carry the country on the strength of the present British promises he would be beaten. If the thing were accomplished and de Valera offered to fight for abandonment of neutrality in the union parliament with the support of the Cosgrave party they would carry the country 85 to 15 per cent. But de Valera at present *will not even promise to advocate the abandonment of neutrality in an accomplished union parliament*; but he will accept British arms and fight if invaded, inviting British help immediately.

O'Kelly (yesterday) told me what I had surmised but had been unable to confirm, namely that the German minister had made definite pledges to Éire that she would not be molested if she remained neutral. They don't believe him but would like to.

He said nothing about getting Northern Ireland from the Germans.

Dillon says the feeling is growing that England is beaten unless we should come in and they don't believe we will.

What might have happened had not Mr de Valera first refused the proposals, remains academic until the British Foreign office opens its files. But there is evidence suggesting that what coercion talk there was did not emanate from 'the top', that there was never disagreement between

Craigavon and the British prime minister. The story as told to me by a friend of Craigavon was that he was informed of the rise in submarine sinkings as the British navy evacuated the French channel ports. He knew the grave import to British interest in the Mediterranean of Mussolini's declaration of war. He had advance information of the French collapse. Craigavon like Churchill was cast in a large mould. He was not appalled at the prospect of Britain standing alone. There was no sacrifice that he would not make to save the ship and he knew that his people would follow him, but he was equally certain that de Valera would never accept the proposals and he was not going to make sacrifices fruitlessly. In 1940 he certainly knew what General MacEoin[6] told the people of Loughrea in March 1959, that de Valera did not want a block of Ulster Protestants controlling the Dáil in Dublin. It meant his political death. With such knowledge therefore Craigavon played the hand for the empire and won.

We have no evidence that he knew that de Valera had sold Ulster out to Berlin, but he seems to have entertained that complete mistrust of him which Mr P.S. O'Hegarty shared and publicised. Craigavon was a man of action. In his book a man was 'trustworthy or untrustworthy, period'. Why de Valera was untrustworthy did not interest him. Nor was he interested in the psychopathic aspects of Sinn Féin separatism nor in its menace to Western Civilisation.

Craigavon's mission, as he conceived it, was to save Protestant Ulster from expulsion from the United Kingdom and prevent its absorption into the non-cooperating Catholic South. This he achieved. Incidentally also he established the open door through which the secessionists may one day return into the Commonwealth when the separatist illusion is finally dispelled.

Craigavon knew that he was taking no grave risks. If unexpectedly de Valera had accepted the proposals and declared war on Germany, Éire would have been back in the union fighting shoulder to shoulder with Ulstermen, Scotsmen, Welshmen, Englishmen, Canadians, Australians, New Zealanders and in 1941 Americans. 'Independent' Éire would no longer have been a menace to Democratic Western Civilisation or to the North. The Irish problem would have been solved.

[6] General Séan MacEoin (1894–1973), soldier and politician, born in Bunlahy, Co. Longford, where he became a blacksmith: routed the Black and Tans in a famous incident.
General MacEoin, TD, the Fine Gael candidate for president, in a speech at Loughrea, Galway, on 24 March 1959, reported next day in the *Irish Times*, said: 'Just picture 50 Deputies from Northern Ireland, walking into Leinster House tomorrow, and see what happens. The present Fianna Fáil majority ceases to exist and no matter how constituencies should be gerrymandered the Northmen would still have the strength to make or unmake a government.
'Of course', said General MacEoin, 'we are compelled to ask the question, "Does Fianna Fáil want them in an all Ireland?" I doubt it'.

In view of the emphasis with which Winston Churchill on April 3rd, 1940, had asserted that he would never coerce Ulster or tolerate coercion, I ought never have believed that coercion was a possibility. But my reports to the president show that I did. I have had compunctions about publishing the information regarding the proposals which the British government confidentially transmitted to Washington and incidentally to me in Dublin. But upon the president's death, my letters with the rest of his files became at least *quasi-public* documents. They are deposited in the Roosevelt Memorial Library at Hyde Park and may at any time be made available to the public. Since I cannot look forward to much more time in which I may, by courtesy, be vouchsafed some control of these private reports, it seems best to print all that relates to the subject as it stands, if only to forestall its use out of context by unfriendly partisans. The reports were written without suspicion of de Valera's understanding with Germany or of the political reasons which prompted his policy. I believed him when he told me that he wanted a 'very strong England'. I took him literally when he said that he could not send unarmed men against men in armour. I accepted the patent implication that if properly armed, he would 'throw in with England *now*'; that although he naturally wished to avoid war he was on 'our side'. On the basis of his supposed attitude I expressed views to the president, which in the light of the facts, were unwarranted and unfair to Lord Craigavon, to Ulster and to the British government.

Furthermore, so much of the truth about the proposals leaked out at the time and was distorted by Sinn Féin propagandists that I feel an obligation to contribute what little I can to a factual understanding of the episode.

Mr de Valera unquestionably deceived the American mission and scored what his admirers regard as a 'diplomatic triumph'. In doing so, however, he established a record which during any foreseeable future will prevent any British government from forcing Northern Ireland into union with the South.

Finally, if I had not believed what Mr de Valera told me, what line could we have profitably followed? In 1940 it was politically desirable not to exacerbate the professional Irish Anglophobes in the United States, and it was desirable to hold the good will of the Irish people in Ireland, whatever course their government might pursue. To serve this latter end we were shortly to establish in Éire a depot of Red Cross supplies adequate for any Irish emergency which might arise.

That June ended with a telephone call inquiring whether 'Mr Setsuya Beppu, Consul of Japan, Liverpool', might call to the legation and present his compliments. France had fallen. Mussolini had struck, the Berlin-Tokyo Axis was working and the vultures were gathering. Mr Beppu was our first portent of Pearl Harbor.

My letter to the president says:

From letter to President Roosevelt

June/July 1940

The Japanese consul in Liverpool is moving to Dublin and echo inquires, 'why Éire at this moment?' I told him how happy I had been in his beautiful country in 1902 and again in 1927. I asked him if he were interested in religion which is I find a good subject for diplomatic discourse if treated objectively, and we discussed Shinto and then Bushido. I told him that I had made a speech at a Harvard Club dinner at the Maple Leaf Club in Tokyo in 1902 and had said that I could not understand why Japan wanted to adopt western industrialism when they had a civilisation which our dreamers were hoping to attain through socialism—no one rich, no one poor, fine manners and general happiness. I told him Baron Kaneko had presided, but no one had commented upon my oration. He then said that Baron Kaneko was still alive, aged 87, and had made a speech at his (Mr Beppu's) wedding.

The subject was 'a visit to 'Sagamore Hill' and seeing 'Aunt Edith', knitting, surrounded by the (Roosevelt) children. He admired it. It was his idea of womanhood, woman in the home. Mr Beppu doctored his first cup of tea with sugar and lemon and then found it was pretty good China, and took his second cup 'straight'. We'll keep an eye on Hon. Beppu. There used to be an Englishman who acted as Japanese consular agent here but I think they have never had any Japanese representation. I don't think there is any business here with Japan.

Éire had no trade with Japan and Mr Beppu did not explain why he was being established in the Irish listening post. After Pearl Harbor he became one of our minor nuisances. He proved however to be useful in one way. We could measure the antagonism of the Irish government toward the United States at any given time by the degree of affection they showed Mr Beppu.

This solicitude for Nippon was ill-rewarded. It was not Mr Beppu's idea, but when his countrymen were being driven out of Manila by General MacArthur, Japanese troops crucified Irish priests by nailing them to doors with bayonets.[7] This put Mr de Valera's newspaper in an embarrassing position, since in order to spare Japanese sensibilities it had suggested that in the general confusion Americans might have killed the priests.

[7] Ironically, because Setsuja Beppu was the first diplomat to call to give his respects to Dublin's new archbishop, *Irish Times*, 26 November 1940; for the end of his Irish career, see *Irish Times*, 9 May 1946.

CHAPTER XII

JULY 1ST–13TH

The secret British proposals were not long secret in Britain. On July 1st Hore-Belisha in a speech at Devonport said:

> The question may be, who is to get the ports of Ireland first? Is it to be Hitler? This can be prevented only by an united policy in Ireland. Surely in the circumstances a united policy in Ireland is not beyond the wit of the Government to achieve. If Germany should obtain the Shetlands, the Faeroes or Iceland, our North Atlantic routes would be jeopardised. Her occupation of Ireland would cover our only remaining flank and make the arrival of those supplies from America on which we are counting most hazardous. A diplomatic success in Ireland would have a most profound effect in the United States.[1]

Leslie Hore-Belisha had been secretary of state for war in the Chamberlain Cabinet and spoke with authority.

On July 2nd, the *London News Chronicle* in its leader expressed what it called the 'common sense' view. After pointing out that if Lord Craigavon was anxious to save the United Kingdom and de Valera wished Éire to survive, there was but one thing to do: 'Let Craigavon and de Valera meet together at once in person, forget their damnable iterations, and agree upon a United Ireland to resist the enemy at our gates. That is the common sense of the matter. That is the way of Irish salvation now and hereafter'.

---

[1] The Belfast Office of Home Intelligence reported on 2 July: 'Hore Belisha's speech advocating national defence policy for Ireland, received critically by the majority, because it ignores neutrality of Éire'. Paul Addison and Jeremy A. Craig (eds), *Listening to Britain*, 181.

In Dublin the presence of a British Cabinet minister incognito had started the IRA circulating charges that de Valera was selling out Irish neutrality to England.

On July 2nd we dined with the famous blind doctor Moorhead at the Kildare Street club. Before he lost his sight he had worked in the United States with Crile and the Mayos. His wife was a daughter of Stephen Gwynn, the historian. On July 3rd I wrote the president:

From letter to President Roosevelt

Wednesday, July 3rd, 1940

On the way in, we were stopped by a procession. There was a vanguard of several hundred Dublin slum children, bare-legged, dirty, tragic, but apparently not undernourished. Then the band, and then seven hundred men marching to the barracks to enlist as 'emergency volunteers'. We inquired of a bystander and got the answer, 'It's the old IRA going to fight for de Valera'.

From diary entry
Wednesday, July 3rd, 1940

Joe Walshe told me they were cutting the cables that landed at the Mizzen and splicing in British land ends. They think there will be less likelihood of being cut by the Germans. They are going to hang MacCurtain tomorrow. He is the IRA who shot a policeman.

From letter to President Roosevelt continued

Wednesday, July 3rd, 1940

I spent most of the day on speech to broadcast tomorrow the Fourth of July. The invitation had been a gesture to Washington. I took text to Joe Walshe and he cleared it so Department will not have to worry.

From letter to President Roosevelt continued

Thursday, July 4th, 1940

We dined last night (July 3rd) at Jammets with Reuel S. (Dinty) Moore, the *United Press* Correspondent here. He had the Gallaghers among his guests. Frank is the Government's

Information Bureau Chief and close to de Valera. (Reputed to be his *rumour* man.) He was with him in America.

Frank Gallagher was always friendly and helpful to American newspaper men. Everyone liked him personally but since he was chief of Mr de Valera's propaganda factory, behind his back they called him 'Dr O'Goebbels'.[2]

Later we all went on to see *Charlie's Aunt.* I see it every ten or fifteen years and it gets better every time.

News of British action against the French fleet came this morning. Joe Kennedy telephoned us from London.

An Associated Press dispatch from Washington announced: 'Senator Key Pittman, Chairman of the Foreign Relations Committee of the United States Senate, asserted that patriotic Americans would applaud the seizure of the French warships'.

The only expression of sympathy with the French in their agony, which we heard in Dublin, was on the occasion of what the Dubliners called, 'This piece of British treachery'. Yet when Pétain violated the Anglo-French agreement in asking for a separate armistice, instead of going to Africa and taking the French fleet, there was no talk of French treachery.

I had a low opinion of Pétain. I had been Pershing's Liaison Officer with General Mangin and the Tenth French army for five months in 1918. I wrote the president (July 4th):

From letter to President Roosevelt continued

Thursday, July 4th, 1940

You may not know it but in the last war the Foch-Mangin school had Pétain's 'number'. On July 16th, 1918, Pétain ordered Mangin to call off his July 18 offensive until it was clear whether Gouraud would stop the German push at Challons.[3] The offensive had been prepared as a secret attack and Mangin knew whatever happened at Challons, the strategic manoeuvre was to

---

[2] Graham Walker, 'The Irish Dr Goebbels': Frank Gallagher and Irish republican propaganda', *Journal of Contemporary History* 27 (1) (1992), 149–65. See the discussion in Mark O'Brien, *De Valera, Fianna Fáil and the* Irish Press (Dublin, 2001), 76; Adam Sisman, *Hugh Trevor-Roper* (London 2010).
[3] Châlons-sur-Marne.

roll up the Chateau Thierry pocket. Mangin went over Pétain's head to Foch who ordered the attack as per schedule. I asked Mangin how he rated Pétain. He said: 'Il est très bien instruit, mais il est un peu froid'. Captain de Rochbuet, Mangin's Officier d'Ordinance, explained by asking me if I had ever poured molasses in cold weather. 'The Boss', he said, 'means that Pétain thinks like that'.

Letter to President, dated July 4th, continued:

Father Flannagan came to see me this morning to intercede on behalf of Thomas MacCurtain.

Father Flannagan was a cousin of Father Flannagan the American who founded 'Boys Town'.[4] He was a famous orator but had been 'silenced' by his bishop for IRA activities and Mr de Valera had given him a job in the National Library translating Gaelic manuscripts.

He has a fine head and withal is a man of distinction. He took the line that MacCurtain had been attacked from behind by a plain clothes man and had shot in self-defence, that de Valera had done all the things that MacCurtain's friends were doing until he took the oath, etc., etc.

I said that all that might be true but that my government could not interfere in the case of a man, not a United States citizen, who advocated rebellion against a friendly government. That I had great personal sympathy for his twisted soul but I also had great sympathy for Mr de Valera who was a humane man, torn between his sense of duty and his personal feelings.

The Priest said that a strong government could afford to be merciful. I said that this was a crisis and that it had to uphold its police. We had some Irish whiskey and parted friendly enough. (MacCurtain had been reprieved pending the Supreme Court's decision on a habeas corpus proceeding which was denied and he now is to be executed on Saturday, July 13th.)

---

[4] Father Edward J. Flanagan (1886–1948), born in Roscommon, portrayed by Spencer Tracy in the Hollywood movie. A post-war and far-sighted critic of the Irish industrial schools system: Father Michael O'Flanagan (1876–1942), an early clerical defector from the Irish party to Sinn Féin in 1917, was a radical social republican with a streak of pragmatism. He was involved in the earliest 'peace feelers', which led to the Anglo-Irish Treaty in 1921 and was a strong believer in the idea that Ireland was composed of not one but two nations, both with a right of self-determination.

The Nuncio came to lunch and told me Flannagan had been with him most of the morning, also the mother and sister. He said, 'They tell me he is a fine young man. He got an inheritance some years ago from his uncle who lived in Nevada and he went to Paris and spent it in riotous living.

Father Flanagan left with me a four-page leaflet entitled '*Police Persecution of Patriot Family*' which presented the story of young MacCurtain's 'wrongs'.

At nine o'clock on the evening of July 4th I did my broadcast. I developed the idea that the Declaration of Independence must be reaffirmed in deeds by successive generations. Living liberty could not be inherited, wrapped in a dead charter. It carried the suggestion that the American way to freedom had not been by neutrality. No Irish listener protested. Probably no one listened. I had never broadcast before. The studio ran it over for me from a record and I did not recognise my own voice, though I had lived with it for seventy years.

On July 5th Mr de Valera's organ, the *Irish Press*, under the two-column headline, 'Neutrality: No change—Taoiseach', announced (my italics):

THE IRISH PRESS

NEUTRALITY: NO CHANGE—TAOISEACH

An Taoiseach, Minister for External Affairs made the following statement last night. In order to prevent misapprehensions which may be created by *recent press* and *wireless statements* I desire to repeat that this government has no intention of departing from the policy of neutrality adopted last September, as representing the unanimous will of the Irish people.

The Government is resolved to maintain and defend the country's neutrality in all circumstances.

It is interesting that Winston Churchill never made reference to the 'secret proposals' in parliament. Neville Chamberlain was dying, ruminating on the bitter fruits of his 'policy of faith'. Nor yet nine years later in *Their finest hour*[5] does the historian mention the episode. Such, the Churchillian code.

[5] Winston Churchill, *Their finest hour* (London, 1949).

From diary entry

Friday, July 5th, 1940

S.S. *Washington* due today. Klemmer, John Julius Cooper, also Ronnie Tree's boy, Jeremy, arrived this morning. Both fine boys. John, 13, is a curious mixture of Duff and Diana.[6] Charming manners, responsive and intelligent. Motored them over to Galway where we arrived about two, having encountered rain showers on the way. Galway, a mad-house, but had luck in getting a table at the Southern Hotel and some lunch. Klemmer had authority from Joe (the Ambassador) to deal with various cases of British subjects, the Mountbatten children and three people named Synge, who said they had been authorised by the White House. Several painful cases of miserable Irish women and more miserable children without money. Got away a little after six and got home at 9.15 very weary.

The experiment of sending British children to the United States and Canada in order to conserve British food stocks did not work. When the boys realised that their schoolmates were in the Battle of Britain they insisted on returning.

From diary entry

Saturday, July 5th, 1940

Got up late, went to town, got tweed jacket Watkins had made me. Katherine went to Carrigans for weekend. Bob Low[7] and Quentin Reynolds[8] came to dinner. They had been racing at Baldoyle and had found a 'dream girl', Sally H. Low had won thirty pounds. Low represents *Liberty* and Quentin Reynolds, *Colliers*. They were very amusing. Reynolds had just got out of Paris in a Baby Austin which he had bought from a French woman at the Café de la Paix for fifteen thousand francs, the 'most

---

[6] For the background, see John Julius Norwich (ed.), *The Duff Cooper diaries* (London, 2005).
[7] Bob Low, author of 'Hitler's No. 1 headache: Draja Mihailovitch—fighter for freedom', which appeared in *Liberty*, 25 April 1942, and other war-time scoops.
[8] Quentin Reynolds (1902–65), Californian, later made popular satirical broadcasts on the BBC, replying to Lord Haw-Haw.

expensive travel account from Paris to Bordeaux *Colliers* had ever paid'. At Bordeaux the 'Babe' was abandoned with hundreds of other cars, including a very swanky British Staff Officer's Rolls.

Mr de Valera having publicly confirmed his refusal of the proposals, Lord Craigavon at a press conference on July 7th, further developed his statement of June 29th. Americans are familiar with the de Valera propaganda expounding Southern Irish 'right' to the Six Counties. Here is authoritative exposition of the Ulster position, which was the position of our allies during World War Two and constitutes the basis of our present position in NATO:

STATEMENT FOR PRESS CONFERENCE

7TH JULY, 1940.
CONFIDENTIAL

(1) The Constitutional Position—History has proved the impossibility of governing Ireland as a single unit. Under the administration of successive Chief Secretaries, from Arthur Balfour to 1920, Ireland was in a state of perpetual turbulence. Since the constitutional division between North and South agrarian and political outrages have practically disappeared.

Each Government has been able to administer the affairs of its own territory in its own way, and within each area there has been a marked increase in the happiness and contentment of the people. The wisdom of 'Partition' has therefore been fully justified.

Between North and South there are deep-seated differences, racial, political and religious, and the only statesmanlike policy is to recognise them frankly and legislate accordingly.

Northern Ireland refused to break away from Great Britain when the Irish Free State was set up, and her constitutional position was defined and settled by the Government of Ireland Act, 1920.

The majority of the people of Northern Ireland wish this position to continue. The agitation against it comes from the South, and from only a minority in the North.

On the principle of self-determination, Northern Ireland is entitled to remain part of the United Kingdom, its people living under the British flag and retaining their British citizenship.

Do the people of Great Britain realise that if, by political or economic pressure or through the exploitation of the war situation, Northern Ireland were united with Éire the people of the North would be compelled, to live not under the Union Jack but under the Republican flag of Éire, to exchange their British citizenship for citizenship of an Irish Republic, and to accept a Constitution in which the King has no place?

Is any responsible newspaper in Great Britain, or any thoughtful body of opinion, prepared to support a policy which would be tantamount to the expulsion of hundreds of thousands of loyal men and women from the United Kingdom?

Their desire to remain part of the United Kingdom and in full association with the British Empire, is not the product of bigotry and intolerance or of any desire for 'ascendancy', but of genuine devotion to the Throne and complete identification with British ideals.

Would Londoners or Lancastrians, Scotsmen or Devonians, allow themselves to be thrust into another state so radically different in outlook and sentiment from their own?

(2) The Neutrality of Éire—Striking evidence of the fundamental difference between Northern and Southern Ireland is to be found in the fact that whereas the North, as part of the United Kingdom, is participating in the war, the South remains neutral.

On Friday (July 5) the newspapers published a statement by Mr de Valera reiterating the determination of his Government to 'Maintain and defend' the neutrality of Éire 'in all circumstances'. This can only mean that the Éire Government is resolved to keep out of the war at all costs—to remain neutral at any price.

If the Germans invaded Éire the military forces of the country would be used to resist them. If British troops landed in Éire, either to drive out the Germans or to prevent a German invasion, the guns of the Éire Army would be turned against *them*. That, at any rate, is the meaning of Mr de Valera's words.

So long as Éire's neutrality is maintained the British Government is precluded from entering into any arrangement for the defence of Éire or for the combined defence of Éire and the United Kingdom.

Éire's neutrality is therefore a source of great danger not only to Éire herself but to the United Kingdom.

An all-Ireland defence plan on Mr de Valera's terms would be futile. It would mean the neutrality of all Ireland, and as a consequence the withdrawal of British troops from Northern

Ireland. The forces remaining in Ireland would be hopelessly insufficient to deal with a German invasion.

Knowing this, the German High Command would undoubtedly order the immediate invasion of Ireland and use Irish territory as a base of operations against Great Britain.

Is this what the Éire Government wants to see? Is this what the advocates of a united Irish military command, *without any conditions or safeguards*, desire or are prepared to risk?

It is precisely because of the dangers already outlined that Lord Craigavon, in his speech on June 29th, specified the conditions indispensable to co-operation between North and South. They were (1) that Éire should take its stand with Britain in the war, (2) that the Éire Government should expel the German and Italian representatives, and (3) that no issue of a constitutional nature should be raised during the war.

Northern Ireland has been criticised for not offering 'concessions' to the South in order to secure unity. The argument used by the critics is that adequate defence is the paramount necessity, and that political considerations must be subordinated to the task of keeping the enemy at bay.

That is exactly the attitude of the Northern Government. From the beginning of the war it has taken the line that sectional controversies should be silenced, political differences dropped, so that undivided attention could be given to the waging of the struggle against the common enemy. It is the Government's opponents, in Éire and in Northern Ireland, who have refused to take this larger view.

The Éire Government is seeking to use the war situation as a lever with which to force the constitutional issue and secure a political triumph. The Nationalist leaders in the North, in a manifesto recently published, have declared that no issue must be allowed to take precedence of 'Partition'.

Yet, strangely enough, it is the Northern Government and its supporters who are accused of obstructionism, political prejudice, and blindness to the menace of the military position'.

(3) The Facts Summarised

The realities of the defence situation are these:

Éire does not possess the military strength to repel a German invasion. It has a small army but at sea and in the air it is defenceless.

Northern Ireland comes within the United Kingdom scheme of defence. Any plan for the joint defence of Éire and Northern Ireland would involve the use of British forces—the army, navy and RAF. Defence is controlled by the Imperial Government. Therefore any plan for the defence of Ireland, North and South, must form part of a wider plan for the defence of Great Britain, Northern Ireland and Éire.

A common policy presupposes a common aim, and all the partners in that policy must be belligerents. There is no half way house. Belligerency and neutrality are mutually incompatible.

Northern Ireland cannot enter into any military compact with Éire. It has not the constitutional power to do so, seeing that defence is a service reserved to the imperial Government.

It is open, however, to the Éire Government to approach the Imperial Government with a request for military aid. That is the line of approach to the problem of Ireland's defence. The criticisms levelled at the Northern Government on this matter are therefore irrelevant and unjustified.

Until the Éire Government seeks and secures the military co-operation of the Imperial Government, Éire will leave itself open to attack by Germany. Éire's security can best be assured by taking the one step that can make such co-operation effective—the abandonment of neutrality and a declaration of full association with Britain and the Empire in the waging of the war.

Northern Ireland is not acting selfishly in this matter but in the highest interests of Éire and the United Kingdom. A neutral Ireland would be unable to enter into military co-operation with Great Britain, and without British help Ireland would be crushed whenever the Germans chose to launch an attack against it.

With Ireland prostrate the way would be opened for an onslaught on Great Britain from the west. Ulster is not prepared to pave the way for such a calamity.

Of this pattern of confusion what interpretation were we to report to Washington? Was Craigavon bluffing? Was de Valera cow-trading? Or was impasse and tragedy ahead? If we had known about the arrangement for getting Northern Ireland in return for Irish neutrality and Irish influence in America to prevent American intervention, it would have been simple. But we did not know. I had reported strong confidence in de Valera.

In part at least because of my reports the president had allocated to Éire twenty thousand rifles of a shipment urgently needed by the English. Now de Valera had refused the proposals and was insisting that Northern Ireland become neutral if they were to co-operate. If it turned out that he was not on our side, it was a mistake to let him have rifles. I could not escape at least partial responsibility. The possibility troubled me and I asked our London embassy to send over competent military officers to investigate and form their own conclusions as to the intentions of the Irish military chiefs.

We were entitled to military attachés though none had yet been assigned, and the Irish government raised no objection to my borrowing from London. General Lee, therefore, sent over Major MacDonald, US air attaché, and Major Studler, Ordinance Officer.

A diary entry of July 8th notes that they came to lunch. It further states that Inspector Collins, whom they had met and liked in Galway:

From diary entry

Monday, July 8th, 1940

… told them to see General Hugh MacNeill,[9] Assistant Chief of Staff (in Dublin). We telephoned MacNeill and he asked me to bring them around. Had very interesting talk, MacDonald telling him of German tactics in landing troops by air—as many as three thousand per hour. They would drop a few parachutists first around an aerodrome. These would cut the wires and attempt to demoralise the guards and clear the runways. Then more would come and machine gun nests would be established and the wireless set up. MacDonald thought that the best defence was at least two tanks at every landing field, ready to mop up the beginnings without loss of time or men. MacNeill intimated that he was improvising armoured lorries for this purpose. On the whole the thing went off very well and we all had the feeling that the army was acting in good faith.

MacNeill had been Chief of Cosgrave's military Mission to the United States in 1924–5 and, according to my information, had attended the US army staff school at Fort Riley.

[9] Ironically, Hugo MacNeill is the general most suspected of dealings with the Germans, see Eunan O'Halpin, *Defending Ireland*, 178.

Diary entry for the next day notes:

From diary entry

Tuesday, July 9th, 1940

After lunch, Majors MacDonald and Studler came in. They had been lunching with the Irish Chief of Staff and the assistant Chief MacNeill. They had had a very interesting time and were convinced; as I was, that the army is acting in good faith and means to fight. I forgot to say (in yesterday's entry) that after seeing MacNeill the day before, we went to the civilian airport and looked it over with Major O'Carroll who was very kind. He agreed with Major MacDonald that the Pan American Airways could operate practically on the US weather reports till autumn, with perhaps an occasional beam for a few hours to guide the ship in, without giving the enemy any assistance.

The soldiers went back to London well satisfied. They left me with a sense of relief and confidence both in General MacNeill and Mr de Valera.

The diary entry for July 9th reports the arrival of Vinton Chapin as senior career officer to the legation. Jack MacVeagh, whom he replaced, had had no home leave for several years. He was tired out and went home to recuperate. It was a blow to us to lose him but Chapin proved a tower of strength.

I had an appointment to see Mr de Valera at 3 p.m. on July 9th. Diary reports that:

From diary entry

Tuesday, July 9th, 1940

After a little talk with (Fred) Boland (presenting Chapin), we went in to see de Valera. He greeted Chapin very pleasantly and then Chapin withdrew, and I talked with him about getting supplies from the American Red Cross through David Bruce. He told me to see Lemass. (This was the beginning of what seemed to be a very profitable undertaking in mutual goodwill.) He (de Valera) seemed very tired and blue. I congratulated him on the interview which he gave Denny in the *Times* in which he proclaimed Irish neutrality. I said I knew what had taken place (his refusal of the British proposals to end partition) and thought he had done the only thing that could be done. But that I was convinced that Britain was sincere in wishing to end partition and seizing this time to coerce Craigavon. I said I did not think it was their only motive, that they doubtless wanted help, but that they were sincere up to a point.

Seán T. O'Kelly had told me only a few days before that de Valera had refused the proposals because the English *could* not deliver the North. In the light of my knowledge at that time I agreed with him. I believed that Craigavon had turned down the proposals before de Valera had. The reverse was true.

After I had said to Mr de Valera that the English were 'sincere up to a point', my report records that de Valera said:

… *'They could never end Partition now'*, which was a reversal of form for him as he has always insisted that they could do it overnight if they wished. Perhaps I misunderstood him.

Here was confirmation of what Mr O'Kelly had told me, but if Mr de Valera believed that England could not deliver, how could he also believe that England was holding the Six Counties 'by force against the majority will?'

It was confusing but I still believed that de Valera intended eventually to come in, in his own time, impelled by Irish interest. I believed also that he was actuated by prudence. As long as the United States were not in the war, I could not blame him for not coming in though I believed he was making a mistake.

Washington had no representation in the Irish Free State until 1926. This, would explain why the Department had no file on de Valera on which prediction of his course in 1940 could be based on past performance. If the Dublin legation in 1940 had known that on October 25th, 1917, Mr de Valera in addressing a meeting of Irish Volunteers had said that the only hope of another Sinn Féin rebellion lay in a German invasion of England and the landing of German arms in Ireland; that when the First World War was over England would be tottering, the Allies could not win; that all nations at the peace conference would be claiming their right to the Freedom of the Seas, and that Ireland was of such international importance in that respect that her claim must be admitted, I should not have been so ready to believe what he had told me in April about wanting a strong England and being in substantial agreement with my views about Germany. Neither would I have accepted Sinn Féin 'history' which denied the existence of the German Plot in 1916. In his speech de Valera had closed by telling his audience that they wanted an army to back Ireland's claim.

Hitler had occupied Poland the previous winter but the Irish government still recognised the Polish 'Government in Exile', in London. The diary continues:

From diary entry
Tuesday, July 9th, 1940

Chapin and I went on to the Polish Consul General's house, somewhere in the outskirts where we found the Maffeys, Lieut. General Sir Hubert Hartigan,[10] retired, and his lady, also Mrs Gavan Duffy and Mrs Conor Maguire. Maffey wanted to see me and we went into a little room. He said someone from England (he mentioned no name) evidently someone of importance, had been here and had seen Cosgrave; that C. said that they (the Opposition) knew nothing about it (the proposals); that if they had known they would have forced the Government to accept the offer.

I said that I was sure that they (Cosgrave) did know about it; that I had given a tip to a certain person (Dillon) who had then conferred with his *confreres* and had gone to de Valera and demanded to be let into the know and that he had been shown the proposals. My only explanation was that Cosgrave was going to take this line for political purposes later on. Maffey agreed that this was doubtless so. There had been too much talk and rumour for Cosgrave not to have been pretty well informed.

Dublin at that time reminded one of the Grand Central Station in New York. Everybody seemed to be passing through or had come to see what Éire was going to do about the war. The diary for July 9th tells of an evening call from Vincent Sheehan and Virginia Cowles representing the North American Newspaper Alliance: 'They came about ten. She was

[10] Gerard Sir Hubert Hartigan was part of Lord Rosebery's racing set. Founder member with Vincent O'Brien of the Irish Racehorse Trainers Association in 1950.

very pessimistic having just come out of France on the last boat. He had gone to Galway expecting to sail in the *Washington* and then had changed his mind'. Miss Cowles was very intelligent as well as attractive. Her book, *Looking for trouble*[11] which came out at the end of the war was one of the few important ones by a newspaper correspondent.

From diary entry
Wednesday, July 10th, 1940

Lovely day after rain yesterday. Went to Powerscourt for lunch. Extraordinary museum of house. Lord Powerscourt showed us Oliver Cromwell's leather beer flagon, two foot six high and ten inches across, covered with pitch inside and out with silver rim with his name engraved on it; 'Oliver Cromwell, Lord Protector of England, Scotland and Ireland 1653'.

At dinner that week at the Swedish consul general's we met Donal O'Sullivan and his wife. He had been Clerk of the original Free State Senate. This was the legislative body which Mr de Valera abolished for holding up some of his measures. Mr O'Sullivan was a man of talent and character. His history *The Irish Free State and its Senate* is standard source material for the period, objective, temperate and important.

Mr de Valera's refusal of the British proposals for the common defence of the island gave Craigavon an advantage which he was quick to follow up. On July 11th he issued still another statement. If my recollection is correct the censorship banned its publication in Éire,
Lord Craigavon began:

The 'Battle of Britain' is imminent: indeed, the daily air raids on coastal areas in England, Scotland and Wales indicate that the most crucial phase of the war has already opened. How does this situation affect us in Northern Ireland? We cannot consider ourselves immune either from air attack or from an attempted landing by enemy parachutists. I have the fullest confidence in Mr Churchill's brilliant direction of British war policy and in the nation's fighting services, and I have no doubt that our cause will be carried to victory.

[11] Virginia Cowles, *Looking for trouble* (London, 1941).

There has been much ill-informed discussion, in the *Press* and elsewhere, on the possibility of formulating a plan for the joint defence of Northern Ireland and Éire. In my speech at Kirkistown I stated clearly the conditions on which, as the head of this Government, I am prepared to co-operate with Éire on matters of defence. Those conditions are that Mr de Valera takes his stand on the aide of Britain and the empire, that he clears out the German and Italian representatives from Éire and that he undertakes not to raise any issue of a constitutional nature.

What is Mr de Valera's reply? In an interview with a representative of an American newspaper he said: 'We have not the slightest intention of abandoning our neutrality. We intend to resist any attack thereon from *any* quarter. Whoever comes first will be our immediate enemy. ... We are not prepared to join in any such proposal as a defence committee while Ireland is divided'. Mr de Valera has thus *definitely rejected my offer*. He is demanding the subjection of Ulster to Éire 'not in' order to make Ireland as a whole powerful enough to resist an invasion by the strongest military power in Europe, but in order to maintain neutrality. This would mean that the people of the North, against the will of the majority, would be compelled to live not under the Union Jack but under the Republican flag of Éire, to exchange their British citizenship for citizenship of an Irish Republic, and to accept a Constitution in which the King has no place. As loyal citizens of the United Kingdom we scorn any such suggestion. It is repugnant to our very souls.

As Mr de Valera's words were addressed in the first instance to the people of the United States, it is not inappropriate to ask, 'What would the American nation say to a proposal of one of the states to secede from the Union? Would they allow anyone to pluck a star off "Old Glory"?' Of course not. Neither will the loyalists of Ulster agree to the Cross of St. Patrick being removed from the Union Jack, under which they are proud to live, and beneath which they intend to remain.

Let no one misunderstand the meaning of Mr de Valera's demand. The union of North and South on the basis of neutrality would involve the withdrawal of Northern Ireland from the war and the removal of all British forces from this Province. This would encourage the enemy to attempt the immediate invasion of Ireland in order to use Irish territory as a base of operations against Great Britain.

Northern Ireland comes within the United Kingdom scheme of defence. Any effective scheme for the defence of Éire and Northern Ireland would necessitate the use of British forces—army, navy and RAF. Therefore the defence of Ireland, North and South, must form part of a wider plan for the defence of Great Britain, Northern Ireland and Éire.

A common policy presupposes a common aim, and all the partners in that policy must be belligerents. There is no half-way house. Belligerency and neutrality are mutually incompatible.

Northern Ireland has not the constitutional power to enter into any military compact with Éire, seeing that defence is a service reserved to the Imperial Government. But it is open to Éire to approach the Imperial Government with a request for military aid. *That* is the line of approach to the problem of Ireland's defence. Until the Éire Government seeks and secures British military co-operation it will leave Éire open to attack by Germany. Éire's security can best be assured by taking the one step that could make such co-operation effective—the abandonment of neutrality and a declaration of full association with Britain and the Empire in the waging of the war.

These are the realities of the situation. Realising them, we in Northern Ireland are completing our preparations, in common with the rest of the United Kingdom, to resist any attack that may be made upon our shores. At a critical moment in our history the gates of Derry were closed against the enemy. We are closing the gates again. We are maintaining our position in the battle front. Ulster has no intention of abandoning its war effort and seeking illusory refuge in a base neutrality. It is not acting selfishly, but in the highest interest of Éire and the United Kingdom. It will not be a party to exposing Britain's western flank to the enemy.

Our duty, then, is clear—to play our part manfully and faithfully in this momentous struggle, and not to quit the fight until the foe is completely and finally overthrown.

The American Majors from London had restored my confidence in de Valera. On July 13th, five days after they went back, I had a talk with the nuncio. What he told me deflated this confidence. Memorandum for the president says:

Letter to President Roosevelt

Saturday, July 13th, 1940

This is going (by) air mail courier, if there is still one operating next week. That is why it is on light paper and single-spaced. Your letter of June 19th came today. Yes, the proclamation in the Charlottesville speech was exactly what I had in mind. It had very good effect here but I fear the effect is wearing off.

I have just had a disquieting hour with the Nuncio. He told me that Spain would declare war in forty-eight hours, or rather he had been told so; presumably I think by the Italian Minister.

There is a pencilled note in the margin here that says: 'It was Joe Walshe'. On July 26th, the nuncio himself told me it was Mr Walshe. How he, Mr Walshe, learned that, if it is true, is beyond me and is a job for the British Secret Service.

He (the Nuncio) then went on to tell me that people who ought to know better, came to see him telling him that they would like to see Hitler crush Britain. There was a professor at Trinity College and one at the National University, both holding this view and not considering what life under Hitler would be. I am going to try to find out from him what the Germans have promised the Government. I think he knows and he might tell me if I did not ask him. I am pretty sure that something recent has been done by them for he spoke of seeing the German Minister, a thing he has not done before, except when they met at public functions, this by order of the Vatican.

The papal nuncio had a special position with the Irish government and it is probable that Mr de Valera and possibly Hempel also assured him that Germany would not attack Éire if she remained neutral and withheld the ports from England.

I told him that I had been reporting to Washington, that I was convinced of the good faith of the Government in the case that the Germans came first. That is, that when they came, he would invite the English in to repel them. The Nuncio suggested that *I had better not be too sure about de Valera* and spoke of his strange *double standard of conscience*. He will not lie to you but he will not be pinned down and his reservations always allow him to slip out if he believes his interest dictates slipping out.

I recalled after writing the memorandum of this conversation that when I had asked him, the Nuncio, 'Do you mean that de Valera *won't* call in the British and fight *with* them?' he had repeated, 'Never! Never! Never!' with great emphasis.

My letter continued:

> This would mean something like this: If he thought England was down, and the Germans landed and announced themselves as liberators of Ulster, he would say, 'We cannot fight against a liberation of Ulster. If Churchill doesn't like this he should have given us Ulster, no matter what the cost'. He (de Valera) has himself suggested to me that this (such a German proclamation) would put him in a 'very difficult position'. This probably means, according to the Nuncio, that he has an unexpressed policy worked out to fit that situation. His cabled message to the World's Fair on Irish Day stressing the wrong of Partition bears this out. That is his technique. He is giving notice to England. As you know, they offered him everything recently in return for 'non-belligerent' co-operation and he turned it down, asserting that the only way was to have Ulster join them in neutrality; and further that he did not believe that England could 'deliver the goods'. Behind this, I think, is the very natural fear that England is going down and not wishing to be tied to a dead horse. Joe Walshe, his Permanent Under-Secretary, I believe is going definitely pro-German. The Nuncio tells me so, and I have noticed a change in his attitude to me. I still think the only wise course is for Britain to wait till the Germans land, build up overwhelming forces in Ulster and then if de Valera attempts to lie down on his engagements give him the works.
>
> Dr Murphy, the owner of the *Irish Independent*, the most powerful paper in Dublin, told me the other night that there is no 'Irish Mentality' in Dev. He won't make a deal on the one hand, and on the other he never takes revenge or shows bitterness to individuals. I am afraid that in this situation he is very slippery.
>
> In considering your policy, toward such a situation as I have outlined, I believe you ought to consider the *possibility of his finding an excuse to oppose* the British and help the Germans. I hope that some of the correspondents get this possibility before the American people.

> I am glad the State Department does not want to throw me out yet. They will.

This had reference to pleasant things which the president had said in his letter of June 19th.

> My French wine, that I thought was abandoned at Bordeaux, got out and is now in Liverpool. Glory be!

I find a note pencilled at the end of this document, 'not sent'. I have no recollection why, unless no air courier turned up, and the substance of the letter was embodied in other reports. It seems today, that with the help of Archbishop Paschal Robinson, we were not far from the truth if we had only accepted it.

That July 13th had been proclaimed Irish Day at New York's World's Fair. Mayor LaGuardia of New York had sent Mr de Valera a politician's felicitations and Mr de Valera had cabled in reply:

> We would wish our participation in the World's Fair to symbolise our desire for peace and co-operation among the nations. Restoration of the unity of Ireland would mark the beginning of an era of such peace and co-operation between Irish and British people.
>
> We believe the restoration of the unity of Ireland to be of particular interest to the American people, and I would earnestly urge your audience and all those who come to visit the Irish Pavilion to *remember that the partition of Ireland is headline for the unjust use of force everywhere by a strong power against a weaker. Our aspirations for the unity and independence of our nation are identical with those which brought about the greatness and happiness of the American people.*

To the 'Irish Heart', whether in Éire or America, this message meant but one thing: 'England is using force *unjustly* against Ireland. Tell Americans to send no help to England. Permit no help'.

To appraise the ill-will compressed in this message one must recall its time and circumstance. On that July 13th Hitler had been in Paris a month less a day. Since 1066 England had been in no such peril. Englishmen with rifles were preparing to fight upon their beaches. Those without rifles had clubs. Women were mobilising. Since the battle of

Vienna, western civilisation had been in no such danger. The hope of prostrate France, of desperate England lay in help from America, and then the Irish Day message.

The Sinn Féin Heart was exultant. *War News* (July 27) said plainly what de Valera dared only imply on July 13th.

WAR NEWS

ISSUED BY THE IRISH REPUBLICAN PUBLICITY BUREAU

Who would have thought that the day would approach so rapidly, when we should see the Empire broken and our own, carefully picking our steps out of the debris? France will recover her dignity, but England never. England will gnaw her own vitals in famine and we will lift no finger to assuage her want. She is anathema, accursed among the nations. She is become obscene for her bond was the word between man and man for the gain of commerce, not caring for the bond binding of man to God nor for God's promise to man.

The late Pope's view of England's desperate situation differed from that of Mr de Valera and of his former comrades, the IRA. In welcoming a new British Ambassador after the war His Holiness said:

During the War the British People endured what was almost beyond human endurance. They did so not only in defence of their own lives and liberties, but as the vanguard *fighting for those human ideals and human freedoms which must be dear to every right minded man.*

… In the hope that your noble nation may soon be able to report perceptible progress in advancing the cause of afflicted humanity and an enlightened sense of Christian principle, we invite God's gracious protection on the King, on the Royal House, on His Majesty's Government and the entire British people. As their chosen representative you may always count on our complete confidence and ready help.

L'Osservatore Romano, June 30th, 1947

De Valera, like Mussolini, never let his religion interfere with business. Both believed they were businessmen but in reality they were dupes of their own wishful thinking. They believed in what Ciano says his father-in-law called '*cette si belle occasion*'—the 'opportunity which comes but once in five thousand years'. But both misread the political scene. Both were victims of illusion. The 'so wonderful opportunity' proved mirage and disaster. Of the two de Valera was the better businessman, for Mussolini refused the Allied bribes and got nothing out of it but to be hung by the feet like a dead hog. De Valera took all he could get as long as there was anything to get and kept it. But both were inept, for both excluded from their calculations not only moral order but the basic interest of the American people in German defeat. Neither of these factors should have been beyond the understanding of competent European statesmen.

CHAPTER XIII

July 13th–August 14th

The German raids on London set us looking for air-raid shelters. Sunday morning, July 13th, I walked the cook's Sealyham and was practising chip shots on the south lawn when my wife came out. She said James Murphy had told her of an abandoned ice house ideally suited for a shelter. She had the key and my shilling flashlight. Ten minutes later I was at the bottom of a masonry pit fifteen feet deep, on a pile of stones. My legs and back seemed to be splintered. Eventually they hauled me out with a hay rope. Ligaments had torn but no bones broken. In three weeks I was able to golf, fish, shoot but never ride again. The grapevine said 'The American Minister had drink taken and fell down the well'. Seven years later arthritis crippled me.

In bed I could only worry about what the nuncio had told me.

Memorandum, Monday, July 15th, 1940

Telephoned Maffey that I would like to see him. He arrived about 6.15 p.m. and came to bedroom. I told him that the latter part of the week I had felt an atmosphere of uncertainty that 'got the wind up'. That on Saturday (July 13th) I had gone to see the Nuncio and that he had told me that Spain would declare war within forty-eight hours; that he had heard it presumably through the Italian B. (Berardis); that he (the Nuncio) had said that *de Valera would never fight on the side of Britain.* I asked him (Maffey) what if anything was going on? The Irish seemed to be afraid of a British invasion. Was there any ground for it?

He said 'No' the attitude of the British Government *was the same as it had always been. They had no desire to make Ireland suffer for having turned the proposals down.*

In spite of this, however, as came out later, de Valera and his pro-German associates anticipated a British attack.

> Maffey repeated what he had said (at the Polish Consul General's) about an unnamed member or representative of the Government coming over last week and reporting that the Opposition had never been shown the proposals and that Cosgrave was indignant. I said that I could find out (about that) for him.

The memorandum continued the next day, Tuesday, July 16th.

> James Dillon came to lunch. Before lunch I told him I had a feeling that something was up but it might have been the trouble owing to MacCurtain's commutation. (The Government had commuted his death sentence—He, Dillon, thought that bad.) He said that the person who had come over saw O'H (O'Higgins), brother of Kevin O'Higgins. He was as fiery as his brother had been cold. He got frightened when 'this man' offered to show him the proposals and said that they should be shown only to the Government. He reported this to Cosgrave, and Cosgrave, with the advice and consent of his party leaders, wrote a letter to Dev demanding an interview. In the meantime Dillon and two of his confreres had seen Dev. He had been very frank with them and entirely satisfactory to Dillon. They carried back word that Dev would be glad to see Cosgrave and Co.

Neither Dillon nor Cosgrave nor his party lieutenants suspected Mr de Valera's 'arrangement' with Hempel. They believed that he was honestly preparing to call in British help the moment that Hitler launched an attack.

I recalled the nuncio's vehemence when I asked him, 'Do you mean de Valera *won't* call in the British and fight with them?' And he had shouted 'Never, Never, Never!'

From diary entry
Wednesday, July 17th, 1940

Better today. Able to get to bath on crutches. 3 p.m.

James Dillon was here to lunch and has just gone. He told me that he had gone to see Dev yesterday with Mulcahy and

O'Higgins. Dillon asked him (de Valera) if he had changed his view about asking the English to come in at once. He said *not in principle*, but he might hold out for a week or more.

'This is not what you told me ten days ago', said Dillon. 'You said you would summon aid immediately'. 'Well', he said, 'I think it would be best that way'.

Dillon said, 'and you would allow the country to be laid waste on a point of order?'

The possibility of delay in asking England for help was of first importance. The situation resembled that of Belgium. General Spears in his *Prelude to Dunkirk* quotes Reynaud's comment: 'It is as if Belgium had said to us: "Stay in your own country. Don't come into ours as long as you can do so easily; you will be invited to come in when to do so will be a mortal peril for you", forgetting that for Belgium also the peril would be mortal'.[1]

Change Belgium to Éire and it describes the German menace to Ireland.

Dillon thinks that the influence of Aiken, Traynor, Derrig, who control the towns, frighten Dev; also that Joe Walshe has told him that the British were putting up a propaganda campaign against him.

Then he (Dillon) said if the British would make the ending of Partition a fact by sending Craigavon to sit in this Dáil on the promise that in that Dáil de Valera would propose non-belligerency, the use of the ports, the right to send in troops, he does not think de Valera could refuse it. O'K (O'Kelly), MacEntee and probably Lemass would urge it.

Of course at this time James Dillon had no specific grounds for suspecting bad faith.

At 4.05 Maffey came in on his way to the boat. He is going to London for two nights. I outlined Dillon's proposal, emphasising that the other proposals were primarily turned down because twice the Irish had been caught out on definite promises that could not be kept. The Opposition could not in such circumstances support the proposals any more than the Government could. I told Maffey that it was hard for him as an Englishman who kept his word to appreciate this, but such was the fact.

---

[1] Edward L. Spears, *Prelude to Dunkirk, July 1939–May 1940*, 2 vols (London, 1954), 51.

Today I am less sure that this was fact.

He (Maffey) went over the points (the details of Dillon's plan);
(i) U. (Ulster) opting to come in and immediately meeting in the
Dáil with its representatives. (2) Dev giving his word to advocate
non-belligerency, this to be construed as (a) the use of the ports,
(b) as allotment of troop areas, (c) the construction of protective
measures on the Ulster coast. There would be no conscription but
everyone could volunteer as at present. This could be humbug
but let it go at that. Ulster would need no other guarantee than
the superior force of G.B. (Great Britain). If Dev broke faith,
Ulster would walk out. This would fulfil all possible guarantees to
Ulster. Dillon predicted that the most tremendous fuss would be
made over the Ulster members by the TDs and if they were adroit
and co-operative, in six months they would be running all Ireland,
as a centre, independent bloc.

This impressed me at the time as being eminently practical and
statesmanlike. In the perspective of fifteen years, it seems to have been
the one logical solution, assuming the good faith of the de Valera
government. It was impossible because Mr de Valera did not want and
was not acting in good faith.

What James Dillon had stated about England twice breaking her
word to Ireland over Home Rule was true or not true according as one
weighs the circumstances. Lloyd George is on record as a 'twister', but
hardly Asquith and certainly not Winston Churchill. At the time that
I repeated the statement to Maffey, I had accepted the Irish viewpoint
without examination of the historical background. Today I believe that,
as in 1940, de Valera made accommodation with the Craigavon
government impossible, so the same extremist viewpoint and bad faith
during the early years of the century made it inevitable that the Ulster
Protestants would reject Home Rule and make it impossible for the
British liberals to fulfil their pledges. No one can put 800,000 people in
jail for refusing to be disloyal to their country.

On July 16th, Hitler issued his order:

Since England in spite of her military hopeless situation shows no
sign of coming to terms, I have decided to prepare a landing
operation against England and if necessary to carry it out. The

preparations for the entire operation must he completed by mid-August.

On July 19th Hitler made his victory speech in the German Reichstag. He appealed to the common sense of England to sue for peace. He said,

> I consider myself in a position to make this appeal since I am not a vanquished foe begging favours, but the victor speaking in the name of reason. I can see no reason why this war need go on. I am grieved to think of the sacrifices it must claim.

Then he added

> Possibly Mr Churchill will brush aside this statement of mine by saying it is merely born of fear and doubt of final victory. In that case I shall have relieved my conscience in regard to the things to come.

This made a strong appeal to the Irish mind. We caught echoes of it for months afterwards in our official talks.

From diary entry
Tuesday, July 23rd, 1940

Commander Dove, a Christian and pacifist called on me. He was a British naval officer and nephew of Admiral Sir John Somerville who had just attacked the French fleet. He wanted to talk with de Valera about disarming. I advised him that Mr de Valera had trouble enough trying to arm. Then he said how about talking with the IRA? I said that would embarrass both de Valera and his own government. I said that Mr de Valera was lunching with me on July 25th. I would talk to him.

July 23rd, in a letter to the president, I summed up the Irish situation as it then appeared to us:

Letter to President Roosevelt

Tuesday, July 23rd, 1940

The Irish Government turned down the British proposals for ending Partition as the price of Éire abandoning neutrality (it was to be called non-belligerency), first because there was no absolute guarantee, as I had gathered from Sir John Maffey. It was the Cabinet's promise to use 'its utmost influence to bring Ulster into a conference to devise a new all-Ireland constitution'. (Such as James Dillon had sketched out.)

Today, in the light of the available evidence, it seems that the true reason for the failure of the negotiation was that de Valera did not wish it to succeed. He had made his book on German victory.

The letter continued:

Following Irish refusal of the proposals, things took a funny turn. It became evident that Irish defence measures and propaganda were being pointed against England rather than Germany. It seems that the anti-British members of the Cabinet, who said that the proposals were a trap, predicted that their rejection would be followed by a Churchill coup against the ports similar to the destruction of the French warships, and everybody got the wind up. Things are quieting down now. The dangerous situation that Dev has got himself into is, that in his appeal for national unity for national defence which has rallied most of the old IRA he has let it be passed about that he dreads England quite as much as he dreads Germany. Now if and when Germany attacks it is not going to be easy to co-operate with British assistance. He continues to deny in public what he readily admits in private, that the freedom of Éire depends on the British fleet.

Letter to President Roosevelt continued

Friday, July 26th, 1940

Yesterday we had the lunch party for the Cardinal Primate, MacRory. De Valera had to back out. Others present—Papal Nuncio, S.T. O' Kelly, John MacEntee, James M. Dillon, Granard, Monsignor Enricci and Chapin. Maude and Katherine Crocker helped receive, then withdrew .... The Cardinal arrived in a taxi and wrangled over the fare with the driver who had lost his way in the Park. Flynn who was at hand to attend the prelate, remained neutral at a distance till the dispute was over.

Lunch went very well, food good. I had the Cardinal opposite (in the French fashion), the Nuncio on my right and S.T. O'Kelly on my left. Not very successful at general conversation.

The Monsignor insisted on keeping up his prattle, the Nuncio switched to Scotch Whiskey which he said was not as strong as Irish (and not as good) but he made up in quantity. He told the story of spending the night in the restored 10th century castle in Donegal with Mr Biggar. They slept on the floor with their feet to a fire in the middle of the room—no windows, just the embrasures, and the mosquitoes poured in ... .

Toward the end of lunch I spoke of the peace proposals of Commander Dove, nephew of Admiral Sir John Somerville, saying that the Nuncio had passed him on to me. I described his program for disarming: one British plane to be scrapped, one German plane, and so on. They all laughed. Then I said that I had told Dove that there was only one way to follow the directions of Christ: turn the other cheek, submit to the Germans and in two or three hundred years (a moment in evolution) the spirit of God would work it out.

The Cardinal opened his blue eyes in amazement.

'But', I said, 'Americans wouldn't submit to Christianity; I didn't think the Irish would and I knew the English wouldn't. So that was the end of poor Dove's peace program. We went into the drawing room and S.T. asked me to talk to the Cardinal. We gathered together by the sofa and he (Mr O'Kelly) told the Cardinal what I did not know, that Roosevelt had prevented conscription in Ulster and that he could help them end partition; that if Hitler won—

'He's going to win', the Cardinal said, 'He'll beat the British'.

'Well', I said, 'if that's so, there is nothing more to be said. You'll find out what will happen to you. But if you are wrong and England wins you don't want to miss the boat. You want to get Partition ended. Now the way to do that is to cultivate good feeling'.

'I'll do that when we get justice', said the Cardinal.

'I told him he ought to go to the Abercorn's parties, that they felt badly that he didn't.

'I'll go when we get justice', he said, 'But', he added 'Abercorn was not a bad fellow, not like Craig'.

There was no doubt where the Cardinal stood. He did not take his politics from Rome. But he was no 'smiler with the knife'.

I had recently met the late Rt. Hon. James MacMahon, P.C.[2] He had been a high civil servant under the union and between 1918 and 1922 he had been under-secretary to the lord lieutenant. Since the Treaty he had been a member of important boards and commissions. He was openly on the Allied side. He told me that he had gone to school with the cardinal. He was a devout churchman and knew a great deal about the inside of church politics. At a tea party at which we were discussing the world situation I told him that the cardinal's views about Hitler were hard for me to understand. His reply, which I embodied in a report to the president, was as follows:

Letter to President Roosevelt continued

The Cardinal believes that Britain enslaves Ireland by financial control, that Hitler will destroy the capitalistic system and free Ireland. The same propaganda is passing the word that Italy did not attack France but only Free Masonry, Divorce and the causes of French decay; also that Hitler is against these things. Three of the bishops, Browne of Galway, the Bishop of Cork and the Bishop of Killaloe stand up and oppose the Cardinal; the rest follow him:[3] I think de Valera resents this pressure. He accepted our invitation to meet the Cardinal (at lunch) and gave out an hour beforehand.

If Mr MacMahon correctly expounded the Cardinal's views on Irish economy, they were apparently in accord with the economic philosophy of the IRA. The issue of *War News*, dated July 13th, 1940, printed the following:

WAR NEWS

ISSUED BY THE IRISH REPUBLICAN PUBLICITY BUREAU

As everyone knows, but nobody thinks about, the victory of Germany in this war will mean the collapse of sterling and the complete destruction of the world dominion of the Empire financiers. This would mean the collapse of the economic system at present ruling in the 'Free State' and Northern Ireland by

[2] James McMahon (1865–1954), civil servant and former under-secretary for Ireland, an active member of the Catholic Truth Society and the Society of St Vincent de Paul, 'genuine insider'.
[3] Bishops Cohalan of Cork and Fogarty of Killaloe tended to be anti-republican and on bad terms with de Valera.

undermining the foundations on which the banks depend. This collapse would force our people, whether they liked it or not, to do what every Republican has tried to persuade them to do, to fall back on their own resources and develop their own economic life based on the country's own needs. The power of the British Empire must be smashed to *ensure the social and economic development* of a free Ireland without outside interference.

When Mr de Valera had told me that the IRA, though numerically few, appealed to 'something very deep in the Irish heart', I had failed to realise that part of this something was the belief that separatist independence would make the poor rich, end emigration and unemployment, put coal and iron in the Irish hills and make Ireland a great power.

There was much to irritate Cardinal MacRory. He was primate of all Ireland but his See was in the Protestant North. His neighbour was the Protestant Archbishop who had possession of the fine Gothic cathedral, supposed to be Saint Patrick's own church. He himself was compelled to make do with a modem and relatively unimposing structure. I found him impulsive and prone to unsound judgements but at bottom fair-minded and warm-hearted. Above all he was outspoken. You knew where you stood with him. Even during the period when we were 'estranged', I always liked him and my feeling was justified for shortly before his death we had an emotional reconciliation.

James Dillon stayed on for tea that July 26 and I took him to town. He told me that last week word came that the British were moving troops into Derry, *preparing to invade Éire*. Irish troops were ordered north but kept thirty miles back of the line. Then it was explained that the British were merely changing billets and all was well.

This was the first of the unpublished alarms that kept us on tenterhooks.

July 26th, Commander Dove wrote:

I have been guided entirely by your advice. Have put a letter in the post and can now go off to wherever the bombs are falling with a clear conscience but a sad heart, at finding so little moral courage in my native land.

I wrote him:

I have great sympathy with your point of view but feel that the problem is insoluble by measures which attempt to compromise between material and spiritual planes. There is logic in Ghandi's position. The alternative is struggle to the end. But I do not mean that (when peace comes) there can be no organisation to prevent war by establishing the police force of a superstate. Unfortunately now, the world is not at peace and I do not see how disarmament before peace, can be arrived at. I hope some day we may meet in a happier world.

Hats off to the John Doves!

From diary entry
Saturday, July 27th, 1940

Mr X a Fianna Fáil Deputy, to lunch: He said he thought the Government was motivated by a belief, perhaps not very well formulated, that Germany was keeping a book and putting black marks down against small nations that behaved in an unfriendly manner, that if they (the Irish Government) were always very polite they would come out better in the end. He thought it probable that a good many of the Cabinet thought Germany was going to win and that several might be hoping so secretly.

I asked him if he did not think that the Government had got a portion of the IRA in by suggesting or allowing it to be suggested that it was England which was most to be feared. He said he thought not; that in his constituency it was understood that they were preparing to fight the Germans though everyone said, 'You can't say that'.

This view was supported by James Dillon's later success in his Monaghan constituency on a platform attacking neutrality and advocating a war alliance with the United States.

X agreed that the censorship was absurd, that the Irish people could not bear to hear the truth about themselves. He said the *London Post* of this week had been banned because of Tania Long's article which seemed to me to be innocuous. He thought that it was the suggestion that Ireland's future was locked up with Great

Britain's. He said he thought Walshe and Boland were definitely pro-German. He asked me if I thought they ought to be removed. I said it would be an impertinence on my part to express an opinion. I thought Joe was full of suspicions which he passed on to Dev, not always helpfully. However, I said, as long as Éire was neutral someone had to be civil to the Germans and Italians and that was what it amounted to. I asked him if he knew what the Germans had offered the Government. He said that he did not know but that he understood that they had offered the IRA *the whole thirty-two counties and two English counties besides*, 'which ones', he said, 'I do not know'. He said 'Only the very inner circle of the IRA know this;' that is, it was not communicated generally. This bore out the story that we had already picked up.

I said that I had heard that General O'Duffy had been the go-between, between the Germans (Hempel) and the IRA until they had got O'Duffy's number.[4]

He doubted that the Germans were doing much in the way of subversive activities, that the huge staff said to be in their legation was nonsense. He said he thought the Fifth Columnist Movement had been exaggerated very much. He said the IRA rank and file never suspected that Held was a member until he was arrested. He said the Germans and Italians were continually watched and the telephone tapped.

This was doubtless 'routine'. One of our legation pastimes was to surprise our 'monitor' into some kind of response. We were often aware of his presence on the line and sympathised with him; we had no secrets.

Diary July 31st: 'David Robinson to lunch'. This was the British officer who had gone Sinn Féin, whose story I had told to Mr Churchill in London. He lived with Robert Barton on his Glendalough estate. He asked me to shoot with him. He was funny about Mrs Osgood and all the children arriving 'for the duration'. He said he should be the South's emissary to Belfast. His father had been Dean of the Cathedral there.

Mr Robinson made no bones about being strongly pro-British and anti-German. He did us many good turns. It is evident that neither he nor Erskine Childers had any suspicion of the intrigue that de Valera was carrying on with Hempel. It seemed to be general knowledge in political circles that Mr Walshe and Mr Fred Boland were pro-German but no one seemed to suspect de Valera. It is probable that Frank Aiken

[4] See Fearghal McGarry, *Eoin O'Duffy: a self-made hero* (Oxford, 2005), 324, for the background to this claim.

was in Mr de Valera's confidence at this time but no one else. De Valera had a lively sense of Irish communicativeness. He once told me that in Ireland if you told anyone a secret it was no longer a secret.

From diary entry

Thursday, August 1st, 1940

Granard telephoned that he would not come to lunch but Mrs Cameron (Elizabeth Bowen the author) was here and very interesting. Before lunch Maffey came in to talk things over and told me again of the account that was worrying the Bank of Ireland directors. Money from America and very active to suspicious payees.

We were going to Castle Forbes, Granard's place in the country for the weekend and I told Maffey that I would sound Granard out about it. He was one of the governors of the bank.

One of the notable survivals of Victorian Ireland was Miss Sarah Purser. She lived in one of the few houses in Georgian Dublin with its own little park or demesne. The diary entry August 2nd reads:

From diary entry

Friday, August 2nd, 1940

Miss Sarah Purser and her nephew, Mr Gaghahan [*sic*], came to lunch. She is ninety-three and still as active-minded as ever. She used to know George Wyndham (when he was Chief Secretary). She said she had been a hardworking woman painter and glass designer all her life and knew no 'swells'. But she knew intimately everyone in the intellectual life of Dublin.

She and Denis Gwynn[5] were almost the last survivors of the Yeats, A.E./George Moore, Lady Gregory Dublin.

Miss Purser avoided politics and the war. What her political convictions were, I never inquired. Most of the better types of pre-1914

5 Denis Roleston Gwynn (1893–1973) was an Irish journalist, writer and professor of modern Irish history. He served in World War One.

Irish intellectuals were nationalists, but not separatists. Many of them became disillusioned by the failure of 'independence' to produce the promised Utopia, but few of them were unionist in feeling, though not unfriendly to England.

From diary entry

Saturday, August 3rd, 1940

Went to call on the Nuncio about noon for a few minutes. He was very charming.

After lunch, started with Maude and Katherine Crocker (by motor) for Castle Forbes. There we found that the Powerscourts were expected, also Colonel Howard Bury and Mr Odlum. The Powerscourts came by train and were an hour and a half late, not arriving till half after six. Had jolly evening and Maude, Lady P., Beatrice and I played bridge. Cheered me to get out of the sick room. Sunday about noon it began to rain but we had seen the gardens under sunshine. The herbaceous borders were the finest I had ever seen, with great masses of dahlias behind the phlox.

Castle Forbes was one of the few Big Houses able to carry on in the old tradition. Early in the nineteenth century the Forbes had impoverished themselves rebuilding, in the pseudo-castellated fashion of the day, an old, fortified strong house which had stood siege in Cromwellian times. It was said to have been in bad repair when Beatrice Mills, sister of Ogden Mills, secretary of the treasury under Hoover, married the earl of Granard. She got Lernigan[6] over from Paris, gave him free hand and the result was not only a 'great' house but a charming one.

From diary entry

Saturday, August 3rd, 1940 continued

After lunch, Katherine C. and some of the men went out on the Shannon to the 'island'. The rest played bridge. I spoke to Granard about the 'Bronk' account. He seemed surprised that I knew about it and said that a British Secret Service agent had called on the directors and asked to see the account. They (the

[6] Lenygon & Morant, interior decorating company established by Francis Henry Lenygon.

directors) said they would think of it. I advised him to tip off S.T. O'Kelly (Minister for Finance) about it.

Sunday morning I read of the arrest of two people named 'Bont' under the Defence of the Realm Act with bail set at four thousand pounds. The ostensible offence was changing residence without notifying the police. Shall see Maffey about it.

As in the Held case, German activity of this kind strengthened de Valera and put Hempel on the defensive.

The Anglo-Irish in Granard's party thought that 'on the whole Dev was doing very well'. Practically all these former Ascendancy people had a feeling of bitterness toward England though their sons were joining up. They felt that England had sold them down the river in 1922. More than that, people with property in Éire had to make their peace with the government 'or else'. Their position resembled somewhat that of the American tories after the American Revolution.

From diary entry

Monday, August 5th, 1940

Lovely morning after rain. Granard, Bury, Powerscourt and Odlum were off at 11 a.m. to some boat races on the Shannon twenty miles upstream. Mrs Willie Naper (one of the famous Trefusis sisters of Edwardian days) came to lunch. She was a great dear. We left at 2.45 p.m. and got home two hours later.

From diary entry

Tuesday, August 6th, 1940

Went in to see Maffey at twelve o'clock and told him of my talk with Granard about 'Bont' who had been arrested and released on four thousand pounds bail. He was glad I had told Granard to tip off O'Kelly. Everything was going all right as far as he knew.

Joe Walshe came to lunch and we talked very frankly.

This proved to be a revealing talk. The diary reports:

We discussed two possibilities:

1. A German victory: If Britain were crushed he believed it would be to Germany's interest to set up a strong Ireland but not to occupy it. I said that that was wishful thinking; that Germany would occupy it and exploit it and develop the ports.

2. A British victory: If Britain won, which he did not think was a possibility, or fought a draw, which was a possibility, then he thought Ireland would go on as before and that within the framework of the Commonwealth of Nations was Ireland's best chance.

I told him of Father Brown's statement to me, that if the Government gave up trying to make Irish a spoken language he would not care what happened to Ireland. He (Walshe) said that was his viewpoint.

I asked him what he thought was going to happen to Norway, Denmark, Belgium and Holland, not to speak of France? He said he thought they would all be restored in some manner, and that Germany would take from France only Alsace-Lorraine and perhaps a little part of the Channel coast. What Italy would take he did not suggest.

I said that I had heard from an authoritative source that Germany had promised the IRA the whole thirty-two counties and two counties of Britain. What these English counties were, my informant did not know.

Walshe said, 'I don't think I believe that, but' he added laughing 'on the basis of Irish majority we ought to have Liverpool'.

He then came to the point and told me what was on his mind: The English were conducting a propaganda campaign against Ireland, in all probability, preparatory to seizing the ports. The American press *doubtless unwittingly* was taking part in this unfriendly and wicked campaign. He showed me correspondence between him and John Steele, the American newspaper man. He thanked me for my memorandum sent through O'Kelly. He promised to send me a collection of anti-Irish newspaper articles in American papers. I told him that our policy was to be helpful to Ireland and work for a German defeat. That I wanted personally very much to help end partition and since it could not be done by force it must be done by conciliation and that everything that increased bad feeling made the job harder. I said that if the right break came we wanted to help end partition but that we could not do it unless we were convinced that Ireland was *benevolently* neutral.

He said that there could be no doubt about that, that Irish neutrality was to the benefit of England as it happened to be to the benefit of Germany also.

Joe's trouble with the newspapers dated back to June. On the 2nd the *New York Times* had printed a dispatch under the headline 'British Again Fear an Occupied Éire'. It was from Robert F. Post, one of their London correspondents, later shot down and killed in an American bomber over Berlin.[7] It began:

NEW YORK TIMES

BRITISH AGAIN FACE AN OCCUPIED ÉIRE

Once more the ancient threat of Ireland to British security has been raised. Already news from Dublin tells of arrests in connection with supposed Fifth Column activity. Recent proofs of efficiency with which the Germans organise espionage, sabotage, and treachery within a country and then overrun it within a matter of hours have raised an old spectre of an enemy firmly entrenched across the Irish Channel.

He quoted from Mr Churchill's protest during the debate on the proposal to surrender the Irish ports to Mr de Valera. Mr Churchill had explained how important they had been during World War One when the American fleet was based on Cork. And now, he said, 'We give them up to an Irish government led by men whose rise to power is proportioned by the animosity with which they have acted against this country'.[8]

Mr Post called attention to the strategic position of Ireland, to the possibilities of German landing by airplanes and submarines:

The army has been expanded, it is true, and there is a small efficient air force (?) and the rudiments of a navy (?). But any resistance by organised forces to the sort of attack Germany is capable of unleashing could be little more than a gesture ... . At

[7] Robert Post (1910–43), Harvard graduate, worked as a reporter for the *New York Times*. He was part of a group of eight reporters known as the Legion of the Doomed or the Writing 69th, selected to fly bombing missions over Germany.

[8] It is not clear if this misquote of Churchill is from Post's article. See this manuscript, xxxv, note 7.

present the Germans occupy southern Norway and the Channel ports. The Germans have numerical superiority in the air. Should they occupy Ireland too, they would be able to launch attacks on Britain from three directions at once… . Furthermore, Germany could use Ireland as an air base from which to attack the western coast of Scotland, where at present the fleet can seek shelter with comparative safety. From Ireland, planes could bomb not only Belfast but Glasgow, the Clyde, and all the important manufacturing and shipbuilding industries.

From a naval point of view an enemy in Ireland is equally dangerous. The great trade route would be cut; submarines could base there, venturing out to sink ships carrying men, guns and food.

The task of meeting this threat is a peculiarly delicate one for Britain and for Premier de Valera. Ancient hatreds still smoulder. The IRA nursed on hatred for England, still is powerful and has access to arms. Despite the gravity of Ireland's present position any appeal for help to England might well mean the downfall of any Irish Government: the arrival of one British soldier might well precipitate bloodshed.

So far this was but a statement of fact though the Irish people were never allowed to read it. But at the end of the article Mr Post touched off his bomb. He said 'But it may be that the British, sick of dancing to Hitler's pipe, will take the risk'.

External affairs went into a dither. Here was the *New York Times* preparing American opinion for a British occupation of Ireland and what was worse arousing no storm of American protest. Sinn Féin taught that England was the traditional enemy of the United States as she was of Ireland, yet here was America promising all aid to England short of war. The Sinn Féin mind was closed to the possibility that 'traditional enemies' might prefer survival to tradition.

On July 10th there was dropped another newspaper bomb. John S. Steele broadcasting in London over the Mutual Network, repeated the suggestion made by Mr Post. He further intimated that defending England without Ireland was like trying to defend New York without Long Island. If Mr Post had startled Mr de Valera, Mr Steele panicked him. Three days later he sent the Irish Day message. He also instructed his representative in London to take the matter up with Mr Steele. It became a diplomatic incident. Mr Dulanty, as instructed, suggested that Mr Steele might not be able to visit Ireland again.

Thereupon, Mr Steele on July 23rd wrote Mr Walshe (italics mine):

I was very much surprised when John Dulanty called me up yesterday about your objection to my broadcast on July 10th. I must also confess that I resented the implied threat in your statement that I might not be able to come to Ireland again. So let us clear that up first. *I am an American, broadcasting to Americans, and am not subject to any censorship of that kind* but I can't believe that you meant it that way ... etc.

To this Mr Walshe replied:

I was very glad to get your letter of 23rd July. I didn't really believe you could have seriously intended to prepare American opinion for a British reoccupation of Ireland. Yet, mind you, that was a fair interpretation of your motives from an impartial reading of your text. I am writing as an old friend, so you must allow me to be frank ... . We are ready to resist any invader to the last man and our army has now reached a stage of efficiency which makes it a fairly formidable adversary for an invading army. We have, moreover, the enormous accretion in *moral* strength from the fact of defending a country, *every sod of which is already holy* for us because it has been *drenched with the blood of our ancestors fighting against invaders for centuries.* That is not mere rhetoric; it is literal fact ... . You know that the *San Francisco Chronicle* of 25th July had a disgraceful and most un-American attack on our independence. Ludwig Lore in the *New York Post* of the 12th July and Major Elliot, leading American commentator, in a broadcast early in July adopted a similar attitude ... .

We only ask those of them who have shown themselves particularly hostile to Ireland—such as the *San Francisco Chronicle*—to remember that *neutrality is of the very essence of Irish independence at this stage of our history.* And, if we do not act as certain American papers wish us to act, it is not through any sense of perversity or any failure to see where our interests lie. It is simply because of our conviction, founded on a profound knowledge of our own people, that the action in question would put an end forever to the existence of an ordered Irish State. It does happen to be the case, almost by a miracle of history, that our neutrality, though for very different reasons, *suits both sides in the present conflict.*

Mr Walshe's passionate insistence on the holy nature of Irish neutrality would have been more convincing if he had not recently been party to selling it.

The letter which Mr Walshe sent me with the correspondence with Mr Steele and the hostile clippings bore the date of July 31st, 1940.

On July 31st, 1940, Hempel, in a report to Berlin said (italics mine):

Also contact with our Embassy in Washington is greatly desired (by de Valera). Walshe also indicated to me further that closer connection between the Irish element in the United States *and the German element there,* and also with the Italian might be *in the general interest* and he has already stated something like this to the Italian Minister. The Irish Government apparently believes that if the Irish element in the United States is *properly used,* it would constitute a *powerful influence in our favour.* Likewise the Irish-American press. The difficulty is, *as Walshe too pointed* out that if any German participation *became known outside* it could easily lead to an opposite effect (influence on Hearst Press).[9] He also gathered that *Ireland must avoid the appearance of co-operation with us.*

Besides the clippings which Mr Walshe sent me I received a clip sheet of American press comment from the Department all to the same effect. I believed that what the American newspapers were saying about Éire was justified, but probably unprofitable. Not long before this both Mr de Valera and Mr Walshe had told me that if America came into the war it would 'change everything for them overnight'. I believed them and I believed that we would certainly be forced into the war. I believed also that de Valera and Walshe were contemplating an American alliance. On this assumption I had discussed the question of American bases with Mr Walshe and he had been very sympathetic. Hostile American newspaper criticism was anything but helpful. I therefore prepared a memorandum for external affairs in which I pointed out that in peace the American government had no control over the Press and that I was sure that Washington deplored inaccurate and extravagant stories about conditions in Éire. I cited the fantastic yarn that described the German Mission in Dublin as composed of eighty Germans, consuming ten gallons of milk daily. I alluded to the strong pro-English elements in Ireland and to the ignorance of the American Press as to the many acts of co-operation of the Éire government with England.

[9] Hearst Press was influential supporter of Irish neutrality, was very much against US entering the war.

The important part about the unfriendly clippings was that neither de Valera nor Walshe saw in them the 'handwriting on the wall'. Similarly they were blind to the significance of Roosevelt's renomination for a third term. But Hempel saw it. See his telegram (italics mine):

No. 266

91/100311–13

The Minister in Eire to the Foreign Ministry
Telegram

SECRET

No. 437 of July 31   Dublin, July 31, 1940
                                                         Received July 31—7.03 p.m.

For Under State Secretary Woermann
The possible re-election of Roosevelt who is not in favour with the Government here would increase the danger for Ireland, since that consideration (British attack) would then be of less consequence. This would certainly be the case if the United States should enter the war, but also even if that step were not taken. Ireland, however, in my opinion, would benefit by the collapse of the Roosevelt candidacy.

   In the US at present, the Irish element and now even the radical opposition (IRA) is reported to be largely backing de Valera, especially as he recently clung to neutrality even in spite of all British allurements. The Irish Minister of External Affairs (de Valera) *has, as already reported, instructed the Irish Minister in Washington* (Hon. Robert Brennan) *to make contacts with the senators of Irish origin who are friendly to Germany in order to take steps against the agitation against Irish Neutrality.* (vide, Messrs Post, Steele, *San Francisco Chronicle*, etc.)[10]

Mr de Valera's instructions to his minister must have been substantially those which provoked the expulsion of Citizen Genet in 1793.[11] Had this come out, political beans would have been spilled in Washington.

   About this time I asked Mr de Valera if he had confidence in his American sources of information. 'Complete', he said. 'Besides I have a

---

[10] Which is bound up with the suspicions originating from England regarding Germany's intentions to attack Irish neutrality.
[11] Edmund Charles Genet ('Citizen Genet') (1763–1834) was French minister to the United States, expelled for pushing the French revolutionary model too hard in US domestic politics.

brother, a priest, in Rochester, New York'. Whatever his sources, the conclusions he arrived at could not have been more wrong.

Hempel's report, dated July 31st, closes as follows:

From various indications in talks with Walshe and Boland I assume the Irish Government may be placing hope in future German interest in the maintenance and completion of an entirely independent *united* Irish state. They express this in a rather negative fashion by saying that they hope that in a future peace settlement we will *not sacrifice Ireland* to England, so they speak of negotiations which the Irish Government *will have to carry on then*. Their particular anxiety is that England immediately following a defeat might be inclined to reduce Ireland to its old position of dependence since Irish neutrality is regarded as a severe blow to the prestige of the British Empire. This might be done with the support of the United States within the framework of the Anglo-American co-operation.

The appearance must be avoided of any intention on our part to put Ireland into a position contrary to England to an extent *not hitherto* expressed. This was what the entente attempted to do with Czechoslovakia after the World War with known unfortunate consequences. I would suggest that an instruction be sent.

This conception of an independent, Catholic Czechoslovakia controlling and persecuting a Protestant Sudeten German minority, as containing the seeds of failure because of the inevitable urge of the Sudetens to rejoin their mother country, is interesting. Hempel foresees the Northern Protestants and the Anglo-Irish unionists as playing an analogous role in the event that Germany established a united Ireland. Hempel also makes it clear that the 'liberation' of Northern Ireland as a *war* aim and the permanent unification of Ireland as a German *peace* aim were different things. It is probable that if the war ended otherwise, Mr de Valera would have experienced bitter disillusionment. Hempel, writing confidentially to his chief, certainly implies that as between Ireland and England, Berlin would prefer England as an ally.

It is possible that Hempel discussed with de Valera this aspect of the post-war settlement and that it was to avoid the recurrence of a situation like that of the persecution of the Sudetens by the Czechs that de Valera evolved the exchange of populations programme. This could have been the subject of the 'negotiations which the Irish government could have to carry on then'.

Hitler had announced that he would be in London August 15th. Hitherto he had kept his 'engagements'. He still had a week in which to arrive. This and the confidence of de Valera and Walshe in imminent German victory leaking out created an atmosphere of tense excitement in certain Dublin circles. The end of the British empire had arrived. It was some day inevitable and that day was at hand. Announcement of the fact was only a matter of days or weeks.

I recall a small and happy man's lunch party at which was discussed the possibility of an Irish empire supplanting the decadent British empire. The argument was reasonable. The people whom de Valera addressed in his broadcasts as 'our exiles', 'our people overseas', actually existed, they were realities. All they had to do was to rise simultaneously and take over in Australia, New Zealand and Canada. Possibly also in the United States and even in England, and the Irish empire, overnight, would be a fact. It was no more fantastic than Mr de Valera's 'Second Dáil'. At this lunch it was handled with a light touch, but I was aware that pulses were beating faster. It brought to mind the bitter story current in my boyhood along the Niagara Frontier. The Fenian whispers: 'There are thirty thousand Fenians ready to take Canada'. 'Why don't they?' 'The police won't let 'em'.

From diary entry
Thursday, August 8th, 1940

David Robinson came again to lunch, He was to take me to see Gerald Boland, Minister for Justice at 4 p.m.[12]

Boland is the 'strongman' of the Cabinet, a bit of a roughneck but straight from the shoulder and I liked him from the start. He and David Robinson were in jail together and he looked after Robinson when he was on hunger strike. They have an old, close bond.

I began by telling Boland how I had been interested and still was in seeing the partition question settled; that though warned against see[ing] (British) Government officials in London by the State Department, Brennan in Washington, McCauley and MacWhite in Rome, Seán Murphy in Paris and John Dulanty in London had all urged me to see the English and get their views first hand. I told him what Churchill had said about his having

---

[12] Gerald Boland (1888–1973), born in Manchester, founding member of Fianna Fáil.

jeopardised his political future in signing the Treaty, and he and Robinson laughed and said 'that's what he said at the time'. I said, 'Don't you trust him?' and they said 'no'.

I then said that Churchill had told me that he would bless any settlement reached between North and South but would never coerce Ulster or consent to it. I told him how I had gone twice to Ulster and had seen various members of the Government and had received no encouragement except from Harry Mulholland, the Speaker, who said that if the Cosgrave policy of conciliation had been carried on they would have been in by now.

'I'm not so sure of that', Boland said.

I said, 'Of course I don't know, but it's clear you have either to take it by force or take it by conciliation and hardly a government speaker makes an address without saying something that stirs up resentment in the North'.

'That is not so', said Boland, 'What has anybody said lately?'

I said, 'well, perhaps in the past fortnight they haven't been doing it but it has been the practice'.

Senator Robinson said that he agreed with me.

Boland: 'They keep jibing at us all the time'.

Robinson: 'The difference is that they don't want any change and we do. We've got to set the example'.

I said, 'Of course my only interest in it, is that if you don't get good feeling established, it makes it harder for your American friends to help'. Boland agreed that might be so.

We then got on to the probable consequences to Ireland of a German victory. Mr Boland agreed that it would doubtless mean permanent occupation, development of the ports, and a naval base for control of the sea and air routes to the West. Probably also German immigration. He had no illusions as Walshe and some others have.

I said, 'Then if your eggs are in the British basket, why do you try to keep so strictly to the middle of the road?'

'If we didn't', he said, '*The IRA whom we have got in would all leave us in a night*'.

This was from the 'horse's mouth'. The cardinal issue really was party politics.

I said, 'You don't anticipate a British invasion, do you?'.

'No', he said, 'but if there was one, I'd take a gun and go out for what there was left in me'.

Later on I had reason to doubt that he was as ingenuous as I had thought, but there was never any doubt as to his courage. The IRA terrorists never intimidated him. He was like an animal trainer that was always ready to go into the cage.

From diary entry

Thursday, August 8th, 1940 continued

James Dillon came to dinner and was in a delightful mood. (It was my 70th birthday, and he had brought me a cup of Cork silver, dated 1760.)

He regaled us with stories of the 'Tariff Reform' boys who have built up Éire's new industries. They were milking the consumer in the same old way, a shoe trust and a cement trust. I went out with him to his car and he told me two interesting things. One was that the true story of 'The (recent) invasion by Ulster' was: In the afternoon a man who said that he had come from Ulster came to the headquarters of troops south of the line, and said he had just come from the North and had definite information that the British were coming over the border at two o'clock that next morning. There was immediate change of dispositions and digging of trenches. Also one bridge was blown. About the same time a man appeared at the headquarters of British forces near the border and said that he had just come from the South and had definite knowledge that the Éire troops were preparing to invade Ulster at 3 a.m. the next morning. They began digging in.

Along in the evening a major of Éire troops who had been a British civil servant began thinking that this was a horrible thing to be taking place, and as far as he could see with no reason. So he sent an officer over the border to British Headquarters. This officer said, 'what do you fellows mean by invading us?'

'Invading you?' they said, 'You are invading us at 2 a.m. We are digging trenches to resist'. Then it became evident there had been a little IRA work.

The other matter was the information that the government had suppressed reports of the trial of the three German agents, one being a Lascar, picked up in the South on their way from Cork to Baltimore. The Lascar had turned state's evidence and said the two others were

German agents from Brandenburg. He didn't propose to stand the rap and was going to appeal. Hempel disavowed them and the government suppressed the news.

From diary entry
Friday, August 9th, 1940

Joe Walshe, as he had promised when lunching with us on the 6th, sent me another packet of clippings from American papers. He stated that during the past fortnight the tone of the British press had become more friendly and also the American press, especially as regards reports from correspondents in England. He thought this indicated a definite change in English policy. None the less he was very stirred up. To my amazement he quoted from Winston Churchill's speech in the debate on the bill to give the ports to the Éire government, the portion quoted by Robert Post, which set forth that it was proposed to give the ports to 'an Irish Government led by men whose rise to power is proportioned by the animosity with which they have acted against this country. In the event of war the first step of a powerful enemy would be to offer immunity to Southern Ireland on the condition that she stay neutral'.

This is precisely what happened.

From diary entry
Friday, August 9th, 1940 continued

The Nuncio telephoned that John de Salis was coming Saturday for a few days. Asked him to let us have John for dinner.

The Charlie Cavendishes[13] came for the night and after an early dinner we went into town and. saw the film *Rebecca*. I thought it very good. Adele (Adele Astaire, Lady Charles Cavendish)[14] very amusing.

August 10th, wrote Joe Walshe:

[13] For the Cavendish family and Ireland, see David Cannadine, *Aspects of aristocracy* (London, 1995), 58.
[14] Adele Astaire (1896–1981), the American dancer. For a picture of this unhappy marriage see Kathleen Riley, *The Astaires: Fred & Adele* (Oxford, New York, 2012).

It would be beside the mark for me to speculate on the course which my Government would pursue in the event of the seizure of the ports but the tenor of the American press clippings which you have shown me, suggests that American public opinion might accept such an act very much as it accepted the destruction of the French Fleet. It is six months since I have been in the United States and your interpretation of American sentiment with Bob Brennan's assistance might very well be as profitable as mine. There is only one thing which as a friend of Ireland I would suggest that it would be well to keep in mind. That is that the American Government by repeated test votes in Congress have declared themselves ready to assist Britain in all ways short of war. The reason for this obviously is that as indicated by the Gallup polls, 85 per cent of the American people believe that a German victory over England would not only result in an enslaving of all the small independent states whose Christian civilisation has been the most promising feature in an unsatisfactory world, but it would bring the United States into inevitable conflict with Germany, if for no other reason, than over South American trade. This being the case it is obvious that American majority opinion would probably support Britain if it were judged that self-preservation dictated the seizure of say Bantry and Cobh as rendezvous for convoys and as bases for an anti-submarine campaign.

Mr Walshe took my letter in good part but his mind was shut to what was obviously taking place in the United States, a something which menaced the whole base of his Irish policy.

He may have been too young to have understood what happened in the United States in 1914–1916, but as a permanent secretary for external affairs he might have read about it. Mr de Valera must have followed the episode at the time if he read the contemporary newspapers. But in 1940 no one in the Irish government had any comprehension of what was taking place. For that matter no politician in either party except James Dillon understood the forces at work, and he was considered too young and brilliant to be taken seriously. Such stupidity on the part of people noted for their quick intuitions seemed incomprehensible. I only suspected the truth when I read the captured German papers and began to understand that de Valera was interested primarily in destroying his political enemy, the IRA, and retaining power; and that to accomplish this he sold Irish honour and interest to Germany under the label of neutrality.

Later on it became clear that Mr de Valera had ignored the counsel of such American leaders of Irish blood and Roman Catholic religion as the signers of the 'Letter to the *New York Times*', as Cardinals Stritch,[15] Mooney,[16] and Spellman,[17] as Bishops Hurley of Florida and Ready of Indianapolis, as the Hon. John W. McCormack of Massachusetts and Edward J. Flynn, to mention but a few of those who stood staunchly behind their government. Instead he relied on such Anglophobes as the late Senator David I. Walshe[18] and the exhibitionist priests, Fathers Coughlan[19] and Curran and on the organisation 'The Friends of Irish Neutrality'. It was of Senator David Walshe, after the charges made by the *New York Evening Post*, that the president wrote me: 'Poor Dave Walshe, he hates England more than he loves his own country'.

That August 10th was a Saturday and there was racing in the Phoenix Park. Diary notes:

From diary entry

Saturday, August 10th, 1940

Had besides the Cavendishes for lunch, the Adares, Tom Laidlaw and the Meades. All went very well. Afterwards went racing with them. Got on Enchantress in the big race for a pound each way (a pound was about my betting limit) which recouped my earlier loss on Mark Twain and a little more. It was a nice day and good fun. The Cavendishes went off to Lismore at six-thirty.

In our racing party we had two American women besides my wife. Lady Adare had been Nancy Yuille of New York and Lady Charles Cavendish was Fred Astaire's sister, Adele. We had known Miss Yuille, and also Count de Salis on Maude's sister's moor in Scotland. The Adares were delightful people. We saw a great deal of them and they showed us great kindness.

[15] Samuel Alphonsius Cardinal Stritch (1887–1958), Archbishop of Chicago.
[16] Edward Mooney (1887–1958), Archbishop of Detroit.
[17] Francis Joseph Spellman (1889–1967), Archbishop of New York.
[18] David I. Walshe (1872–1947), Massachussetts senator and Boston University graduate; isolationist.
[19] Father Charles E. Coughlin (1891–1979), an early supporter of the New Deal and Roosevelt, by this point an ardent antisemite and 'sneaking regarder' of European fascism.

The Battle of Britain, on which hung the fate of the Democratic World for what would certainly have been a very long period, was approaching its climax, yet on that sunny August afternoon in Phoenix Park it seemed as if there were no war. No one mentioned it. I learned afterwards that Charlie Cavendish had given the English government five thousand pounds to pay for a Spitfire. He was an invalid and troubled that he could not join up.

Just before eight that evening, I drove over for John de Salis at the nunciature. He had had a very interesting time in France as interpreter between the two high commands.

From diary entry
Wednesday, August 14th, 1940

My wife, Mrs Crocker and I lunched with Joe Walshe. He had an attractive little town house and when we came away we agreed that it had been the jolliest party we had been to in Dublin. Also we had boiled Irish bacon and spinach which the teenagers of today would describe as 'out of this world'.

Joe was shortly to take his holiday with Herr Hempel on the Kerry shore. In view of the impending 'German victory', and the possible landing of German paratroopers, to be with Hempel was a good idea. But he did not talk about his holiday.

CHAPTER XIV

AUGUST 15TH–31ST

In August 1940 it was not admitted in Dublin that the Pope was anti-Hitler. Yet Count de Salis, a British soldier, was stopping with his nuncio.[1] One straw shows how the wind blows. When de Salis left the nunciature he made us a visit. During the winter 1939–40 he had been a military liaison officer in France, interpreting for the British high command. He had accompanied the duke of Windsor when he toured the front. I wrote the president:

Letter to President Roosevelt

John tells me that as early as October 1939 he had reported in writing that the Maginot Line would be broken between Valenciennes and Maubeuge. It lacked gun power and was otherwise vulnerable. (This was within a few miles of the breach.) Not much later he found out that Pétain had been a defeatist from the beginning and had been arranging for an armistice commission in the early winter. Then he went to Spain and fixed up his fascist understanding with his old friend Franco. John says he told most of this to Sherman Miles (American Military attaché in London), whom he greatly admires. I suppose Bullitt has also told you. Apparently the political dissension in France turned largely on the rows between the Catholic Rightists and the 'Grand Orient', the Masonic group.

Since Sir John Somerville's attack on the French fleet, Pétain had become a hero in Dublin. I was interested to find out that Mangin's estimate of him in 1918 was supported by de Salis.

---

[1] The de Salis family were large landowners in Armagh and London. John Eugene de Salis inherited the Holy Roman title in 1939; he died on 21 October 1973.

Letter continues:

John says he knows de Gaulle and feels that he is not a strong man, and has undesirable friends but that the British have to make the best of him.

De Salis was Romanischer Swiss. His ancestors had been soldiers in the Roman legion left stranded in the Alps after Rome fell. Americans who ski at St Moritz know Bondo, the de Salis château. John explained that de Salis was a clan, not a family name. At Bondo, the postman, the cook, the gardeners were all de Salis. His branch of the family had become British over a century ago. His father, the seventh Count, was related to many of the great European families. John had cousins everywhere in Europe and special facilities for picking up inside political information. He was trilingual. From an Irish grandmother he had inherited a ruined castle on the shore of Lough Gur in Limerick. That summer, Seán P. O'Riordain, Professor of Celtic archaeology at the National University, Cork, was excavating on John's property.

From diary entry

Friday, August 16th, 1940

U.P. Bureau telephones two IRA members, Patrick McGrath and Thomas Green, alias Francis Harte, have shot and killed two policemen. They contend that they were 'Soldiers of the Republic' rightfully defending their post, a room over a Dublin shop when the police of 'a Government they did not recognise' intruded.

From diary entry

Saturday, August 17th, 1940

We all drove down to Limerick to see what O'Riordain was finding at Lough Gur.

The diggers were undergraduates who had volunteered for the summer vacation, and they sifted each spadeful of dirt with loving care. The stratum they were working in was but two feet deep, but at the bottom were traces of the Neolithic civilisation of the original Irish; then the Bronze Age. On top of this were remains of the Gaels who arrived in historic time with iron spears. We saw the post holes preserved in the clay in which they had inserted the props that held up the roofs of their wattled clay-plastered huts. It told the story of the subjugation of an inferior civilisation by a superior one. In their turn the Gaels were subdued by superior cultures. We wondered what the National University students thought, who had been brought up on the Sinn Féin doctrine that 'God Made Ireland for the Gael'.

While at Lough Gur we came across a curious piece of German propaganda. Diary reads:

From diary entry continued

Someone is passing the word among the farm labourers that Hitler will redistribute the land, that is, break up the twenty-five and fifty-acre holdings into three- and four-acre plots (presumably this was IRA work intended to embarrass the de Valera Government).

De Valera had tried the small plot system but reluctantly came to the conclusion that the 'labourer minded' labourer could not run a farm. They are now encouraging the larger landholders to employ more labour and till more land. They are not bothering the Anglo-Irish farmers who employ all their labour.

August 20th, four days after the IRA patriots had killed the two policemen, they had been tried, found guilty and sentenced to death.[2]

The Cosgrave government at the close of de Valera's Civil War had devised a procedure of trial without jury. They set up a 'Military Tribunal'. It worked. Mr de Valera and his followers were unable to intimidate the Tribunal and public order was restored. It was in effect the system that Arthur Balfour had introduced in Land League days. Mr de Valera had denounced Cosgrave's Tribunal as 'Coercion', but public order was established.

When he came to power and let out the 'patriots' whom Cosgrave had jailed, he discovered that he needed the Military Tribunal and re-established it.

The verdict and sentence on McGrath and Green, alias Harte, appeared to meet popular approval. But execution was held up by habeas corpus proceedings. *War News* printed this account:

[2] See Seosamh Ó Longaigh, *Emergency law in independent Ireland 1922–1948* (Dublin, 2006), 254–6, for a good discussion of his case.

WAR NEWS

ISSUED BY THE IRISH REPUBLICAN PUBLICITY BUREAU

YOU HAVE STARTED THIS SHOOTING

As reported in our last issue two Republican volunteers were captured by the police following the skirmish in Rathgar Road, Dublin. One of these, Green (Thomas Harte of Lurgan) was wounded in the leg. The other Volunteer was Patrick McGrath who said to his captors, 'I am surprised at you men coming to a house where there are Republican Soldiers, knowing they are armed. You have started this shooting by shooting two of our leaders. We are taking no chances now'.

The Captured Volunteers were taken before the Free State 'Military Tribunal' and 'tried' for the 'murder' of the two detectives who were killed in the encounter. Mr de Valera recently made a law which prevents the Military Tribunal from inflicting any sentence other than death. Harte and McGrath were therefore sentenced to face a 'Free State' firing squad.

In 1922 when de Valera encouraged the IRA to fight against the 'Free State Dominion', Joe McKelvey and his comrades were attacked in the Four Courts by 'Free State' soldiers with English guns. The Republicans defended themselves in arms and for doing this Joe McKelvey, Rory O'Connor, Liam Mellows and Dick Barrett died in front of a Free State Firing Squad. Today in confirming the sentence on McGrath and Harte, de Valera has himself condemned two Republican soldiers to death for defending themselves against the forces of the Free State Dominion and their English guns.

When habeas corpus produced a stay of execution, I received notice that an IRA deputation would call on me on Friday, August 23rd. On August 25th I reported the murders to the president and continued:

Letter to President Roosevelt

Saturday, August 25th, 1940

The Nuncio ducked out of town when the postponement occurred and is still in the country with Seán T. O'Kelly. (We lunched with him yesterday at Roundwood.) As a consequence the full force of the patriots descended on this legation. They predict very serious reprisals (shooting a few Cabinet ministers) if not open civil war if the sentences are carried out. It is generally believed that the government must abdicate if it does not go through with the executions, as these murders came on the heels of the commutation of MacCurtain who also shot a policeman.

I get along pretty well, as I can tell them (the IRA) truthfully that these men, not being American citizens, it would be an impertinence for me to make representations to their Government, and I might be sent home. I also tell them that to protect myself I tell the government of their visits, which in fact I do. I don't want to get into Irish politics. I wish you could sit in on these sessions. The one last Friday comprised:

1. Mrs O'Moloney, formerly Miss 'Kattie Barry' on the staff of the Irish Republican Army. Believe me she is a grand girl.
2. Father Flannagan, the brilliant, radical priest who has been 'silenced' and is now a librarian in the National Library. Father Flannagan thinks one piece of ice produces enough water for a tumbler of fifteen-year-old Jameson.
3. A Dublin barrister, Mr Mullane.

At one point in the discussion I said: 'It is nonsense to pretend that Mr de Valera likes to execute people. He is a very humane man'. 'Yes', said the barrister. 'He forgives and forgets. He forgives his enemies and forgets his friends'.

I didn't put it in the letter but this brought a big laugh and we had another drink. Miss 'Kattie' would only sip a little sherry.

The letter went on:

Letter to President Roosevelt continued

Saturday, August 25th, 1940

These people were all with de Valera till lately. They are bitter now because he condemns them for doing just what he did, for many years, that is, insist on the right of a minority not to bow to majority rule. I find that by being honest with them and telling them that their philosophy is impossible for an American to sympathise with, one gets on fine. They want to talk and when they get going you find out a good deal.

I never saw Mr Mullane again. A little later on Mrs O'Moloney telephoned me in regard to the same unfortunate men, and the next year I met her in the street on the morning after Dublin experienced its first German bombing. Her ideas from my American point of view were 'cockeyed' but she was a very superior and attractive young woman. I was told she had carried dispatches during the Civil War for the de Valera rebels.

A diary note for August 22nd reads:

From diary entry
Thursday, August 22nd, 1940

Wrote Mr de Valera a brief account of this interview and told him that I cannot be rude to such visitors but that I want him to know that I appreciate the danger of getting involved in Irish politics and will see no one opposed to his government without making it clear that it is not a confidential meeting which I cannot discuss with the Government.

What made the McGrath case particularly difficult for Mr de Valera was that as in the case of the hunger striking son of Count Plunkett, young McGrath had been a close personal friend of many of them during their attempt to overthrow the Free State government.

August 23rd Patrick McGrath's brother sent me a copy of a letter which he had written Mr de Valera. In it he deplored the strife which was dividing the nation, especially when '*a few more months may place the whole Irish question in a different perspective and automatically put an end to the fratricidal encounters*'. The letter continued: 'The IRA hold that they were established to secure the freedom of *all Ireland*'. The writer then argues that if the de Valera government pursues a policy of non-violence toward the North and tolerates 'British occupation', pending the success of conciliation, why should not the same policy be pursued toward the IRA ?

My letter to Mr de Valera further reported an incident which had more meaning to him than to us. It said:

Letter to President Roosevelt continued

Saturday, August 25th, 1940

About 10.30 on the evening of the same 22nd of August (that is the day Father Flannagan's deputation called on us) I received a typewritten communication, purporting to come from 'Córas na Poblachta' and signed by the chairman and secretary. This communication stated that the organisation in question was endeavouring to bring about a 'truce' to the unnatural conflict between Irishmen, but that in the opinion of the organisation the executions, if carried out, would render agreement impossible.

Coras na Poblachta, ('Towards the Republic') was the legal or constitutional organisation that 'fronted' for the IRA. It did not employ or openly advocate violence.

The letter to President Roosevelt went on:

Yesterday (August 24) I had another IRA leader with me for three hours. (Rather he was an ex-leader). He came to discuss some scheme for developing Irish-American trade on which he was very sound; and then we went on to politics. He says that de Valera lost Irish-American political support by high-hatting it and neglecting to keep in touch with it after he got into power. That is why McGarrity left him.[3]

This probably was true. One of the reasons for replacing MacWhite in Washington with Robert Brennan was to mend political fences. The letter continued:

My visitor claimed to have broken Seán Russell's hold on the IRA in America. He worked eight or nine years 'downtown' in New York and is a clever fellow. I have an idea for an Irish-American Export and Import agency backed by Irish Government credit, the management to be paid on a commission basis. The curse of Irish bureaucracy is salaried inefficiency. Under this plan no results, no pay. This guy thinks well of it and he is working out a detailed scheme which we will take to de Valera. They want to do a lot of business with us after the war and of course have got to sell to us—tweeds, whiskey, bacon, ham, baled peat and stout, if they are going to buy.

Word has just come (Aug. 26) by telephone that a German bomber has dropped bombs in Wexford, I'll have to stop and see what has happened.

---

[3] For Joseph McGarrity's break with de Valera see T.P. Coogan, *De Valera: long fellow, long shadow*, 484–5.

But to finish up with Mr X, my radical trade friend. He says that conditions in the Dublin slums are unspeakable, far worse than ours, that some four thousand Jews from Germany have got in here and established sweat shops cutting the minimum legal wage of eight shillings and sixpence a week in many cases to five shillings. They have seduced some Catholic girls which is bad business here and according to him there is a big undercurrent of pro-Hitler sentiment in the slums on the anti-Semitic issue, but *not* anti-British. This is another element that complicates the situation.

The report of the bombing in Wexford turned out to be true. On a midsummer morning, August 26th, a warplane circled over the peaceful fields of County Wexford and dropped bombs on three defenceless villages. At Campile the pilot made a bag. He killed three Irish girls employed in the creamery. The plane flew low and German markings were clearly seen, but word was passed that 'just as Churchill had sunk the *Athenia* and blamed it on Hitler so he was sending disguised English planes to create anti-German feeling'. The IRA in the issue of *War News* dated August 29th printed the following under the heading 'British Bomb Wexford',

WAR NEWS

ISSUED BY THE IRISH REPUBLICAN PUBLICITY BUREAU

BRITISH BOMB WEXFORD

Our readers will remember that in our issue of July 30 we warned them of the possibility of camouflaged British planes bombing Belfast. We did so after certain information had been passed on to us by Republican intelligence officers in England. It was known that certain specially selected English pilots were in conference with Cabinet ministers and 'M.I'., the British secret service, on the subject of bombing raids over Ireland. On Saturday, 24th August, one of these pilots was ordered to report at M.I. Headquarters where he received instructions for a special commission. The identity of the man chosen is believed to be Flt. Lieut. Maurice J. Hall. Acting on his orders the pilot motored from London on Monday, 26th August, to a deserted spot on the Welsh coast where mechanics awaited him at a concealed hangar. He transferred to a camouflaged plane, on the wings of which black crosses had been painted, and took off for the Irish coast. In the course of earlier conversations with M.I. the suggestion that the outskirts of Dublin be taken as the objective was vetoed. It was decided that the objective must be such that there would be no chance of the plane being brought down by anti-aircraft fire with the subsequent fear of identification. The objective was therefore to be a small village a few miles inland from the Irish coast. The raid must take place in broad daylight in order that the painted marks on the wings and tail would be clearly seen by eye-witnesses. The pilot was ordered to destroy his plane in the event of its being attacked in such a way that escape was impossible and to shoot himself with a German automatic pistol to avoid capture.

The English pilot actually reached Ireland, dropped bombs in the Co. Wexford, killing and injuring several people and returned to the Welsh coast without being molested. Immediately on his return the identification marks on his plane were again changed and the pilot returned to London. The object of the raid which was of course to stir up the Irish people against Germany, succeeded to this extent that several people identified the plane as German. The mentality of the British led them to believe that Germany would deliberately bomb a country which although its 'Government' claims to be neutral is actually bitterly antagonistic toward England.

The official German news agency in Berlin comments that all squadrons operating over England on Monday have been questioned and not the slightest grounds have been discovered for the report that German aircraft had chosen the route over Ireland. It would be a singular proceeding for Germany to disturb her relations with Éire by dropping bombs on that country. And Germany has not the slightest interest in this act of provocation which is only in accordance with British policy.

The *War News* story was convincing but it had one weakness. Dr Hempel admitted that the plane was German.[4] Germany accepted responsibility, apologised and said that it was a regrettable mistake.[5] Mr de Valera accepted the mistake theory and asked for 15,000 pounds damages.

[4] Duggan, *Herr Hempel*, 112.
[5] See *Irish Times*, 27 August 1940.

It may be that the German pilot was lost. English authorities guessed that he thought he was over Pembroke in Wales. The important fact is that even if he believed he was over Wales he was guilty of deliberately bombing defenceless country villages miles from any military objective in violation of the rules of civilised war. Here was German 'kultur' which was in fact the basic issue of the world conflict. It was the kultur which Mr de Valera's neutrality was upholding. His government was suggesting that 'the Germans are our friends, the English our enemies. You mustn't let English lies weaken your loyalty to our German friends'. The Censor even deleted references to Hitler which did not address him as 'Herr'.

A month later Katherine Crocker who had been visiting in Kilkenny, came back with the story that the German bombing of Campile had been according to plan. Memorandum reports:

MEMORANDUM

I asked Dillon what he thought. He said that a Colonel Chubb had indeed written the Ministry of Justice some time before the bombing saying that he had received a stenographic rescript of a warning issued by German wireless to the effect that Campile Creamery and two others that were sending a great deal of butter to Britain would continue at their peril. Dillon took it up with Gerry Boland who at first said that he had received no such notice, but later found Chubb's letter in his files. Chubb refused to reveal the source of his document which presumably was British. None of this has been allowed to get out here. The Irish have a listening bureau but had no record of this. The English record everything. What is one to think?

Whatever the truth, the Campile bombing embarrassed Hempel and played into de Valera's hands. It was daily becoming clearer that Irish neutrality, which kept England out of the ports, was of first importance to Germany. Undoubtedly de Valera made it clear to Hempel that if this kind of bombing went on he could not be responsible for the consequences, meaning that he might not be able to continue being neutral.

Six years later, on February 13th, 1946, after the Allies had defeated 'Herr' Hitler and saved Éire, Mr Aiken, speaking for the government, announced that they had collected 12,000 pounds from Irish citizens who owed debts to German nationals. Germany had never paid. Hitler had 20,000 dollars to give to Goertz, the spy, but nothing for the

Campile victims. Of the 12,000 pounds which the government got from Irish citizens, 4,000 was allocated for personal injuries.

At the time I had expected that Campile would open the eyes of the Irish government to the kind of people they were dealing with, that every red-blooded Irishman would be filled with indignation. Their much publicised pride and their notable gift for regarding themselves insulted seemed to me inevitably to forecast strong anti-German feeling. But nothing came of it. It was another of those opportunities for mobilising public opinion against the Axis which Mr de Valera refused to accept. When he told me after 'playing down', the Campile incident that the people would not have followed him if he had taken any other course, I could only suggest that he had never tried.

Although a majority of the plain people reluctantly accepted the government's announcement that the Campile plane was German, a large minority believed the *War News* version. They believed that 'English gold' had corrupted de Valera.

Before the end of August, the legation had still another IRA visitation. This one had a direct bearing on 'American Interest'. The spokesman informed us that the government of Northern Ireland was interning Irish patriots in a 'prison hulk'. They had anchored it in the Lough conspicuously to invite bombing attack. 'Did this not contravene the Geneva convention regarding prisoners of war'?

As every American schoolboy of my generation knew, during the American Revolution the British used 'prison hulks' in New York Bay to incarcerate American prisoners of war. Lord Howe's scoundrelly Irish quartermaster, Captain Cunningham, stole their food and provided no medical attention. The death rate was a scandal. 'British Prison Hulks' had become a symbol of British 'brutality and oppression'.

Washington had an efficient American consul general in Belfast. He was the bearer of a historic Virginian name, John Randolph.[6] We worked happily together, and I wrote him for advice and help. In my letter I said:

This Legation is worried about the possible effects of interning IRA members in the ship as proposed. I have already had a protesting delegation to deal with. The ship has already become a 'prison hulk moored in a position to invite destruction by the enemy'. If this gets publicised in the United States you and I know

[6] Francis M. Carroll, *The American presence in Ulster: a diplomatic history 1796–1996* (Washington DC, 1996), 143–4.

that very serious consequences for our British friends may follow. For that reason, unless the use of this ship should be a prime military necessity, it seems hardly worth the risk that it involves.

I would be very grateful if you would let me know your personal reaction to this matter and whether there is much discussion in the circles you frequent. I am suggesting to 'our friend' (Abercorn) that it may cause trouble in America.

Mr Randolph replied that the one thing which the Northern Ireland government did *not* want was to have a group of IRA internees exterminated by a German bomb while in their custody; also that they wanted no 'grievance' over health conditions. No jail was as healthy and as safe as a ship moored offshore away from anything which could be construed as a military or industrial objective. By publishing the nature and position of the ship and the fact that the inmates were IRA allies of Germany it was thought that the most had been done. After such public notice, it was a German responsibility.

This was all true, but the facts would make no impression on an Irish-American public opinion inflamed by the 'Prison Hulk' story. We hoped the Northern Ireland government would realise this.

I sent Mr Randolph's letter to Sir John Maffey. He wrote:

It is a very interesting account, but he seems to miss the danger which was in our minds, namely that the Germans would bomb the ship without any regard for the opinions of the people on board, if they thought that by so doing they could make trouble for the British in Ireland.

Eventually the Northern Ireland government brought the internees ashore.

On the last day of August, I prepared a report for Washington on the events of the month. It was impossible to forecast anything with confidence. Was there going to be an IRA insurrection? Was there going to be a German landing of paratroops with submarine support? Would the Irish army fight? Against whom? All we knew certainly was that the army had nothing to fight with against paratroops. England was trusting de Valera with such arms as she could spare but had no spare tanks or anti-aircraft or field guns, or fighter planes.

In July Dubliners thought England was beat but while ruthlessly bombed, England was unshaken and each week growing stronger. The RAF was tearing the Luftwaffe to pieces. One day the bag was 185. Hitler had not arrived in London on the 15th, the New Order was still at the end of the rainbow. Each week, Weygand's amiable prediction that Hitler would wring England's neck 'like a chicken' seemed less likely to be fulfilled. 'Some chicken', Mr Churchill had observed.

We hoped this would have a sobering effect on the Pro-German group in the Irish government but there was no change in policy to report. The most I could say with confidence was that Éire could never have been more divided or confused in mind. Only one thing seemed certain which was that neutrality was not paying off as the farmers had been led to expect. The myth that England was dependent on Ireland for food was being exploded.

I closed my report by saying:

MEMORANDUM

Finally, the unemployed, amounting to some 61,000 this August, are a fruitful field for IRA propagandists and create in the larger cities and town what might be called an unstable element easily inflamed by radical promises coupled with appeals to traditional hatred of Britain.

A further grievance which is exploited by radical agitators is the fact that about a third of the land tenures in Dublin are ground rents, mostly held by absentee owners. Many other Irish towns are similarly circumstanced. The Government feels the danger of this, but is not prepared for confiscation and can devise no scheme of penalising taxation that would not open Irish holders of British securities to reprisals.

Against all this are the naturally conservative groups, the farmers, merchants and manufacturers. But the farmers, though not doing badly are discontented because they are not getting the prices from Britain they got in the last war, the merchants with a rise in all price scales are not profiting, and the same is true of most of the industries. Beyond that as members of property-owning classes they are all dismayed at the rising costs of government and its failure to solve the nation's economic problems. In view of all this it becomes evident that there is no united, vital, nationwide consensus of opinion behind the Government which it can mould to its own policy. National defence has gone a certain distance in restoring Mr de Valera's leadership, but the novelty is wearing off, and as some of those who respond and believe they have enrolled to fight the British and others to fight Hitler, it has not made for national unity as might have been expected.

One observer, a prominent Judge, has said to me, 'the best thing that could happen to Ireland would be to have Hitler invade us. It would at least force a show-down'.

On August 27th, 1940, *War News*, under the headline 'Freedom', had defined its political and economic programs:

WAR NEWS

ISSUED BY THE IRISH REPUBLICAN PUBLICITY BUREAU

FREEDOM

With the assistance of our victorious European allies, and by the strength and courage of the Irish Republican Army, Ireland will achieve absolute independence within the next few months.

The Government of the Republic is determined that our freedom will be used solely for the benefit of the Irish people—in Tone's words: 'The greatest happiness of the greatest numbers in this island, the inherent and indefeasible claims of every free nation to rest in this nation—the will and the power to be happy to pursue the common weal as an individual pursues his private welfare'.

We do not intend to tinker with the existing system, the system that seeks to make Mammon and not God rule this world—in one word, the 'English or famine system'. All the machinery of the British Capitalist system will be utterly and ruthlessly destroyed. Those vile creatures who have waxed fat on the sweat and misery of the Irish workers will be forced to disgorge their ill-gotten gains. We will not go cap-in-hand to the Financiers, Landlords, and Titled Pickpockets who rule and rob this land. The wealth and resources of the country belong to the Irish people by right of birth, and will be restored to them.

We are done with 'Commissions' on this and that! Red Tape must be abolished! '*Direct Action and to Hell with Bureaucracy*' must be the slogan of the Government of the Irish Republic. We will not measure our actions by a host of archaic laws and shibboleths, but by the need of the people. If a thing is good and necessary, it shall be done!

We shall break away completely from the English Money System. Money is not wealth, but only the pale reflection of it. We have *real* wealth—the fertile soil of Ireland, and the brawn and brains of the Irish people. Under the Republic, Money will perform its legitimate function as a ticket-of-exchange.

All the thousands of acres of rich soil at present used to fatten the cattle of thieving ranchers or preserved for the fishing and shooting of absentee landlords and English tourists, will be restored to the people. Slums must be pulled down—no more damp, dark and dirty rooms, and sunless tenements. Our children shall grow up in clean and healthy homes. Thousands of families will be planted on the land regained by the opening of the big demesnes and ranches.

Hospitals must come under the supervision of Government, so that there will no longer be a cure for the rich and a coffin for the poor. Railways must be developed and used for the people and not for the private profit of individuals. Re-afforestation will be undertaken on a national scale, and within a few decades our country will possess valuable tracts of timberland.

The restoration of the land to the people, and the abolition of unemployment, will stop the constant drain of emigration. Our young people will be enabled to marry and to live in happiness and moderate comfort. Our marriage-rate, for years the lowest in the world, will at last rise to normal, and we shall see a natural increase of healthy and intelligent children, born with economic security and freedom as their heritage. Equal educational opportunities will be afforded each child, the chance to develop his mental and physical powers, to engage in the vocation for which he is best suited, and to serve the Nation by so doing.

This is *Freedom* Is it not worth fighting for? If we fail now, we betray the unborn generations—but we shall not fail! *Freedom within a few months! Long live the Republic!*

The printed circulation of *War News* was probably but a few hundred, but each copy was passed from hand to hand. Its contents circulated by word of mouth. It expressed the aspirations of that 'Irish Heart' in which de Valera put his trust. And the philosophy which it promulgated was

Marxian communism and dictatorship of the proletariat. This confirmed and explained the reports that during de Valera's Civil War his followers had hoisted the red flag on the Heffernan Mills in Cork.

As always in crisis and confusion, the cinemas and play houses were crowded, but government made no effort to revive the 'classical' Abbey plays as propaganda for national unity.

De Valera and Sinn Féin regarded the Irish Literary Revival as an Anglo-Irish business. With 'Liberation', 'Separatism' and 'Restoration of the Irish Language' would come a flowering of the Irish genius which would make the Abbey period insignificant. In August 1940, eighteen years had passed since the Treaty, and eight since de Valera had become 'Liberator' of the Twenty-six Counties. And what had happened? The veteran artists of the Abbey who survived still gave brilliant performances in the old tradition.[7] But the dead hand of 'party line' control was killing the Abbey as an institution.[8] It was producing nothing new. There was nothing new that was important. The Irish creative genius was as sick as the Irish economy. Fire mercifully destroyed the old play house before the smell of spiritual death became public scandal, but in 1940 admirers of the past were still hopeful of resurgence and reinvigoration. They were looking to the Gate and the Gaiety where new coteries were working. Word had got to New York that great things were in the making.

From diary entry

August 31st, 1940

Wrote Micheál MacLiammóir, Dublin playwright, producer, actor, wit, that I had just received letters from Bob Kane of Twentieth Century Fox film corporation and Julian Johnson, head of their literary department. Both said they were much interested in new Irish creative writing and would be glad to see the script of MacLiammóir's play *Where stars walk* about which I had written them.

---

[7] Micheál MacLiammóir (1899–78), born Alfred Whitmore in London, playwright, actor and man of letters, *Where stars walk* was published in Dublin in 1962. Opened in the Gaiety Theatre in Dublin on 19 February 1940. A tour of Canada and the US ended with a performance in Mansfield Theatre in New York in 1948.

[8] As early as 1935 it had been a kind of conventional wisdom in the literary world that the Abbey was 'past its prime'. See Louis MacNeice to Rupert Doone, 22 July 1935, in Jonathan Allison (ed.), *Letters of Louis MacNeice* (London, 2010), 255.

I had said that this seemed to be a play that portended the looked for resurgence. It had wit and high comedy. It was clever theatre. It was poignant and moving. It 'acted'.

The curtain rises on the drawing room of a retired actress, one of the Abbey 'greats', now a patron of 'les jeunes'. There is 'discovered' a playwright and his actors trying to find out what the 'matter' was with their play. The characters lack reality. But was reality possible with such a plot? It was based on the Gaelic legend of Aethan,[9] the beautiful wife of the King of Tara and her lover in a former life. He came back to Tara, persuaded her to leave this world and go away with him. They were last seen in the moonlight as two swans, bound with a golden chain, flying to Tír na nÓg.

There is a planchette belonging to the mistress of the house on a table, and the leading lady as she listens to the discussion idly plays with it. It writes. She receives a message in Gaelic of which she knows nothing. When the mistress of the house uses the toy, one of the housemaids goes into trance. Presently word comes from the kitchen that the housemaid is asleep. It is late and at midnight a strange young man knocks at the door and asks for a job. The mistress asks him if he is answering her advertisement for a kitchen boy. He says 'no', he has come because he has recognised 'the house'. The audience now knows that there is a 'relation' between the collarless boy from the bog and the psychic kitchen maid. And so the story of Étain, re-enacts itself while the playwright struggles to make his characters 'real'. The final curtain falls as the two servants disappear into the garden late at night. The company follow and see, silhouetted against the moon, two swans flying into the west.

Another MacLiammóir play, not *Where stars walk*, was eventually produced in New York. But what we had taken for the light of tomorrow proved to be afterglow of yesterday. Sinn Féin had settled the hash of the Irish Literary Revival. James Joyce died in self-imposed exile, O'Casey lives in England, Pádraic Colum in New York. Frank O'Connor has done nothing notable since *Guests of the nation*,[10] Seán O'Faoláin[11] goes on as an 'essayist'.[12] Every aspiring young Irish author domesticated in

[9] Edain on title page of published playscript. Micheál MacLiammóir and John Barrett, *Selected plays of Micheál MacLiammóir* (Buckinghamshire, 1998), 1. Modern spelling Etáin.
[10] Frank O'Connor (1903–66), short story writer and man of letters, *Guests of the nation* was published in 1931.
[11] A republican in his youth, O'Faoláin, by the 1940s, regularly accused de Valera of being enslaved to an 'antique notion of Gaelic culture that had no solid basis in reality'. See Joe Cleary, 'Distress signals: Seán O'Faoláin and the state of twentieth-century Irish literature', *Field Day Review* 5 (2009), 50.
[12] Pádraic Colum (1881–1972), a significant contributor to the Abbey prose realist tradition.

England and the US becomes 'Shane' or 'Liam' and hurries to catch the market for the stuff which the English-speaking public accepts today as Irish 'literature' before Honor Tracy[13] debunks the 'racket'.

---

[13] Honor Lilbush Wingfield Tracy (1913 –1989). Novelist, columnist and travel writer. Her novels satirised Irish and British society.

BIOGRAPHY OF DAVID GRAY
by Bernadette Whelan

Gray, David (1870–1968), diplomat and playwright, was born 8 August 1870 in Buffalo, New York state, of Scottish parents; his father was editor of the *Buffalo Courier*. He graduated from Harvard University in 1892. Between 1893 and 1899 he worked as a reporter and leader writer for several Rochester and Buffalo newspapers. Admitted to practise at the Bar in 1899, he nevertheless earned his living as a writer and was the author of several plays, articles, one novel, and an unpublished work, 'Behind the green curtain'. In 1914 he married Mrs Maude Livingston Hall Waterbury (1877–1952), youngest sister of Eleanor Roosevelt's mother. She had been married to Lawrence Waterbury for twelve years and had two children, Lawrence and Anne. The Grays went to live in Maine, but US participation in the First World War disrupted their life. He served as a captain in the American Expeditionary Forces in France and received the Croix de Guerre and Chevalier de la Légion d'honneur for his work as a liaison officer with the French army. Maude worked in one of the intelligence bureaux of the post office department in New York city. Towards the end of the war, Gray broke his leg in two places and was helped to return to the US through the good offices of Eleanor Roosevelt, who requested her husband, Franklin Delano Roosevelt, assistant secretary of the navy, to have Gray return stateside with them on board the *George Washington*. Both he and Maude remained close to the Roosevelts, with FDR describing David as his 'cousin'. After the war, Gray returned to writing; he received a doctorate of letters from Bowdoin College in 1925.

President Roosevelt appointed the 69-year-old Gray as US minister in Dublin on 16 February 1940 to replace John Cuddahy. An amateur in the world of diplomacy, Gray faced a difficult situation in a neutral state, at a time when Northern Ireland, as part of the UK, participated fully in the war with its ports, airfields, and manufacturing industries playing vital roles in the war effort. Gray held definite views about Ireland: he resented the influence exercised by Irish nationalists with those in Irish-America who were critical of Roosevelt's pro-British policy, and he opposed Irish neutrality. His views mirrored those of Roosevelt. Neither of them, nor indeed the US public in general, fully understood the rationale behind neutrality, despite the efforts of Robert Brennan, the Irish minister in Washington. From the time he arrived in Dublin, and particularly from June 1940 to July 1941, when a German invasion was a real possibility, he worked in cooperation with British officials and ministers to persuade and intimidate the de Valera government into the war or, to use Roosevelt's words, 'to fish or cut bait' (Coogan, 543). But his effectiveness was lessened because Eamon de Valera came to detest him and Joseph Walshe, secretary for External Affairs, believed he 'brandished the big stick too much' (Fisk, 305). Gray was actively involved in summer 1940 in moves to offer Irish unity in return for Irish entry into the war. Unusually for a diplomat accredited to Dublin, he tried (unsuccessfully) to persuade Northern Ireland government ministers to accept such a deal.

His relationship with de Valera was further damaged when the taoiseach blamed Gray for the negative reaction that Frank Aiken encountered from Roosevelt, from Dean Acheson, assistant secretary of state, and from officials during his arms- and equipment-buying trip to the US in April 1941. Although Roosevelt relented and agreed to sell two ships and wheat through the American Red Cross, it was clear the US government was unwilling to support Éire so long as it denied the military use of its ports to Britain and appeared to be tolerating Axis espionage activity (in fact, all German agents landed in Ireland were captured). Following the near-failure of the Aiken visit, Gray learned that de Valera was furious, blaming him for misrepresenting Ireland to Washington, and that he would ask for Gray's recall were it not for his connection to Roosevelt.

Once the US entered the war in December 1941 and the German threat of invasion to Britain and Ireland began to recede, the 'testy old gentleman' (as Ervin Marlin of the US Office of Strategic Services described Gray; Fisk, 531) refused to acknowledge the Irish policy of benevolent neutrality towards the Allied side. Gray contributed to Roosevelt's 'absent treatment policy' of Éire and the 'American note' affair that represented the crisis point in US-Éire relations during the war. On 21 February 1944 Gray delivered a note to de Valera requesting the recall of German and Japanese representatives in Dublin. De Valera regarded the request as an ultimatum and rejected it. Irish neutrality remained intact, but there was to be one last round to the de Valera-Gray match on 30 April 1945, when the US minister requested the keys to the German legation in Dublin before the German minister, Eduard Hempel, could destroy its archives. When de Valera declined, it provided Gray with further evidence of Irish refusal to cooperate with the Allies. But the extent of de Valera's personal and political dislike of the US minister emerged two days later, when the taoiseach visited Hempel to express his condolences on the death of Adolf Hitler. This provoked Allied outrage but de Valera explained his action as part of the courtesies of neutrality, remarking that Hempel 'was always friendly and inevitably correct—in marked contrast to Gray' (Coogan, 610).

Roosevelt had believed that Gray was doing 'exceedingly well' in Dublin. He accorded him a go-between role between the White House and Queen Wilhelmina of the Netherlands. Despite Roosevelt's death in April 1945 and lobbying by Irish-American Democrats for his removal, Gray's personal connection with the Roosevelts allowed him to remain in office until June 1947. In his last two years in Ireland he supported the negotiation of the bilateral air agreement (for the sake of US security) and Irish requests to the Truman administration for food supplies, but he was furious at de Valera's efforts to 'pressure-group our government' (Gray memo, June 1947; Gray papers, box 9, file 'Ireland') on the anti-partition issue. After his return to the US he retired to Siesta Key, Sarasota, Florida, remaining interested in Irish politics. He died 12 April 1968.

Bernadette Whelan is a senior lecturer in the Department of History, University of Limerick. Her latest book is *American Government in Ireland: a history of the US Consular Service in Ireland, 1790–1913* (Manchester, 2010).

This biography is copyright of the *Dictionary of Irish biography from the earliest times to the year 2002*, edited by James McGuire and James Quinn (9 vols, Cambridge University Press, 2009; and online at dib.cambridge. org).

Notes
Franklin Delano Roosevelt Library, New York State, papers of David Gray; ibid., Franklin Delano Roosevelt, official file; ibid., Pare-Lorentz

chronology; ibid., president's secretary's file; Eleanor Roosevelt, *The lady of the White House: an autobiography* (1938); Robert Fisk, *In time of war: Ireland, Ulster and the price of neutrality, 1939–45* (1983); Tim Pat Coogan, *De Valera: Long Fellow, long shadow* (1993); Joseph Carroll, 'U.S.-Irish relations, 1939–45', *Ir. Sword*, xix, no. 75–6 (1995), 99–105.

PUBLISHER'S NOTE

The editor and publisher are grateful to the John J. Burns Library and the Trustees of Boston College for permission to reproduce David Gray's memoir 'Behind the Emerald Curtain'. The text was transcribed and typed from photocopies of the original manuscript. It has been annotated by the editor to offer an introduction to less-known members of the diplomatic community in Ireland and America.

This work, which Gray wrote at the age of 89, is described here by Gray as 'an interpretation of accepted history' and as 'the raw material of history in the making'. It is as accurate and reliable as a memoir allows, and opinions on that 'accepted history' will differ from those now current. With this in mind the publisher has taken care to retain the author's style, while standardising terms and spellings and Gray's distinctive use of capital letters and/or scare quotes when discussing weighted issues. These include 'Irish Friendship' and 'Gentleman's Agreement'; the 'Split' (or Anglo-Irish Treaty); 'Separatism' and 'Partition', and 'Uprising' (or 1916 Easter Rising). Conversely, 'the emergency' has been left in lower-case as this was not yet an agreed term for the war years in Ireland. Some errata have been left—'till' is retained where the author meant 'until', and tenses are liable to change throughout the narrative. Irish and German language in letters and telegrams is understandably erratic; for instance, 'Eirean' and 'Eire' have been left as recorded—misspelled and without fadas.

ACKNOWLEDGEMENTS

In the course of editing this text I have incurred a number of profound debts. Professor Robert Stout of Queen's University Belfast very kindly alerted me to the existence of the copy of David Gray's manuscript which had been in the possession of his late father, a distinguished Northern Irish civil servant. During the process of editing I received much help and advice from a great scholar, Dr Patrick Maume. In the Royal Irish Academy I was fortunate to receive initial support from Pauric Dempsey and Helena King. Jennifer Berg carried out wonderful research in the US archives. At a later date Roisín Jones, Maggie Armstrong and Fidelma Slattery were tremendously helpful in the advice and support they gave. Because David Gray lived in a number of different worlds—artistic and political, Irish and American—this has not always been an easy work to edit. In the book a unique and highly diverse cast of characters is brought together in one place at a critical moment in world history, arguably the critical moment in twentieth century history. We have become accustomed to acknowledging the role in the recent peace process of White House envoys like Senator George Mitchell and Ambassador Mitchell B. Reiss who helped bring affairs to a triumphant conclusion. We should not forget earlier important figures like David Gray. It is a pleasure to thank all those who assisted in the process of preparing the book.

Paul Bew

BIBLIOGRAPHY

PRIMARY SOURCES

Archives

'Behind the Emerald Curtain', David Gray memoir, William F. Stout
    Collection (MS.2007.020), box 1, folders 5 and 6, John J. Burns
    Library, Boston College.
Dominions Office Records, National Archives, Kew.

Papers of

Carl W. Ackerman, Library of Congress, Washington, DC.
W.A. Carson, Public Record Office of Northern Ireland, D1507.
G.C. Duggan, Public Record Office of Northern Ireland, T3251.
David Gray, University of Wyoming, American Heritage Centre.

Newspapers and periodicals

Atlantic Monthly
Belfast Newsletter
Belfast Telegraph
Boston Sunday Globe
Connaught Telegraph
Connaught Tribune
County Cork Eagle
Daily Telegraph
Dundalk Democrat and People's Journal
Irish Independent
Irish Times

Liberty
Mayo News
National Review
New Yorker
New York Times
Northern Whig
Roscommon Herald
Sunday Express
Sunday Independent

Documents on foreign policy

Crowe, Catriona, Fanning, Ronan, Kennedy, Michael, Keogh, Dermot and O'Halpin, Eunan (eds) 2008 *Documents on Irish foreign policy: volume VI, 1939–1941*; 2010 *Documents on Irish foreign policy: volume VII, 1941–45.* Dublin. Royal Irish Academy.

Baumont, Maurice, Beddie, James Stuart, Bonnin, George, Duke, K.H.M., Fisher, M.H., Kent, George O., Kogan, Arthur G., Lambert, Margaret, Ronau, K., Scherer, André, Smyth, Howard M., Stambrook, F.G., Sweet, Paul R. (eds) 1956 *Documents on German foreign policy 1918–45, series D (1937–1945).* Washington. US Department of State, British Foreign Office and the French Government.

Official publications

Dáil Éireann debates
Hansard—House of Lords debates
Seanad Éireann debates

SECONDARY SOURCES

Books

Addison, Paul and Craig, Jeremy A. 2010 *Listening to Britain: home intelligence reports on Britain's finest hour—May to September 1940.* London. Bodley Head.

Allison, Jonathan (ed.) 2010 *Letters of Louis MacNeice.* London. Faber.

Barone, Michael 1990 *Our country: the shaping of America from Roosevelt to Reagan.* New York. Free Press.

Barrington, Brendan (ed.) 2000 *The wartime broadcasts of Francis Stuart, 1942–1944*. Dublin. Lilliput Press.

Berardis, Vincenzo 1950 *Italy and Ireland in the Middle Ages*. Dublin. Clonmore and Reynolds.

Bew, Paul 1989 *The dynamics of Irish politics*. London. Lawrence and Wishart.

Bew, Paul 1994a *Ideology and the Irish question: Ulster unionism and Irish nationalism*. Oxford. Clarendon Press.

Bew, Paul, Gibbon, Peter and Patterson, Henry 1994b *The state in Northern Ireland: political forces and social classes*. London. Serif.

Bew, Paul 2008 *Ireland: the politics of enmity, 1789–2006*. Oxford. Oxford University Press.

Bew, Paul and Maume, Patrick (eds) 2008 *Wilfrid Ewart: a journey in Ireland in 1921*. Dublin. University College Dublin Press.

Bowen, Elizabeth 1999 'Notes on *Éire*': espionage reports to Winston Churchill 1940–2. Aubane. Aubane Historical Society.

Bowman, John 1982 *De Valera and the Ulster question*. Oxford, New York. Clarendon Press.

Burleigh, Michael 2010 *Moral combat: a history of World War II*. London. Harper Press.

Cannadine, David 1995 *Aspects of aristocracy*. London. Penguin.

Carroll, Francis M. 1996 *The American presence in Ulster: a diplomatic history 1796–1996*. Washington DC. Catholic University of America Press.

Carson, W.A. 1956 *Ulster and the Irish republic*. Belfast. W.W. Cleland.

Churchill, Winston 1949 *Their finest hour*. New York. Houghton Mifflin Company.

Ciano, Galeazzo 1946 *The Ciano diaries 1939–1943: the complete, unabridged diaries of Count Galeazzo Ciano, Italian Minister of Foreign Affairs, 1936–1943*. New York. Doubleday.

Clifford, Angela 1985 *The constitutional history of Éire/Ireland*. Belfast. Athol Books.

Coogan, Tim Pat 1993 *De Valera: long fellow, long shadow*. London. Hutchinson.

Cowles, Virginia 1941 *Looking for trouble*. London. Harper.

Davis, Troy D. 1998 *Dublin's American policy: Irish American diplomatic relations 1945–52*. Washington DC. Catholic University of America Press.

Dobrzynska-Cantwell, Krystyna 1998 *An unusual diplomat*. London. London Polish Cultural Foundation.

Douglas, R.M. 2009 *Architects of the resurrection: Ailtirí na hAiséirighe and the fascist New Order in Ireland.* Manchester. Manchester University Press.

Duggan, John P. 2003 *Herr Hempel at the German legation in Dublin 1937–45.* Dublin. Irish Academic Press.

Dunleavy, Janet Egleson and Dunleavy, Gareth W. 1991 *Douglas Hyde: a maker of modern Ireland.* California. Berkeley Oxford University of California Press.

English, Richard 1994 *Radicals and the republic: socialist republicanism in the Irish Free State.* Oxford. Clarendon Press.

Gifford, Lewis 2005 *Edith Somerville: a biography.* Dublin. Four Courts Press.

Gilbert, Martin 1983 *Winston S. Churchill, volume 6: finest hour 1939–1941.* London. Heinemann.

Girvin, Brian 2006 *The Emergency: neutral Ireland 1939–45.* London. Macmillan.

Gonne MacBride, Maud 1938 *A servant of the queen: reminiscences.* London. Victor Gollancz.

Hardy, Henry and Holmes, Jennifer (eds) 2009 *Isaiah Berlin: enlightening letters 1946–60.* Oxford. Random House.

Harkness, D.W. 1976 *History and the Irish.* Belfast. Queen's University Belfast.

Haverstock, Nathan A. 1996 *Fifty years at the front: the life of war correspondent Frederick Palmer.* Washington DC. Brassey's Inc.

Herdman, Rex 1970 *They all made me.* Omagh. S.D. Montgomery Ltd.

Hess, Stephen 1966 *America's political dynasties: from Adams to Kennedy.* New York. Transaction Publishers.

Hirsch Chajes, Zevi 2005 *The students' guide through the Talmud: a pre-eminent scholar's overview of Talmudic literature and history.* New York. Yashar Books.

Horgan, John J. 1949 *Parnell to Pearse: some recollections and reflections.* Reprint 2009. Dublin. Browne and Nolan.

Hughes, Harry and Ryan, Áine 2007 *Charles Hughes: Lankill to Westport 1876–1949.* Westport. Charles Hughes Ltd.

Hull, Cordell 1948 *The memoirs of Cordell Hull.* 2 volumes. Reprint 1993. New York. Macmillan.

Johnston, Joseph 1913 *Civil war in Ulster: its objects and probable results.* Reprint 1999. Dublin. Sealy, Briars & Walker.

Kennedy, Michael 2008 *Guarding neutral Ireland: the coastwatching service and military intelligence.* Dublin. Four Courts Press.

Kehoe, Elizabeth 2004 *Fortune's daughters: Jennie Churchill, Clare Frewen and Leonie Leslie*. London. Atlantic.

Lee, Celia and Lee, John 2009 *The Churchills: a family portrait*. London. Palgrave Macmillan.

Lee, J.J. 1989 *Ireland 1912–85: politics and society*. Cambridge. Cambridge University Press.

Leslie, Anita 1954 *The remarkable Mr Jerome*. New York. Henry Holt & Co.

Lukacs, John 1999 *Five days in London: May 1940*. New Haven. Yale University Press.

MacLiammóir, Micheál 1962 *Where stars walk*. Dublin. Progress House.

MacLiammóir, Micheál and Barrett, John 1998 *Selected plays of Micheál MacLiammóir*. Buckinghamshire. Colin Smythe Ltd.

McGarry, Fearghal 2005 *Eoin O'Duffy: a self-made hero*. Oxford. New York. Oxford University Press.

McMahon, Deirdre 1984 *Republicans and imperialists: Anglo-Irish relations in the 1930s*. New Haven. Yale University Press.

McMahon, Paul 2008 *British spies and Irish rebels: British intelligence and Ireland 1916–45*. Woodbridge. Boydell Press.

McNamara, Robert (ed.) 2012 *The Churchills and Ireland 1660–1965*. Dublin. Irish Academic Press.

Manning, Maurice 1999 *James Dillon: a biography*. Dublin. Wolfhound Press.

Marra, Kim 2006 *Strange duets: impresarios and actresses in the American theater 1865–1914*. Iowa. University of Iowa Press.

Nolan, Aengus 2008 *Joseph Walshe: Irish foreign policy*. Cork. Mercier Press

Norwich, John Julius (ed.) 2005 *The Duff Cooper diaries 1915–51*. London. Pheonix.

O'Brien, Mark 2001 *De Valera, Fianna Fáil and the* Irish Press. Dublin. Irish Academic Press.

O'Connor, Frank 1931 *Guests of the nation*. New York. Macmillan.

Ó Drisceoil, Donal 1996 *Censorship in Ireland 1939–1945: neutrality, politics and society*. Cork. Cork University Press.

O'Halpin, Eunan 1999 *Defending Ireland: the Irish Free State and its enemies since 1922*. Oxford. Oxford University Press.

O'Halpin, Eunan 2008 *Spying on Ireland: British intelligence and Irish neutrality during the Second World War*. Oxford. Oxford University Press.

O'Hegarty, P.S. 1998 *The victory of Sinn Féin: how it won, and how it used it.* Introduction by Tom Garvin. Dublin. University College Press.

Ó Longaigh, Seosamh 2006 *Emergency law in independent Ireland.* Dublin. Four Courts Press.

O'Neill, William 1993 *A democracy at war: America's fight at home and abroad in World War II.* New York. Free Press.

Patterson, Henry 2007 *Ireland since 1939: the persistence of conflict.* London. Penguin.

Pihl, Lis 1994 *Signe Toksvig's diaries 1926–37.* Dublin. Lilliput Press.

Powell, Anthony 1996 *Journals 1982–1992.* London. Heinemann.

Price, Stanley 2002 *Somewhere to hang my hat.* Dublin. New Island.

Rauchbauer, Otto 2009 *Shane Leslie: sublime failure.* Dublin. Lilliput Press.

Riley, Kathleen 2012 *The Astaires: Fred & Adele.* Oxford, New York. Oxford University Press.

Roberts, Andrew 2009 *The storm of war: a new history of the Second World War.* London. Allen Lane.

Roosevelt, Eleanor (ed.) 1950 *F.D.R.: his personal letters 1918–45.* New York. Duell, Sloan and Pearce.

Ruppe, Richard A. (ed.) 2002 *Robert Brennan, Ireland: standing firm: my wartime mission in Washington.* Dublin. University College Dublin Press.

Ryle Dwyer, T. 1992 *De Valera: the man and the myths.* Dublin. Dufour Editions.

Ryle Dwyer, T. 2009 *Behind the green curtain: Ireland's phony neutrality during World War II.* Dublin. Gill & Macmillan.

Savory, Douglas 1958 *A contemporary history of Ireland.* Belfast. Ulster Unionist Council.

Shannon, Elizabeth 1983 *Up in the Park: diary of the wife of the American ambassador in Ireland.* Dublin. Gill & Macmillan.

Sisman, Adam 2010 *Hugh Trevor-Roper.* London. Weidenfeld & Nicolson.

Spears, Edward L. 1954 *Prelude to Dunkirk, July 1939–May 1940.* 2 vols. London. A.A. Wyn.

Stuart, Francis 1933 *Try the sky.* London. Gollancz.

Tully, John Day 2010 *Ireland and Irish Americans: the search for identity 1932–1945.* Dublin. Irish Academic Press.

Vidal, Gore 1995 *Palimpsest.* London. Penguin.

Walsh, Maurice 1941 *Thomasheen James: man-of-no-work.* London. W. & R. Chambers.

Walsh, Colonel Maurice 2010 *G2: In defence of Ireland—Irish military intelligence 1918–45*. Dublin.

Walshe, Joe 2008 *Irish foreign policy*. Cork. Collins Press.

Articles and papers

Acton, Carol 2010 'Stepping into history': reading the Second World War through Irish women's diaries, *Irish Studies Review* **18**, 39–56.

Baker, Andrew 2005 Anglo-Irish relations 1939–41: a study in multilateral diplomacy and military restraint, *Twentieth-Century British History* **16**(4), 359–81.

Bew, Paul 2012 What did Churchill really think about Ireland?. *Irish Times*, 8 February.

Cleary, Joe 2009 Distress signals: Seán O'Faoláin and the state of twentieth-century Irish literature. *Field Day Review* **5**.

Jeffery, Keith 2009 Review of Eunan O'Halpin, 'Spying on Ireland: British intelligence and Irish neutrality during the Second World War', *Irish Historical Studies* **XXXVI**(143), 471.

Fisk, Robert 2011 German U-boats refuelled in Ireland? Surely not. *Independent*, 17 September.

Foster, R.F. 1980 To the Northern Counties Station: Lord Randolph Churchill and the prelude to the Orange Card. In F.S.L. Lyons and R.A.J. Hawkins (eds), *Ireland under the union: varieties of tension*. Oxford. Clarendon.

Girvin, Brian 1998 The forgotten volunteers of World War II. *History Ireland* **6**(1).

Hale, Korcaighe P. 2009 The limits of diplomatic pressure: Operation Safehaven and the search for German assets in Ireland', *Irish Historical Studies* **XXXVI**(143) (May).

Horgan, John J. 1957 'Ireland: new problems, old policies'. *The Round Table* **48**(189) (December), 71–5.

McCarthy, Patrick 2011 The Treaty ports and the battle of the Atlantic. *Irish Sword* **XXVIII**(111), 75–100.

Maume, Patrick 1996 Ulstermen of letters: the unionism of Frankfort Moore, Shan Bullock and St John Ervine. In Richard English and Graham Walker (eds), *Unionism in modern Ireland: new perspectives on politics and culture*. New York. Macmillan.

Maume, Patrick 2009 Dreams of empire, empire of dreams: Lord Dunsany plays the game *New Hibernia Review* **13**(4) (winter), 14–33.

Ottonello, Paola 1999 'Irish/Italian diplomatic relations in World War Two', *Irish Studies in International Affairs* **10**, 91–113.

Roberts, Geoffrey 2000 Three narratives of neutrality: historians and Ireland's war. In Brian Girvin and Geoffrey Roberts (eds), *Ireland in the Second World War: politics, society and remembrance*. Dublin. Four Courts Press.

Roberts, Geoffrey 2004 Neutrality, identity and the challenge of the Irish volunteers. In D. Keogh and M.O. Driscoll (eds), *Neutrality and survival: Ireland in World War Two*. Cork. Mercier Press.

Sloan, Geoffrey 2007 Ireland and the geopolitics of Anglo-Irish relations'. *Irish Studies Review* **15**, 239–75.

Walker, Graham 1992 'The Irish Dr Goebbels': Frank Gallagher and Irish republican propaganda. *Journal of Contemporary History* **27**(1), 149–65.

White T.J. and Reilly, A.J. 2008 Irish neutrality in World War Two: a review essay. *Irish Studies in International Affairs* **19** (2008), 142–250.

INDEX